THE LIFE OF WOMEN

IN ANCIENT ATHENS

*

*

*

JOSEPH R. LAURIN

authorHOUSE®

AuthorHouse™
1663 Liberty Drive
Bloomington, IN 47403
www.authorhouse.com
Phone: 1-800-839-8640

Published by AuthorHouse   12/26/2012

ISBN: 978-1-4772-9616-5 (sc)
ISBN: 978-1-4772-9615-8 (e)

Library of Congress Control Number: 2012922992

ACKNOWLEDGMENT

My gratitude goes first to the innumerable scholars
who transmitted, in the original or translation,
the texts used as sources of this book.
My indebtedness goes also to the libraries that assisted
me in my research, especially at
California State University San Bernardino
and Universiy of Redlands.

To my wife Joan and all the friends,
especially the graphics artist Alfred Lau,
who encouraged and supported me
in the pursuit of this project,
I express wholeheartedly
my appreciation and sincere thanks.

Joseph R. Laurin

GENERAL CONTENTS

MAP OF ANCIENT GREECE

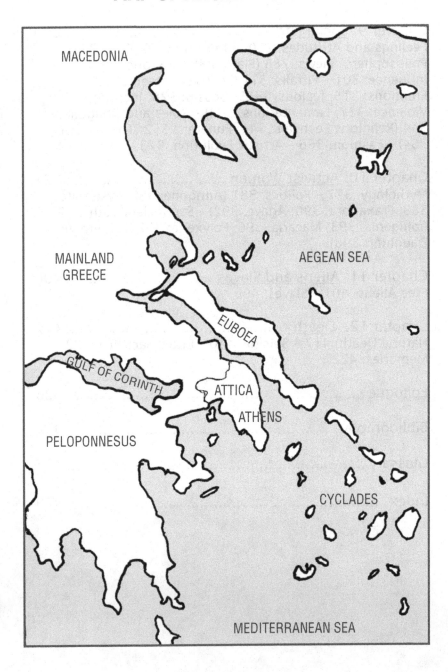

MAP OF ATTICA

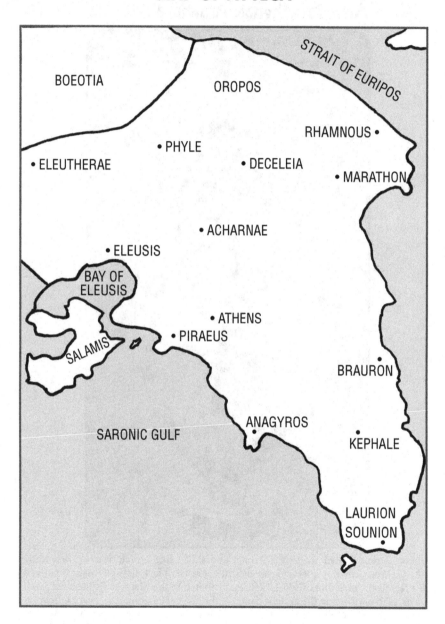

Image of Athena Promachos
Attic Panathenaic Amphora with Lid

Athena is represented wearing a helmet and shield like a male warrior defending Athens (Promachos), yet wearing an elegant dress. Her black-figured image is painted on a terracotta amphora of 340-339 BCE, attributed to the Marsyas Painter and given as a prize to a winner in the athletic games at the festival Panathenaea, every four years in the month of Hecatombaion (July/August). The dimensions with the lid are 89.5 cm (35,1/4 in.) in height and 38.5 cm (15,1/8 in.) in diameter. This image is reproduced here from the J. Paul Getty Museum, Villa Collection, Malibu, California, 79.AE.147.

FOREWORD

Until the 20th century, the life and roles of men and women remained substantially the same. Then, in the more industrialized countries, a change began to develop in the life of women, from being one of subordination to men to one of collaboration and competition with men. The rights of women to live a more emancipated life and to participate in public affairs of the workplace, heretofore reserved to men, became gradually recognized by society. As a result, men and women shared in more traits such as wearing pants, driving cars and traveling alone freely and, more importantly, emulating each other in the practice of medicine, engineering, scientific research and the Law. Also, the skills women displayed at managing the household broke the barriers of prejudice and penetrated the world of manufacturing, services, business, commerce, politics and, for a few among them, in positions at the highest level of leadership. As citizens, not only did they fight for and acquired the right to vote but also to serve in elected offices from members of school boards to leaders of countries.

All in all, this new status in the life of women was good and well, but it was recent and for a very short time in comparison with the millennia during which women were considered inferior to men and restricted to roles related to sex appeal and motherhood. The common women of the long past worked at home and stayed home, except when specific tasks called upon chosen ones to emerge, like Joan of Arc (1412-1431) in war, Maria Theresa (1740-1780) in political power and Marie Curie (1867-1934) in science.

The women of Ancient Athens belonged to this long past, yet some among them, like Antigone and Lysistrata whose stories were related by men, demonstrated more courage than any women of the entire Ancient World when they ventured into activities reserved to men.

This book is an attempt at describing the life of girls and women in the city-state of Athens at the time of her greatest glory from Pericles to Alexander the Great, and her most devastating defeat in the Peloponnesian War, all in the fifth and fourth centuries BCE. [1]

Research and reflection have been our sources: research for the facts in literature, archaeology and art, and reflection upon the findings and their implications for the interpretation. The novelty and value of this book are in the plan and its components of data and thoughts. For this purpose, the readers will appreciate the use of the best texts available, especially those presented in the Loeb Classical Library for the Greek text and the English translation, and the Encyclopedia of World Art, especially for the illustrations (In abbreviation: Loeb and EWA). Other illustrations and texts will be identified by name. In critical cases, the Greek text will be examined closely and given the translation considered best.

The territorial target of our study is Attica, a peninsula of about 1560 sq. miles jutting south into the Mediterranean Sea, between the Aegean Sea to the east and the Saronic Gulf to the west, where Athens was the only major city and, for this reason, the hub on which all eyes in Attica and the colonies were focusing their sight. It was the center of all social, religious, political and cultural activities.

All male citizens living in Attica were Athenians and the women under their tutelage were Athenians by proxy. No major aspect of culture, language and social organization differentiated the lives of the citizens in urban and rural Attica. Compared to Athens, the countryside had a small population scattered in a great number of towns, villages and hamlets where most of the farms were small. The important cities surrounding Athens, proceeding clockwise from the west coast, were Piraeus, Eleusis, Eleutherae, Phyle, Deceleia, Rhamnous, Marathon, Brauron, Sounion, and Acharnae in the center, north of Athens. The communications between them were easy, none of these farms being much further than fifty miles from Athens. Only the pace was slower and the freedom of movement greater in the rural areas. The country folks loved it the way it was. At the beginning of the Peloponnesian war, in the summer

---

[1] The Christian dating by the letters BC and AD and the secular dating by the letters BCE and CE are a matter of choice. The latter is used here in order to convey the thought that the ancient Greek culture preceded by several hundred years the birth and rise of the Christian culture In the Roman World.

of 431, they resented being forced to move inside the walls of Athens. Thucydides reported:

> They were dejected and aggrieved at having to leave their houses and the temples which had always been theirs – relics, inherited from their fathers, of their original form of government – and at the prospect of changing their mode of life, and facing what was nothing less for each of them than forsaking their own town. [2]

The city of Athens was more crowded with small houses and plots. On the other hand, its public buildings were more spacious and all resplendent of harmony and elegance. The activity was also more intense. Behind closed door, however, where women spent the major portion of their time, the style of living was essentially the same in the city as it was in the countryside.

Estimates of population are pure approximations inasmuch as they are based only on inferences and comparisons, easier to make about men than about women. During the fifth century, dramatic fluctuations in population took place from the final victory over the Persians at Salamis in 480 to the defeat of the Athenians in the Peloponnesian War in 404 BCE. Choosing as stepping stones the following three dates -- first, 451 when the Periclean law of dual parentage was enacted; second, 431 when the Peloponnesian War began; third, 404 when Athens capitulated -- the following estimates may be offered without the corroboration by any direct records. [3]

Year	451	431	%	404	%
Population	300,000	354,000	(+18)	253,000	(-29)
Citizens	30,000	42,000	(+40)	30,000	(-29)
- Upper Class	4,000	26,000	(+650)	3,000	(-89)
- Married or widowers	2,265	4,860		1,920	
- Unmarried adults	1,735	11,140		1,080	
- Lower Class	26,000	16,000	(-39)	27,000	(+69)
-Married or widowers	14,735	9,140		17,225	
- Unmarried adults	11,265	6,855		9,775	

---

[2] *The Peloponnesian War*, 2, 16, 2: Loeb 108, 292.
[3] See A.W. Gomme, *The Population of Athens in the Fifth and Fourth Centuries B.C.*, p. 3 and passim.

Wives or widows	17,000	24,000	(+41)	21,000	(-13)
Children	51,000	60,000	(+18)	64,000	(+7)
- Girls	21,640	25,455		27,150	
- Boys	29,360	34,545		36,850	
Other Adults	31,000	36,000	(+16)	38,000	(+6)
Foreigners	25,000	30,000	(+20)	13,500	(-5)
Slaves	146,000	162,000	(+11)	86,500	(-95)

The following notes may help explain this Table:

1. Citizens: Our estimate is based on Plato's data in the fourth century about a military force of "about twenty-thousand" [4] and a citizenry of about thirty-thousand which was near the same made for 451 and 404 BCE.

2. Upper Class: wealthy enough to not have to work as farmers or artisans. Lower Class: working for a living. The partition between the two classes was not tightly sealed. Nevertheless, the Peloponnesian War increased the lower class by some 69 percent.

3. Married and Unmarried: The number of married citizens is based on citizenship at 20 years of age, the male average life span of 45 years and an average marrying age at 32.5 years old. The percentage of 30,000 citizens varies roughly from 57% (17,000) in 451 to 64% (19,145) in 404.

4. Athenian wives: the number of married women and widows is based on an average life span of 36 years and marrying age at 15. The number of widows, mostly from the loss of their fallen husbands during the Peloponnesian War and from the plague, is estimated in 404 at about 1,855, an increase of nine percent.

5. Children: the number of girls through 14 years old and boys through 19 years old, the number being divided per age about evenly, is based on an average of 3 children per household in 451, 2.5 in 431 and 4.3 in 404.

6. Athenian Adults who were non-citizens came from mixed marriages or were illegitimate boys and girls or unmarried girls.

7. Foreigners were Free Residents: freeborn and manumitted aliens (metics).

---

[4] Plato, *Critias*, 112D: Loeb 234, 276 and *Symposium*, 175E: Loeb 166, 92.

8. Slaves were of all ages and marital status.

During the Periclean age, from his rise to power in 451 to the Peloponnesian War in 431, the number of Athenian wives living in Attica increased by about 41 percent, from 17,000 to 24,000. This estimate makes for some 24,000 households (*oikoi*) with 48,000 parents, some 60,000 children, 18,000 unmarried citizens and 36,000 other Athenian adults.

The number of Athenian wives who lost their husbands during the Peloponnesian War, from 431 to 404, is unknown but it would not be wrong if it were placed at about twelve thousands. We estimate that the war and its immediate aftermath caused the male citizen population to decrease by about 29 percent, from 42,000 to 30,000, and the wives' and widows' population by about 13 percent, from 24,000 to 21,000, favoring the right of men to have more than one wife.

Barring some fluctuations, the number of male citizens remained about 30,000 during the 4th century. The number of Athenian adults and children remained about 120,000 while the number of metics dropped a little from about 13,500 to 10,000 (-26%) and the number of slaves dropped a lot from about 86,500 to between 20,000 and 30,000, a two-third decline. The cheap way to acquire slaves by military conquests was then greatly reduced.

Although still approximate, the rate and timing of growth and decline are more accurate than the numbers. Nevertheless, the demographic change in Athens at the turn of the century is obvious and not only significant in itself but also as indicator of new responsibilities befalling women.

With the end of the Peloponnesian War in 404 and the following period of internal crisis and uncertainty, the social life of women changed slightly toward more freedom and permissiveness. Philosophers, especially Plato (427?-347?) and Aristotle (384-322), and the artists, especially Zeuxis (fl. Late 5th century) and Praxiteles (fl. 375-330), developed theories and practices that testified to such a change which, nevertheless, affected none of the men's feelings of superiority and the ways they continued to govern their private household and the public affairs of the State.

Our time begins approximately with the year 480 BCE when the Greeks, led by the Athenians, destroyed the Persian fleet at Salamis, thus securing the freedom of Greece and launching the Athenian course to glory. Nevertheless, the statements made about women by prior writers, especially Homer and Hesiod of the eight century will be brought up because of the familiarity and reverence given to them during the Classical Age of Athens. The women of Athens joined the men at public recitations of Homer's war stories, especially at the Panathenaic games. The Athenians were less familiar with Hesiod's poems *Theogony* and *Works and Days*, also of the eighth century, because the same public recognition was not given to them. In any case, they had a bearing on the views of the writers, especially the playwrights, and will be introduced with relevant caution. The playwrights of the fifth century were the heirs of Homer and Hesiod like Pericles was of Solon and Cleisthenes and the artists who produced the idealized beauty of the Classical *Korê* (maiden) were the heirs of the artists who carved the demure *Kourê* of the sixth century.

Our time ends in the late fourth century, at about the time of the death of Alexander the Great in 323 and before Menander's floruit in New Comedy. By then, considerable changes in Athens were ushering in a new period of her history.

Important, yet almost needless to say that all our contemporary sources of information about women of Ancient Athens were male. Only men told us about women, even when they told us what women thought about themselves. Their representation of women may appear to some readers utterly appalling by the standards women have painfully won for themselves during the climb of the centuries, especially in the past hundred years. Greek men had the usual male prejudices, especially the ones caused by their strong feeling of natural superiority. Furthermore, their reputation as virile men required that they speak of women as being inferior to them. For these reasons, our prejudiced male sources provided us only with a partial and biased view of the condition of women in Ancient Athens. Literally, history is "his-story". [5]

---

[5] See P. Cartledge, *The Greeks*, 66.

Justice to the ancient times, however, cannot be satisfied with broad strokes. Nuances of depth and coloring must be carefully applied. The first of these pertains to the status of the major source of our information which is not history but drama where aggrandizement, the "dramatic", is the rule in order to produce the effects of pity and fear in Tragedy and laughter in Comedy. Furthermore, another nuance applies to the prejudices of the male sex in Ancient Athens since they were tempered in real life by a sense of moderation, humaneness and love of family equal to none in Antiquity.

Although all the known plays of the Classical period were written and produced by men, all these plays, except Sophocles' *Philoctetes* and Euripides' *The Cyclops*, featured female characters. The irony was in assigning these female characters to male actors. For the sake of the tradition of relegating women in all things behind the scene, figuratively, a firm convention had to be made with the audience, especially when women held the leading role, for example in *Antigone, Hecuba, Medea* and *Lysistrata*. Each female character represented an aspect of the women's role and status in society as well as of the men's views and attitudes toward them.

Let it be said also at the outset that, although the location of the action in the plays may have been anywhere away from Athens, like Thebes or Delphi, the play itself was produced on the Athenian stage and, for this reason, was written for an Athenian audience, therefore having a strong connection with the real lives of men and women in the audience, otherwise the plays would not have been understood or well received. [6] The playwrights cared to please their audience in Athens because they needed approval if they wanted, as they did, to entertain and be recognized as writers and producers of substance, with adequate financial support for their future productions. They needed to cater to men's pride while not offending women's dignity. Preservation of their careers required such a caution, not only about women but about other characters they featured, including the gods. For this reason, the subtlety of some of their statements requires of us a careful interpretation in relation to the general context.

---

[6] Plato, *Gorgias*, 502A-E: Loeb, 166, 448-453.

The women of Athens had on stage a voice they never had in life, even in the private life they had with their husbands and children. Some fictitious public demonstrations of women's independence were included in the lore of subjects the male playwrights presented on stage and would not care to describe in other forms of literature. The stage had the advantage of telling the truth, or portions of the truth, in a make-believe setting of fantasy. Yet the contemporary events that contributed to inspire the playwrights and were recognized by the audience, made mostly of male citizens, probably with their wives, ran above an undercurrent of thoughts and emotions that was neither history nor theory. The audience soaked their feet into the stories while their eyes and ears enjoyed the poetry and imagery of the stage production. Antigone and Electra could not have done in real life what they did on stage but their actions, although extremely dramatic, were not the only subject mediated on stage. Their underlying message was also an important part of the subject conveyed through the medium of tragedy, namely, in one case, the right of every Athenian citizen to receive a respectable burial and, in the other, the right to avenge the murder of a father by murdering the perpetrators of the crime, although justice should prevail in the end only in a court of law, the Areopagus, instituted by Athena herself, the guardian of Athens.

As a source of information, the voice of the dramatists was "polyphonic". [7] Some sounds were base and demeaning, other sounds high and noble. Even the words and actions of the same characters, especially those of Euripides, were often ambivalent: for example, The Asiatic Hecuba showed in words and deeds a tender care for her daughter Polyxena in contrast with the bloody retribution she inflicted upon king Polymestor. Both sounds with some ampliation echoed the Athenian society of the fifth century where caring was given and cruelty committed in real life. By representing such scenes on stage, the dramatists went beyond reflecting the cultural elements of their society: they contributed to reinforcing them in the minds of their audiences. No surprise, then, that certain traits such as

---

[7] Aristotle, On Poetics, 13, 1453a, 33-35: Loeb, 199, 72; see E. Hall, The Sociology of Athenian Tragedy, in The Cambridge Companion to Greek Tragedy, ed. by. P.E. Easterling, 118-126.

female inferiority, which were the results of men's decisions, were interpreted, even by philosophers as conscientious as Aristotle, as being natural and therefore necessary. There lies the tension between history and theory, between the real society of Athens and its desired state.

Euripides was a primary witness of women's behavior. He was known for his misogyny and rightfully so during a period of his career. His wife's infidelity was for him a traumatic experience that caused him not only to divorce her but also to hate all women for a while. He wrote for Hippolytus words that could have reflected his own thoughts:

> A curse on you all! I shall never take my fill of hating women, not even if someone says that I am always talking of it. For they too are always in some way evil. Let a man accordingly either teach them to be chaste or allow me to tread upon them forever! [8]

According to a woman attending the festival *Thesmophoria*, he called women "lover-keepers, man-chasers, wine-oglers, traitors, chatterboxes, utter sickies, the bane of men's lives." [9]

In his days, If a woman was assertive, like Antigone, she was considered masculine; if she was courageous, even for evil deeds, like Clytemnestra, she was viewed as having a man's attitude; if she was clever at planning activities, like Electra, she was said to have a man's mind; if she was a good administrator, like Penelope, she did a king's job. In all these instances, the heroines were exceptional women who did not reflect the character and role of the common Athenian women in ancient times. The masculine tag placed upon them reflected the interpretation of the male writers. Yet the same writers described the assertiveness of Alcestis, the courage of Iphigenia and the cleverness of Medea without ever seeing them as unfeminine. The playwrights of Tragedy used the base notes and the high notes in a symphony of dramas that included the full scale of harmony from love to hate, trust to suspicion and indeed from cooperation to domination. The cultural reality certainly

---

[8] *Hippolytus*, 664-667: Loeb 484, 188.
[9] Aristophanes, *Women at the Thesmophoria*, 390-394: Loeb 179, 506.

restricted women to a space where they seemed to live an unflattering life as housewives and mothers.

We would not be pressing too hard, however, if we were to think that the culture prevalent in Athens of the Classical Age kept hidden in the minds and hearts of women some vague aspirations toward greater freedom and that the playwrights reflected not only the reality of women's life but also its possibilities. Life in Athens was not complete with only the subdued Ismene but needed also the anarchist Antigone. Sophocles introduced both to his audience, making Antigone the heroine because Classical theater was poetry and poetry was about dreams.

Euripides despised the villainous women but pitied the deprecated ones. How could he, a man, write choral lines as prophetic as those in *Medea* without having any thought that his picture of heroines could help improve the lot of ordinary women? Although a foreigner, but not unlike a Greek woman, Medea did not take for granted to be abused and rejected by her Greek husband Jason, yet, when she used the murder of their sons as his punishment, she committed a crime a Greek woman would have never done, an evil deed greater than the rejection that produced slanderous rumors against her. Nevertheless, the dramatist did not have her punished for her evil deed. On the contrary, not only did he call upon a god to take her away and save her but lent her words about honor to justify it:

> Honor is coming to the female sex: no more will women be maligned by slanderous rumor. The poetry of ancient bards will cease to hymn our faithlessness. [10]

The playwrights never intended to be historians, theorists or teachers of the masses about women's roles and status. However, when they were by force of their literary genre exposed on a stage to thousands of spectators, delivering words of poetry and calling for emotional rather than mental responses, they were clients to what they understood to be a slice of history and became conveyors of ideas and de facto teachers of the masses. Their dramatic stories had a by-product of views that

---

[10] *Medea*, 420-425: Loeb 12, 320.

modern commentators sometimes extolled for the benefit of their own theories of structuralism, feminism or deconstruction. To impose our own theories upon the assumed views of the playwrights is not only unfair to them but unhelpful to us in our effort to understand the Classical Theater and women's life in Athens. The playwrights' approach to their poetic art was much more simple, genuine and unsophisticated than we may tend to make it.

Yet, when they made male hegemony a cultural label, It was superimposed on a daily reality, more real in fifth-century Athens than at any other time of her history because of the democratic movement bringing the common citizen, not only the aristocrats, into the process of decision-making. By sublimating the role of the *polis* (city-state) to the detriment of the role of the *oikos* (home), the playwrights fell into the rut where the role of women was restricted to the private sector of procreation, rearing of children and management of the household. Nevertheless, although excluded from the government and the courts, these same women had definite roles in the religious and funerary life of their city, not to say anything about their personal influence upon the affairs conducted by men in public offices and businesses.

Furthermore, the theater productions, especially the kind staged by Euripides and Aristophanes, were set in the mold of democracy, so tightly that it seemed at times to crack the walls for the sake of freedom of speech about the behavior of people and the gods. It matched the democratic aspirations of the citizens by featuring on stage not only royalties and aristocrats but also lowly women such as mistresses, servants, maidens and beldames. "It was a democratic act", declared Euripides in his contest with Aeschylus. And Aristophanes explained:

> By staging everyday scenes, things we're used to, things that we live with, things that I wouldn't have got away with falsifying, because these spectators knew them as well as I and could have exposed my faulty art. [11]

---

[11] Aristophanes, *Frogs*, 948-956 & 959-961: Loeb, 180, 152-157; see Aristotle, *On Poetics*, 25, 1460b, 33: Loeb 199, 128.

The picture on stage was more real because it was closer to the common life of the audience, even in the context of the theater. The playwrights were aware of the perimeters of influence between the genders and were not out to change them. They were primarily concerned with entertainment and with the politics of domestic relationships and international conflicts. Like all the other citizens of Athens they were active members of the city-state, engaged in its functioning primarily as teachers of the masses. Such an involvement, unprecedented in all history, marginalized the public role of women, but epitomized their role as mothers and managers of the households.

Bernd Seidensticker is on target when he sees a resemblance between the main traits of the general role of women in reality and the one that the male dramatists gave them to play on stage. [12] There exists, therefore, a similarity between the information gathered from the stage productions and the information provided by other sources. To use the words and actions of the stage as a source of information is appropriate and valid, provided one cares to strip from it, first its poetic form, although it is at times quite helpful toward understanding the prosaic reality and, second, its aggrandizements either into epic salvos or comedic clashes, or simply the exceptional circumstances which are part of the ordinary life of every human being, albeit rare and unusual. The underlying behavior and belief held by a Clytemnestra, Medea, or Antigone were conventional, while the dramatic circumstances in which they were embroiled were totally exceptional. The latter should not discredit the former.

Most major statements about women can be extracted especially from two playwrights: Euripides (c. 484-406 BCE), a writer of Tragedy who projected the image of a misogynist, and Aristophanes (c. 445-385/75 BCE), a writer of Comedy who assigned to women certain roles they could not have dared assuming except in fantasy.

The references to laws and singular events related to women, reported by historians Thucydides (c. 460-c. 400 BCE), Herodotus (c. 485-c. 425 BCE) and Xenophon (c. 428-354 BCE) and by orators Lysias (c. 450-380 BCE), Isaeus (c.

---

[12] *Women on the Tragic Stage*, in *History, Tragedy, and Theory*, ed. by B. Goff, 151-173.

420-350 BCE), Aeschines (390-c. 314 BCE) and Demosthenes (c. 384-322 BCE) will be important also, especially
for the fourth century. The philosophers Plato (c. 427-347
BCE) and Aristotle (384-322 BCE) will also be called upon to
testify about their respective views concerning women's life
in Ancient Athens. Finally, the physician Hippocrates (c.
460-c. 370 BCE) and his followers who made up a corpus of
writings will be consulted about women's health problems
and their natural cures.

In addition to writings, art productions from the
seventh through the fourth century BCE will provide a flow
of valuable information about women. Among the few
painters and sculptors known by name, none is a woman.
The male painters, however, have been generous with their
choice of women's scenes, especially weddings, for their
paintings on a variety of vases. The male sculptors were
also very prolific depicting the female body, either nude or
in draperies and adornments. Aphrodite was a favorite
deity, the Amazons favorite mythological figures and the
Kourê (maiden) the favorite human model. The evolution in
sculpture, as well as in painting, went from the idealized
model to a more realistic representation of women in more
relaxed, theatrical and sensuous poses.

These are our major sources of information. Now,
before leaving this Foreword, a few comments about
linguistic seem appropriate. Since the time of Homer in the
eight century BCE, the Greeks had two words for "man",
namely *anthrôpos* for any person of the male gender and
anêr for a male person of the elite, especially as leader or
hero. A concise passage of the *Iliad* brings the two together
in a manner that challenges every translator. In Greek: "ê
themis anthrôpôon pelei, andrôn êde gunaikôn". [13] In this
phrase, any circumlocution or reference to humankind in a
generic sense is inexact. The meaning is that, although any
and every man (*anthrôpos*) would have sexual relation with
a concubine acquired as war prize, I, Agamemnon, a man-
leader (*anêr*) and because I am a man-leader, have not done
it with Briseis as my wife. Both terms refer to individual
men. Our modern languages do not convey this dual
meaning for individual men, but several of them, including

---

[13] *Iliad*, 9, 134: Loeb 170, 404; see *Ibid.*, about *anthrôpos*: *Iliad*, 1,
   250; 5, 442 & 9, 134: Loeb 170, 30, 238 & 404 and about *anêr*:
   Iliad, 1, 7: Loeb 170, 12 & *Odyssey*, 1, 403: Loeb 104, 42.

English, distinguish between a generic and a specific meaning of man, a distinction not carried in the Ancient Greek language. [14]

In the Attic language of the fifth century, the two words continued to be used but *anêr* lost the vigor it had in the prior language: it was sometimes Homeric [15] but, other times, referring only to a husband. [16] The word *andrôn* for the men's quarters in the house was a derivative of *anêr* in this softer meaning. Or is it that the husband viewed himself as his family's hero?

The name *gunê* for woman did not convey the double meanings, neither like the Ancient meaning of *anthrôpos* and *anêr* nor like the Modern meaning of generic and individual carried for man since the Roman times. It always meant the individual woman with some variations to indicate her status, for example *akoitis* or *gunaikos* for wife or legally-married woman. [17]

The confusion between the generic and the specific meaning of "man" continued throughout the centuries. The context usually clarified the meaning in which the word was taken. Such a problem does not exist with the word "woman" which always signifies a female member of the human race. As human beings, however, women are included in the generic word "man". The same confusion exists in other modern languages under the influence of Latin. For example, the French "La déclaration des droits de l'homme" includes women (*femmes*) because "homme" is understood here in its generic sense. The words of the American Declaration of Independence may carry the modern ambiguity: "All men are created equal". It took two

---

[14] See Homer, *Iliad*, 5, 442: Loeb 170, 238. Special care should be given to translations of passages such as Sophocles, *Antigone*, 332-333: Loeb 21, 34 and Plato, *Theaetetus*, 152A: Loeb 123, 40.

[15] Herodotus, *Histories*, 5, 63: Loeb 119, 68. The title "Histories", in the sense of Inquiries, is preferred to "Persian Wars": see John Marincopa's Introduction to the translation by Aubrey de Sélincourt, published by Penguin Books, p. xv-xvi.

[16] *Ibid.*, 1, 146: Loeb 117, 186 and Aristotle, *Politics*, 1, 1253b, 10: Loeb 264, 14.

[17] Homer, *Iliad*, 1, 348: Loeb 170, 38 (*gunê*); Id., *Odyssey*, 24, 193: Loeb 105, 426 (*akoitis*); Aristotle, *Politics*, 1, 1253b, 10: Loeb 264, 14 (*gunaikos*).

millennia, and not yet in all countries of the world, to recognize that women also are created equal to men and to each other.

In the eyes of Greek men, the womanhood of their wives, mothers and daughters was an object of inferiority of body and soul, respect for its role, warmth for its tenderness and admiration for its beauty. It was also one of torment, either for pleasure or for pain. Aristophanes, a male writer, minted their feelings like a coin in his blown-up comedic words: "Can't live with the pests or without the pests either." [18]

This book is a remodeling and updating with several additions, revisions and corrections of *Women of Ancient Athens* published in 2005 as a textbook. Although the text is often similar to the previous one, the structure is totally different and the presentation more suitable to the interest of college students and readers of all ages.

*   *   *

---

[18] *Lysistrata*, 1039: Loeb 179, 410.

CHAPTER ONE

GIRLS

Mythology

In the mythological genealogy of the gods known to the Athenians, goddess Gaia came first and procreated all the Pre-Olympian deities. The most famous of them all was Zeus who established his residence on Mount Olympus and generated a large community of gods and goddesses. By Hera, he had a son Hephaestus who made the first woman Pandora by mixing earth and water. He made her beautiful. Unfortunately, she became baneful to men after she opened the jar her husband, Epimetheus, kept closed because it contained all evils to mankind. Hesiod sounds vindictive:

> He made an evil thing [Pandora] for men as the price of fire. ... the beautiful evil to be the price for the blessing. ... From her is the race of women and female kind: of her is the deadly race and tribe of women who live amongst mortal men to their great trouble. ... So Zeus who thunders on high made women to be an evil to mortal men, with a nature to do evil. [1]

The mythical birth of Pandora was represented on a bas-relief below Athena *Parthenos* on the east side of the high Acropolis of Athens. [2] The myth of Pandora as the first woman may have been known to the Ancient Greeks a thousand years before the story of Eve became known to the Hebrews. Pandora, however, was never considered the mother of all mankind, like Eve was. The Greek myth devised by men about the origin of mankind, not only made women a mixture of good and evil but bypassed them entirely because men already viewed themselves as

---

[1] Hesiod, *Theogony*, 570, 585 & 590-593: Loeb 57, 120-123.
[2] Pausanias, *Description of Greece*, 24, 7: Loeb 93, vol. 1, 124.

members of the divine race and the ones who created all other women.

From this time of Hesiod who narrated his story in the eight century BCE, the moment the baby girl was born, she was put in her place of inferiority to boys. She was already cast for a lifetime of homebound activities in submission to men. As Athenian she had no name of her own interfacing with *Athenaios*, the name of the male citizen.

The myth of goddess Athena was consistent with a representation of the two genders, male and female, yet with the subdued claim that the female was subservient to the male, like the body is to the soul. She was motherless and remained a virgin by choice. She was depicted with the attributes of a male warrior, wearing a helmet and aegis and holding a spear. [3] On the other hand, she was attributed the invention of weaving, a function typical of the housewife. For this reason, Athena was viewed as female in body and skill but as male in mind and courage. [4]

Plato imitated Hesiod when he offered his own version of the origin of man and woman. He explained that the gods created the souls, "equal in number to the stars". With the bodies, they are of two kinds: the superior one to be called man and the other, woman. Man and woman have the same faculty of sensation, but woman is prone to evil. If man behaves in evil ways, he will have a second birth as a woman and, if he does not correct himself he will be reborn as some brute. [5] Therefore, woman appears as a creature between man and beast, not only inferior to man, but needing to be disciplined by him because of her proclivity toward evil. Near the end of his career, speaking of public meals, Plato still professed that, without State control, women, more than half of the population, were disorderly and, in this respect, inferior to men in goodness. [6]

The same Plato reported that Aristophanes, the Comedy playwright, offered another myth when he attended a symposium on love in Agathon's house with Socrates and

---

[3] Homer, *Iliad*, 5, 115 ff.: Loeb 170, 214 and Euripides, *Fr.*,
   Unidentified Play, 1009a: Loeb 506, 574.
[4] See image of Athena on p. 8.
[5] *Timaeus*, 42B-C & 91A: Loeb 234, 92 & 438
[6] *Laws*, 6, 781A-B: Loeb 187, 486-489.

a few other friends. He spoke about "the nature of man and what has happened to it" and said:

> For our original nature was by no means the same as it is now. In the first place, there were three kinds of human beings, not merely the two sexes, male and female, as at present; there was a third kind as well, which had equal shares of the other two, and whose name survives though the thing itself has vanished. For 'man-woman [androgunos = hermaphrodite] was then a unity in form no less than name, composed of both sexes and sharing equally in male and female; whereas now it has come to be merely a name of reproach. [7]

Aristophanes continued with a description of man in a fantasy of his best vintage. When men revolted against the gods, Zeus decided to

> slice every one of them in two, so that while making them weaker we shall find them more useful by reason of their multiplication. [8]

So Zeus cut each of the three sexes in half and, like a shoemaker, smoothed all parts over. The two segments, namely man and woman, became mates and procreators of the human race while the others, man and man and woman and woman, found intermittent satisfaction in their unions also, but without being able to procreate.

> These parts he [Zeus] now shifted to the front, to be used for propagating on each other – in the female member by means of the male; so that if in their embracements a man should happen on a woman there might be conception and continuation of their kind; and also, if male met with male they might have some satiety of their union and a relief, and so might turn their hands to their labours and their interest to ordinary life. Thus anciently is mutual love ingrained in mankind, reassembling our early estate and

---

[7] Symposium, 189D-E: Loeb 166, 134.
[8] Ibid., 190D: Loeb 166, 136.

endevouring to combine two in one and heal the human sore. [9]

Aristophanes continued explaining that love is the desire to be constantly together, like being one. So if it were possible to be one in life and in death, there would not be a man who

> would unreservedly deem that he had been offered just what he was yearning for all the time, namely, to be so joined and fused with his beloved that the two might be made one. The cause of it all is this, that our original form was as I have described, and we were entire; and the craving and pursuit of that entirety is called Love. Formerly, as I have said, we were one; but now for our sins, we are all dispersed by God. [10]

Aristophanes concluded:

> What I mean is – and this applies to the whole world of men and women – that the way to bring happiness to our race is to give our love its true fulfillment; let every one find his own favourite, and so revert to his primeval estate. [11]

Love restores us, men and women, to our original state in which we were one. On Aristophanes' myth, Eryximachus commented: "I thought your speech charming." Charming it was but with a deeper meaning like all Greek myths. After Hesiod's misogynist myth, it was refreshing to hear Aristophanes, always brilliant and funny, bring a measure of balance with his own myth of love in all forms.

Female

Historically, the autochthonal race inhabiting Attica was Pelasgian. [12] It was killed or displaced, however, by the

---

[9] *Symposium*, 191C-D: Loeb 166, 140.
[10] *Ibid.*, 192E-193A: Loeb 166, 144.
[11] *Ibid.*, 193C: Loeb 166, 146.
[12] See Herodotus, *Histories*, 2, 51: Loeb 117, 338 and Thucydides, *Peloponnesian War*, 1, 2, 5-3, 2: Loeb 108, 4-7.

Ionian invaders from the north, probably during the twelfth century BCE, in search for arable land and good communications by sea, the latter found in Attica. So, the Athenian baby girl was likely to be Ionian by race, with a fair complexion and a stocky frame. As she grew up, she became as strong and energetic as a female can be.

The word *kourê*, the feminine form of *kouros*, referred to a young unmarried girl, either virgin or concubine. [13] A young child was called *pais* or *tekos* and a young girl *meirax, parthenos* or *neanis*.

The representation of the maiden (*Kourê*) in the art of the Classical period can be deceptive. The artists represented the ideal women as tall, usually svelte, and elegant. They were goddesses, mythical females or idealized maidens. They were gorgeously beautiful when young or in middle age, and always matronly and dignified when more advanced in age. The statues of Greek women represented the common women of the time no more than the fashion models of today represent the common women of our time. They represented the ideal image the male artists had in their minds and probably hoped to find in women of their embraces.

By nature, females were considered physically different from males only in some respects. They have a more delicate frame and, as Aristophanes put it, a voice that sounds feminine at all ages. [14] One Hippocratic physician described a woman's flesh as "more sponge-like [porous] and softer than a man's," more like wool than cloth. Another believed that a woman's body absorbs more easily the water and blood needed for pregnancy and menstrual discharges; a man's body absorbs less and is more compact and hard, for example in the breasts. These male physicians attributed the difference not only to nature but also to life style, a woman being perceived as less active than a man. Their main interest was with diseases, especially the abnormalities of the womb. [15]

Simple observation, without instrumentation other than the knife for dissection, guided Aristotle in his description of the human genders. He concluded that

---

[13] Homer, *Iliad*, 1, 111 & 470: Loeb 170, 20 & 48.
[14] *Women at the Thesmophoria*, 268: Loeb 179, 494.
[15] See M.R. Lefkowitz and M.B. Fant, *Women's Life in Greece and Rome*, 96, p. 89 & passim.

animals and humans bore a close physical resemblance and that male (*arrên*) and female (*thêlus*) in both kinds resembled each other in most aspects, except in the size and strength of the upper body, the musculature and the extremities, [16] and especially in the organs of reproduction, commonly called *splanchma*. [17] This last element of the gender differences, enumerated above, is the most obvious, constant and important; therefore it calls for some scrutiny under the guidance of Aristotle, the most articulate of all Classical writers in biology as well as philosophy.

Aristotle raised the question whether the difference between male and female is essential, i.e. one of *genos* (genus or species) like between human and animal, or accidental, i.e. one of *eidos* (gender or race) like between contraries within the same *genos*. Simple observation indicates that male and female share in the same *genos* and, therefore, are different only in *eidos* as contraries or opposites. Aristotle explained that one contrariety makes things different in species (genos) and another does not, for example to have feet is essential to humans and to have wings is essential to birds, thus making humans and birds different in species, but to have a black or white skin is accidental to both of them and does not make them different in species. [18]

A question then arises: Is the difference between man and woman like the difference between a white man and a black man, since both are accidental? First, Aristotle believed that the difference by *genos* (essential) was always one in soul (form and definition), like between a man and a dog, but the difference in *eidos* (accidental) was always one in body but could be sometimes in body and soul. Second, he refined his explanation by distinguishing accidental differences as either perishable like between being a child first and an adult later or imperishable like between a person of pale skin and another of dark skin. [19] In these two examples, only the body (matter) is involved.

The difference between man and woman is one of *eidos* (gender or race), accidental and imperishable yet,

---

[16] *History of Animals*, 4, 11, 538a, 23-30 & 538b, 1-24: Loeb 438, 92-95.
[17] *Generation of Animals*, 1, 2, 716a, 19 ff: Loeb 366, 10.
[18] See *Metaphysics*, 10, 8-10: Loeb. 287, 40-51.
[19] *Ibid.*, 10, 10, 1058b-1059a: Loeb 287, 51.

unlike being black or white, involving both the body and the soul. Therefore, the difference stands between *genos* and only the bodily kind of *eidos*. In her elaborate chapter on this subject, Giulia Sissa concluded rightly that

> the difference between masculine and feminine is neither accidental [in body only] nor essential but some ambiguous combination of the two. [20]

Some of the ambiguity may be dispelled by the following observations. The kind of difference Aristotle recognized between man and woman is twofold: first, they are opposite and complementary, each being equipped with matching organs required to generate a child and, second, they are unequal: in body, woman being weaker and colder than man and, in soul, less intelligent and courageous. Therefore, being deficient by the nature of her body and soul, i.e. having the same qualities but to a lesser degree, woman is by nature inferior to man. [21]

According to Aristotle, humans have the highest form of life and the human male is the most perfect living being when he has reached sexual maturity. [22] Therefore, he assumed that the human male is the prototype and, as a result, the female is described only in comparison to the male: he has testes, she has a uterus, and both are double; [23] he has semen, she has menstrual blood, and both contain a seed. [24]

> The female contribution, of course, is a residue too, just as the male's is, and contains all the parts of the body potentially, though none in actuality. ... The female is as it were a deformed male; and the menstrual discharge is semen, though in an impure condition; i.e. it lacks one constituent, and one only, the principle of Soul (*psuchês archên*). [25]

---

[20] *The Sexual Philosophies of Plato and Aristotle*, in *A History of Women in the West*, ed. by P. Schmitt-Pantel, vol. 1, p. 64.

[21] *Generation of Animals*, 4, 6, 775a, 14-22: Loeb 366, 458-461.

[22] *History of Animals*, 1, 6, 490b, 18-19: Loeb 437, 32.

[23] *Generation of Animals*, 1, 3, 716b, 33-35: Loeb 366, 16.

[24] *Ibid.*, 10, 637a, 38: Loeb 366, 521.

[25] *Ibid.*, 2, 3, 737a, 23-30: Loeb 366, 172-175; see *Ibid.*, 1, 19, 726b, 30-37: Loeb 366, 92-95.

The so-called deformity or mutilation of the female is not like the amputation of a limb. Both sexes are physically and functionally complete. It is the lack of the "principle of soul" in the female that prevents her from being able to generate a new life. The soul (*psuchê*) is the principle of life in both animals and humans: in animals it is purely sentient while in humans it is both sentient and rational. Both the human male and female have a rational soul, but it is not fully operative in the female.

In the Platonic view, the soul (form or idea) has an existence separate from the body but, when it "in-forms" the body, it makes it what it is. Aristotle retained only the latter part and accepted that the soul is what makes the body what it is, but he gives it a biological, instead of an ideological, origin.

The male and female organs correspond to their specialized functions in procreation, functions that can be fulfilled only in complementarity. Genital dimorphism makes for a difference but not a separation. Only in the union of the two genital components can procreation take place: a process to be considered later in Chapter Four.

In summary, the Aristotelian view of the difference (*diaphora*) between the sexes is as follows:

1. An essential difference, called *genos*, exists between humans and animals.
2. An accidental difference, called *eidos*, exists between all male and female, therefore between man and woman.
3. An accidental difference can be perishable, for example when the male or female grows from child to adult without changing its identity.
4. The same accidental difference can also be imperishable, as between a white person and a black person. In this case, the difference is purely in the body.
5. Between man and woman, the difference is accidental and imperishable, and it is such in the soul as well as in the body, because woman has a soul that contributes to generating not only the body but also the soul indirectly through a seed of her own. Therefore, the difference between man and woman is imperishable, yet stands between essential and accidental, i.e. not as much as between humans and animals but more than between child and adult and between white person and black person.

6. The Aristotelian theory of sex may be extended to homosexuals, either gays or lesbians, in that the accidental difference in this case lies between the soul and the body, when the soul is of one sex and the body of another.

Guardian

On the day they were born, both girls and boys fell under the tutelage of a guardian (*Kurios*), the girls for as long as they lived, the boys until the age of twenty when they became emancipated through education in civic and military matters and assumed responsibilities in the public affairs of the city-state (*polis*). A *kurios* was a provider and a guardian, not a slaves' master. Before the maiden's marriage, he was usually the father or, in his absence, an emancipated brother, a grandfather or a paternal uncle.

Plato indicated in his *Laws* that, if necessary, another person, always a male, could fill this function of *kurios*, namely a relative or a friend, whom the woman's father would have named, for example in his will. [26] On his deathbed, Demosthenes' father assigned two of his nephews as *kurioi*: Aphobus for his wife and Demophon for his daughter. [27] Demosthenes was barely past twenty years of age when he became famous for his speeches against Aphobus in 363 BCE.

A short time after birth, the father or, in his absence, the guardian introduced to the phratry (*phratia*), a subdivision of the *polis*, the newborn child, boy or girl, and named the child as a legitimate offspring of Athenian parents. All their lives, the citizens were known by a personal name and the father's name, even after the father had died and the daughter had married, as it is still customary in many cultures of the world.

The notion of *kurios* was closely related to that of *oikos*, which meant family, household and property as a social and economic institution. Aristotle defined the *oikos* as "the partnership therefore that comes about in the course of nature for everyday purposes. [28]

The word *genos* always referred to some blood relationship in the immediate family, like the bond between

---

[26] *Laws*, 6, 774E: Loeb 187, 466.
[27] Demosthenes, *Against Aphobus I*, 4-5: Loeb 318, 8.
[28] Aristotle, *Politics*, 1, 1252b, 13-14: Loeb 264, 6.

parents and children, and in the larger family, identified as *anchisteia* or clan or, still sometimes on a larger scale, in the human race. In the *genos*, the father was always considered the source that generated the flow of genes into the children but, in the household (*oikos*), another man could be the head and guardian (*kurios*).

The immediate family consisted of the direct line from grandparents to parents and their children. The mother was the center of the family. The father was at the top as *kurios*, to wit guardian and provider of his wife and children not only as a personal responsibility to his family but also as one assumed to the state, because his family was the cradle of citizenship.

Maidens were expected to be always submissive to their *kurios*, even in the personal affair of their own marriage, and he, as well expected, to the state because of the public consequences it carried. The case was made on stage after the fifty Danaids resisted marrying their fifty cousins who were pursuing them in their own right. These girls did not and could not have resisted by themselves. Their father Danaus made the decision and their resistance to the fifty suitors was an act of obedience to him, whether they concurred with him or not. Their father warned them to remain in their place as women by staying at the altar and appearing submissive. [29] Obedience to father as guardian and provider was the golden rule of girls even in normal circumstances.

If a *kurios* was negligent or abusive, he could be charged by any adult male, never a female, before an *Archôn* (ruler and magistrate) who could impeach him and even take away from him the right of tutelage. Obviously, the male prosecutor had to obtain his evidential information from the aggrieved woman, either unmarried or married. The hearing was done privately, in the home where a woman had a right to testify in front of a magistrate. She could even take a private oath (*horkos*) in a religious setting as a sign of the veracity of her testimony. Such action was more political than judicial.

In about 400 BCE, the orator Lysias defended in court a widow's children who had been deprived of their father's inheritance by their new guardian, Diogeiton, who was their

---

[29] Aeschylus, *Suppliant Maidens*, 176 ff.: Loeb 145, 16-19.

paternal uncle. Their mother rendered such a passionate testimony against him in court that the jury wept and departed in silence, after restoring the children's inheritance. [30]

Young girls were also vulnerable to sexual abuse by their *kurios*, either father or substitute. The detail of information is lacking but the assumption is valid, knowing human nature. [31]

The responsibility of the Archon in all these matters was well established in the Athenian Constitution, as follows:

> He also supervises orphans and heiresses and women professing to be with child after the husband's death, and he has absolute power to fine offenders against them and to bring them before the jury-court. He grants leases of houses belonging to orphans and heiresses until they are fourteen years of age, and receives the rents, and he exacts maintenance for children from guardians who fail to supply it. [32]

This piece of legislation focused on the needs of children. Mothers were involved only indirectly, as child-bearers. The goal was to have healthy citizens for the state.

<u>Life Style</u>

Before being nubile at about the age of fourteen, girls had more freedom than women to dress with a shorter tunic (*peplos*) and go outside the house to play and meet girlfriends in the neighborhood. Little girls played with dolls and cared for pet animals, like a goose as shown on the grave stele of Plangon, dated of 325-320 BCE. [33] Through Procne's words, Sophocles acknowledged the easy life of girls before marriage:

---

[30] Lysias, *Against Diogeiton*, 12-18: Loeb 244, 666-671.
[31] See below p. 218-221.
[32] Aristotle, *Athenian Constitution*. 56, 7: Loeb 285, 156.
[33] See Fantham, E. et al, *Women in the Classical World*, 104-106.

> In childhood in our father's house we live the happiest life, I think, of all mankind; for folly always rears children in happiness. [34]

Every unmarried girl, however, was bound by some restrictions. Euripides told us, for example, that "it's not good for unmarried girls to appear in public" [35] or even to be seen on the roof of the house. [36] In these matters, the Athenian girls did not have as much freedom as the Spartan girls

> who leave their houses in the company of young men, with bare thighs and loosened tunics, and in a fashion I cannot stand they share the same running tracks and wrestling places with them. [37]

Euripides objected to this practice on moral ground, arguing that girls could not remain chaste even if they wanted to, because the boys in their company would make it impossible.

Athenian girls of the fifth century were never permitted to associate with boys and probably did not want to do it, even during their early teenage years, when their parents were supervising their behavior very closely. At this age, they were ready to be married and knew that their father or his substitute was looking for a suitable husband who would replace him at the helm.

Courtship was absent from the lives of young girls. This restriction, however, did not quench their natural thirst for romance. Especially when they reached the age of twelve or thirteen and became interested in boys, they were closely watched and confined to the house, except on the rare occasions when they appeared in public, for example, at religious festivals, funerals and perhaps the theatre. Everywhere in public, however, they were surrounded by parents who guarded them like hawks guard their young. Everyone knew that the eyes of men were focusing on them. [38]

---

[34] *Fr., Tereus*, 583: Loeb 483, 292.
[35] *Orestes*, 108: Loeb 11, 422.
[36] *Phoenician Women*, 88-103: Loeb 11, 218.
[37] Euripides, *Andromache*, 597-599: Loeb 484, 328.
[38] See Aristophanes, *Acharnians*, 257: Loeb 178, 90.

The guardian and another man, such as a physician, for special reasons and never alone, may enter the women's room. Lysias reported an instance in the early fourth century when a young man, a relative who had been drinking too much wine, forced himself at night into the women's room. It was his own house where his sisters and nieces, some of them orphans, were sleeping. They were "ashamed to be seen by their kinsmen". The other men in the house were alerted at once and "drove him out by force." [39]

This is all very well but the ingenuity of young girls should never be underestimated when they were under the spell of infatuation caused by either the sight of an attractive man or a wooing gift from a male admirer. [40] The sight of a young and mature man in uniform of war, with a crested helmet, breastplate, short tunic and shin guards could cause a tingling of joy in a young girl's heart. Also, the sight of one at the games -- handsome, strong, agile and beautiful in shape and elegance, his body nude and glistening in the sun -- could cause in a young girl's flesh a new and exciting feeling. Love could not grow without courtship, but infatuation could flourish even better. At puberty, when the prospect of being married was sure and near, girls must have been like a swarm of bees hunting for nectar. We can imagine them clustering, whispering comments, giggling, holding hands in total exhilaration. They would not scream like today's teenagers at a Rock concert but would vibrate like leaves in the breeze on a spring day.

The mother, for sure, was first to notice the bright light in her daughter's eyes. She noticed also that she was spending less time helping in the kitchen or playing games and more time adorning herself in front of a mirror and dying her hair blond. [41]

How could an unmarried girl break through the walls surrounding her? Most young girls were not as lucky as Nausicaa who found Odysseus lying on the bank of a nearby river. She was of age to become a wife and a mother; he was a mature man of about forty years of age. She felt at once the excitement in her limbs and the passion in her heart, but her mind had not yet deciphered the meaning of these

[39] Lysias, *Against Simon*, 6-7: Loeb 244, 74.
[40] See Aristophanes, *Assemblywomen*, 611-612: Loeb 180, 324.
[41] Euripides, *Fr.*, *Danae*, 322: Loeb 504, 330.

feelings. She was shy but not without desires, she was eager but not without self-control.

In Homer's story, Nausicaa had asked her father to go to the river for the purpose of washing clothes for the family. Homer was explicit also about her inner thoughts: "She was ashamed to name the joys of marriage to her father; but he understood all." [42]

At the beach, Nausicaa and her maids washed the clothes and spread them to dry in the sun, then they frolicked, playing ball, singing and dancing. Shouts of the girls awoke Odysseus from his sleep. They found him naked, only thick leaves covering his body. The girls scattered in fear but Nausicaa stood right in front of him. She listened to his praise of her beauty and to his plea for her help. Then, they all retreated a distance so that he could modestly wash himself in the stream. When he finished,

> he went apart and sat down on the shore of the sea, gleaming with beauty and grace; and the maiden marveled at him. [43]

Then Nausicaa said words of hope and a wish:

> Would that such a man as he might be called my husband, dwelling here, and that it might please him to remain here. [44]

Finally, Nausicaa agreed to take Odysseus to her father, Alcinous, king of the Phaecians. But, because of the risk of causing a scandal by letting a male stranger ride with her in the wagon, she started first, followed by the maids on foot and behind them Odysseus who stopped to pray at a sacred grove of Athena and only later proceeded to town . [45]

Most girls never had Nausicaa's advantage to be near a man they desired. For contact, they could only use as a carrier a discreet and devoted slave who could wander outside unhindered and deliver a message of interest and hope. In his diatribe against women, Hippolytus referred to

---

[42] Homer, *Odyssey*, 6, 66-67: Loeb 104, 224.

[43] *Ibid.*, 6, 236-238: Loeb 104, 236.

[44] *Ibid.*, 6, 243-245: Loeb 104, 238.

[45] *Ibid.*, 6, 320-323: Loeb 104, 242. Nausicaa's mother was Arete who was her father's wife and niece.

servants who carry women's wicked plot abroad. [46] His complaints applied to women of all ages. The orator Lysias referred also to married women who conducted romantic affairs through slave intermediaries. [47]

In spite of all the efforts, the segregation could not be enforced in the neighborhood so strictly as to prevent girls from seeing boys and falling in love. "Puppy Love" is a part of growing up. Aristotle was thinking about it when he wrote that young people were amorous and fickle; so "they form attachments quickly and give them up quickly, often changing before the day is out". [48]

Young girls needed to be protected, since their lives could be destroyed by the indiscretion of wild male pursuers whose passion had overcome their good sense of respectability.

The story of Creusa is an example of such a disastrous encounter. She was a young girl, unmarried and virgin, when god Apollo forced himself upon her and made her pregnant. A rape was cruel enough, but not for Apollo: he made her abandon her child to die of hunger and be devoured by wild animals. What happened to baby Ion later, being saved and raised in the precinct of the temple of Delphi, unbeknownst to his mother Creusa, did not alleviate her pain and remove the injustice. When she returned to Delphi, some fifteen years later, tears filled her eyes when she saw the temple and remembered the pain inflicted upon her as a young girl and still felt to this day. [49]

What god Apollo did to Creusa, some men could also do to other unmarried girls, if the opportunity presented itself. It came rarely, with difficulty and considerable risk. If it happened and the family became aware of it through any gynecological consequences, it was kept very quiet. By Solon's law, revealing the secret would force the girl into slavery, [50] which was an option the family usually refused to accept. The documentation is indeed very scarce and cloudy. However, we know of one instance during the fifth century, when a male physician was called by a guardian, Timenes, to examine his niece. He found her asthmatic. The

---

[46] Euripides, *Hippolytus*, 649-650: Loeb 484, 186.
[47] Lysias, *On the murder of Eratosthenes*, 20: Loeb 244, 12.
[48] *Nicomachean Ethics*, 8, 3, 5: Loeb 73, 460.
[49] Euripides, *Ion*, 241-254: Loeb 10, 344.
[50] Plutarch, *Parallel Lives, Solon, 2, 1-2*: Loeb 46, 466.

pertinent part of his report was the following note he added: "And if she had an infant, I do not know". [51] The physician would not have made this note if he had not had a suspicion, almost equal to a certainty. Then, why did he not ask, since a pregnancy was relevant to his diagnosis? The answer lies in the social blemish the admission would have placed upon a male guardian whose reputation was more important than the health and reputation of the girl.

Euripides attributed to Melanippe the thought that the raped girl, in fear of the adverse consequences from her father, would not only do all she could to hide her pregnancy but also attempt to make her newborn baby disappear or die. [52] Euripides probably remembered the story he wrote about Creusa, how she feared her parents' reprisal, gave birth alone to a baby boy,

> then carried the child to the same cave where she was ravished by the god, and left him to die in the round hollow of a cradle. ... Well, the girl put upon the child what adornment she possessed, thinking he would die, and left him. [53]

The pain this girl endured carrying to term an unwanted child and giving birth in secrecy was little to compare with the guilt she felt for having abandoned her child to die, which meant nothing less than committing the murder of a baby that was part of herself, all in secret even from her husband of later years. How many of those secrets were kept hidden by girls of Ancient Athens and remained secrets to this day, we will never know. The close supervision of girls within the family probably kept the opportunity rare and the frequency low.

The beauty of love and the sweet desirability of a mate's attention were expressed, perhaps as a reaction, in the seventh century BCE by lyric poets such as Sappho, Anacreon, Archilochus and Alcman. The initiation of young girls to adulthood provided to them the occasion for expressing their libidinous desires. Such a literary phase did not become a trend because of the severe reforms of

---

[51] *Epidemics*, 4, 26: Fantham, E. at al., *Women of the Classical World*, 183.
[52] *Fr.*, *Melanippe Wise*, 485: Loeb 504, 582.
[53] *Ion*, 15-27 & 1372: Loeb 10, 322-325 & 482.

Lycurgus in Sparta and Solon in Athens. The Classical age of the fifth century admired beauty and allowed sexual liberties, but kept itself on the high ground of respectability and moderation. The undercurrent of sensuality in the expression of beauty returned in the fourth century.

In spite of the dangers inherent to the human condition and, as we have noticed, not alien to the divine condition also, the family remained the cornerstone of the Athenian society. Even when he flirted with the fantasy of sharing women as a common resource, Plato recognized in the fourth century the importance not only for families to grow by marriage but also for young people who would commit their entire lives to it to get acquainted before the wedding. He said so:

> For, in view of the fellowship and intercourse of marriage, it is necessary to eliminate ignorance, both on the part of the husband concerning the woman he marries and the family she comes from, and on the part of the father concerning the man to whom he gives his daughter; for it is all-important in such matters to avoid, if possible, any mistake. To achieve this serious purpose, sportive dances should be arranged for boys and girls; and at these they should both view and be viewed, in a reasonable way and on occasions that offer a suitable pretext, with bodies unclad, save so far as sober modesty prescribes. [54]

It seemed important to Plato that the bride and groom be acquainted and attracted toward each other. This was the wishful thinking of an aristocratic mind. In daily reality, the consideration of status and wealth was paramount in the minds of the groom and father. The bride's feelings did not matter much, if at all. The scenario in Aristophanes' play *The Clouds* was probably typical. The wealthy farmer Strepsiades and the aristocratic Coesyra were married, he for status and she for money. [55] Peter Green commented: "He wants her class, she needs his cash". [56]

---

[54] Plato, *Laws*, 6, 771E-772A: Loeb 187, 458.
[55] Aristophanes, *The Clouds*, 46-52: Loeb 488, 14.
[56] *Classical Bearings*, p. 141.

Girls had a golden opportunity to step out of their sheltered life at the religious festivals they shared with other children and families. There, they could be active participants, dancing or carrying gifts to a goddess. Such was the case at Brauron where they attended with their vigilant mothers the festival of goddess Artemis, the protectress of young girls. For sure, the goddess being honored was not the only object of their attention. In his *Lysistrata*, Aristophanes let women's chorus use memories to describe the girl's religious functions at this festival:

> As soon as I turned seven I was an *Arrêphoros* [one of the two girls who weaved and carried a robe offered to the goddess]; then when I was ten I was a Grinder (*aletês*) [of ritual cakes] for the Foundress [Artemis]; and shedding my saffron robe I was a Bear (*arktos*) at the Brauronia [dancing naked, between the age of five and ten]; and once, when I was a fair girl, I carried the basket, wearing a necklace of dried figs [symbolizing fertility, probably at the age of eleven]. [57]

Young girls participated with their mothers in other religious festivals in Athens, especially the *Panathenaea*, the *Anthesteria* and the *Great Dionysia*, in several active ways such as singing and dancing, even drinking wine, always separately from boys.

Let it be said now, in conclusion, that all mothers guided their children to play (*paidia*) with toys, dolls and pets, and made them share fun games with other children. The toys and games were simple, yet plentiful: for example, wooden horse, roller or cart, rattle, hoop, balancing stick, swing, see-saw, knucklebones, balls, spinning tops. Girls had an inclination to jewelry boxes. Jointed dolls were a favorite, especially in puppet shows. Cats and dogs were pets of choice, but goats, piglets and birds, like doves and fighting cocks, were also well liked. Children enjoyed riding on adults' shoulders, running, playing tag or hide-and-seek and, best or all, dancing which they enjoyed to do either

---

[57] *Lysistrata*, 640-646: Loeb 179, 356; about bearing a basket, see Thucydides, *Peloponnesian War*, 6, 56, 1: Loeb 110, 280.

alone or with older men. [58] More will be said later about the education of girls by their parents.

Let it be said also that, in all things everywhere and for the rest of their lives, girls were "in second place, always at a distance from [boys and] men", in one way or another. [59]

*

*

*

---

[58] Euripides, *Fr.*, *Erechtheus*, 370, 10: Loeb 504, 388.
[59] *Ibid.*, 319: Loeb 504, 330.

CHAPTER TWO

BRIDES

Expectations

The word *parthenos* meant simultaneously unmarried woman, virgin and nubile young woman, with a shifting emphasis. According to the Hippocratic physicians, the young girl who had reached the age of menarche experienced at this time severe bodily and mental distress, unless the accumulation of blood flowed out normally in menstrual discharge. In order to facilitate it, they recommended getting married, having sexual intercourse and especially becoming pregnant.

A husband can in this fashion help alleviate the pains beginning with a girl's puberty. The men's perception was also that she was at this time better suited to become a mother. Therefore, a girl's unmarried stage was one to be terminated as soon after puberty as possible. She needed a man to do it, as she needed a man in all other phases of her life. Girls rehearsed in their minds their future role as wives and mothers, and nothing else.

Like the model goddess Athena chosen by boys and men for the city, the model favored by girls was related to her future role as wife and mother. Goddess Artemis protected their virginity and helped it blossom until they could offer it as brides. [1] The classic intervention of her power occurred when she snatched Iphigenia from under the sword as she was offered in sacrifice for the troops held at Aulis. [2] She saved the girl's virginity from being shed in blood and used it for the role of priestess of her cult among the Taurians. Artemis was a virgin herself, a female capable of becoming a mother, yet never being one. Her resentment made her jealous and possessive toward the virgin girls who placated her with gifts on their wedding day.

---

[1] Plato, *Cratylus*, 406B: Loeb 167, 80.
[2] Euripides, *Iphigenia at Aulis*, 1582 ff.: Loeb 495, 336 ff.

Another goddess, Hecate, whose origin was traced to Caria in Asia Minor, was so closely related to Artemis, whose famous temple was in nearby Ephesus, that she seemed to share with her the role of protectress of girls from the age of their puberty to the time of their wedding. A shrine was erected on the doorway of the house to protect them from unwelcome intruders. [3]

A wedding day was the greatest desire of a pubescent girl, as it was also of the society of Athens. The blind Oedipus was reflecting his society's views when he estimated it was shameful for Antigone to accompany him in his exile, not as much because his daughter would be wandering in public as because she would remain unmarried. Antigone had her own views about the family bond: she found exile with her father "not disgraceful but noble – provided she is sensible". [4] Later, she will marry at the time of her suicide but never become a wife and mother.

The girl's desire to get married was matched by her guardian's ambition to find for her the best male partner as a husband and the suitors' desire to strike the best deal for a good wife. It seems that family relations were more important in this pursuit than the simple acquisition of a bride. The implications were honor, wealth, political standing and indeed the values of honesty, industriousness and loyalty.

When a girl became a wife, she did not lose the family ties she had with her father and siblings, as she still shared in the same blood relation (genos), but acquired with a husband a new guardian (kurios) and, thus, initiated with him a new family home (oikos), separate from their prior ones.

This subject must be approached with a broader scope. Man was expected to domesticate all the women in his family, wife and daughters, but not do it in the same manner he domesticated his animals or dominated his slaves. He never doubted women's humanity although he repeatedly, in words and actions, reminded them of their lack of authority or immaturity and, as a result, of their inability to rule and make binding decisions like men do, now as guardians or suitors.

---

[3] Aristophanes, *Wasps*, 804: Loeb 488, 324.
[4] Euripides, *Phoenician Women*, 1692: Loeb 11, 386.

Agreement

A major responsibility of the guardian was to find suitable husbands for the girls and other unmarried women under his tutelage. He had only one far-reaching alternative and one choice highly preferable and more common than the other: it was for the girl to be married by contract and the other by cohabitation. Most Athenian men, were they guardians or suitors, preferred marriage by contract because the financial and social arrangements were clear, instantaneous and public. A marriage by cohabitation had no official recognition except socially and in the court of justice where it could have a legal standing, like in today's cases of palimony. Nevertheless, in both cases there was a permanency for which the Greeks had no special word. Aristotle explained the basic notion and purpose of the permanent union of man and woman:

> The first coupling together of persons then to which necessity gives rise is that between those who are unable to exist without one another, namely the union of male and female for the continuance of the species (and this not of deliberate purpose, but with man as with the other animals and with plants, there is a natural instinct to desire to leave behind one another being of the same sort as oneself). [5]

If the choice of a bride was between an Athenian and a foreign girl the advantage was in favor of the Athenian girl because she could produce citizens for the state. The law of dual Athenian parentage, sponsored by Pericles in 451 BCE, was sound for two reasons: first, because it restricted the citizenry at a time of influx of immigrants from the colonies in the aftermath of the victory over the Persians in 480 and, second, because it served him well politically. By this law, he secured for himself the top leadership in Athens against Cimon whose mother was a foreign woman married to the famous general Miltiades, his father. It is not clear whether the law was retroactive. In any case, Cimon was not deprived of his citizenship because no one attempted to

---

[5] Aristotle, *Politics*, 1, 1252a, 24-30: Loeb 264, 4.

challenge it in court before he died in Cyprus in 449, shortly after the law was enacted.

It made no sense to Athenian citizens, whether guardians or suitors, to allow two Athenians to marry by cohabitation. This latter kind of marriage occurred only with a foreign girl, either long-term companion (*Hetaira*), like Aspasia was for Pericles, or concubine (*pallakê*), like Andromache was for Neoptolemus, namely serving all his general needs. A prostitute (*pornê*) enjoyed no permanence in her relationship even if she remained with the same man for a while. The word *gunê* meant both woman and wife because, in the Greek mind, only the wife was the real woman.

Briseis was only a war-concubine whom Achilles took after he killed her husband. They came to love each other. Propriety prevented her from suggesting the idea of marriage to Achilles himself but, as Homer implied, she discussed her secret wish with Patroclus, the closest of all Achilles' friends. When he died on the battlefield, she revealed his promise to her:

> You [Patroclus], when swift Achilles slew my husband and sacked the city of godlike Mynes, you would not even let me weep, but said that you would make me the wedded wife of Achilles and that he would lead me in his ships to Phthia, and make me a marriage feast among the Myrmidons. [6]

A man could find some advantages in keeping a female companion (*hetaira*) without marriage contract and any legal and family ties, but she, especially the maiden who was forced to be one like Briseis, probably yearned to be married and recognized by all as the legitimate wife.

Although most girls earnestly desired to be married, they feared some hardships associated with the change of identity and status from maiden to married woman and wife of a certain man. In the words of Aristotle, she became a part of his nature. [7] By contrast, nothing worse could happen to a married woman than to be divorced by her husband. She became nobody any more, back under the

---

[6] *Iliad*, 19, 295-299: Loeb 171, 356.
[7] Aristotle, *Nicomachean Ethics*, 5, 11, 1138b, 9: Loeb 73, 320.

guardianship of her prior *kurios* or his next of kin. For this reason, all participants in the agreement considered marriage as monogamous and permanent although, as we shall see later, it could be dissolved and expanded under certain conditions.

Nevertheless, both the *Kurios* and the suitors took a risk when they agreed to a marriage contract. The guardian did not know everything about the suitors to prevent making a bad choice, althought he knew more about them than most suitors knew about the wife they were agreeing to take. Nothing was more important to them than finding a good and virtuous wife who could deliver reputable children. [8] In the fifth century, they took only one wife and, as Euripides stated, "they risk[ed] much on the throw; for people take wives into their houses like ballast, with no experience of their ways." For this reason, he preferred to allow the suitor to take as many wives as he could afford "so he could throw the bad one out of his home and be pleased at keeping the one who actually is good." [9] This may have been the case for a time after the end of the Peloponnesian War in 404 BCE.

Contract

The marriage contract was made like a business contract, not between bride and groom but between the bride's *kurios*, usually the father, and the suitor. Like a traded good, the bride was the subject of the contract, not a partner in its negotiation and conclusion. The case of the sixth century Olympic winner who allowed his three daughters to choose their husbands is surely an exception, if the source of this information is not an interpolation. [10] Customarily, the consent of the girl was not required, but the consent of the man always was, and yet, in one instance, it may have been different, so the case was challenged in court, as Demosthenes reported. One of the witnesses testified about the groom having said:

---

[8] Euripides, *Fr., Oedipus*, 543: Loeb 506, 14-17; also, *Ibid.*, 545a: Loeb 506, 16.

[9] *Fr., Ino*, 402: Loeb 504, 446 & *Fr., Protesilaus*, 657: Loeb 506, 116.

[10] Herodotus, *Histories*, 6, 122: Loeb 119, 276.

> As for me, he [my father] forthwith persuaded me, for I was about eighteen years of age, to marry the daughter of Euphemus, wishing to live to see children born to me ... so [I] obeyed him. [11]

In this case, the persuasion can be explained, if not justified, by the young age of the son and the ill health or old age of the father.

The contract consisted usually of only a few words of exchange, for example, as Herodotus reported, the brief words uttered by Cleisthenes, the ruler of Sicyon in northern Peloponnesus, in the contractual delivery of his daughter to her future husband, Megacles: "To Megacles, son of Alcmeon, do I betroth my daughter, Agarista, as by Athenian law ordained." [12]

On occasions, however, the contract was more specific about certain details such as the place where the couple would live, as it appeared in the contract of 311-310 BCE between Heracleides of Temnos and Leptines of Cos, father of the bride Demetria. [13] Nevertheless, the essence of the contract was always to transfer the right of guardianship over the future bride from the present guardian to her future husband, thus cementing before the wedding the relationship between the two families under the watchful eye of the state and, on occasions, of the groom's father. The contract did not yet make the groom the guardian of his new wife, i.e. not until the wedding celebration that included consummation.

A vase painting of about 425 BCE shows that the verbal agreement was followed by a handshake between the bride's guardian and the groom. [14] Not only was the bride's consent not required but also her presence. The presence of witnesses was not required either but recommended in view of testifying later about the progeny. [15]

---

[11] Demosthenes, *Against Boeotus II*, 12: Loeb 318, 488-491.
[12] *Histories*, 6, 130: Loeb 119, 286.
[13] J. Neils and J.H. Oakley, *Coming of Age in Ancient Greece*, 122b.
[14] See J. H. Oakley and R. H. Sinos, *The Wedding in Ancient Athens*, fig. 1. p. 51.
[15] Demosthenes, *Against Onetor I*, 30, 21: Loeb 318, 1, 140.

Dowry

The contract involved a dowry (*phernê*) from the bride's guardian (*kurios*). It was negotiated according to his financial ability, like a business transaction. It was neither a pay off nor a rental fee. It was a security to be administered by the husband for his wife's eventual needs. Even after the transfer of the dowry the bride's guardian kept the right to dissolve the marriage contract or order its dissolution and reclaim the dowry, if he could prove the inability of the groom to provide for his wife. The odds were in favor of a successful marriage if the groom and his bride were of the same rank and equal wealth, as Euripides suggested from his own point of view:

> Men who marry wives above their rank, or marry great wealth, do not know how to make a marriage. The wife's interests prevail in the household and make a slave of the husband, and he is no longer free. Wealth acquired from marriage with a woman is unprofitable, for divorces are (not) easy. [16]

If the husband died or divorced when his wife was childless, or if the wife died childless, the dowry returned to the original guardian or his next of kin. If she was a mother when her husband died or divorced, her dowry remained for her and her children while it was administered by her guardian until an adult son could assume the responsibility. If her husband outlived her and had at least one child in his charge, her dowry remained for the girl until her wedding and the boy until his maturity. The protection of both the mother and the child was the purpose of the dowry.

The sum of money was large in the dowries supported by evidence, like the one paid by the elder Demosthenes who was a very wealthy man. In his will, he bequeathed two talents (12,000 drachmas) to his daughter and to his wife 8,000 drachmas which was added to her original dowry of 5,000 drachmas. Such a wealth was rare in Athens. Ninety percent of the people lived in poverty or frugality. The Spartan life was a reality not only in Sparta

---

[16] *Fr., Melanippe Wise*, 502: Loeb 504, 606 and *Fr., Phaeton*, 775, 158-9: Loeb 506, 344.

but also in Attica. Therefore, the dowries were more often in drachmas than in talents.

The equivalent in our modern currencies can be guessed only by comparison. For example, setting the current minimum wage for an unskilled beginning employee at 25,000 American dollars per year and the unskilled Ancient Athenian worker at 225 drachmas, and the top wage of a skilled beginning worker, either employed or independent, at 65,000 American dollars per year and the skilled Ancient Athenian worker at 600 drachmas per year, we may be warranted to estimate that the middle-range dowry was roughly between 225 and 600 drachmas, by comparison between 25,000 and 65,000 dollars, with the poor below this range and the comfortable middle class above this range, therefore an average of 330 drachmas (45,000 dollars). Of course, the size of a family will reduce the level of financial comfort.

The dowry could be paid in coins, possessions, business shares or land. The amount was not regulated by law but subjected to the combined forces of tradition, guardian's generosity, economic prosperity, and supply and demand -- a greater supply of brides tended to increase the dowries in order to attract the fewer men seeking marriage. As a result, the amount probably oscillated over the short waves of peace and wars. In any event, the details are lacking and our estimates cannot be more than conjectures.

At least during the Homeric times of the late eighth century, it appeared that, for special interest, the suitor himself paid the bride's guardian a certain amount of money as a price (*hedna*), making the financial deal a kind of bartering. Strait-laced Penelope, the wife of Odysseus, commented on the custom followed by wooers competing for a lady's hand:

> Those who wish to woo lady of worth and the daughter of a rich man and vie with one another, these themselves bring cattle and fat sheep, a banquet for the friends of the bride, and give to her glorious gifts; they do not devour the livelihood of another [the bride's *kurios*] without atonement. [17]

---

[17] Homer, *Odyssey*, 18, 276-280: Loeb 105. 220

Mythology is also indicative of the ancient culture. After god Hephaistos exposed the adultery Ares committed with his wife Aphrodite, he claimed from Zeus, her father, the bride-price he had paid him. He warned:

> The snare and the bonds shall hold them until her father [Zeus] pays back to me all the gifts of wooing that I gave him for this shameless girl [Aphrodite], since his daughter is beautiful but faithless. [18]

This bride-price was like a payment for purchase, entirely private and to be used for the benefit of the bride's guardian as he saw fit. It did not resemble the dowry kept as security. Did the practice become a tradition in the later period of the Classical Age? The evidence is lacking. However, the importance of being well connected in the financial world of land ownership and trade, and, in the fourth century, of banking, and in the political world of leadership, probably kept the practice alive but also very secret. This is the kind of activity a Greek man found embarrassing, even damaging to him if revealed to other men.

The dowry may have been like a thorn in the side, inserted more deeply into the recipient's side than into the provider's side. The new husband had no right to dispose of it as he wished and could feel enslaved by it, especially if he married above his wealth. Plato favored abolishing the dowry practice entirely. [19] But he also proposed to fine the men who refused to marry for such a reason and to deprive them of all honors due to elders. On the other hand, the guardians whose poverty prevented from giving a dowry may be compensating the new household with a greater favor, because there "will be less insolence on the part of the wives and less humiliation and servility on the part of the husbands because of money". [20]

When a matchmaker, man or woman, was involved in bringing together the bride's guardian and the suitor, some monetary compensation to the matchmaker was probably in

---

[18] Homer, *Odyssey*, 8, 316-319: Loeb 104, 204.
[19] *Laws*, 5, 742C: Loeb 187, 372.
[20] *Ibid.*, 6, 774D: Loeb 187, 466.

order. This portion of the contract was also handled privately and secretly. [21]

Love

Was the Greek marriage based only on business or was it also based on love, in both senses of affection (*philia*) and sexual desire (*erôs*)? In his *Oeconomicus* of the early fourth century, Xenophon did not include love as contributing to the wife's success in the management of her husband's estate. Also, love was absent from Plato's conditions for the choice of a husband by a *kurios*. He referred only to "nearness of kin and the security of the lot [property] ... A person suited by character and conduct." [22]

Marriage could hardly be based on love since the bride and groom had little opportunity to know each other at all before the wedding. The sexes lived parallel lives. To make citizens for the state and add to the family wealth were the only goals that seemed to matter.

Yet, love has always been a major part of life in all situations. Sophocles' chorus of Elders in *Antigone* of 443/441 BCE celebrated the unrestricted power of love, for good or bad results. The brothers Eteocles and Polynices had killed each other in their struggle for power. Then, against the decree of king Creon, Antigone performed the ritual of burial for the attacker Polynices, and was ready to die for it. Knowing she was promised in marriage to Creon's son, Haemon, the chorus personified Love and chanted:

> Love invincible in battle, Love who falls upon men's property, you who spend the night upon the soft cheeks of a girl, and travel over the sea and through the huts of dwellers in the wild! None among the immortals can escape you, nor any among mortal men, and he [Haemon] who has you is mad.
> You wrench just men's minds aside from justice, doing them violence; it is you who have stirred up this quarrel between men of the same blood [the brothers]. Victory goes to the visible desire that

[21] Aristophanes, *Clouds*, 41: Loeb 488, 14 and Xenophon, *Memorabilia*, 2, 6, 36: Loeb 168, 144.
[22] Plato, *Laws*, 11, 924D: Loeb 192, 426.

comes from the eyes of the beautiful bride [Antigone], desire that has its throne beside those of the mighty laws; for irresistible in her sporting is the goddess Aphrodite. [23]

Given a choice between being married for love or for money, the viewpoints of the guardian and the suitors, on the one hand, and of the daughter, on the other hand, were different, the first for wealth and prestige [24] and the second for love. Wealth and love never cease to be in the match of life and the match of life has no other purpose, except for the totally selfish participant, but to share

oneness of heart in all its excellence. For nothing is greater and better than this, than when a man and a woman keep house together sharing one heart and mind, a great grief to their foes and a joy to their friends, while their own fame is unsurpassed. [25]

These words about a young girl, Nausicaa, revealed the flame of her burning desire to be married, perhaps to this stranger, Odysseus, and chart also the path toward a successful and happy married life. Every congenial marriage was preferable to a wealthy disagreeable one, even to a sexually passionate one. All adversities will thus be overcome when women share with their husbands in all the pleasures and pains of life, some coming to her from parents, siblings, children and even husbands, others mostly of her own. Most girls, however, married a husband they did not know and learned to love only while married to him.

Whether with love or without it, a dowry had to be paid and it could make a rich couple richer but never turn a poor couple into a rich one. Nevertheless, Greek marriages were probably sealed frequently and only in money. The family wealth, the dowry, the financial connections and influence were all assets carefully reckoned in the arrangement of a marriage. Plato warned the men of his time to avoid marrying rich women lest they become "mean and subservient to them on account of property". To keep

---

[23] *Antigone*, 781-800: Loeb 21, 76-79.
[24] Euripides, *Fr.*, *Thyestes*, 395: Loeb 504, 434.
[25] Homer, *Odyssey*, 6, 181-185: Loeb 104, 232.

control seemed to have been more important than to
acquire wealth. But his complete advice was really more
balanced than this first statement would let us believe:

> You must make a marriage that will commend itself
> to men of sense, who would counsel you neither to
> shun connexion with a poor family, not to pursue
> ardently connexion with a rich one, but, other things
> being equal, to prefer always an alliance with a
> family of moderate means. Such a course will benefit
> both the State and the united families. [26]

Whether rich or poor, of a noble or humble origin,
the husband was always the master of the household. No
one ever referred to him as "that woman's husband" but,
like Electra stated, everyone referred to her as "that man's
wife". She explained:

> Yet it is a disgrace for the woman, rather than the
> man, to be the head of a house. I loathe any child
> who derives his name in the city not from his father
> but from his mother. For when a man marries a wife
> of greater eminence than himself, no account is
> taken of the man but only of his wife. [27]

Electra had in mind her mother, Clytemnestra, who
dominated her marriage to Aegisthus. Such a relationship
was not acceptable in Athenian society. The husband was
the ruler of the household and of all who belonged to it,
wife and children.

A fragment from the fourth century seems to indicate
that some wives did not forget the dowry they brought to
their husbands for safekeeping and had their ways of
reminding them. One husband, Alexis, admitted it: "We can't
say we don't pay a price for their dowries: bitterness and
women's anger". [28]

Another fragment from a lost comedy introduces a
wife whose father was more of a money-grubber than she
was. He first married her to a well-to-do man who really

---

[26] *Laws*, 6, 773A: Loeb 187, 460.
[27] Euripides, *Electra*, 932-937: Loeb 9, 254.
[28] In M. R. Lefkowitz and M. B. Fant, *Women's Life in Greece and
Rome*, 35, p. 18.

cared for her. They had a happy life together but, for some unknown reason, the husband became bankrupt. When his father-in-law wanted to take his wife away from him and marry her to a rich man, she objected:

> Explain to me how, by whatever he has done, he has done me wrong. There is a covenant between man and wife; he must feel affection for her always till the end, and she must never cease to do what gives her husband pleasure. He was all that I wished with regard to me, and my pleasure is his pleasure, father. ... How can it be just and honorable that I should take a share in any good things he has, but take no share in his poverty? [29]

Some suitors were willing to ignore marrying for love or money, because their bride may not be beautiful enough to excite their passion or wealthy enough to satisfy their financial ambitions but, according to Euripides, they preferred high birth and good reputation "for the children's sake". [30] Besides, as he also wrote, "This is the best kind of wealth, to find a noble spouse" [31] and "what need of a beautiful wife, unless she had good sense?" Remember that beauty does not last, but good sense does. [32]

Laws

Romantic and financial thoughts, although pertinent, should be accompanied by thoughts of laws and traditions (*nomoi*), never far from some contractual arrangement.

As early as the eighth century BCE, Hesiod advised the father to wait until the fifth year of his daughter's puberty, at least after the age of fifteen, before marrying her to a man of about thirty years of age, who had then attained some status among his fellow-citizens. Besides, "males' vigour is longer lasting, while a women's youth abandons her body more quickly." [33] On the other hand, an

---

[29] In M. R. Lefkowitz, *Women in Greek Myth*, 68.
[30] *Fr.,Ino*, 405: Loeb 504, 448; see *Fr.,Alexander*, 59: Loeb 504, 54.
[31] *Fr., Andromeda*, 137: Loeb 504, 146.
[32] *Fr., Antiope*, 212 & 213: Loeb 504, 222.
[33] *Fr., Aeolus*, 24: Loeb 504, 24.

older husband would be older yet when his children needed his attention and, therefore, became burdensome, so his wife would have to carry a greater burden. [34] Such a difference in age between about fifteen and thirty became a custom, like a law (*nomos*). As a result, it gave the bride's father the advantage over his counterpart to become a living grandfather.

Hesiod preferred also that the bride lived nearby and was looking well, "for a man wins nothing better than a good wife and, again, nothing worse than a bad one." [35] The odds of success increased if the marriage was within the family, at least the same clan. This arrangement smoothed away the hardship of moving from her current home to her husband's household and kept the family wealth intact in spite of the dowry. We do not know how often this larger family arrangement prevailed, although our guess is that it prevailed very often. The closeness of the family relationship, however, was probably rarely as close as it was, for example, for Cleopatra, daughter of king Philip of Macedon and sister of Alexander the Great, who married her maternal uncle, Alexander of Epirus, in 336 BCE, the day before her father was assassinated at the theater.

The wedding contract could be legally enforceable, yet it could also be broken before the wedding ceremony by mutual agreement between the girl's guardian and the suitor, without involving the courts and, of course, the girl.

On the other hand, to falsely pretend to have a marriage contract and a wedding ceremony certifying the legal marriage was a crime, as the case of Stephanus and Neaera amply demonstrated. [36] In this case, an Athenian man pretended to be married to an Athenian woman when she was a foreign companion (*hetaira*). He was found guilty of this deception in the court of *graphê* (written document) and sentenced to pay a fine of one thousand drachmae. [37] The *kurios* who gave the foreign woman away and pretended she was an Athenian woman lost his civic rights and his property. [38] What happened to the woman, a pawn in this men's game? Since the foreign woman had no legal

---

[34] Euripides, *Fr., Phoenix*, 804 & 807: Loeb 506, 412-415.
[35] *Works and Days*, 695-705: Loeb 57, 53-55.
[36] Demosthenes, *Against Neaera, 14 & passim*: Loeb 351, 360 ff.
[37] *Ibid.*, 16: Loeb 351, 362.
[38] *Ibid.*, 52 & 87: Loeb 351, 390 & 418.

rights or property to lose, she simply returned to her true status of foreign woman.

If the case had been the reverse, namely that a foreign man would have been found guilty of pretending to be legally married to an Athenian woman, he would have been sentenced to be sold as a slave and his property confiscated. As for the Athenian woman who had been duped into marrying a foreign man, she was the victim of a crime and punished enough by the stigma of an illicit and embarrassing conjugal union. In spite of the wounds inflicted on the legal marriage in the fourth century, this legislation demonstrated the vigor of the marriage contract, as displayed in the previous century: "mightier than an oath (*horkos*) and Justice (*Dikê*) is its guardian." [39]

Although the mother had no legal standing in the negotiations of the marriage contract for her daughters, she probably watched closely and advised dutifully her husband who was the *kurios* in charge in this matter.

It was considered a duty to the state for the girl's *kurios* and the suitor to implement the marriage contract with a wedding ceremony and then for the couple to try to have children. The law allowed the contract to take place long before the wedding. For example, the elder Demosthenes betrothed his daughter when she was an infant of only five years of age to her cousin Demophon who was then about twenty-five years old. [40] Nevertheless, the contract remained valid until fulfilled or annulled.

Solon, the lawgiver of the sixth century BCE, made no law against bachelorism. In his *Parallel Lives*, Plutarch told the fictional story of Solon visiting the philosopher Thales of Miletus who was unmarried because he felt the pains of having children were too much to bear. Nevertheless, as Plutarch added, he adopted his nephew Cybisthus. [41]

It appeared that the unmarried status among men older than twenty years of age became more frequent during the Periclean age of prosperity in the fifth century. According to the best estimates, from 451 when Pericles enacted the law of dual parentage to 431 when he engaged Athens into a war against Sparta, the number of bachelors increased by 38 percent, from 13,000 to 18,000. The girls'

---

[39] Aeschylus, *Eumemides*, 217-218: Loeb 146, 292.
[40] Demosthenes, *Against Aphobus III*, 43: Loeb 318, 110.
[41] *Solon*, 6, 2: Loeb 46, 418.

guardians had a better choice among the suitors. On the other hand, more girls were left waiting and wanting. During the subsequent period of the Peloponnesian war, and especially after the disaster of the Sicilian expedition of 415 BCE, the number of bachelors fell by 53 percent, from 18,000 to 8,500. Such a threat to the Athenian population prompted the legislators to allow the men who survived the war to have more than one legal wife.

Of course, the disaster of war and the low birth rate could have been corrected if only the men would have married at a younger age. But it appears that they did not. Five hundred years after Hesiod, the marrying age was still a matter of social consideration. In the fourth century, Plato recommended the ages of 12 to 20 for the women and 30 to 35 for the men. It seems, however, that tradition and his exhortation were not entirely successful because he also suggested imposing a fine, commensurate to the men's wealth, if they were still unmarried at 35 years of age. [42] Worthy of note is the fact that no law forbade a man to marry at a younger age if he had the financial resources to open a new household. It probably occurred rarely because men had little incentive to give up their careless freedom and marry before reaching the thirty-year mark.

In his *Republic* of about 367 BCE, Plato suggested which years were more appropriate to have children: between 20 and 40 for the wife and between 25 and 55 for the husband. [43] The fulfillment of this duty may have been neglected when, several years later, Aristotle approved of a more mature age, delaying the age of marriage to 18 for the woman and 37 or a little before for the man. [44] Like Plato before him, he implied that some men were marrying younger and deplored it. He believed his proposal would improve the quality of the offsprings, but neglected to think that it placed the burden of educating the children on the mother alone, because most men found it difficult to be involved when they had reached their 40s and 50s. Furthermore, if the first son could be ready for marriage only at 37 and raised his family in his forties, his father would then be in his late seventies and his grandparents already deceased. The result was that paternal

---

[42] Plato, *Laws*. 6, 774A-B: Loeb 187, 464.
[43] *Republic*, 5, 460E: Loeb 237, 464.
[44] *Politics*, 7, 14, 1335a, 29: Loeb 264, 620.

grandparents, already scarce in the fifth century, completely disappeared in the fourth century.

Wedding Celebration

The Greeks had only one word, *gamos*, to signify the wedding and the ensuing permanent status of marriage. [45] According to the full meaning of the verb *gameô*, to be married involved sexual consummation, in the sense that it legitimized the marital relations.

The earliest paintings of weddings in black-figured style dated back to the third quarter of the seventh century BCE, the vases from Sophilos on the same subject dated of 580-570 [46] and those from Kleitias a decade later. [47] They sublimated the human wedding by introducing deities like Dionysus, Hermes and Apollo, by uplifting the appearances, for example substituting a chariot for a cart in the procession, and by focusing on the transfer from a lower status to a higher one in society.

After about 480 BCE, wedding scenes appeared on vases of the red-figured style. A noticeable change in subjects and shapes took place with the change in style. The range of subjects grew wider, covering a variety of scenes related to the wedding celebrations, from the preparations to the final nuptial encounter of the newly-weds. During the Classical period of the fifth and fourth centuries, the procession and the adornment of the bride became favorite subjects.

Also, the vases selected for paintings were more directly connected to the wedding: for example, instead of the general vases like the water jar (*hudria*) and the two-handle liquid jar (*amphora*), the more specific vases like the slender jar to carry bathwater (*loutrophoros*), the wedding bowl (*lebes gamikos*), the round-bottom bowl on a stand for mixing wine and water (*dinos*), and the cosmetics box (*puxis*) were selected by the painters.

After about 440 BCE, when Phidias was carving the figures of goddesses and Lapith women at the Parthenon of Athens, the number of wedding scenes increased and their romantic aspects gained in importance, as deities like Eros

[45] Aristotle, *Politics*, 1, 1, 1253b, 9-10: Loeb 264, 12-15.
[46] EWA 2, Pl. 46
[47] EWA 2, Pl. 36 and 14, Pl. 295.

and Aphrodite played a greater role. The association of the human with the divine became more obvious in the Late Classical period of the fourth century. Also, the selection of scenes became more pointed, for example on carrying the bathwater, presenting the gifts, and dancing. In the process, the scenes appeared more human and less sublime.

These changes were very much in keeping with the changes taking place in the society of Athens and of Greece in general. The Peloponnesian war of 431-404 inflicted on the common people some mental confusion and disillusionment which they did not feel before and from which they never recovered completely in later years. They became more realistic, romantic, even seductive in the fourth century and less involved in the heroic and divine symbols of the past. The bride became more often the focus of attention and her beauty more often exploited by the artists.

On the other hand, when the artists depicted myths of erotic pursuits, for example by the hero-king Theseus, they added to reality an ingredient that fed the imaginations of Greek men and women who carried in the recesses of their minds erotic fantasies related to the culture of the wedding celebration.

Like the wedding in every other culture, the Athenian wedding included three elements of ritual: the preparations (separation), the actual wedding (transition) and the consummation (incorporation). The Greek wedding was an exciting and joyous event well documented in literature from Homer in the eighth century down the centuries to the times of Alexander the Great in the late fourth century BCE.

Preparations

The last function a mother performed for her daughter was to manage the preparations for her wedding. In a manner never used by humans yet indicative of the role of a mother, Hera, goddess of marriage, is represented on a red-figure column-mixing bowl (*kratêr*) of about 470-460

BCE sending her daughter Hebe in a chariot to fetch Heracles for their wedding. [48]

After the handshake of the girl's guardian and the suitor, sealing the agreement about the marriage, a wedding date was discussed and agreed upon. In due time, the preparations began in earnest under the supervision of the bride's mother.

When Agamemnon called his daughter Iphigenia to Aulis, it was allegedly to do the preparations for her wedding to Achilles. Her mother Clytemnestra was there ready to take charge. [49] A messenger reported:

> They are performing the maiden's consecration to Artemis, mistress of Aulis [before the wedding]. ... But come now, in view of these things prepare the basket, garland your heads, and you, lord Menelaus, get ready the Hymen song! Let the pipe sound in the tents and let there be the sound of dancing feet! This day is a blessed one for the girl! [50]

Before dying and leaving her daughter to a resentful stepmother to care for the inevitable wedding preparations, Alcestis worried, perhaps without cause, about not being there to assist her with all the attention she will need. [51] It was natural for her to worry about a stepmother's intentions and interests.

The sacrifice to the virgin goddess Artemis was only half the preparations but it was an important one. Lest the bride would offend Artemis for leaving her state of virginity, she should first placate her with the proper sacrifice of gifts, like dolls and trinkets.

The next step was to deliver herself to the goddess of love, Aphrodite. The offering of childhood things, such as toys and clothing, or of a lock of hair, to Aphrodite and some other goddesses of choice was also a part of the

[48] Attributed to the Cleveland Painter and kept at the Cleveland Museum of Art. See J. Neils and J.H. Oakley, *Coming of Age in Ancient Greece*, 128-129.
[49] Euripides, *Iphigenia at Aulis*, 691 ff.: Loeb 495, 238 ff. and *Iphigenia Among the Taurians*, 818-819: Loeb 10, 236.
[50] Id., *Iphigenia at Aulis*, 432-439: Loeb 495, 210.
[51] Id., *Alcestis*, 313-319: Loeb 12, 184; see Id., *Fr., Phrixus*, 824: Loeb 506, 452.

preparations to the wedding. So both passages, from virginity to motherhood and from childhood to adulthood, were signified in the preparations.

The sacrificial ceremony consisted of a procession depicted on a fragment of a round-bottom bowl, called *dinos*, by Sophilos of the first half of the sixth century BCE. He showed the participants in the marriage of Peleus, king of the Myrmidons, and the Nereid Thetis, future parents of the hero Achilles, marching toward the altar where will take place the sacrifice of animals, usually small but, according to the wealth of the family, sometimes as large as an ox. The bride is wearing a fine dress and a veil. Standing by her, the groom is accompanied by other men, including guards. We cannot expect absolute clarity from only one silent painting preserved only in fragments. Nevertheless, we can expect that any representation of mythical events will reproduce events in real life, because the latter were the only ones known by the artists. [52]

The ritual bath followed the sacrificial offerings. It was elaborate and ceremonial for the bride. The groom had his own ceremonial bath, simple and, of course, separate. Special water from a spring or river was required. A child carried it in a vase, both called *loutrophoros*, in a scene frequently shown on pottery. [53] On a red-figure cosmetics box (*puxis*) of about 425 BCE, the bride is shown bathing, dressing and receiving final advice from Aphrodite with the help of Eros. [54]

In his play *The Phoenician Women* of about 425 BCE, Euripides exploited the grief of the Theban queen Jocasta for the exile of her son Polynices and his marriage, away from home, to a princess of Argos, and referred to three elements of the marriage ceremony: the torches, the bath and the procession. Jocasta was addressing the chorus of Phoenician maidens:

> I did not kindle for you the blazing torch that custom requires [in marriages], as befits a mother blessed. The Ismenus River made this alliance without the

---

[52] EWA 2, Pl. 46.
[53] J. H. Oakley and R. H. Sinos, *The Wedding in Ancient Athens*, Fig. 15, p. 28.
[54] In A. Richlin, *Pornography and Representation in Greece and Rome*, Fig. 1, 9, p. 25.

luxurious bath, and in the city of Thebes none cried aloud at the entrance of your bride. [55]

In this passage, Euripides referred to three elements that belonged to the wedding celebration, the first two from the preparations: first the lighting of the torch by the groom's mother and, second, her son's ritual bath with water not drawn from the river Ismenus at Thebes. The wedding ceremony itself, which we will soon consider, included the procession with songs and dances.

The last phase of the nuptial preparations was the adornment of the bride and groom. The bride received more attention since her wedding was the time in her life when she could be as extravagant as her family could afford, therefore wearing a necklace and rings of gemstones, a purple dress, a flowery crown covered by a veil over her head, elegant wedding sandals, and a perfume fragrant enough to overcome the man's perfume, as Socrates suggested. [56] One woman, called *numphokomos* (bride's hairdresser), took charge of the adornment of the bride with the assistance of some other women friends and relatives. [57]

A scene from Homer's *Iliad* depicted in human images the divine strategy of Hera to lure Zeus into making love to her. Our attention should focus on the adornments that were of the kind a bride would wear for her wedding.

With ambrosia first, she cleansed every stain from her lovely body, and anointed herself richly with oil, ambrosial, soft, and of rich fragrance; if this were but shaken in the palace of Zeus with threshold of bronze, its scent would reach to earth and heaven. With this she anointed her lovely body, and she combed her hair, and with her hands plaited the bright tresses, fair and ambrosial, that streamed from her immortal head. Then she clothed herself in an ambrosial robe which Athene had worked and smoothed for her, and had set on it many

[55] *Phoenician* Women, 344-349: Loeb 11, 244; also *Trojan Women*, 308-341: Loeb 10, 46-51.
[56] Xenophon, *Banquet*, 2, 3: Loeb 168, 542.
[57] Oakley, J. H. and R. H. Sinos, *The Wedding in Ancient Athens*, Fig. 23, p. 64 and A. Richlin, *Pornography and Representation in Greece and Rome*, Fig. 1, 9, p. 19.

embroideries; and she pinned it at the breast with brooches of gold, and she girt about her a belt set with one hundred tassels, and in her pierced ears she put earrings with three clustering drops; and abundant grace shone from them. And with a veil over all did the fair goddess veil herself, a veil fair and bright, all glistening, and it was white as the sun; and beneath her shining feet she bound her fair sandals. [58]

Ceremony

When the preparations were completed, the wedding (*gamos*) could take place. The first day of the wedding celebrations began with sacrifices to the gods (*proteleia*) which were usually conducted outdoors by the bride (*numphê*) and her retinue. [59]

The famous "Francois vase", signed by the painter Kleitias and the potter Ergotimos of the second quarter of the sixth century BCE, displays the image of the divine wedding of Peleus and Thetis. The bride is sitting inside the house while the groom stands in front of the house ready to greet the guests, some arriving on foot and others on a chariot pulled by a team of horses. [60]

No private celebration compared with the wedding extravaganza both families put up for their son and daughter, usually at the house of one of the parents and preferably in gamelion (Jan./Feb.) and at full moon which was understood to be a fertile time. It was an ostentatious feast, with food aplenty, including meat from the sacrifice, and wine to prompt the loud shouts and songs, and the dances at the beat of the tambourines and sweet sound of the flutes. Men and women were guests, yet they were entertained separately. The dances were particularly elaborate, swift and elegant. Although men and women danced separately, they could observe each other with joy and enthusiasm. Plato recommended that the list of guests be limited to ten friends and ten kinsfolk or connexions, evenly divided from each side, both sexes being

---

[58] *Iliad*, 14, 170-187: Loeb 171, 78-81.
[59] EWA 7, Pl. 21.
[60] EWA 2, Pl. 36 and 14, Pl. 295

represented, and that the expenses for the wedding festival be kept according to the groom's financial means. [61]

Aristophanes provided examples of wedding celebrations with obvious ridiculous exaggerations, seldom with marital contract. In his play *The Peace*, he described how god Hermes gave as a wife the beautiful maiden Harvesthome, a Dionysiac symbol of fertility and joy, to the peacemaker Trygaeus. "Beetle! Let's fly home now, home!" ordered Trygaeus, [62] and the whole party followed them to his home where he first entrusted his bride to his servant for the nuptial preparations, [63] then offered a lamb in a bloodless sacrifice to Peace.

On his way to the wedding feast, Trygaeus dismissed from attending the celebration a certain Hierocles, known only as a soothsayer warmonger. At the feast, he greeted the guests and urged them to "pile on the cookies and thrushes, and lots of the rabbit, and the roles". [64] Trygaeus chimed:

> Let us speak auspiciously, and escort the bride
>   outside here,
> and fetch torches, and all the people rejoice with us
>   and cheer us on,
> and move all our equipment back to country right
>   now,
> dancing and pouring libations and driving
>   Hyperbolus [despicable politician] away,
> and making prayers to the gods
> that they grant prosperity to the Greeks
> and help us produce lots of barley,
> all of us alike, and lots of wine,
> and figs [for fertility] to nibble,
> and that our wives bear us children,
> and together we recover all that we lost
> just as it was to begin with,
> and have done with the shining blade. [65]

---

[61] *Laws*, 6, 775A: Loeb 187, 468.
[62] *Peace*, 720: Loeb 488, 518.
[63] *Ibid.*, 842: Loeb 488, 532.
[64] *Ibid.*, 1195-1196: Loeb 488, 578.
[65] Aristophanes, *Peace*, 1316-1328: Loeb 488, 596. The last lines allude to the Peloponnesian War.

Finally came the happy moment of union of bride and groom. The chorus blasted the familiar song: "Hymen, Hymenaeus O! Hymen, Hymenaeus O!." [66] Thus ended the wedding feast described in comedy by the playwright Aristophanes.

This extravagant ceremony was not repeated for a second wedding. Also, marital union, as we previously explained, usually occurred by contract but sometimes also by cohabitation. In this latter situation, the celebration was always very discreet, even when some degree of solemnity gave it credibility. Aristophanes' celebrations at the end of his plays appear to be one step below the *gamos* by cohabitation, because it was no more than one sexual encounter, like a one-night stand or a short affair by both parties.

In the rare occurrence that the marriage contract had not yet been executed, it was done at nightfall of this second day. Then, for the first time, the bride joined the groom and removed the veil off her face. [67] No doubt, the new husband looked at her with a good measure of emotions. This moment was the center of all the nuptial celebrations. Now the groom and the bride were officially, but not yet in reality, man and wife.

In a court action of the fourth century, the orator Isaeus presented the evidence that his mother was the legitimate wife of his father, Ciron. He explained how public the event had been:

> When our father took her in marriage, he gave a wedding-feast and invited three of his friends as well as his relatives, and he gave a marriage-banquet to the members of his ward according to their statutes. [68]

Now the bride could be taken to her new home, followed publicly by the procession of all the guests. [69] With the songs and dances, the torches added an element of

---

[66] Aristophanes, *Peace*, 1332-1333: Loeb 488, 598.
[67] See J. H. Oakley and R. H. Sinos, *The Wedding in Ancient Athens*, Fig. 85, p. 97.
[68] Isaeus, *On the Estate of Ciron*, 18: Loeb 202, 298.
[69] EWA 2, Pl. 135 and S. Hornblower & A. Spawforth, *Oxford Companion to Classical Civilization*, 423.

mystery and legitimacy to the marriage. The procession took place after sunset, yet in the clear view of all spectators. The lighting of the torches was the responsibility of the two mothers. [70]

The scene of the procession ending the marriage ceremony was a favorite theme of the vase painters as early as the seventh century when the black-figured style appeared and, long after it, when it was replaced by the red-figured style, until as late as the fourth century. Although very useful to our understanding of this important event, it is more symbolic -- like depicting the wedding of Peleus and Thetis instead of a human wedding -- and, therefore, not as accurate as some of the literary testimonies about it.

A fragment of Sappho (seventh century BCE) describes this solemn procession from the house of either parent, or sometimes from a sanctuary where the feast took place, to the new home the bride and groom will occupy and, as husband and wife, will start their own family (*oikos*). The fragment deals with the marriage of Hector and Andromache of Troy:

> At once the sons of Ilus yoked the mules to the smooth-running carriages, and the whole crowd of women and (tender?) and led maidens climbed on board. Apart (drove) the daughters of Priam ... and unmarried men yoked horses to chariots, ... and greatly ... chariotees ... [gap of several verses] ... like gods ... holy ... all together ... set out ... to Ilium [Troy], and the sweet-sounding pipe and cithara were mingled and the sound of castanets, and maidens sang clearly a holy song, and a marvelous echo reached the sky ... and everywhere in the streets was ... bowls and cups ... myrrh and cassia and frankincense were mingled. The elder women cried out joyfully, and all the men let forth a lovely high-pitched strain calling on Paean, the Archer skilled in the lyre, and they sang in praise of the god-like Hector and Andromache. [71]

---

[70] Euripides, *Iphigenia at Aulis*, 734: Loeb 495, 244; *Trojan Women*, 310: Loeb 10, 46 and *Phoenician Women*, 344-345: Loeb 11, 244.

[71] *Greek Lyric: Fr., Sappho and Alcaeus*, 44: Loeb 142, 89-91.

In Euripides' play *Alcestis*, king Admetus grieving for the loss of his wife Alcestis, recalls the day he walked into his house with her as his bride:

> Once I entered with pine torches from mount Pelion and bridal songs, holding the hand [72] of my dear wife, and a clamorous throng followed, praising the blessedness of my dead wife and me, because she and I, both nobly born, had become man and wife. Now groans of grief in answer to those songs and black robes in place of white escort me in to a desolate bed chamber. [73]

A more sober description of the same festive procession appeared in a court case of the fourth century BCE. A certain Lycophron had been accused of approaching a bride during the wedding procession and trying to win her to himself, away from the groom. Hyperides defended him by showing how impossible it was for a stranger to do it when the bride's two brothers, Dioxippus and Euphraeus, both famous wrestlers, were standing by her. [74]

Also, Plutarch told that a drunken youth, a close friend of the groom, once jumped onto the bride's carriage during the procession, just to be facetious, and was killed instantly by the other friends of the groom. [75]

The bride and her two attendants seated on both sides of her were riding in a carriage drawn by a mule or an ox. Not only was she completely covered with garment and veil, as women always were in public, but she was also well protected by the surrounding crowd, cheering and throwing flowers onto her, and by the man whose charge it was to walk beside her carriage, so that no foul-play could take place. The groom could not provide this protection himself, since he was either riding with his bride in the carriage or preceding her in order to receive her on the threshold of their new home. Some paintings on vases show the bride and groom not riding in a carriage but walking together.

---

[72] Represented in iconography as the wrist: see H. S. Lonsdale, *Dance and Ritual Play in Greek Religion*, 214-216.

[73] *Alcestis*, 915-925: Loeb 12, 248.

[74] See S. Usher, *Greek Oratory*, 330.

[75] Plutarch, *Moralia, On the Virtue of Woman*, 244E: Loeb 245, 484.

Either riding or walking, the bride was safe and the painter had an opportunity to depict the couple in one scene.

The well-wishers of the cortege accompanying the newlyweds from the wedding site to their new house were singing:

> Hymen, Hymeneus O!
> Hymen, Hymeneus O!
> You will live happily,
> and free of troubles
> gather in your figs.
> Hymen, Hymeneus O!
> Hymen, Hymeneus O! [76]

Friends and relatives were dancing their way, as the Trojan princess Cassandra wished they would at her wedding with the Greek king Agamemnon:

> Lift your foot and shake it, strike up the dance (*Euhan! Euhoi!*) just as in my father's happiest days! The dance is holy; do you, Phoebus, lead it. ... Dance, mother [Hecuba], dance, lead off and whirl your foot this way and that, joining with me in the joyful step! Shout the cry of Hymen with songs and shouts of blessedness to the bride. Come, you daughters of Phrygia, with your lovely gowns sing for me of the one destined for my marriage bed, my husband! [77]

Mature women enjoyed the glamorous dances and joyous songs at weddings. Even girls participated in them, celebrating Aphrodite. [78] They competed with each other for attention. In one voice, one of Euripides' choruses of Greek women exclaimed:

> May I take my place in the choruses where once as maiden of illustrious family near my dear mother I whirled in dance, and competing in grace with the throngs of my agemates and vying with them in the luxury born of soft-living wealth I put on a veil of

---

[76] Aristophanes, *Peace*, 1344-1350: Loeb 488, 600.
[77] Euripides, *Trojan Women*, 325-341: Loeb 10, 48-51; see Id., *Iphigenia at Aulis*, 1036-1057: Loeb 495, 280.
[78] Id., *Fr., Phaethon*, 229-235: Loeb 506, 354.

many hues and let down my tresses to shade my cheek. [79]

The cortege of revelers, rich and poor, filed between the houses,

By the light of the blazing torches they were leading the brides from their rooms through the city, and loud rose the bridal song. And young men were whirling in the dance, and with them flutes and lyres sounded continually; and the women stood each at her door and marveled. [80]

With their relatives and friends, the newlyweds were now heading for their new house, usually a very humble house but, for the wedding ceremony, all decked with garlands and branches. The groom preceded his bride and, with his mother, welcomed her at the door. [81] He guided her to the hearth, sometimes indoor, as we noticed in the house of the Acropolis, but more often in the courtyard. There, all the relatives and friends who could squeeze into this small area sprinkled the newlyweds with fruits and nuts as a sign of prosperity, especially figs as a symbol of fertility.

Solon instructed the "bride to nibble a quince before getting into bed", while attendants adorned her head with "a chaplet of asparagus." [82] By these rites she signified her acceptance of the sexual love (erôs) her new husband had pledged to her. Plato recommended also that the newlyweds abstain from too much wine, lest they be intoxicated and, as a consequence, their offspring be unfit in mind and body, nothing said about the quality of their first marital intercourse. [83]

---

[79] Euripides, *Iphigenia Among the Taurians*, 1143-1152: Loeb 10, 270-273.

[80] Homer, *Iliad*, 18, 492-496: Loeb 171, 322.

[81] See J. H. Oakley and R. H. Sinos, *The Wedding in Ancient Athens*, Fig. 106, p. 110.

[82] Plutarch, *Moralia, Advice to Bride and Groom*, 138d: Loeb 222, 300 and *Parallel Lives, Solon*, 20, 3: Loeb 46, 458.

[83] *Laws*, 6, 775B: Loeb 187, 468.

Consummation

In mythology, the voluptuous Aphrodite with the assistance of her son Eros presided over the union of male and female for the procreation of divine children. [84] On this wedding night, she presided also over the union of the human newlyweds.

Now was the time for all attendants to leave and the groom to take into the bridal chamber his new wife all spruced up for the occasion. The bed was a low couch with pillows, sometimes with a canopy over it.

One male friend of the groom, having closed the door behind the newlyweds, stood guard because the crowd was slow dispersing, as they continued to sing and dance outside well onto daybreak, a comfort to the bride's apprehensions. [85] As for the new husband, he often sponsored a special feast for the men of his *phratria* (group of families) as a way of informing them officially that a new *oikos* (family) had been formed. The Greeks respected the privacy of the bride and groom, especially for the sake of the bride who became on this wedding night a woman and a wife (*gunê*), as well as the manager of a new household and perhaps member of a different clan in society.

Keeping in mind the usual age difference of fifteen or twenty years between a virgin bride and an experienced groom, one would think that this first night called for his loving care and patience. It would not be totally facetious to say that his first child was in reality his own bride. Many married lives may have been seeded with happiness or sorrow on this first wedding night. The responsibility rested almost entirely on the new husband.

In some cases, the bride was not so young because the wedding ceremony was delayed for some reason. For example, king Menelaus of Sparta and his wife Helen had a daughter, Hermione, before the whole affair of the Trojan War broke out. If we allow a few years after Helen's elopement for the expedition to Troy to get under way, then more years for the war itself, Hermione must have been about fourteen years old when her father promised her to

---

[84] Hesiod, *Theogony*, 194-206: Loeb 57, 92-95.
[85] See J. H. Oakley and R. H. Sinos, *The Wedding in Ancient Athens*, Fig. 107, p. 111.

Neoptolemus during the last year of the war. The return of
Menelaus to Sparta and Neoptolemus to Phthia after the war
took several more years, at least seven or eight. By this
time, Hermione was in her early twenties, a mature woman
by Greek estimates. [86]

In any case, a marriage contract did not make a real
marriage without consummation. Electra was really
unmarried when she lived with a peasant husband who
respected her virginity. [87] Her name implied her status: *a-
lektron*, namely "without marriage bed". Only later, after the
divine Castor gave her away to Pylades, Oreste's friend, did
she become a wedded wife. Antigone also was promised in
marriage to Haemon, king Creon's son, but was really never
married to him because their union was never consum-
mated.

According to customs, the marriage festivities
continued outside all through the night. Then, a third day of
celebrations began at dawn -- when did they sleep? -- and
continued all day with songs and dances, enlivened by good
food and wine. This day was called *epaulia* to signify the
leftover tasks to be performed on this day, like driving on
the shoulder of a road before exiting. One task was for the
new wife to visit a shrine, for example the Nymph shrine,
south of the Acropolis, where she would dedicate some of
her household pottery; another task was for her to receive
the wedding gifts from the guests, such as perfume and
cosmetics, sandals and clothing. A few paintings on vases
show the husband standing near, sometimes holding hands
with his seated wife, no doubt in appreciation for the gifts
being presented. [88] If the dowry had not yet been delivered,
it was done on this third day of the wedding festivities,
according to the agreement made prior to the wedding.

From this moment, the festivities could continue for
more than a third day, into a fourth and a fifth day,
according to the wealth of the families and the mood of the
guests.

When the wedding celebrations were over, one more
party, called *Gamelia*, was for men only. As for the bride,
she was left out and happy to have reached her most

---

[86] Homer, *Odyssey*, 4, 5-14: Loeb 104, 118.

[87] Euripides, *Electra*, 44-53: Loeb 9, 154-157.

[88] See J. H. Oakley and R. H. Sinos, *The Wedding in Ancient Athens*,
Fig. 117, p. 118 and Fig. 125, p. 124.

cherished goal, yet somewhat confused and frightened, having been so sheltered before and now so alone under the domination of one man she did not know well. A good measure of apprehension was mixed with her pride and joy. She probably resorted to some face-saving ways, out of consideration for her husband and the guests. No doubt, she felt bewildered, like a character represented in Sophocles' *Tereus*:

> But when we have understanding and have come to youthful vigour, we are pushed out and sold away from our paternal gods and from our parents, some to foreign husbands, some to barbarians [a rare occasion for an Athenian girl], some to joyless homes and some to homes that are opprobrious. And this, once a single night has yoked us, we must approve and consider to be happiness. [89]

Also from the pen of Homer we learn of a dream in which goddess Athena warned Telemachus:

> For you know what sort of a spirit there is in a woman's breast; she wishes to increase the house of the man who marries her, but of her former children and staunch spouse she takes no thought, when once he is dead, and asks no longer concerning them. [90]

The reason for it is clear and simple: "When a woman has left her ancestral home she belongs not to her parents but to her marriage-bed" with her husband [91] which means that she adds fuel to only one fire at a time. [92]

The period of transition from being a girl sought by suitors and a newlywed was one of waiting, rarely for very long, as it was for Deianeira. as Sophocles said: "And suddenly she is gone from her mother, like a calf that has wandered." [93]

---

[89] *Fr.,Tereus*, 583, 6-12: Loeb 483, 294.

[90] *Odyssey*, 15, 20-23: Loeb 105, 76-79.

[91] Euripides, *Fr., Danae*, 318: Loeb 504, 328.

[92] Aristophanes, *Fr., Polyidus*, 469: Loeb 502, 336 and Euripides, *Fr., Hippolytus Veiled*, 429: Loeb 504, 478.

[93] *Women of Trachis*, 530: Loeb 21, 180.

Plato's Communism

Moving now from reality to utopia, we turn to Plato of the early fourth century. His so-called communism of women whereby men could share them equally, without a wedding contract, was nothing but a dream that ought to be interpreted in the context of his political philosophy and the social climate of the time, although it was not entirely new since Pythagoras of the sixth century already suggested it as an aristocratic ideal. When Aristophanes held it to ridicule in his play *Assemblywomen* of 392 and *Wealth* of 388 BCE, [94] Plato was in Athens in both years and probably sitting in the audience. He was then in his mid-thirties and already making waves with his theory, before he advocated it as a viable system of state organization, first in the 5th book of the *Republic* (c. 367 BCE), then in the 6th, 7th and 8th books of the *Laws* (c. 348 BCE).

Plato's premise was that a State is a community of friends and, among friends, everything is common property, including women and children. [95] Therefore, nothing is "mine" and "not-mine" for an individual, except one's own person. [96] The point is that "to own" means "to care for" and one cares only for oneself.

Antisthenes (444-365 BCE), a contemporary of Plato and like him a disciple of Socrates, reached the same conclusion by way of a return to the simplicity of nature. He founded the Cynic school of thought made famous by the philosopher Diogenes (c. 412-323 BCE). The Cynics advocated that men may share their women without any of the restrictions imposed by marriage or social modesty.

The political and social climate of the time in Athens favored the growth of such outlandish ideas. The plight inflicted on the survivors of the Peloponnesian War after the surrender in 404 BCE led everyone to seek some measure of uninhibited happiness in ways that affected the life of women as men's sexual pleasure. The common access to women fostered the freedom of both sexes from the constraints of marital bondage, as displayed also more

---

[94] *Assemblywomen*, 1013-1022: Loeb 180, 388-391 and *Wealth*, 959 ff.: Loeb 180, 560 ff.
[95] *Republic*, 5, 457C-D: Loeb 237, 452-455.
[96] Plato, *Republic*, 5, 464A-D: Loeb 237, 474-477.

openly in the permissive manners in which salons and symposia were conducted. In his Dialogue *Symposium*, Plato acknowledged Aristophanes' attendance at one on love. [97]

With his lectures and writings, however, Plato brought the discussion to a higher level and gave the subject a serious tone. As entertainment, the comedies of Aristophanes may have given the impression that this sexual communism was nothing more than a farce or a fad, although it should have never been considered so lightly after Pythagoras, as mentioned above, presented it as an aristocratic ideal and the Cynics, contemporary of both Aristophanes and Plato, accepted it as a sympathetic practice without much theory. Plato himself was aware of the novelty of his theory.

When scantily clad women shared their physical exercises with scantily clad men, he called the objections "a wave" of misplaced modesty. He called it a "greater wave" when he had to overcome the widespread opposition to a law he proposed

> that these women shall all be common to all these men, and that none shall cohabit with any privately; and that the children shall be common, and that no parent shall know its own offspring nor any child its parents. [98]

Plato was not sure that such a law was ever possible, but he seemed convinced that it would be useful to the state. Here is how he described in practical terms how the lawgiver of the state would select the men and women to live together: he will first pick these men and then "select to give over to them women as nearly as possible of the same nature." [99] They will have their houses and meal in common and have no private possessions.The necessity of sexual unions will be guided by love. However,

> disorder and promiscuity in these unions or in anything else they do would be an unhallowed thing in a happy state and the rulers will not suffer it. [100]

---

[97] 185 ff.: Loeb 166, 120 ff.
[98] *Republic*, 5, 457C-D: Loeb 237, 452-455.
[99] *Ibid.*, 5, 458C: Loeb 237, 456.
[100] *Ibid.*, 5, 458D-E: Loeb 237, 458.

The next question in Plato's mind was: How can the institution of marriage survive in such a communistic arrangement? Taking as a model the process of animal breeding, which includes bringing together the best with the best, he felt the same practice should be used with humans. He realized, however, that this practice will not come naturally. The rulers of the state must intervene with their best methods of influence, even with "considerable use of falsehood and deception for the benefit of their subjects." [101] For this reason, the rulers will regulate marriages and births by appropriately matching the couples, the young men "who excel in war and other pursuits [be given] the opportunity of more frequent intercourse with the women ... having them beget as many of the children as possible." [102] Population control must constantly be present in the rulers' minds. But these arrangements, Plato confessed, must be kept secret, lest the ignorant folks rebel against it.

The children will also be nursed and raised in common. Nurses will be employed for the care of the children. Mothers will give their milk to any child indiscriminately, "employing every device to prevent anyone from recognizing her own infant." [103] Plato concluded:

> Then it is the greatest blessing for a state of which the community of women and children among the helpers [guardians] has been shown to be the cause. [104]

Aristocratic and elitist prejudices led Plato to such a utopian conclusion that he admitted was hardly applicable in practice. Besides, he never had the power to implement it. Under the guise of ethnic purity and political domination, the Nazi experiment of our modern times found its base in Plato's theory. Holding absolute power, Adolph Hitler attempted its selective practice and drowned it under the wave of abusive regimentation, accompanied by a disastrous loss of human rights and family stability.

The relevance of our review of Plato's sacrifice of the marriage institution on the altar of communism of female partners, only as a theory never implemented in Ancient

---

[101] *Republic*, 5, 459D: Loeb 237, 460.
[102] *Ibid.*, 5, 460B: Loeb 237, 462.
[103] *Ibid.*, 5, 460D: Loeb 237, 462-465.
[104] *Ibid.*, 5, 464B: Loeb 237, 476.

Athens, is relevant as one of the significant symptoms of the changes in attitude not only of men but also of women about marriage and the family, starting at the turn of the century and continuing throughout the fourth century. [105]

Plato's dream of sharing women for sex and reproduction had nothing to do with polygamy which is the practice of plural marriages. Euripides defined the Athenian custom when he wrote that "everyone who wants to live decently is content to look for a single mate for his bed", [106] except as a tolerated temporary practice in time of shortage of men, like it was in the aftermath of the Peloponnesian War, and only for those men who could afford it.

Aristotle was aware not only of the intellectual ferment of his time but of the special contribution of Plato when he gave him the credit for this outlandish theory: "Nobody else", he admitted, "has introduced the innovation of community of children and women." [107]

*   *   *

---

[105] See below, p. 292-294.
[106] *Andromache*, 179-180: Loeb 484, 288,
[107] *Politics*, 2, 4, 1266a, 35: Loeb 264, 110.

CHAPTER THREE

WIVES

Transition

When the wedding celebrations were completed and the revelers gone home, the newlyweds settled down in their own home. The word *oikos* meant home, family and household as well as married life.

When a girl left her family to join the new one to be created by her husband she moved from childlike dependency, a well-set home, and a trust shared among blood relatives, to a new status of marital dependency, responsibility and unknown association not only with her husband but with his own family. It was natural for her, at least for awhile, to keep bending her trust toward her own kin, like her husband's trust did toward his father and brothers more than toward his wife. As she had done while growing up, she tended to share problems, anxieties, and feelings with her mother and sisters rather than with her husband. And if she needed the counsel or assistance of a man, a brother with whom she had spent her early years at home was more likely to give her a greater satisfaction than her husband who was not only discovered later in life but was twice her age. Besides, the obstacles of judgment and authority did not exist with a known kin.

At the beginning of her married life the new wife was facing many challenges of adjustment to a new environment of people, site and things. More than her husband she needed comfort and inspiration from divine powers. Because of her inferiority, she sought the protection of goddess Hera who, as the first female Olympian deity, wife of Zeus and mother of divine children, was chosen as guardian of marriages and, as a result, protectress of motherhood.

Divorced by Jason, Medea was bitter about a woman's lot: "Of all creatures that have breath and sensation, we women are the most unfortunate." Married to a stranger, twice her age, a girl must bring a dowry and move to a new home, coming as she does "into the new customs and practices of her husband's house." [1] Marriage was indeed a major challenge for a young woman as it was also for a man twice her age. It was like sailing into a "dangerous harbor". [2]

The attitude of the husband toward his new wife, half his age, was usually warm and tender. Thinking of them, the great orator Demosthenes exclaimed: "For what is sweeter to a man than these [including his mother and children], or why should one wish to live, if deprived of them." [3]

Love

From the wedding day forward, the couple was expected to develop some earnest love as lovers and companions. Love was making married life an ideal to pursue and conquer. Love [*Erôs*], as Euripides wrote, breathes "two kinds of breath", for he

> is the pleasantest of all the gods for mortals to consort with, for he possesses a pleasure that brings no pain, and so leads them to hope. May I not be among those uninitiates in his toils, and may I also keep clear of his savage ways! To the young I say, never flee the experience of love, but use it properly when it comes. [4]

As early as the eighth century, when Homer was composing his *Iliad*, a praise of a man's love for his wife was lent to the warrior Achilles:

> Do they then alone of mortal men love their wives, these sons of Atreus? Whoever is a true man, and sound of mind, loves his own and cherishes her, just as I too loved her [Briseis] with all my heart, though she was but the captive of my spear. [5]

[1] Euripides, *Medea*, 228-229 & 236: Loeb 12, 304.
[2] Sophocles, *Oedipus King*, 422-423: Loeb 20, 366.
[3] Demosthenes, *Against Polycles*, 62: Loeb 351, 44.
[4] Euripides, *Fr.,* Unidentified Play, 929a & 897: Loeb 506, 520 & 496.
[5] *Iliad*, 9, 340-343: Loeb 170, 418.

Short of a law, Solon of the sixth century recommended to marry only for love. If the bride was not an heiress, he encouraged the new husband to abstain from requiring a dowry and thus marry only for love. She needed to bring to her new house no more than the essentials:

> The bride was to bring with her three changes of raiment, household stuff of small value, and nothing else. For he [Solon] did not wish that marriage should be a matter of profit or price, but that man and wife should dwell together for the delights of love and the getting of children. [6]

If the bride was an heiress, Solon preferred that the husband be a kinsman, in order to keep the wealth in the family.

Solon was a wise lawmaker and, at the same time, a poet and a dreamer. He did not change the reality that married life was a partnership made for convenience and cooperation, rarely for love (*philia*) at the outset. Mutual love was apt to grow with time, as husband and wife shared in the "great mysteries" of living together under one roof. [7] For the rest of his life, barring a divorce, the husband was the guardian and leader of his wife, even in a loveless marriage. If love came only from the wife, without any response from the husband, unfortunate heartaches would be the wife's fate to endure, as Ino said: "Oh, women's hearts! What a great affliction we have acquired in love." [8]

The playwrights of the fifth century pointed out several mental traits which, in their view, made women by nature different from men but none seemed to be more important than falling in love more easily than men. This kind of love (*erôs*) which included sexual desire was different from affection (*philia*) which was as strong in men as in women, for instance in fathers and mothers toward their children. Both kinds of love from her husband were required to making a wife completely happy. [9]

---

[6] Plutarch, *Parallel Lives, Solon*, 20, 4: Loeb 46, 458.
[7] Id., *Erotikos*, 769a: Flaceliere, R., *Love in Ancient Greece*, 162 and 185.
[8] Euripides, *Fr., Ino*, 400: Loeb 504, 444.
[9] Id., *Fr.*, Unidentified Play, 1062: Loeb 506, 596.

Romantic love could flourish even in a relationship of ruler and ruled, but literature did not express it before the late fourth century, in New Comedy. Earlier in this century, in Plato's *Symposium*, [10] Aristophanes commented only on the myth of the pristine unity of woman and man. Later, Aristotle stated that it meant the "desire to grow together and both become one instead of being two." Such a unity, he specified, can exist only in extreme affection, not in sexuality, lest the affection of either one perish. [11] Socrates believed that Niceratus and his wife had reached such a state of mutual love. [12]

As for the wife's love for her husband, whether it existed in the heart or not, it had to be shown by being not only faithful to him but also attentive to all his needs in food and clothing, even to the death. If the story of Alcestis, presented on stage in 435 BCE by the playwright Euripides, has any element of reality, she was one who saved the life of her husband Admetus, by sacrificing her own. Alcestis was a wife of unusual devotion. She laid down her life out of love not only for her husband but also for their children and the kingdom he ruled. For her generous and unselfish deed she was rewarded by returning alive to earth.

If a good reason, like a god's demand, presented itself, would a husband accept a similar sacrifice for the benefit of his wife? No Greek man ever imagined such a situation could take place, except when he was called upon to fight on the battlefield for the good of family and state. This, however, does not mean that Greek men in times of peace did not sincerely love their wife and were not devoted to her. Some funerary monuments were the purest expression of grief for the loss of a dearly beloved wife. One inscription of the fourth century reads like a tender parting of two partners in love:

Farewell, tomb of Melite, a good woman lies here. Your husband Onesimus loved you and you loved him in return. You were the best and so he laments your death, for you were a good woman. And to you farewell, dearest of men; love my children. [13]

---

[10] *Symposium*, 189 ff.: Loeb 166, 132 ff.
[11] *Politics*, 2, 1, 1262b, 12-14: Loeb 264, 82.
[12] Xenophon, *Banquet*, 8, 3: Loeb 168, 612.
[13] M. R. Lefkowitz, *Women in Greek Myth*, 67.

The comments made by the avant-garde Plato about Alcestis some seventy-five years later were consistent with his general views. He suggested that husbands also should be willing to die for the sake of saving the life of their wives, if it was required for a greater good and sanctioned by the gods. Nevertheless, he placed the emphasis on Alcestis' sacrifice because he knew of no example of a similar sacrifice in reverse. In his Dialogue *Symposium,* he lent these words to Aristophanes:

> Furthermore, only such as are in love will consent to die for others; not merely men will do it, but women too. Sufficient witness is borne to this statement before the people of Greece by Alcestis, daughter of Pelias, who alone was willing to die for her husband, though he had both father and mother. So high did her love exalt her over them in kindness. [14]

Another sacrifice of life was willfully caused and executed for love by a married woman when no outside pressure or intervention made it happen. After Evadne had lost a brother, Eteoclus, and a husband, Capaneus, in the war between the two brothers, Eteocles and Polynices, she decided to join her husband in death. She leaped into the fire where his body was being cremated. She did it not for her brother's sake, but for her husband's. She did it against the prayers of her father Iphis who needed her help in his old age. She did it "in glorious victory", she said, "over all women the sun looks on." [15] Her mind was on womanhood that she understood and advocated to be totally subservient to the husbands. Since she had no identity of her own, being in everything only a part of her husband's life, she could not have any identity beyond his death. In the Greek culture of the fifth century, such a victory carried the sense of what men expected of women.

More profoundly than men, women experienced the emotions of love as if their minds were imbued by them through and through, so thought the seer Tiresias even about sexual love *(erôs).* The emotions hidden in the dark

---

[14] *Symposium,* 179B-C: Loeb 166, 102-105.
[15] Euripides, *Suppliant Women,* 1059-1061: Loeb 9, 118-121.

recesses of their minds were often used, so men believed, as effective weapons against them.

A model of soft manipulation of men was Hera, the goddess of married life, who conspired, intrigued and beguiled in order to outmaneuver Zeus, her husband. Once, she adorned herself and lured him to make love to her so that he would fall asleep and all this she did for an Achaean victory on the battlefield. [16]

The same goddess Hera devised another ploy that caused great pain and fame to the Argive princess Io and gave the Greek people a fascinating myth. [17] When Hera's husband Zeus fell in love with the princess, she accused him of infidelity. So he changed his dulcinea into a white cow and made himself a bull. But Hera was not so obtuse and certainly not yet defeated. She made the cow Io possessed with madness from a fly (oistros) that bit her; then, as she started wandering, Hera appointed Argus, "the all-seeing one" [18] to watch over her and keep her away from her pursuer. Io wandered through northern Greece and Asia all the way down to the banks of the Nile. There, Zeus avoided Argus long enough or waited until god Hermes killed him; then, he returned her to womanhood, forced himself upon her by a touch of his hand, and "she conceived a burden, in very truth of Zeus, and bare a blameless child", [19] by name Epaphus, who begat also many generations of sons and daughters, among them the fifty Danaids of Egypt. Hera's emotional plans were thwarted. She succeeded, however, in harassing the great god whose lust was always thunder and lightning.

Irritability and madness were attributed to the physical nature of women as baneful coordinates of their propensity to love. If the blood, absorbed in their bodies more abundantly than in men's bodies, does not find its release, it causes some affliction in the mind, a condition that is either temporary or pathological. Therefore, healthy women experience such mental distress only moderately. However, when the distress is severe, for example in the case of Medea, it is much more severe in women than it could ever be in men.

---

[16] Homer, *Iliad*, 169 ff.: Loeb 171, 78.
[17] Aeschylus, *Suppliant Maidens*, 291 ff.: Loeb 145, 28.
[18] *Ibid.*, 303: Loeb 145, 30.
[19] *Ibid.*, 580-581: Loeb 145, 62.

Indeed, a wife's love for her husband sometimes bred madness when it grew out of bounds. Although pushed to its limit, Alcestis' love for her husband was calm and rational. Medea's love, on the contrary, was out of bounds, as it was purely and wildly emotional in all its sincerity. It seemed, however, that she cared more about the emotion of being in love than about her husband. If he had died, she could and probably would have offered her youth in marriage to any royal prince of Thessaly. Such a consideration made her cruel reaction to abandonment even more significant when she killed their two sons to punish him. [20]

The Athenian wives identified themselves with the Greek Alcestis rather than the Barbarian Medea. Most of them would have accepted the ultimate sacrifice of death or separation if a good reason presented itself and all men would have expected it.   When Jason left Medea, a foreign woman, for a Greek princess of Corinth, his wish that she would quietly go away became lost in the cesspool of her jealousy. He then vented his own bitter feelings not only toward her but also toward all women:

> You women are so far gone in folly that if all is well in bed, you think you have everything, while if some misfortune in that domain occurs, you regard as hateful your best and truest interests. Mortals ought to beget children from some other source, and there should be no female sex. Then mankind would have no trouble. [21]

Parties involved in a bitter divorce are not suited to lecture on gender psychology. But they do, like Jason did with a disarming candor and a male bias tending to equate love with sex. Regardless of his extreme disappointment, however, Jason was willing to provide generously for Medea and their two sons. She turned him down. Baffled, the Chorus of Corinthian women blamed this impasse on her excessive love:

---

[20] Euripides, *Medea,* 1280-1281: Loeb 12. 398.
[21] *Ibid.*, 569-575: Loeb 12, 332.

Love that come to us in excess brings no good name or goodness to men. If Aphrodite comes in moderation, no other goddess brings such happiness. [22]

The outcome of Medea's excessive love was an utter and most despicable madness when she killed her two young sons to take revenge of her husband. Why turn two innocent boys into victims for the offence committed by their father! She should have gone against him personally, if she thought he deserved it, probably like other wives did when they quietly killed their husbands by poison or other secret means, as Euripides once seemed to suggest: "Well, go on and get married, get married, and then die either through poison or plot from your wife!" [23] Killing her husband would have been explicable, if not condoned, since she had already killed her half-brother Apsirtus for what she thought was necessity, but killing her innocent children was a complete aberration.

Love was a two-edge sword that pierced the heart of lovers, sometimes for good and some other times for bad outcomes. The story of Medea, as those of many other women featured by the dramatists, showed the ambivalent power of love. On their wedding day, the bride and groom hoped for love with the best of outcome for a lifetime. But their anticipations did not always come true.

Inferiority

No more than a touch of misogyny appeared already in Homer's writings. But, In his own times of the eighth century, a full embrace of it took place in Hesiod's writings and began to be imitated throughout the Greek world. [24] The lyric poets Archilochus (714?-676 BCE), Simonedes of Ceos (c. 556-468 BCE), Hipponax of Ephesus (fl. sixth century BCE) shared in their distrust of and antipathy toward women. The latter was allegedly the one who showed more arrogance than wit when he said:

---

[22] *Medea,* 627-631: Loeb 12, 338.
[23] *Fr., Cretan Women,* 464: Loeb 504, 524.
[24] Hesiod, *Works and Days,* 405: Loeb 57, 32 and Aristotle, *Politics,* 1, 1, 1252b, 10-14: Loeb 264, 6.

There are only two days in your life that your wife
gives you pleasure: the day you marry her and the
day you bury her. [25]

Greek poets frequently degraded women with tales of
their misgivings and foibles. From this time on, Greek men
had ambivalent expectations of women: they expected them
to be either weak and manipulative in Hesiod's tradition or
strong and loyal, always behind the scene and never to be
completely trusted, in Homer's tradition.

In colors darker than the ones usually used by the
other dramatists of the Classical Age, Euripides depicted the
feelings of the Athenian men when he wrote:

[Men's] hatred of womankind is a most grievous
thing. Those [women] who have fallen bring disgrace
on those who have not, and the bad ones share their
censure with the good, and where marriage is
concerned men think they have no integrity at all. [26]

In his own analytical style, Aristotle of the fourth
century BCE excavated the foundations of these feelings
when he described the male attitude of superiority and
explained how man rules over woman, according to nature
and in a special way. She must obey in her manner of
cooperating with her husband in the management of the
household. Her obedience, however, is not like that of a
slave, a child or an ox. A slave, either male or female, is a
possession on the same level as an animal, like an ox,
therefore, being without deliberative power, it is ruled
arbitrarily by the master. Woman and child who are free
persons have deliberative power but differently: in a woman
it is without authority, because she is more emotion-driven
and irrational than man, and in a child it is still immature.
So, the rule of the husband over his wife must be different.
Aristotle wrote in his *Politics*:

The science of household management has three
divisions, one the relation of master to slave, ... one
the paternal relation, and the third the conjugal

---

[25] F. A. Wright, *Feminism in Greek Literature*, 39.
[26] Euripides, *Fr.*, *Melanippe Captive*, 493: Loeb 504, 594.

relation – for it is a part of the household science to rule over wife and children (over both as over freemen, yet not with the same mode of government, but over the wife to exercise republican (*politicôs*) government and over children monarchical (*basilikôs*); for the male is by nature better fitted to command than the female (except in some cases where their union has been formed contrary to nature) and the older and fully developed person than the younger and immature. It is true that in most cases of republican government the ruler and the ruled interchange in turn (for they tend to be on an equal level in their nature and to have no difference at all), although nevertheless during the period when one is ruler and the other ruled they seek to have a distinction by means of insignia and titles and honours. ... The male stands in this relationship to the female continuously. [27]

According to Aristotle, the father's rule in the household is affectionate and absolute over his children but only political over his wife, yet it is not completely political, like in the city-state of Athens, because the husband is permanently the ruler of his wife while the rulers of Athens are democratically elected into office and therefore temporary. Why do husband and wife not rule in turn in the household, like citizens do in Athens? Because they are not equal in all respects, the husband being always better fitted for command. Therefore, although they are mature in their own ways, the wife is always without authority.

Further down in his discourse, Aristotle asked himself whether the difference between man and woman was one of kind, or only one of degree and, therefore, whether the difference of virtues in the exercise of their proper functions was also one of kind or only of degree. He answered by comparing the relationship of husband and wife to the relationship between reason and emotions in the soul. Reason must rule, he declared, and emotions obey, therefore the difference is one of kind. [28]

---

[27] *Politics*, 1, 5, 1259a, 1-1259b, 10: Loeb 264, 56-59.
[28] *Ibid.*, 1, 5, 1260a, 5-8: Loeb 264, 62.

It is not that the souls of husband and wife are not equal in components and virtues. They both have reason and emotions and the domination of reason over emotions is manifested in virtues, such as temperance, courage and justice but, seemingly caught in a vicious circle, Aristotle explains that "the one is the courage of command and the other that of subordination, and the case is similar with the other virtues." [29]

Strange as it may sound, this philosophical comment may echo the dichotomy of feelings that a poet like Euripides had many years earlier about women, one time perceiving them as good and another time as bad. Once he lent these words to Melanippe:

> Vainly does censure from men twang an idle bowshot at women and denounce them. In fact they are better than men. ... For my part, I will make a distinction: on the one hand nothing is worse than a bad woman, but on the other nothing excels a good one in goodness. The natures of each are different, [30]

The playwright Euripides used the word *phusis* for nature in the sense of inborn quality. The philosopher Aristotle used it in the sense of essence that defines every individual thing or being. Therefore, the difference between man and woman was neither one of nature, in its philosophical sense, because both the rational and the irrational are parts of every human soul, nor one of degree because their virtues can be equally great when the irrational is always subservient to the rational, but the difference was one of kind (*eidos*) for man to command and woman to obey. As an example of a difference in kind, Aristotle quoted the words Sophocles lent to Ajax -- "Silence gives grace to woman" -- to which he added: "though that is not the case likewise with a man." [31] Lysias, his senior by only a few years, stated the same conclusion as a fact that

---

[29] *Politics*, 1, 5, 1260a, 24-25: Loeb 264, 62 and Plato, *Meno*, 73A-E: Loeb 165, 272-275.

[30] *Fr., Melanippe Captive*, 494, 1-29: Loeb 504, 594-597.

[31] Aristotle, *Politics*, 1, 5, 1260a, 30-31: Loeb 264, 64 and Sophocles, *Ajax*, 293: Loeb 20, 58.

women are not "accustomed to speak in the presence of men." [32]

Socrates of the late fifth century BCE briefly acknowledged the difference between man and woman with regard to their respective ability and virtue. As he was considering the ability of female acrobats, he summarized the two natural differences, physical and mental, that made them, and all women, weaker than men. He said:

> Woman's nature (*phusis*) is not a whit inferior to man's, except in its lack of judgment [*gnômê*] and physical strength (*ischus*). So if any one of you has a wife, let him confidently set about teaching her whatever he would like to have her know [because she can learn]. [33]

Aristotle corrected some of the beliefs held by his predecessors, especially Plato, when he advocated that women are not equal to men in kind of virtue, because the virtue of one is in commanding and of the other in obeying, and rejected Plato's utopian type of egalitarian republic.

Aristotle was a scientific philosopher who used observation as the starting point of his theories. It served him well, although his observations were far from being as sophisticated as they can be today, thanks to our efforts to conduct elaborate experimentations and use the most advanced instrumentation. He observed the similarities of relationship between male and female in the two realms, animal and human. This approach fell short of providing an adequate foundation for understanding the functions of the human soul in man and woman. He then resorted to a common observation of the rational and the irrational in both man and woman, and concluded that, inasmuch as the rational prevailed in man, he should be ruler and that, inasmuch as the emotional prevailed in woman, she should be ruled permanently. In his view of woman's relationship to man, she was, unlike a boy, permanently inferior to man.

In summary, from Hesiod in the eighth century to Aristotle in the fourth, the Greeks modified their view of the nature of woman as compared to man's nature. Hesiod

---

[32] *Against Diogeiton*, 11: Loeb 244, 666.
[33] Xenophon, *Banquet*, 2, 9: Loeb 168, 546.

described her in unsophiscated terms as different in nature and a necessary evil in the life of man. The playwrights of the fifth century saw in her diminished physical strength the cause of her mental inferiority to man. They characterized her inferiority by less courage, more lamentations, greater propensity to love and irritability. In the fourth century, the philosopher Aristotle accepted the traditional belief that woman is inferior to man, both physically and mentally. For the first time, however, he dissected this belief into the following tenets: One: woman is inferior to man, neither in nature nor in degree but in kind, as between the rational and the irrational (emotional) in the soul; two: because of this inferiority, woman does not rule, but is ruled by man; three: man's rule over woman is political, not monarchical, which means that, although woman's deliberative power is not authoritative, it can contribute to man's decisions as a ruler; four: the virtues of man and woman are different in that man's virtues are in commanding and woman's virtues in obeying. Such a difference is in kind, not in degree.

The stereotype of woman being physically weaker and mentally more emotional than man led to her status of inferiority at home and exclusion from the Athenian society. Aristotle's philosophy carried an enormous weight of influence on the physician Hirophilus of about 300 BCE and his successors, especially Galen in the second half of the second century CE, and throughout the centuries of European Christianity.

Female Attraction

From the early times of the beautiful Pandora and the gorgeous Helen down to the generations of the Classical Age, physical beauty was one of the main assets of the Greek women not only, as Lysistrata said, "when we ought to be having fun and enjoying our bloom of youth" [34] but also when women had reached a mature age. The fact is that some of the most attractive women in literature and art were women of a mature age. Lysistrata herself must have been of middle age when she became the strong leader that she was. Some sculptures of Aphrodite represented women of mature age, like the Aphrodite of Knidos and the

---

[34] Aristophanes, *Lysistrata*, 591: Loeb 179, 350.

Aphrodite of Melos. Beauty was indeed women's major contribution to her husband and society for most of their life span.

Demosthenes thought of women as "the most beautiful of all beings", [35] especially The Athenian women who distinguished themselves by being more feminine than the Spartan women well represented in Aristophanes' Lampito whose beauty was not only in "rosy cheeks" but also in "firmness of physique [that] could throttle a bull." [36]

Women's beauty was admired and enjoyed in literary descriptions, sculptures and paintings, and more so in person when it was an enticement to touch and embrace. In erotic situations, women enticed men also by their charms and adornments, not by their words (*peithô*), like men did. Women and men knew it and both used it to their own advantage: men to win and hold their exclusive possession and women to gain and assure their protection and fulfillment, including their own erotic desires. An Athenian jug, called *pelikê*, with two handles and a greater width at the base, shows in red-figure painting a middle-aged woman, fully dressed, sprinkling water over a row of phalli, like plants in the garden of Adonis. [37] Women's beauty sprinkled desire in men's minds and limbs, and thus made the world go round for better and for worse.

Since the Trojan War in the late thirteenth century, men viewed Helen, the wife of king Menelaus of Sparta, as the most beautiful, the least chaste and the most disastrous of all women. Paris of Troy saw her as the most beautiful woman in the world. She fell for his amorous advances and was unfaithful to her husband Menelaus and her child Hermione when she eloped with him. As a result, a ten-year devastating war was fought to return her from Troy to her family in Sparta.

In a post-war scene of Euripides' play *Trojan Women* of 415 BCE, Menelaus decided first to sentence Helen to die for her crime, and to bring her back home to serve her sentence, only after admonishing all women:

> But when she reaches Argos the wretch will die a
> wretched death, as she deserves, and will cause all

---

[35] Aeschines, *On the Embassy*, 112: Loeb 106, 242.

[36] *Lysistrata*, 78-81: Loeb 179, 278.

[37] J. J. Winkler, *The Constraints of Desire*, 36-37.

women to be chaste. To be sure, this is not easy. But her death will make foolish women afraid, though they be still more reprobate than she is! [38]

In Euripides' play by her name, Helen admitted that beauty was "woeful" (*dustuchestaton*). [39] In her case, it certainly was when it caused a ten-year war and her own death sentence. This sentence was not carried out, however, because her beauty and charm were enough to assuage the most indomitable of husbands. So, she seemed to have been forgiven by him who let her live a peaceful life with him in Sparta. He married their daughter Hermione to Neoptolemus, son of Achilles, and also witnessed the marriage of the son Megapenthes whom he had had in a prior year by a slave girl. [40] For this indiscretion, one of many for sure, he needed no forgiveness. The men's sexual style made it acceptable.

The disparity in marrying age of men at about thirty and women at about fifteen was not only reinforcing the double standard but challenging the sexual purity of women. At the age when young women were already married and tied to the home where their only duty was to obey their husbands, the young men for at least fifteen more years sprinkled their attention on female prostitutes and boys.

Furthermore, the newly-married man still in the prime of his vigor could not give up for more than a short while the liberties he had taken freely prior to his marriage, not only with other women but also perhaps with men and boys. Was this situation a cause for his wife's alarm, whether she was newlywed or mother of children by him? It did not seem to be, so entrenched was the culture of disparity of standards between women and men. If it was for wives a cause for alarm, they followed about it the practice of silence expected of them by men in this matter, as it was in all other matters where the male superiority could be challenged. Since only men could speak and they had no interest in speaking, we know nothing about their wives' feelings concerning their own extramarital affairs. Perhaps

---

[38] *Trojan Women*, 1055-1059: Loeb 10, 114.
[39] *Helen*, 236-237: Loeb 11, 38.
[40] Homer, *Odyssey*, 4, 5 & 11: Loeb 104, 118.

as a correction, Euripides would have made marriage a matter of pure economics. He wrote:

Laws are not well made concerning wives; the prosperous man should be having as many as possible if his house could maintain them, so he could throw the bad one out of his home and be pleased at keeping the one who actually is good. Now, however, they look to one wife, and risk much on the throw; for people take wives into their house like ballast, with no experience of their ways. [41]

Sexuality

The history of sexuality is an important part of the history of culture. The latter is not defined by sexuality but cannot be defined without it. Our present interest in describing the sexual style of women in ancient Athens is for the purpose of locating it in the context of all the cultural elements already considered and relating it to the moral standards established by customs and the law. This endeavor will involve men in some of their sexual activities having an impact, directly or indirectly, upon women. The double standards will appear as blatant here as in the exercise of political leadership and in the conduct of social and financial affairs.

Our present focus is the sexual activities of husbands and wives within the confines of their marital life. Later, our focus will be the sexual misbehavior of women outside their married life and of men as it affected the feelings and behavior of their wives.

One comment on this subject ought to be made at the outset, as it applies particularly to the young society of Athens in the fifth and fourth centuries BCE, a society in search for its own identity. The sources of information about sexuality are sometimes ambiguous, some other times even contradictory. On the other hand, every interpretation must take into account the general spirit of the Athenian society in the Classical Age and recognize not only the apparent contradictions in the letter of its pronouncements but also the consistency it displayed in its popular

---

[41] *Fr.*, *Ino*, 402: Loeb 504, 446.

behavioral applications. All societies, not only the ancient ones which have provided sometimes so little information but also the modern ones exposed in full view, are often replete with conflicts. The courts are the theaters of surgical reconcilement, neither always clear in their decisions nor easy to understand.

Sexual activities in and out of married life always took place in the framework of a hierarchical and democratic society. Men were equal under the law but they were always the rulers of women. The Athenian husband used his wife for procreation and no other man had a right to her sexual attention. On the other hand, every man either voluntarily or on command had a right to sexual relations with any woman, whose status was inferior to that of any Athenian woman, of course excluding his wife, because all Athenian men were equally superior to women and therefore ruled over them by justice. Every man had also a right to having relations for a time as mentor and lover of boys and as lover of another adult man, in honorable circumstances.

Because of women's presumed romantic disposition, most men seemed to perceive women as more erotic than they were. Several conflicting legends about the seer Tiresias, who had a prominent role in the Oedipus saga, include the story of his transformation into a woman and his return to be a man after a few years. He then reported that women enjoy love-making in full ten times when men only once, which goddess Hera flatly denied, so she blinded him for making such a claim. [42]

In his play *Trojan Women* of 415 BCE, Euripides tied together the women's sorrows and their erotic love, as the latter helped them assuage the former. Andromache became the slave-woman of Neoptolemus whose father Achilles had killed her husband Hector on the battlefield. The belief of this new bedroom master was indicative of men's general belief about women inasmuch as "they say that a single night dispels the hatred a woman feels for her bedmate." To this statement, the playwright promptly added that Andromache did not agree with what "they say", because she rejected "with contempt a woman who casts her former husband aside because of a new connection and

---

[42] Hesiod, *Melampodia*, 3: Loeb 57, 269.

loves another." [43] Andromache contended that, even in the embrace of Neoptolemus, she never ceased to love her husband Hector.

Our interest here is in the words Euripides put on Andromache's lips. He suggested, on the one hand, that men believed and said that women care only about their satisfaction in bed and, on the other hand, that Andromache disagreed with this belief. The "single night" statement he attributed to men in general probably applied to men's behavior rather than to women's, in view of the free reins all men had with their sexual activities as compared to the sheltered life of most women. So, Andromache was probably right when she disagreed. Euripides himself seemed to admit that she was right when he attributed his statement to "they say". Nevertheless, he revealed by the same words a new, sexual and demeaning facet in the misogynist attitude of Greek men toward women in Ancient times.

On the other hand, the same Euripides could not have been more explicit when he lent the following statement to Andromache, in this case addressing Hermione about the women of Thrace, in the northeast of Greece, where men share their bed with many women:

> If so, you would have branded all women with insatiable lust. This is a disgraceful thing. We women suffer worse from this disease than men, but we do well to veil it decently from sight. [44]

The case of a healthy marital sexual life, allowances being allotted for exaggerations, was probably made well by Aristophanes in his *Lysistrata* of 411 BCE. The plot was whether the withdrawal of marital sex from husbands will persuade them to negotiate peace instead of wage war. At the beginning, Lysistrata convened her lady friends. She asked: "Don't you all pine for your children's fathers when they're off at war?" [45] Yes, they replied. Then, one of the lady friends, Calonice, revealed by her remark a reality often ignored about the conduct of Athenian wives: When their husbands were gone, they had no consolation because "the

---

[43] Euripides, *Andromache*, 665-668: Loeb 10, 80.
[44] *Andromache*, 218-221: Loeb 484, 292.
[45] *Lysistrata*, 99-100: Loeb 179, 282.

lovers have vanished without a trace." [46] As a result, when Lysistrata announced that the strategy for peace was to abstain from marital sex when their husbands were home, she could not miss the general consternation falling like a dark cloud upon the gathering of wives.

> Why are you turning away from me? Where are you going? Why are you all pursing your lips and shaking your heads? What means your altered color and tearful droppings? Will you do it or not? What are you waiting for? [47]

Myrrhine and Calonice replied at once that they simply will not do it! After some coaxing, they finally accepted the bargain for peace. However, after five days of squabbles between a group of husbands and their wives encamped on the Acropolis, the separation had become unbearable to both spouses: The women were husband-sick, wanting to defect one by one and go home under pretenses: one to spread her wool, another to peel her flax, a third one to give birth to a baby today when she was not even pregnant yesterday. Desperate, Lysistrata confessed: "The truth is. I can't keep them away from their husbands any longer; they're running off in all directions." [48] She realized that this rout must be stopped at once, lest peace should be lost. She pleaded with them one more time:

> Just be patient, good ladies, and put up with this only a little bit longer. There's an oracle predicting victory for us, but only if we stick together. [49]

When Lysistrata produced the oracle written on a papyrus roll, the women yielded and remained on the Acropolis. These scenes were all in jest. Aristophanes focused on peace and took for granted that the audience allowed for some exaggerations. Our present viewpoint is different: we are focusing our attention on sexual attitudes of women and, although we too allow for some

---

[46] *Lysistrata*, 107-110: Loeb 179, 282.
[47] *Ibid.*, 125-128: Loeb 179, 284.
[48] *Ibid.*, 718-720: Loeb 179, 364.
[49] *Ibid.*, 765-768: Loeb 179, 372.

exaggerations, we detect the reality of healthy sexual relations between husbands and wives of Ancient Greece.

In the same *Lysistrata*, Aristophanes expressed the belief, probably on behalf of all Ancient Greek men, that wild and passionate craving for sex was not peculiar to men but that women had more of their fair share of it. For this reason, they were often viewed as dangerous if left unbridled. Regardless of this apparent common belief, the fact is that Greek men and women had a great sense of respectability and moderation but, inasmuch as their sense was based only on nature and social order, it was interpreted more freely than it was and still is in cultures directed by prophets and teachers inspired by God. They were not any worse for it, except those who did not abide by the norms of nature, civility and mutual respet, because as long as men and women set those norms and abide by them, they are worthy to be called what they really are: decent human beings. For example, to accept the norms of the Judeo-Christian ethics and live by the norms of the Ancient Greeks would be a cause for reprobation. But for the majority of Ancient Greek men and women to live according to their norms indicated no fault either in their character or in their social order.

The law itself was silent about sexual conduct between husband and wife. We know of no direct law or decree addressing the conduct of women, such as the manner of sexual activity or birth control. Therefore, women's behavior was regulated by customs rather than by written laws. It was a private matter left to the husband to control. His standing in the community mattered first. Her legal rights were restricted to her status in the economics of the family (*oikos*), not the politics of the city-state (*polis*).

Since the law was silent, some other dynamics of control had to come to the fore and regulate interpersonal behavior. Then, even the most private activities, especially those related to sexual behavior, fell under the normative rules of approval and disapproval, honor and shame, propriety and deviance. Reputation based on these rules which define the view one person has of another became a norm in itself, albeit ambiguous, yet clear enough to carry social consequences. On the other hand, reputation has feet of clay because the person who grants it tends to accept or reject the conduct of another person only if it conforms to personal norms of evaluation. These norms may grow into a consensus in a specific society but they never have complete objectivity and permanency. The mores of successive times tend to evolve and change.

In sexual matters, the activities may be called private because they take place between two individuals in absolute privacy, and yet the moment any activity involves more than one person as spectator or participant it becomes public and subject to rules of social conduct. The law covers only a portion of the public domain, the one in which society at large is impacted. The other portion is loosely regulated by taste, inclinations, appearances and values often expressed by the voice of conscience and by the so called "chemistry" or harmony experienced in the relationship between individuals, whoever they are, in this case between husband and wife.

Therefore, sexual relations between married couples never appeared to be acts of sexual abuse or violence by the husbands or even by the wives, if they behaved according to the norms of propriety in social interaction. In sexual intercourse, both sexes had their means of control. In Aristophanes' *Lysistrata*, the husbands who drooled and the wives who wanted to defect shared equally in the same erotic enthusiasm. Xenophon seemed to confirm this observation when he introduced the wife who "is willing to oblige, whereas the girl's [slave] services are compulsory." [50]

Adultery

In translation, the words "adultery" and "adulterer" are too weak and vague to render well the Greek words *moicheia* and *moichos*. In English, adultery means voluntary sexual intercourse with a married spouse not one's own. In Ancient Greek, *moicheia* meant also voluntary sexual intercourse, not with any married woman but only with an Athenian woman, married or virgin, and by entering another man's house. Shame, dishonor and violation, not only of a person but of a space, were integral to the concept of the Greek *moicheia*. The word *moichos* had in Ancient Greek no feminine correspondent to signify adulteress because she did not really matter as passive participant. The fact is,

---

[50] *Oeconomicus*, 10, 12-13: Loeb 168, 450.

however, that there were probably more adulteresses than adulterers, although not many of either sex.

Marital fidelity was the rule for Athenian women, but not for Athenian men who were blameless for keeping a concubine for daily care, frequenting prostitutes for pleasure and enjoying the company of female companions (*hetairai*) or young boys (*erômenoi*). Wives were only expected to bear legitimate children. As a result, the sexual behaviors of men and women were guided by different standards, much more restrictive for women than for men. Such standards were applied less for the protection of women than for the reputation of men whose honor depended on two appearances: one, of their manliness and, the other, of their ability to ensure their wife's fidelity and daughters' virginity. Appearances meant prestige, power and success. They were worth some lies and manipulations when reality was not cooperating adequately. These were the social expectations the Athenian husbands placed upon their wives.

There were indeed blatant double standards between men and women, not only in the activities of public life, but also in their sexual habits. Clytemnestra took a paramour, Aegisthus, to the palace of Argos and Agamemnon returned to the same palace with a concubine, Cassandra, "the fairest of the daughters of Priam," [51] who gave him "loving embraces in bed." [52] His wife was blamed for having a lover but he was not for having a concubine.

When Clytemnestra responded to the deceptive invitation to visit her daughter Electra, she immediately confessed her despicable folly which fractured her family. "I do not feel", she said, "such great joy at the deeds I have done," [53] after she took Aegisthus as lover and consort in the palace and, together, murdered her husband. Nevertheless, with her daughter Electra she defended herself skilfully and vigorously. She killed her husband Agamemnon, because, she explained, he deceived me when

> Enticing my child with a marriage to Achilles, [he] went off with her to the harbor at Aulis, and there ... slit her pale white throat ... only because Helen was a

---

[51] Homer, *Iliad*, 13, 365: Loeb 171, 28.
[52] Euripides, *Hecuba*, 830: Loeb 484, 474.
[53] Id., *Electra*, 1106: Loeb 9, 272.

whore. ... [then] came home with the god-possessed
seer girl [Cassandra] and installed her in his bed and
meant to keep two women at the same time in the
same house." [54]

At once, Clytemnestra added: "Woman, to be sure, is
a thing of folly, I do not deny it." [55] Yet, shall we ask, why
was she not allowed to do what her husband did? Why was
she blamed for taking a paramour to the palace in his
absence when he had with impunity a concubine away from
home and even took one home with him to live with his
wife? She can herself help us place the answer in the
context of the Trojan War and, more broadly, of the
Athenian culture of the time. In matters of relationship
between husbands and wives, double standards were a way
of life recognized by custom.
    Clytemnestra challenged these double standards with
her argument by reverse about the sacrifice of her daughter
Iphigenia, and her murder of the perpetrator, her husband
Agamemnon. She raised the question: if, instead of
Menelaus having lost his wife Helen, it would have been
Helen who had lost her husband Menelaus, would a war had
been waged and, if it had, would her son Orestes, instead of
her daughter, had been sacrificed for its success? Certainly
not on both counts. Therefore, when Agamemnon vowed to
avenge his brother Menelaus and advocated this reason for
killing Iphigenia, he should have given his wife, by the same
token, the right to kill Orestes, if she had to avenge her
sister Helen. In this case, Agamemnon would have been
justified to murder her in retaliation because her son was
his also. Why then was she not justified to murder him in
reparation for his killing of her daughter? She argued that
the reasoning should be valid both ways. If custom would
make the murder by Agamemnon hypothetically right and
just, it should equally make her own really right and just,
lest custom, equal to the law, be uneven and unfair. [56] She
concluded by challenging her daughter to refute her
argument by reverse: "If you so desire, speak and tell me in

[54] Euripides, _Electra_, 1020-1034: Loeb 9, 264.
[55] _Ibid._, 1035: Loeb 9, 264.
[56] _Ibid._, 1036-1045: Loeb 9, 264-267.

perfect liberty how it was unjust that your father was killed."
[57]

Electra did not refute directly her mother's argument, specious because it assumed wrongly that custom was weighing evenly on the scale of justice yet true if one holds the anachronistic belief in equal rights. She correctly responded by endorsing the practice of double standards according to custom: killing Iphigenia was justified but murdering Agamemnon was not. Therefore, as Electra declared, "if one deed of murder decrees another in requital" [58] in order to avenge her father, she must slay her mother who not only murdered her father but lived with another man in his palace while he was away at war. She was now using the illicit sexual behavior of her mother to justify her plan for murder. By linking the two, she reached the Greek cultural foundation for the asymmetry in sexual practices of men and women and thus made the balance fall heavily in favor of men's side. A wife, she stated, "has no need to show a lovely face to those outside the house unless she is looking for mischief." [59] And the chorus of women chanted the ultimate reason for it: "A woman, one who is sound in mind, ought to accede in all things to her husband's wishes." [60] His first wish was indeed his wife's absolute fidelity.

The Ancient Greeks projected the same perception of disparity upon their gods and goddesses. Calypso bitterly complained that goddesses were begrudged by Zeus for loving a man when all the gods take women as paramours all the times. [61] Also, the violence inflicted on rape victims was more than once recorded in mythology. As he did with Io, Zeus disguised himself as a bull and abducted Europa from Phoenicia to Crete, making her the mother of king Minos. Hades also, Zeus' brother, abducted Persephone to the Underworld. Apollo raped the virgin Creusa and abandoned her to her dire fate.

The heroes featured in mythology had also affairs of their own. For example, the lesser Ajax, son of Oileus, dragged and raped Cassandra, daughter of king Priam. In

---

[57] Euripides, *Electra*, 1049-1050: Loeb 9, 266.
[58] *Ibid.*, 1094: Loeb 9, 270.
[59] *Ibid.*, 1074-1075: Loeb 9, 268.
[60] *Ibid.*, 1052-1053: Loeb 9, 266.
[61] Homer, *Odyssey*, 5, 116 ff.: Loeb 104, 190.

this case, as expected, the Greeks did not censure or punish him. God Poseidon did it, however, for another reason, namely because he, a god, had been treated with contempt by him, a man, so he stirred violent storms that battered his fleet returning home and made him drown in the sea. [62]

The husband was the only man who had a right on his wife. When Deianeira was newly wed to Heracles, he resorted to the centaur Nessus to carry her across the treacherous waters of the river Evenus in the northwest of Greece. The centaur took advantage of her when "In midstream he laid lustful hands" upon her. She shrieked and Heracles killed him with his arrow. [63] Anybody who touched one's wife deserved to be killed. Yet, the same Heracles later took the young princess Iole as concubine and sent her home for a ménage à trois. Both situations were carried within the rights of the husband and were accepted in made-up myth because they were accepted by custom in real life.

Some cases called abduction or rape seemed to have taken place with the consent of the victim: for example, certainly Helen by Paris and perhaps the innumerable women and goddesses that god Zeus won into his amours. The men of Ancient Athens preferred to think that women were consenting to an affair even when they were forced into it. Most men did not experience their sexual pleasure out of brutalizing women but out of winning them into participation. They loved beautiful women and loved them even more when they were a conquest.

Aristotle explained that adultery was intrinsically bad and not made good by the circumstances, like being done "with the right woman, at the right time, and with the right manner; the mere commission of any of them is wrong" when it is done with another man's wife. [64] It was considered a crime, not of sexual misconduct but only of injustice against the husband.

For one who considered adultery evil, the gods were rated the worst perpetrators of it. Zeus had innumerable affairs with goddesses and mortal women. Whether they were married or not, their violation never seemed to bother him. Since men devised these stories, they sounded like

---

[62] Euripides, *Trojan Women*, 70 ff.: Loeb 10, 20.
[63] Sophocles, *Women of Trachis*, 565 ff.: Loeb 21, 184.
[64] Aristotle, *Nicomachean Ethics*, 2, 6, 18: Loeb 73, 96.

bells ringing a call to women to cooperate and satisfy their sexual desires.

The most dramatic and sad story was the rape of Creusa, daughter of king Erechtheus of Athens, by none other than god Apollo. He forced himself on her, a virgin, and violated her in a cave on the side of the Acropolis of Athens. She remained there hidden the full term, until she gave birth to a baby boy. Then, according to customs, she abandoned her baby born out of wedlock, perhaps to die in the same cave as a prey to beasts and birds. The rest of the story concerned this baby boy, called Ion, and was told by Euripides in his play *Ion* of 418-417 BCE. As we already know, Euripides had little respect for the gods. He lent Amphithryon these words about Zeus who violated his wife: "In goodness, I though mortal, surpass you, a mighty god." [65]

Euripides, however, did not believe that the gods "have illicit love affairs". These stories are nothing, he said, but "wretched tales of the poets." [66] The poets invented such fictions knowing that they would be well received by their male audiences. The sexual mores of the gods created by the poets were only the reflection and muted justification of the sexual desires in the heart and mind of the Athenian men.

When Demosthenes of the fourth century quoted the law-giver (*thesmothetês*) Draco of the end of the seventh century BCE on the matter of death and divorce, he not only made a leap of some three-hundred years but recognized an evolution in the mores of Athens. [67] Draco made a bizarre distinction between seduction and rape as the cause of adultery. If a man seduced a married woman and, after having been accused of it by any citizen, has been proven to be guilty, he was punishable by death, because such a man alienated a wife from her husband. His offense was more against the husband than against the wife who had, in fact, only yielded to the seduction. If, on the other hand, a rapist forced a woman to submit, he was not punishable by death, because the wife remained in her mind faithful to her husband, but was only sentenced to pay a fine to the husband in reparation for violating his property. In the early

---

[65] *Heracles Mad*, 342: Loeb 9, 338.
[66] *Ibid.*, 1341-1344: Loeb 9, 444.
[67] Demosthenes, *Against Aristocrates*, 23, 53: Loeb 299, 246-251.

fourth century, Xenophon rephrased this statement from the point of view of the husband onto his wife:

> When a wife has sexual intercourse by accident [usually interpreted as rape], husbands do not honor them the less on this account, if the wives' affection [*philia*] seems to remain unaffected. [68]

It seems obvious that in either case the Athenian husband considered his wife a possession without any rights rather than being a partner in marriage. He owned his wife for the sole purpose of procreation and household management. Adultery, either as seduction or rape, was not a crime against a woman, but against her husband and the state: the husband for the violation of his property and the state for the obstacle to the legitimacy of the children.

Draco's legislation reflected the inferior status in which women were kept in the seventh century BCE. In the first quarter of the fourth century, Draco's law was used in a court case reported in a speech written for it by the orator Lysias. The defendant was Euphiletus who murdered Eratosthenes for seducing his wife into adultery. True to customs, the wife's name was not given. The incident occurred after she had had one child and had gained the trust of her husband. But another woman, Eratosthenes' previous mistress who felt cheated, whispered in Euphiletus' ear some unsettling information about his wife's infidelity. So, one day, he came home unexpectedly and, at once, interrogated his slave-girl who revealed the affair after she realized that he already knew about it. When he burst into the bedroom, he found the seducer naked in bed with his wife. He murdered him on the spot after hearing his admission of guilt. [69]

The adulterer's relatives took Euphiletus to court for murder. He argued that his action was not only justified but required as punishment. He used the old law enacted by Draco in 621 BCE to the effect that

> those who use force deserve a less penalty than those who use persuasion ..., considering that those

---

[68] *Hiero*, 3, 4: Loeb 183, 22.
[69] Lysias, *On the Murder of Eratosthenes*, 8-29: Loeb 244, 6-17.

who use force are hated by the persons forced; while
those who used persuasion corrupted thereby their
victims' souls, thus making the wives of others more
closely attached to themselves than to their
husbands, and got the whole house into their hands,
and caused uncertainty as to whose the children
really were, the husbands' or the adulterers'. [70]

Euphiletus pointed out also that his killing of
Eratosthenes was not premeditated and for any other reason
but the flagrant adultery. To prove it, he reminded the jury
that he killed this evil man in front of his wife, the servant
and a few male neighbors. They were witnesses of the exact
intent of his action. The jury acquitted him of any crime.

A social comment, however, may be useful in order
to help understand some of the pitfalls affecting the proper
management of a household. In this case, all barriers of
caution had broken down: the husband was too trusting,
the wife too free after her mother-in-law died, the servant
too corrupt, so the adulterer, sex-crazy with all women, had
a field day with Euphiletus' wife. A greater measure of
vigilance and restraint may have helped preventing this
unfortunate incident.

On a much larger scale, the Trojan War also could
have been avoided if Menelaus had only kept watch more
closely on his wife, Helen, knowing, on the one hand, that
she was attractive and wild and, on the other hand, that
Paris of Troy was on the prowl when he visited Sparta. After
the fact, these observations appear sensible and wise.

The use of Draco's law, although successful in
Euphiletus' defense, was anachronistic in the fourth century.
Draco's successor, the lawmaker Solon, softened Draco's
law. Any man, he declared, was permitted but not required
to kill an adulterer caught in the act against a free woman. If
he was not killed, the husband could charge a fine against
him: a hundred drachmas for a rape and only twenty for a
seduction. [71] Plutarch, who reported this law, commented
that it was a "very absurd" law because Solon reversed
Draco's law. The laws of later years, the ones Plutarch knew
and approved, followed Draco's spirit instead of Solon's,

[70] Lysias, *On the Murder of Eratosthenes*, 32-33: Loeb 244, 18-21.
[71] Plutarch, *Parallel Lives, Solon*, 23, 1: Loeb 46, 466.

namely that a seducer was more culpable than a rapist and always deserved a more severe penalty.

In 333 BCE, another court case involved Lycophron, a wealthy Athenian cavalry commander, accused of breaking the law in different ways, including by acts of adultery (*moicheia*). Except for the orator Lycurgus (c. 390-324 BCE) who preserved a few prosecutorial fragments, the defense orator Hyperides was the only one who provided some details about the case. He explained that his client was accused of

> making many women grow old unmarried with their houses [because he violated their virginity] and many marry against the laws those whom it is not fitting [namely foreign men]. [72]

The dominant charge, however, was not Lycophron's adulterous behavior, which he vigorously denied, but his ability to be trusted in public office and in the service of democracy. In Athenian law, adultery and public office crossed at the junction of public justice. Yet, for adultery to jeopardize a career in public office, it seems that it had to be a behavior considered habitual, thus a reflection of one's character pattern, as it was in the two cases of Eratosthenes and Lycophron.

In order to understand how one can subvert public justice and Athenian democracy by committing adultery, we ought to return to the Eratosthenes' court case, previously examined. Caught in the act, Euphiletus' wife bit back like a snake. She accused her husband of having his sexual ways with the slave-girl, dragging her around. [73] If it is so, she implied, why does her lover deserve to be murdered for being found in bed with her? She knew the answer: because the wife is her husband's possession. In the law, adultery was not a sexual crime but a crime against public justice by depriving another man's ownership. Sexual misconduct alone did not involve public justice. So, Euphiletus neither denied nor admitted the truth of his wife's accusation, but only laughed at it as irrelevant because she did not have him as her possession.

---

[72] *In Defense of Lycophron*, 12: Loeb 395 (Minor Attic Orators, vol. 2), 388.

[73] Lysias, *On the Murder of Erastosthenes*, 12: Loeb 244, 8.

The possession of the wife by the husband, called objectification in modern language, was the reason why the Ancient Greeks did not need a word for adulteress. A wife was unable to commit adultery even when she indulged in illicit sex because she was created by nature, not custom, to sexually submit to a man. [74] Nevertheless, like her adulterous partner who could be murdered, she could be physically punished; yet neither for sexual misconduct nor for injustice but for the profanation of a religious sanctuary, namely the home. The adulterer's wife also, being deprived of every title of ownership, including that of her husband, could not lose him away to another wife. Therefore, she had no justified claim of any kind.

Solon treated the adulteress kindly. If she was caught in adultery, she was only forbidden to adorn herself and barred from attending public sacrifices and, if she attended, "any man who meets her shall tear off her garments, strip her of her ornaments and beat her (only if he may not kill her or mame her)." [75] The purpose of such a punishment was only to disgrace the adulterous wife. However, if she had been a daughter or a sister, still an unmarried virgin, she could have been sold as a slave. [76]

The enforcement of Solon's laws against adulteresses did not last, as Demosthenes recognized in his days after the mid-fourth century. The laws, then, stood as follows: the married woman who had been proven guilty of having willingly entered into an adulterous affair was divorced, excluded from all ancestral and religious festivals and returned to her parents who could treat her like a slave. [77] Her life was not worth living any more. [78]

In the case of the famous courtesan Neaera, the punishment was severe: First, her husband may not continue to cohabit with her, lest he be disfranchised; second, as an adulteress wife, she will be barred from attending public sacrifices and, if she is caught attending, "any person whatsoever may at will inflict upon them any sort of punishment, save only death, and that with

---

[74] Euripides, *Fr.*, *Auge*, 265a: Loeb 504, 268.
[75] Aeschines, *Against Timarchus*, 1, 183: Loeb 106, 146.
[76] Plutarch, *Parallel Lives*, *Solon*, 23, 2: Loeb 46, 466.
[77] *Against Neaera*, 85-87: Loeb 351, 414-419.
[78] Aeschines, *Against Timarchus*, 1, 184: Loeb 106, 146.

impunity." [79] This punishment was more severe than the one enacted in the sixth century by Solon who did not include divorce but only exclusion from participation in the sacrificial rites.

The enforcement of either one of these laws against an adulteress must have been very rare, even in cases of seduction. No case has been recorded during the period between the seventh and the fourth centuries. When it occurred, it was probably handled privately with a divorce and nothing more. Also, the possibility of mistaken activity or identity was ever present in the minds of the accusers unless they caught the culprits in the act. Aware of the dire consequences, most adulterers were more cautious than Eratosthenes. Besides, if a man was accused of adultery, he could contest the charge in court and, if he succeeded in proving his innocence, the punishment was reversed. The orator Apollodorus in about 340 BCE was probably covering laws of prior centuries when he described the situation in these terms:

> If a man unlawfully imprisons another on a charge of adultery, the person in question may indict him before the Thesmothetae [court magistrates] on a charge of illegal imprisonment; And if he shall convict the one who imprisoned him and prove that he was the victim of an unlawful plot, he shall be let off scot-free, and his sureties shall be released from their engagement; But if it shall appear that he was an adulterer, the law bids his sureties shall be released from their engagement; but if it shall appear that he was an adulterer, the law bids his sureties give him over to the one who caught him in the act, and he in the court-room may inflict upon him, as upon one guilty of adultery, whatever treatment he pleases, provided he use no knife [to castrate, mame or kill?]. [80]

Because of the manly pride of Greek husbands, we can assume that the number of incidents kept secret

---

[79] Demosthenes, *Against Neaera*, 86: Loeb 351, 416.
[80] *Ibid.*, 66: Loeb 351, 400.

exceeded by far those that ended up in court. [81] Besides, men did not need to take the dire risk of being caught and punished when they could find their satisfaction without any risk at all with any non-Athenian women.

In *The Clouds* of 423 BCE, Aristophanes used the setting of Socrates' school to describe the kind of education he provided. At one point, he entrusted the pupil Pheidippides to two male characters, one impersonating Better Argument (*kreittôn logos*), the worse kind, old and ugly, and the other, Worse Argument (*êttôn logos*), the better kind, young and handsome. [82] The two Arguments argued with each other for a while, one for the old-fashioned ways and the other for the new ways of life. As they came to the subject of chastity, Better Argument pointed out that king Peleus' chaste life gained him to marry Thetis, mother of Achilles. Worse Argument replied:

> And then she [Thetis] up and deserted him because he wasn't a roughneck, and no fun to spend the night with between the sheets. A woman enjoys being lewdly used. But you're just a king-sized Cronus [old-fashioned]. My boy, do consider everything that decency entails, and all the pleasure you stand to lose: boys, women, dice, fine food and drink, laughs. If you're deprived of all this, what's the point of living? Now then, I'll proceed to the necessities of nature. Say you slip up, fall in love, engage in a little adultery, and then get caught. You're done for because you're unable to argue. But if you follow me, go ahead and indulge your nature, romp, laugh, think nothing shameful. If you happen to get caught in *flagrante*, tell him this: that you've done nothing wrong. Then pass the buck to Zeus, on the ground that even he is worsted by lust for women, so how can you, a mere mortal, be stronger than a god? [83]

If we believe only a portion of what Aristophanes is stating here in the fifth century, we can infer that adultery, although severely punishable, was not only humored but

---

[81] Aristotle, *Rhetoric*, 1, 12, 1372a, 5-10 & 1373a, 34: Loeb 193, 130 & 138.
[82] *Clouds*, 891 ff.: Loeb 488, 130 ff.
[83] *Ibid.*, 1068-1082: Loeb 488, 152-155.

also often tolerated. In fact, according to Diogenes Laërtius (second century CE), the Athenians of the late fifth century BCE, confronted with the shortage of men, passed a decree to allow the citizens to marry one Athenian woman and have children also by another. Socrates and Aristotle may have taken advantage of this new law. [84]

The laws of Draco and Solon concerning adultery gave the picture of an ideal society. Their laws were impractical, without balance and not enforceable. The "do-as-you-please" policy of Pericles tended to prevail in the fifth century if some arrangements could be negotiated quietly between the parties involved, which did not include the wife. Furthermore, the death penalty for adultery was flexible: neither totally public because it was executed by the offended husband, on the basis of justice (*dikê*), and not by the court, on the basis of a written law (*graphê*), nor totally private because the recourse to the court was available, yet only if the prosecution came from the injured party, namely the guardian (*kurios*), not by any citizen as in the procedure of *graphê*.

The punishment by death extended beyond strict adultery. Any man who had sexual relations with any woman, married or not, free or slave, could be punished by death by the offended *kurios*, whose property had been violated, and the murder was forgiven by the state. Therefore, the murder was a justifiable homicide, regardless of whether the case was one of a married or an unmarried woman, Athenian or not, having been seduced. Demosthenes quoted a statute that listed the possible victims:

> If a man kills another ... [caught] in intercourse with his wife, or mother, or sister, or daughter, or concubine kept for procreation of legitimate children, he shall not go into exile as a manslayer on that account. [85]

Homicide was considered justifiable whether the case was adultery or fornication because it caused an injustice to

---

[84] Diogenes Laërtius, *Lives of Eminent Philosophers*, Socrates, 2, 26: Loeb 184, 156.
[85] *Against Aristocrates*, 23, 53: Loeb 299, 246-249.

the *kurios*, husband or father, and not because of a sexual violation of a woman "kept for procreation". What was the crime then if the woman was known to be infertile or had passed the age of procreation? The law failed to answer, as it did also to explain how a concubine could produce a legitimate child unless she was Athenian. It remains clear, however, that every intercourse with a woman claimed by another man as his own was a crime of injustice punishable by death or some other vindication chosen by the offended guardian. If the chosen penalty was questionable, the court could be petitioned to review it and redress it. The Athenian Constitution, as reported by Aristotle, read as follows:

> One who admits homicide but declares it to have been legal (for instance, when he has killed a man taken in adultery) ... is tried at the Delphinium. [86]

This court, probably seated southeast of the Acropolis, was one of the lower courts in Athens, like the courts of Palladium, Prytaneum and Phreatto, and therefore the case was not considered of the highest importance.
In every case of adultery from the sixth through the fourth century, the husband had a right to punish the adulterer but, by force of tradition, must divorce his wife caught in adultery, lest he loses his civil rights. [87] If he did not kill the adulterer, because he did not want to or could not do it, he could privately negotiate a monetary compensation. When this option between murder and a financial settlement was available, it seems natural that the husband preferred the latter. As long as his honor was upheld, it meant less trouble and less danger of retaliation, while some tangible advantage resulted for him. Aristotle went further when he suggested that some adulterers pay the husbands a fine, not in reparation but for the service of their wives. The real adulterers then were the pimping husbands, as he wrote:

> Again, suppose two men to commit adultery, one for profit, and gaining by the act, the other from desire, and having to pay, and so losing by it; then the latter

---

[86] *Athenian Constitution*, 57, 3: Loeb 285, 158.
[87] Demosthenes, *Against Neaera*, 87: Loeb 351, 418.

would be deemed a profligate rather than a man who takes more than his due, while the former would be deemed unjust, but not profligate; clearly therefore it is being done for profit that makes the action unjust. [88]

In this situation, the pimp was the one who acted against justice and should be penalized, not the adulterer who was simply culpable of sexual self-indulgence.

A husband who was the victim of an adulterer's injustice had a third choice, namely to prosecute the culprit in the court. The procedure is not clear. The gap between the ideal and the practice may interfere and cause some confusion on this point. There must have been very few prosecutions of this kind in Athens. In any case, the documentation is lacking. Aristotle did not clarify the issue when he stated that a man may commit adultery, yet not be an adulterer, therefore unjust, if he did it "not from the motive of deliberate choice but under the influence of passion." [89]

A child that resulted from an adulterous union was considered illegitimate, yet could be free if both parents were not slaves. If the child was a boy, he could be legitimized by an act of legislation, as it was the case for the son Pericles had with his alien *hetaira*, Aspasia.

In accord with the law reported by Diogenes Laërtius, as previously quoted, [90] we may assume that a bigamous husband could keep the second family in the shadow of the first one, although the children of both families were considered legitimate.

Women accepted men's sexual habits as a fact of life. They were not consumed by it. They even did not feel it was worth their attention by way of comments of approval or disapproval. Euripides who better than any other playwrights dissected his stage characters offered an innuendo about the attitude of women towards men's liberties. In his play *Electra* of 415 BCE, he made his heroine utter the following statements after she and her brother Orestes murdered Aegisthus but before they murdered their mother Clytemnestra. Addressing his corpse, she said first:

---

[88] *Nicomachean Ethics*, 5, 2, 1130a24-28: Loeb 73, 262.
[89] *Ibid.*, 5, 6, 1134a, 20-22: Loeb 73, 290.
[90] *Lives of Eminent Philosophers, Socrates*, 2, 26: Loeb 184, 156.

You shamefully married my mother ... Imagined that if you married my mother you would find in her no bad wife, though she was unfaithful to the bed of my father. [91]

Then, in this context, she cautiously revealed her knowledge of his escapades with other women: "Your conduct toward women (since it ill befits a virgin to describe it) I pass over in silence, but I shall give an intelligible hint." [92]

Electra hated her mother Clytemnestra, but utterly despised her lover Aegisthus who took her father's place in the palace during the Trojan War. His behavior terrified her when he was alive. But, as soon as her brother Orestes murdered him, she cried out her revulsion for the shameful marriage he had with her mother, thus wronging her father's honor.

Nevertheless, Electra was even-handed in attributing the blame for this illicit marriage. She attributed it to both, her mother Clytemnestra and her lover Aegisthus. In general, however, it appears that men who took the liberty to indulge in extramarital affairs tended to blame the women for enticing them. Women resented this charge. No doubt some of them did what is required to appear coquette and alluring, but it was not the case of most Athenian women.

Still, if the man's sexual appetites were not completely satisfied at home, the women's sexual appetites may not have been satisfied either. Euripides lent these words to Andromache, a princess from Troy, about the insatiable sexual lust of married women:

This is a disgraceful thing. We women suffer worse from this disease than men, but we do well to veil it deceitly from sight. [93]

Being as sequestered as she was, the Greek wife had no opportunity to satisfy herself except with her husband. She had no brothels to frequent, no symposia to attend, no open place to roam around freely. If she was to fall for a

---

[91] Euripides, *Electra*, 916-920: Loeb 9, 252.
[92] *Ibid.*, 945-946: Loeb 9, 254.
[93] *Andromache*, 218-221: Loeb 484, 292.

man other than her husband, it was at such great risks that she rarely accepted to cooperate.

In an aside in the play *Ion*, Euripides addressed writers and performers. For this reason, his words ring true to contemporary feelings among women, especially because they come from the man whom women perceived as their misogynist enemy. A handmaiden of the chorus interrupted the story, turned toward the audience and said:

> All you that with defaming songs
> travel the path of minstrelsy,
> singing of the unholy unions
> and unlawful loves of our sex,
> see how in piety we excel
> the unrighteous brood of males!
> Let songs reverse its course,
> and the muse of blame
> assail men for their amours! [94]

No man but the husband had the right to respond to his wife's sexual attraction. So no man who was not the husband would be left alone in the house with a married woman or would attempt to flirt with one in public places. Society condoned a man's escapades, even expected him to yield to his impulses, but not any Athenian woman. So if she showed the slightest interest in another man but her husband, she was found wanting as a wife. The fact is that, even if she never failed in this matter, she could never be trusted by her husband simply because she was a woman with attractive attributes. [95]

When the peasant husband of Electra found her standing at the door and speaking to Orestes and Pylades, two young men he did not know, he exclaimed: "Who are these strangers I see at my door? ... It is quite shameful for a woman to stand about with young men." [96]

Close family friends or relatives tended to take the role of husbands when the legal husbands were absent. They not only supervised the management of the household but occasionally indulged in some adulterous affairs which

---

[94] *Ion*, 1090-1098: Loeb 10, 450.
[95] Euripides, *Fr.*, *Hippolytus Veiled*, 440: Loeb 504, 482; also *Fr.*, *Cretan Women*, 463: Loeb 504, 524.
[96] Euripides, *Electra*, 341-344: Loeb 9, 188.

created problems especially when illegitimate children
resulted from them. The legitimate children must have
resented this arrangement when it was protracted, because
they naturally loved their father and resented the intrusion
of another man replacing him in their home.

The members of the larger family (*anchisteia*), as far
as the second cousins, could not be kept at a distance
because of the close ties and frequent interactions among
them. They could not be avoided either in the house or in
places of social gathering. Besides, marriages were allowed
between a man and his patrilateral half-sister and, of
course, with any other kin relatives, like between uncles and
nieces, and between cousins. This latter situation was
probably frequent, out of loyalty to the larger family. [97] Even
though they were thorough rascals, relatives like
Dicaeogenes were given more regard than was given to
money. [98]

The major challenge to a husband's honor and a
wife's fidelity came not only from relatives but also from all
the male neighbors and friends for whom access was easy
and the guards down. Friends stood between private and
public life. They were chosen and sometimes preferred to
relatives for their help. [99] They shared in family celebrations,
like weddings, festivals and funerals. Although such
closeness of friends was recommended as good for both the
state and the family, it was also dangerous when the
supervision was overly relaxed. [100] Not that it was always
easy to do it, especially because husbands spent so little
time in the house even when they were not away on
business or military duty for long periods of time. "There is
no wall, no wealth, nothing else so difficult to guard as a
woman." [101] The fact is that women always had to guard

---

[97] Isaeus, *On the Estate of Apollodorus*: Loeb 202, 248-279 & *On
the Estate of Menecles:* Loeb 202, 40-67 and Demosthenes,
Against Neaera, 2: Loeb 351, 350-353.
[98] Isaeus, *On the Estate of Dicaeogenes*, 30: Loeb 202, 180.
[99] Aristotle, *Nicomachean Ethics*, 5, 9, 1137a, 6 & 20: Loeb 73,
310-313; Lysias, *On the Murder of Eratosthenes*, 1, 23-24: Loeb
244, 14 and Demosthenes, *Against Aristocrates*, 23, 56: Loeb
299, 248.
[100] Plato, *Laws*, 5, 738E: Loeb 187, 360 and Demosthenes, *Against
Theocrines*, 40: Loeb 351, 322.
[101] Euripides, *Fr.*, *Danae*, 320: Loeb 504, 330.

themselves and withdraw when male friends entered the house or became aggressive in their presence, especially under the spell of wine or passion. Euripides' lost play *Stheneboea* was about a wife falling in love with a younger man while he was the house guest of her husband. [102]

In Sophocles' *Electra*, Clytemnestra rebuked her daughter for rejecting the guardianship of Aegisthus in the absence of her father, Agamemnon:

> You are ranging about once more, it seems, at large; because Aegisthus is not here, he who always used to prevent you from shaming your family at least outside the house. [103]

Since men could not be trusted in the management of sex, women had to protect themselves by allowing no close contact, even with male relatives and friends. Their quarters (*gunaikonitis*) in the house were forbidden to all men except the father and the husband. When the brothers Thrasylochus and Meidias came to visit Demosthenes for an exchange, they were his friends in his household and yet they violated the women's quarters doing something even relatives would not have dared doing: they forced the door open and used foul language in the presence of his unmarried sister. [104] Needless to say that he did not tolerate it.

The sequestration of Athenian women, however, did not go as far as it currently goes with some Muslin women who cannot even leave the house unless a man accompanies them. Greek women could go out on the streets and in the agora as long as they were veiled and cautious. They usually went in pairs or with their children or a slave girl. Such isolation of women can be viewed as a form of birth control.

It is not the place to relate the escapades of men, especially the unmarried ones, even if it was to justify the precautions prescribed by customs and society in order to protect women. The fact is amply established that Greek men of the Classical Age found sexual satisfaction when and where they needed it. They found their models from on

---

[102] See E. Hall, *The Sociology of Athenian Tragedy*, in *The Cambridge Companion to Greek Tragedy*, ed. By P.E. Easterling, 118.
[103] *Electra*, 516-518: Loeb 20, 212.
[104] Demosthenes, *Against Meidias*, 21, 78-81: Loeb 299, 56-61.

high: Zeus among the gods and Heracles among the demi-gods. There is also hardly a name that we know -- Pericles, Alcibiades, Sophocles, Socrates -- that is not associated consistently with some sexual affairs. Alcibiades was the worst because he was an adulterer (*moichos*) who, at least once, made a married woman pregnant, queen Timaea of Sparta, while her husband, king Agis II, was campaigning in northern Attica. [105]

Plato said of Sophocles that in his youth he was under the force of love, "a raging and savage beast of a master". His interest was in both women and boys. [106] Already in 467, Aeschylus had recognized the existence of bisexuals and homosexuals as a group in the society of Athens when he wrote: "Man or woman or whosoever is betwixt." [107] Some twenty years later, Sophocles expressed kind feelings toward homosexuality since himself behaved bisexually.

Sophocles kept a concubine also until he died: Theoris when he was an old man and Archippe shortly before he died at the age of ninety. This life style was in no way objectionable until it threatened the public rights of a citizen. His legitimate son Iophon prosecuted him unsuccessfully on the ground of senility in order to ensure the inheritance for himself and prevent it from going to Theoris' illegitimate son, Ariston. Inheritance was a mixture of private and public elements. The line between public and private, as well as between freedom and the law, was not clearly drawn during the fifth century.

As aleady mentioned, Pericles professed a "do-as-you-please" policy in the public conduct of democratic government. Equality and justice among all the citizens required such a policy, applied under the guidance and not without the demagoguery of leaders like himself. He extended it also to all spheres of private and sexual activities, except when it infringed on equality and justice among all citizens. He understood the tension between freedom and the law, and he deliberately favored the pull of freedom. [108] In the fifth century, the enacted law covered rarely the private affairs of citizens, including their sexual

[105] Plutarch, *Parallel Lives, Alcibiades*, 24, 2: Loeb 80, 66.
[106] *Republic*, 1, 329C: Loeb 237, 10.
[107] *The Seven Against Thebes*, 197: Loeb 145, 336.
[108] Thucydides, *Peloponnesian War*, 2, 37, 2-3: Loeb 108, 322-325.

behavior regulated at best by customary norms of moderation, respect and fidelity. When the law addressed sexual conduct, it was not to prevent immorality but to correct injustice against a property worth keeping and defending. Such was the case when a man committed adultery or resorted to pimping his wife or children.

The orators and philosophers of the fourth century repeated the Periclean "do-as-you-please" policy but accepted some legal limitations to its effectiveness in the private sector. They recognized the value of freedom, yet tilted on the side of the law because of their painful experiences with tyranny at the end of the Peloponnesian War. They continued to set their standard of morality in the control of all human appetites by way of self-restraint (sôphrosunê) and of freedom from the enslavement of passions. [109] Sexual enslavement could afflict women as much as men, but the social conditions and mores prevented it and, for this reason, made it less detectable. No one can enter the minds and hearts of people, especially those of cultures distant in the past and of different places, but only see and hear their external revelations. Some women in the Lysistrata story seemed to have suffered of this enslavement as much as their husbands. If we tend to think that the exaggerations for comedic purposes were put upon the women more than the men it is because to this day we are conditioned to think in this way.

On the other hand, the orators of the fourth century in many court summations and the philosophers in several dissertations, while preserving the customary standards of the past, emphasized the value of legal decisions and government rules concerning marriage, adultery, rape and every form of sexual exploitation.

The common people of Athens followed a permissive line of conduct, resisting every form of excess on one side or the other. They avoided abstinence and profligacy, attempting to strike a middle ground in all things within the limitations of human frailty. Women knew their place in society and the kind of relationship they were bound to entertain. Did they always succeed in real life? Probably more than they wanted to because of the physical and social restrictions put upon them.

---

[109] Xenophon, Oeconomicus, 1, 22-23: Loeb 168, 372.

One last question: Did the Greeks believe that permanent sexual relations between husband and wife were only for the purpose of procreation? Plato seemed to believe so in the following advice about it:

> A natural use of reproductive intercourse, -- on the one hand, by abstaining from the male and not slaying of set purpose the human stock, nor sowing seeds on rocks and stones where it can never take root and have fruitful increase; and, on the other hand, by abstaining from every female field iin which you would not desire the seed to spring up. [110]

But then he knew that such a prescription was wishful thinking. He immediately added that, if it could be enforced as a law, it "would be the source of ten thousand blessings." A good wife did not deserve to be cheated of the warm embrace of her husband because she was infertile. As one of the Danaids said: nothing is more precious to her than when her husband

> would fall into and play in my arms and at my breast, and win my heart with a host of kisses; for these things hold the biggest spell over people, their intimacies. [111]

A wife's sexual fulfillment remained uncertain because it depended only on the interest of her husband who married her primarily to become the mother of his children and had many opportunities outside his marriage to satisfy his libidinal desires. He could even divorce her easily, if he so desired. As a wife, she could not play the field or divorce him. No doubt, her life without motherhood was meaningless and probably miserable.

---

[110] Plato, *Laws*, 8, 838E-839A: Loeb 192, 158.
[111] Euripides, *Fr.*, *Danae*, 323: Loe 332.

CHAPTER FOUR

MOTHERS

Procreation

The official status of the Athenian wife was measured by her relevant responsibilities. The first one was to give birth to legitimate children. The new wife looked forward to becoming pregnant at once with her first child. She hoped for a son in order to please her husband and fulfill better her role in the city. [1] The cycle of transmission of life will be repeated as often and successfully as possible in the primitive conditions of the time and place.

Husbands as well as the state expected the wives to perform their public duty. Demosthenes summarized it well in the court case of Neaera:

> For this is what living with a woman as one's wife means -- to have children by her and to introduce the sons to the members of the phratry (*phratêras*) and the deme (*dêmotas*), and to betroth the daughters to husbands as one's own. ... Wives to bear us legitimate children and to be faithful guardians of our households. [2]

Husbands looked at their wives only as the soil where they grew sons and daughters, not simply because it was their natural role in the family structure but because it was their responsibility in the larger structure of the city-state (*polis*). The city-state had a vital interest in the birth of a sufficient number of good sons and daughters. If natural fertility was lacking, husbands and wives resorted sometimes to extraneous means, such as consultations with

---

[1] Aristophanes, *Lysistrata*, 651: Loeb 179, 356 & Id., *Women at the Thesmophoria*, 832: Loeb 179, 558.
[2] *Against Neaera*, 59, 122: Loeb 351, 444-447

the oracle of Delphi, like Xuthus and Creusa did [3] or drugs, like the ones Medea offered king Aegeus. [4] For the same reason, Plato recommended that

> the opportunity of marriage will be more readily provided for the good man, and that he will be more frequently selected than the others for participation in that sort of things, in order that as many children as possible may be born from such stock. [5]

Aeschylus portrayed the men's arrogant attitude toward women when he endorsed the belief that women were not parents, but only enablers for men, and called as a witness no less than Athena herself, the Olympian Zeus' own created child, that grew not in the womb's dark coverture. [6]

So, as we discover through myths, the story of the origins of mankind, devised by men bypassed women or made her evil to men. Pandora originated the race of women, without being considered, like Eve, the mother of all human beings. Men traced their mythological ancestry to Gaia (Earth). They were the only natives of the land and therefore the only ones with the right and responsibility to rule. Prometheus who represented men in the fight against Zeus freed Pandora from a prison in the Underworld, using a mallet, the symbolic tool of agriculture. In this context of mythology from the time of Athens' origin, the Athenian females were relegated in the background and made subservient to the male citizens. As female residents of Athens, they did not even have a name of their own, interfacing with *Athenaioi*, the name for male Athenians, citizens of Athens.

Hecate, however, extended her protection beyond the wedding until the birth of the first child. For this reason, among others, the couple had a shrine for Hecate before the doorway of their home. [7] The goddess was expected to guard from intruders the home where the bride conceived

---

[3] Euripides, *Ion*, 66: Loeb 10, 326.
[4] Id,, *Medea*, 717: Loeb 12, 348.
[5] *Republic*, 5, 468C: Loeb 237, 488-491.
[6] *Eumenides*, 663-664: Loeb 146, 334; see Euripides, *Ion*, 454-457: Loeb 10, 374.
[7] Aristophanes, *Wasps*, 804: Loeb 488, 324.

and bore her first child.   The   protective   role   filled   by Hecate contributed to the fecundity of mothers and their healthy childbirths.

Goddess   Demeter   also,   fulfilled   the   role   of protectress of motherhood, like her sister Hera did, but in a manner more responsive to human life in which joys are often marred by some sufferings. She experienced the joys of motherhood but lost her daughter Persephone when Hades took her away. She retrieved her and thus restored the blood bond she had made as her mother. For this reason, she became the model and protectress of mothers in their role in the family. She was honored in a special shrine at Eleusis, north of Athens.

In spite of such protection from the goddesses, nature thwarted sometimes their divine efforts and suborned them for evil doings. Some virgins died unmarried, some brides died before becoming pregnant, or during pregnancy, or in childbirth. The Ancient Greeks had no explanation for these failures and were eager to deflect the responsibility to ghosts who roamed the world under the guidance of goddess Hecate. Sarah Iles Johnston has extracted from the meager information available about these ghosts (aoroi) an extensive review and analysis which need not be repeated here. [8]

Let it be said only that these ghosts had experienced in myths the pain of either dying in childbirth, like Gello, or remaining childless, like Mormo and Lamia. Inasmuch as they understood such tragedies, they could supply men and women with a deflection of responsibility for similar tragedies in real life. The Greeks enwrapped them in evil myths of wandering between the upper and the lower worlds in search of victims for premature deaths. So they caused the deaths of virgins and mothers with babies. Among them they recruited more of the same envious ghosts willing to disrupt the maternal course of nature.

For protection, young women implored Demeter and Hecate with supplications and gift offerings in shrines, especially on their wedding day. They thus wished the goddesses would change the evil power of these ghosts into protection against it, somewhat like Athena did when she

---

[8] Restless Dead, esp. p. 161-287.

changed the wandering punitive Erinyes into peaceful Eumenides with a dwelling beneath the earth. [9]

These female models belonged to the realm of the divine or its borders. Very few mortal women were deified and honored with a shrine and a cult after their death. None ever had the prestige male heroes received after death, especially Heracles who may have been a historical figure whose achievements of strength and courage catapulted into myth where the borderline between divine and human is often blurred. His origin was half divine as he was attributed a mortal mother, Alcmena -- daughter of Anaxo and Electryon, and wife of Amphitryon -- and the Olympian god Zeus as a father. Alcmena, was a very beautiful woman but more chaste and faithful than Helen. The legend has it that Zeus had to pretend to be her husband when he first approached her. With his mother, Heracles received in Athens the sacrificial offerings reserved to the gods.

Helen of Sparta had a place of choice among all the mortal women whose excellence entitled to divine honors after death. Like Heracles, she was given in mythology a divine origin from Zeus and Leda who was the daughter of Thestius and wife of Tyndareus. The Dioscorus Pollux and his sister, Clytemnestra, Agamemnon's unfaithful wife, shared the same parentage with her. No more than her sister, however, was Helen taken as a model of womanhood, for example like Penelope who was considered a model but had a human origin and was identified only as the wife of Odysseus and the mother of Telemachus. Helen was placed on a higher pedestal not for breaking her marital bond of fidelity but for vindicating her marriage to Menelaus, a marriage she violated and yet proved to be unbreakable when she returned home to him, her legal husband. Thus the matrimonial bond was respected and the husband's right to own his wife was affirmed inalienable forever. Helen's cult at Therapne, near Sparta, reminded the wives of their most important obligation as they were preparing to become mothers.

Aristotle observed his fellow-humans and found between them and the animals so many similarities that he described them as a superior form of the same kind of living beings. When he considered the process of

---

[9] Aeschylus, *Eumenides*, 1021 ff: Loeb 146, 368.

procreation, he found it also to be similar except for one major difference, namely in *philia* which is the affection binding husband and wife. He was probably wrong when he deprived certain animals, mates or parents, of some kind of affection. He was also generalizing too readily a feeling that needed to be nurtured by humans more than some partners cared to do. He was right, however, in understanding the role of such a feeling of affection and love between husband and wife as the crowning of a successful relationship. [10]

Pregnancy and childbirth were natural functions of women who were known in Ancient Greece to be hardy and strong. They expected no public assistance, such as clinics to visit and consultations with physicians, almost all male. They had midwives, like Socrates' mother, who assisted in the delivery and probably also during the pregnancy if any complications occurred. Athens did not assume the charge of providing the means to bring every pregnancy to a safe and healthy childbirth, but left it to both father and mother to do it for the sake of their family and the state. Both parents hoped for a beautiful and healthy child to be born. [11]

In view of this, from the wedding days to the birth of the first child, husbands were expected to make life easier for their new wife by only spending the nights in the house. They worked outside the house in the daytime and ate "at the common tables, just as they did before marriage." Wives would have resisted eating out because, as Plato explained with some unfair arrogance, they take offence when strangers notice how much they eat and drink. [12]

Nothing was more sacred than motherhood in the life of a woman and nothing more important than new citizens for the survival of the state. So much so that a temple dedicated to the Mother -- the *Metroôn* -- was erected on the Agora next to the *Bouleutêrion* where the citizens' Council met. Motherhood performed a civic function. For this reason, Electra's scheme to lure her mother Clytemnestra, queen of Argos, to visit her in the hills was so deviously clever. When Orestes asked how he should slay their mother she answered firmly: "I shall manage my mother's death". [13]

---

[10] Aristotle, *Nicomachean Ethics*, 8, 12, 1162a, 7: Loeb 73, 502.
[11] Euripides, *Fr.*, *Aeolus*, 15 & *Danae*, 316: Loeb 504, 18 & 328.
[12] *Laws*, 6, 781A: Loeb 187, 486.
[13] Euripides, *Electra*, 647: Loeb 9, 222.

Then, carrying out her plan which she executed with him, she ordered her servant:

> Go to Clytemnestra, old man, and say the following to her. Tell her that I have given birth to a boy ... ten days ago, the time a woman who has given birth keeps pure [by abstaining from intercourse]. [14]

The tenth day (*dekatê*) after childbirth was an official landmark: it was the day of the mother's customary sacrifice of purification and of the child's naming. [15] On this day, the Athenian father introduced to his clan and deme his baby newly born "of an Athenian mother duly married." [16] The witnesses of the marriage contract may be present again at this proud moment if their testimony was needed to prove that the child was "of citizen on both sides", namely father and mother. [17]

Hard evidence is not available to indicate whether girls as well as boys were introduced on this tenth day. Surely, because girls were considered less important to the state than boys, their introductions were probably done rarely or with less fanfare. It was a father's duty and pride to have his sons, future citizens and warriors, recognized with a feast of food and wine for the witnesses. The private ceremony of acceptance of newborn children by their parents at the household hearth (*amphidromia*), held on the fifth or the seventh day after birth, probably sufficed in most cases to recognize girls' births.

Athenian parents never felt a responsibility to have as many children as their resources could allow, except in time of great losses of lives, for example after the plague of 430 BCE and the military disaster of the Sicilian expedition of 415 BCE. Their determinant, in good and bad times, was the good life of all the citizens. If a crisis jeopardized it and a greater number of citizens was required in order to sustain it, the husbands and wives of Athens filled the needs. According to the best estimates, the number of children carried to viable terms by Athenian wives during the

---

[14] *Electra*, 651-654: Loeb 9, 224.
[15] *Ibid.*, 1126: Loeb 9, 274.
[16] Isaeus, *On the Estate of Ciron*, 19: Loeb 202, 300 and *On the Estate of Pyrrhus*, 80: Loeb 202, 122.
[17] Aristotle, *Athenian Constitution*, 26, 3: Loeb 285, 78.

Peloponnesian war almost doubled: from 2.5 per household at the beginning in 431 to 4.3 at the end in 404, in spite of the absence and loss of thousands of Athenian men.

These numbers are small because family size was controlled by two other factors: first by the limited resources of Attica, a land which was one of the poorest among all the Mediterranean regions and, second, by the philosophy of life endorsed by the Athenian people. Of all the philosophers, Aristotle is the best interpreter of such a philosophy. Here is his premise:

> Men, individually and in common, nearly all have some aim, in the attainment of which they choose or avoid certain things. This aim, briefly stated, is happiness and its component parts. ... For one should do the things which procure happiness or one of its parts, or increase instead of diminishing it, and avoid doing those things which destroy or hinder it or bring about what is contrary to it. [18]

Aristotle has made two points: first, the means are chosen in view of the end or goal and, second, the goal of life is happiness. He still needed to define happiness. He wrote:

> Let us then define happiness as well-being combined with virtue, or independence of life, or the life that is most agreeable combined with security, or abundance of possessions and slaves, combined with power to protect and make use of them; for nearly all men admit that one or more of these things constitute happiness. [19]

How fascinating! A philosopher gives a definition by listing the meanings on which everybody agrees. He follows through, however, with his own long list of the "constituents" of happiness, like noble birth, friends and children, wealth, and so on. These constituents of happiness that make for prosperity cannot be preserved without family planning by way of a reasonable control by

---

[18] *Rhetoric*, 1, 5, 1360b, 5, 1-2: Loeb 193, 46.
[19] *Ibid*. 1, 5, 1360b, 5, 3: Loeb 193, 46-49.

the parents, especially the fathers. Therefore, a choice had to be made between either having or not having and raising a child. Such a choice implied a more fundamental choice concerning the end or goal of life, namely happiness.

In the aftermath of the Peloponnesian War (404 BCE) until the death of Aristotle in 322, the population of Athens continued to decline from some 30,000 to 21,000 (-30%), according to Raphael Sealey, [20] setting the average family size at three children. Several factors certainly contributed to this decline, such as the political instability of the time and the poverty and insecurity of the Athenians. It is clear also that the good life of the citizens combined with some personal selfishness were the primary goal of every household in determining both the number and the quality of its offspring.

Biology

The biology of procreation was understood in the fifth century as a very simplistic process. Human and animal procreation was compared to agriculture. The parent seeds transmitted life and imprinted their characteristics, like the seed of wheat or of oak produced a plant of the same kind and quality. The Greeks believed that the man provided the primary seed and, for this reason, was the primary parent of the child's life and main source of its characteristics. The woman's role was primarily to nurture the man's seed. Her womb was like the soil into which the seed was sown, where it germinated, grew and, after complete gestation, produced a similar offspring. Procreation was, therefore, a function of the man who needed an enabler, the woman's womb. The healthier it was, like the richer and well irrigated the soil, the stronger the child, like the plant was.

This kind of perception led to the strangest of arguments in Orestes' case of his mother's murder in which the Furies prosecuted, Apollo testified for the defense and the Areopagus acted as court jury and judge. The judgment of the court was not on the crime itself that Orestes confessed but about its gravity. [21] The Furies argued that Clytemnestra "was not of one blood with the man she slew",

---

[20] *Women and Law in Classical Greece*, 7.
[21] Aeschylus, *Eumenides*, 587-588: Loeb 146, 324-327.

[22] her husband Agamemnon and therefore the murder of her husband was not a capital crime. Quite true: husband and wife are not of the same blood and, in Greek law, the murder of a victim not related by blood was less grievous and, for this reason, did not call for punishment by death. Therefore, unlike Clytemnestra's murder, Orestes' murder of his mother was excessive and unwarranted. Apollo countered in his defense that a crime on fatherhood – Agammnon by Clytemnestra -- was more serious than one on motherhood – Clytemnestra by Orestes -- and, therefore, should not be punished when the latter rectified the former. Why so? Because, if fatherhood can exist without motherhood, as Zeus himself has proven by giving birth to Athena from his head alone, then fatherhood is the only essential party to procreation and, as a result, to the perpetuation of the family and the state. [23] Apollo's specious argument was simply revealing the Greek view that justified in the fifth-century the male superiority, even about procreation and, to boot, in a court of law. In Apollo's words:

> The mother of what is called her child is not its parent, but only the nurse of the newly-implanted germ [sperm]. The begetter is the parent, whereas she, as a stranger for a stranger, doth but preserve the sprout, except God shall blight its birth. [24]

In this case, the Furies sided for the prosecution against Apollo but, when the jury of judges hung divided equally, goddess Athena broke the tie by acquitting Orestes, in favor of the defense by Apollo.

The same Aeschylus said of king Oedipus in the choral words of the Theban women:

> The same [Oedipus] who sowed his seed in a hallowed field, his mother's womb, where he was

[22] *Eumenides*, 605: Loeb 146, 328.
[23] *Ibid.*, 640-643: Loeb 146, 332; see Euripides, *Ion*, 452-456: Loeb 10, 372-375.
[24] Aeschylus, *Eumenides*, 657-661: Loeb 146, 334.

nurtured to life, -- and he came to endure a growth of blood. [25]

So spoke Aeschylus, the first in time among the classical playwrights, comparing procreation to agriculture. About Oedipus, being married to his mother, Sophocles made the chorus of elders mix the same imagery with another one:

Ah, famous Oedipus, whom the same wide harbour served as child and as father on your bridal bed! How, how could the field your father sowed put up with you so long in silence? [26]

Elsewhere, Sophocles acknowledged with these words Deianeira's complaint against her husband, Heracles:

We had, indeed, children, whom he, like a farmer who has taken over a remote piece of ploughland, regards only when he sows and when he reaps. [27]

In spite of his travels throughout Greece and in Asia Minor, performing twelve labors, visiting friends like Admetus and fighting enemies like Lycus, Heracles had according to the myth seventy-one sons and – perhaps in a moment of weakness or distraction – one daughter. [28]

The story of Oedipus' daughter Antigone provided Sophocles another occasion to compare procreation to agriculture. King Creon of Thebes had decided to kill her for disobeying his order when she buried her brother Polynices. Antigone's sister, Ismene, remonstrated to her uncle Creon that he will kill the bride promised to his son, Haemon. Creon replied: "Yes, for the furrows of others can be ploughed!" [29]

---

[25] Aeschylus, *The Seven Against Thebes*, 753-756: Loeb 145, 384; see also *Fr., Kares and Europe*, 50, 3: *Loeb 146, 414-417* and *Addendum*: Loeb 146, 601-603.
[26] *Oedipus King*, 1207-1213: Loeb 20, 454.
[27] *Women of Trachis*, 31-33: Loeb 21, 134.
[28] Aristotle, *History of Animals*, 9, 585b, 23-24: Loeb 439, 452.
[29] *Antigone*, 569: Loeb 21, 56; see also Euripides, *Orestes*, 551-553: Loeb 11, 472 and Aristophanes, *Lysistrata*, 1173: Loeb 179, 424.

Euripides was more explicit than Aeschylus and
Sophocles when he compared procreation to agriculture. For
example, when Orestes, his mother's murderer, was
addressing his maternal grandfather Tyndareus, he tried to
justify his crime in these terms:

> My father engendered me, and my mother,
> ploughland receiving the seed from another, gave me
> birth. Without a father there could never be a child. I
> reckoned that I should come to the defense of the
> author of my begetting rather than of her who gave
> me nourishment. [30]

In the fourth century, Plato was more cerebral in his
description of procreation, but his mind in this matter was
like that of a child. He explained that man and woman
secrete their respective animated substance, endowed with
respiration, and this becomes the reason why they naturally
seek intercourse. He returned to the traditional imagery
when he commented:

> The desire and love of the two sexes unite them.
> Then, culling as it were the fruit from the trees, they
> sow upon the womb, as upon ploughshed soil
> animalcules that are invisible for smallness and
> unshapen; and these, again, they mold into shape
> and nourish to a great size within the body; after
> which they bring them forth into the light, and thus
> complete the generation of the living creature. In this
> fashion, then, women and the whole female sex have
> come into existence. [31]

The traditional interpretation of another passage
from Plato is subject for debate. Hephaistos, the lame god
with consummate skill as master craftsman, [32] molded
Pandora like pottery. He used earth and water like potters
do and fashioned her with his own hands. In this Greek
myth, woman is molded into a beautiful figure, a work of art
totally dependent on a male god for her existence and

---

[30] *Orestes*, 551-556: Loeb 11, 472.
[31] *Timaeus*, 91C-D: Loeb 234, 250.
[32] Homer, *Iliad*, 1, 607-608: Loeb 170, 58.

appearance. [33] As an aside, we may recall the Biblical story of the first woman, Eve, who came from Adam's rib, his own self, at God's command. This biblical story suggests companionship more than subservient collaboration, as it appears in the Greek myth.

Woman fulfills the functions of procreation like earth moist with water. Like earth she is the receptacle of a seed therein deposited. Nourished in the soil mixed with water, the seed germinates and grows inside her womb until it is ready to come out into the world. It continues to grow, man or woman, to maturity. Mothers, therefore, imitate the earth in which farmers dig furrows and sow seeds from which the plants grow out into the light.

Plato further explained that women who are mothers possess nourishment like the land that produces wheat and barley as nourishment for men. Then he concluded: "It is not the earth which imitated women in conception and generation, but women the earth." [34]

If the earth comes first and is exemplary to the role of women in procreation, women are reduced to the resources of imitation not only because they are like earth the enablers of seeds to germinate and grow but because this is the only one contribution the men of ancient Athens were willing to acknowledge. Women's imitation of earth points toward a similarity or resemblance in the functions of generation. Greek men brought together the images of two events and found between them a similarity, one helping in understanding the other. In this case, plowing the soil, sowing the seed in a furrow, growing inside and coming outside independent from the soil yet still nourished by it were images which served the purpose of explaining the process of sexual intercourse, conception, pregnancy and childbirth. The association of earth and motherhood was first a popular perception before it was expressed by the playwrights and Plato whose talents were not in biology but, as literates, in the use of imagery for understanding and style. No doubt, a degradation of women does lie in the Ancient Greeks' perception of similarity of process whereby the women's procreative functions are subordinated to

---

[33] Hesiod, *Works and* Days, 70 ff.: Loeb 57, 6 and Aeschylus, *Fr.*, (Uncertain Play) 204: Loeb 146, 496.
[34] N. Loraux, *Born of the Earth*, 85.

those of men to the extent of making him the only parent, like the seed is the only parent of the fruit.

After the many references presently known, those quoted above and many more, for sure, that we do not know, it is impossible to assume that the agricultural metaphor was not a part of the popular belief, at least among men who were the only ones to think and speak publicly. It seemed that it was accepted not only for the procreation of children but also in reverse – the earth imitates woman – as a way to emphasize the Greek autochthony of the Athenians, inasmuch as they belonged to the land of Attica and always did, alive or dead, all others being strangers. Thus reversing the metaphor, the Ancient Athenians made the soil their first mother who gave them their authority and citizenship rights and responsibilities. In this view, their human mothers were kept in the background, behind the soil, and the metaphor had a patriotic purpose as it favored the supremacy of the state, without interfering with the metaphor – woman imitates the earth -- applied to motherhood for the production of its citizens.

The ancient Greeks understood that the female made a unique contribution toward procreation, although she was unable to generate life by herself. Every child appreciated the privilege of having grown in her womb. Sharing in such a sacred shrine of life made brothers and sisters so close that they would never marry each other and have intercourse, although they would if they shared only in the same father. To her descendant, the mother could also transmit inheritance and power, in the absence of a male descendant. Creusa made the case, as Euripides presented it in his play *Ion*. She was the only daughter king Erechtheus of Athens had not sacrificed [35] and he had no son, brother, or nephew. His daughter gave birth to Ion by god Apollo who, as a god, had no bloodline and no right to name his child. Furthermore, Creusa's husband, Xuthus, was an alien in Athens. [36] How could Ion inherit the throne of Athens his grandfather Erechtheus occupied? Only through his mother Creusa. [37] Therefore, the diminished role of the mother in procreation was not so limited, even in this primitive view,

[35] Euripides, *Ion*, 277-280: Loeb 10, 348-351.
[36] *Ibid.*, 589: Loeb 10, 396.
[37] *Ibid.*, 1585 ff.: Loeb 10, 506.

that she could not be recognized as a transmitter of life and of certain rights. It is not the imitation of earth, as pure mimesis, that makes a mother's role demeaning to her, because her role is not a copy of the original earth but only its resemblance. Her role is demeaning in relation to man when it is understood by men for whom the mimesis was perfectly suited as an expression of their arrogant sense of superiority.

These simplistic and somewhat incoherent views of procreation will remain intact until Aristotle wrote in the third quarter of the fourth century his remarkable treatises about the generation and the history of Animals. [38] He was explicit about the positive contribution of the mother, although he still used here and there words reminiscent of the traditional comparison. As the son of a physician and a conscientious biologist in his own right, he used observation to validate his theories. First, he observed that man and woman belong to the animal kingdom in which they are the highest class.

Then, Aristotle offered the premise that "the female, as female, is passive, and the male, as male, is active and the principle of the movement comes from him." [39] On the other hand, an observant researcher like Aristotle could not miss the resemblance that occurs between some children and their mother, rather than their father. A pure enabler could not produce such similar traits.

So he concluded that she bore a seed of her own, less potent than the husband's semen, because, being mixed with her menstrual blood, it has no vital heat. "She too emits a fertile seed", he wrote in his *History of Animals*. [40] When it is lacking entirely, sterility ensues with some mental consequences, such as distress and irritability.

The production of seeds in both boys and girls begins at about "the completion of twice seven years": which means about the age of fourteen. For the girls, it is also the age when the first menses is released, the breasts have risen and the voice changes to deeper. [41] The moralist who

---

[38] Especially Book 2, chapter 4 of *Generation of Animals*: Loeb 366, 176-201.

[39] Aristotle, *Generation of Animals*, 1, 21, 729b, 12-14: Loeb 366, 112.

[40] *History of Animals*, 10, 637a, 38: Loeb 439, 520.

[41] *Ibid.*, 9, 581a, 33-581b, 13: Loeb 439: 416-419.

wrote two books on Ethics was never far behind the biologist so he added at once that boys and girls are then

> In most need of guarding too about this time; for their impulse toward sexual activities is strongest when they begin, so that if they do not take care causing further movement.

He is now referring to bodily changes, especially those facilitating intercourse and also thinking of exciting memories fostering profligacy that

> is likely to continue into their later life. For the females who are sexually active while quite young become more intemperate, and so do the males if they are unguarded either in one direction or in both [male and female]. [42]

Normally, after the male seed has been deposited in the womb by copulation, it appears that the mother contributes jointly with the father in producing the offspring and determining its genetic characteristics in body and soul. Aristotle and everyone else could observe the transmission of heredity to children, as they resemble their parents either in physical appearance, mental ability or character traits.

Hippocrates was first at the turn of the fifth century to deal briefly with heredity. Both male and female, the physician explained, produce a sperm. The stronger in quantity determines the offspring's gender, either boy or girl [43] and the resemblance. [44] In other words, the quantity of each parent's seeded contribution determines the sex and the resemblance of the offspring,

Later in the fourth century, Aristotle may have been inspired by Hippocrates when he advocated a similar theory, based on his own observations. He repeated then the same simplistic explanation: a son resembles his father when the father is the stronger and a daughter resembles her mother

---

[42] *History of Animals*, 9, 581b, 13-22: Loeb 439, 418-421.
[43] *On the Generation Seed and the Nature of the Child*, 7: M.R. Lefkowitz and M.B. Fant, *Women's Life in Greece and Rome*, 87.
[44] *Ibid.*, 8: J. Longrigg, *Greek Medicine*, 5, 16, p. 57.

when the mother is the stronger of the two. [45] Aristotle concluded that a son usually takes after his father and a daughter after her mother, without investigating the interaction of nature and nurture. [46] He observed also that the resemblance sometimes jumps over a generation or more, in one case up to the seventh generation. [47] In the case of an Ethiopian father and a Greek mother, the daughter, who did not resemble her father, was the conduit of heredity from him to her son, his grandson. Aristotle made several other observations, for example that certain parental traits, like macrocephaly, and certain diseases, like gout and epilepsy, were transmitted by heredity, as the Hippocratic physicians (*iatroi*) confirmed. They never raised the following questions: how, why and from which parent. Every reference to genetics seemed to be irrelevant to the treatment of disease.

Aristotle set his views on procreation within the scope of his theory of the so-called "four causes" – formal, material, efficient and final -- and of the process of change from potentiality to actuality. He explained, as traditionally accepted, that the father is the sole agent of procreation because he provides the sperm, the principle of life, and the mother only the receptacle and the material for it to grow. Therefore, if the father's action generates life, he is the one who provides the soul, to mean the form that shapes and defines each individual offspring. Therefore, the father contributes the efficient and the formal causes when he initiates the process and shapes its outcome.

The mother contributes the material cause and the potential in her blood to change the ovum into a fetus and a child. In this context, she seems to provide only the material cause and, If it is so, only the body (*soma*) originates from her, while both body and soul (*psuchê*) originate from the

[45] *Generation of Animals*, 4, 3, 767b, 16-30: Loeb 366, 402; Id., *History of Animals*, 9, 585b, 32-586a, 3: Loeb 439, 454 and Hippocrates, *On Generation*, 8: J. Longrigg, *Greek Medicine*, 5, 16, p. 57.
[46] *Generation of Animals*, 4, 1, 766b, 9-12: Loeb 366, 392; 1, 17, 721b, 13 ff.: Loeb 366, 50; 1, 18, 725a, 21 ff.: Loeb 366, 80; 4, 3, 767a, 36-767b, 5: Loeb 366, 400 and 4, 3, 768b, 16-23: Loeb 366, 410.
[47] *Ibid.*, 1, 18, 722a, 9: Loeb 366, 52.

father. [48] On the other hand, the material exists in the female before the male initiates the movement of procreation and, in this material, there must be a kind of seed, similar to the man's seed, which explains the child's features transmitted from the mother. Hippocrates and Aristotle said so. If the latter, as a clever biologist, had pursued further, he would have attributed to the mother a minor contribution with the father to the efficient and formal causes, in addition to the material cause. He understood the question and it may have been nagging him when he seemed to prefer a new comparison taken from craftsmanship, either the carpenter and the wood or the potter and the clay, to explain the process of procreation. [49] Then, the material has a much greater significance in craftsmanship than the earth has in agriculture and, therefore, the mother also has a greater role in procreation than is given to her by the traditional comparison to seed and earth. The soil is not a component of the end product, but the wood and the clay are.

Aristotle professed that functions reveal the nature (formal cause) of every thing, including the nature of man and woman in soul and body. Virtue (*aretê*) consists in performing according to functions or nature. [50] He attributed to the woman the function understood as nurturing the fetus and body formed by the soul and given by the man, and yet he perceived also that this common view fell short of explaining all that is taking place and of giving the woman her fair share in the procreation of a child. The common men were complacent, the poets were pleased with their imagery and the biologists had no means to pursue their inquiries. The question was raised but remained pending in Antiquity.

The last of the four causes, the final cause -- the procreation of a child -- came first in the man's mind but was last to be achieved at delivery by the mother. [51]

[48] *Generation of Animals*, 2, 4, 738b, 20-28: Loeb 366, 184.
[49] *Ibid.*, 1, 22, 730b, 6: Loeb 366, 118.
[50] *On the Soul*, 2, 1, 412a, 13: Loeb 288, 66-69.
[51] *Generation of Animals*, 2, 4, 740b, 15-38: Loeb 366, 198-201.

Health

    The Hippocratic physicians seemed to believe that the diseases that afflicted a woman's body and hastened her death were all related to gynecology, therefore of a kind a man finds more difficult to understand. The ten most frequently quoted female diseases in the case studies of these physicians were the following, in alphabetical order: Asthma, Epilepsy, headaches, hysteria, malaria, menstrual suppression, mental depression, pneumonia, puerperal infection, and tuberculosis which was usually fatal.[52] The main symptoms were the wandering womb and the obstruction of menses. Aristotle mentioned also spasms of the uterus being distended: normal if they occur in childbirth but pernicious if they come from inflammation. [53] The female diseases explain why the women's average lifespan was estimated at 36 years of age, some nine years shorter than the lifespan of men.

    The Hippocratic physicians of the fourth century viewed menstruation as a normal function of the female body, a benefit to its well-being from menarche to menopause. On the other hand, any abnormality in this function could have baneful effects on the body in the form of illness and on the mind in the form of madness, erratic behavior, and even suicide. They estimated that, were it not for the ordeal of childbirth, women would outlive men, thanks to menstruation that releases bad humors.

    Aristotle estimated that the periodic episode of menstruation was troublesome for women, "for they suffer during these days. ... in all of them   the body feels burdened until it has been discharged." Then he added a redeeming factor:

> Now by nature conception takes place in women after this discharge is completed; and those who do not have the discharge remain childless as a rule. Nevertheless some conceive even without its occurrence. [54]

---

[52] Hippocrates, *Epidemics*, 2, 10: Loeb 147, 148.
[53] *History or Animals*, 10, 636a, 28-35: Loeb 439, 504.
[54] *Ibid.*, 9,582b, 8-15: Loeb 439, 426; see also Hippocrates, *Diseases of Women*, 1, 17: W.H.S. Jones, *Philosophy and Medicine in Ancient Greece*, 8, 57.

Pregnancy interrupts the menses which resume for some women after thirty days or forty days depending on whether the embryo is female or male, and for all women at normal intervals after the birth of the child. [55]

The Hippocratic medicine usually dealt with patients as men (*anthropoi*) except about women's reproductive functions which are so different that they required being isolated in discourses and spoken about only to physicians (gynecology: *gunê-logos*). [56] Warm or cold winds and water were often perceived as the causes of such female problems as infertility, miscarriage, irregular and painful menstruation, difficult childbirth, inability to nurse, fluxes from the bowels, and consumption (*phthisis*) especially of the lungs. [57]

The major female diseases addressed by the Hippocratic physicians concerned the womb that they considered "the cause of all ailments." [58] The first ailment was the "wandering womb". They argued that, when the womb becomes dry, it tends to move toward other organs that are moist, such as the heart, the liver or the bladder. Then it gets to become painful because of its dislocation and wandering up, down, or sideways. They believed that intercourse and pregnancy would stabilize the womb in its proper position. For this reason, unmarried women and widows, especially after menopause, were prone to this disease. Surgery was never recommended but there was a plethora of folk-remedies easily available: for example, garlic, ewe's milk after meals, purgation, fennel and absinthe to fumigate the womb, massage, and pessaries made of one or more ingredients such as boiled squill, opium poppies, bitter almond oil, rose oil, cantharid beetles, peony seeds, cuttlefish eggs, parsley seeds in wine, honey mixed with water, mercury plant, foul-smelling or sweet-smelling herbs depending on the position of the womb. [59]

A second major female ailment was dropsy in the womb, the accumulation of fluid called *oidêma*. They

---

[55] *History or Animals*, 9, 583a, 28-34: Loeb 439, 432.
[56] Euripides, *Hippolytus*, 295: Loeb 484, 150.
[57] Hippocrates, *Air, Waters, Places*, 3, 3 ff.: Loeb 147, 74.
[58] Id., *Places in Man*, 47: J. Longrigg, *Greek Medicine*, 16, 11, p. 195.
[59] See J. Longrigg, *Greek Medicine*, 196-197 & 200-201.

noticed that it occurred more frequently after a miscarriage. They believed that the use of warm bath, purgation, fumigation of the womb and pessary-douche could cure it in one day. If it did not, they recommended continuing the treatment until the fluid had dissipated or menstruation taken place. The final cure, however, was again intercourse and pregnancy. [60]

The physicians and biologists of classical Athens did not verbalize the private stages of procreation. Marital relations were natural, unplanned and unprotected. In spite of the wishes expressed by Hippolytus and Jason that children be born in a manner that would in no way involve women, like buying them for gold or iron in the temples of the gods, [61] the three stages of procreation never changed: copulation, pregnancy and childbirth. The men figured that this process was always good for the women's health and happiness.

Copulation

Aristophanes preferred the mixture of crude and lewd colors for his depictions of sexuality. Obviously his male patrons and fans enjoyed the frequent double-entendres and bawdy scenes on his stage. He was a part of the Greek culture we are attempting to understand. The feast (gamos) at the end of The Peace is typical. [62] The translation into English is tamer than the original Greek, but the meaning is clear about the men's libidinous urge and the availability of certain women, none of them Athenian.

Plato in his later years and his contemporary Aristotle understood that the mating of male and female humans was similar to the mating of animals. [63] They saw the male being active and the female passive, but not to the degree of one dominating the other into a submissive collaboration. The affection (philia) that was the bond between a man and a woman in coitus was considered natural to humans but not to animals. Therefore, every tendency in the human male to

---

[60] Hippocrates, Nature of Woman, 2: J. Longrigg, Greek Medicine, 13, 7, p. 159.

[61] Euripides, Hippolytus, 618-624: Loeb 484, 184 and Medea, 573-575: Loeb 12, 332.

[62] Peace, 885 ff.: Loeb 488, 538 ff.

[63] Plato, Laws, 8, 840D-E: Loeb 192, 164 and Aristotle, Generation of Animals, 2, 4, 737b, 27-28: Loeb 366, 178.

extend his active role into domination was blocked by his natural feeling of affection and gratitude for the pleasure given to him by his female partner, "and if a man allows the memory of a kindness (*charis*) to slip away, he can no longer be accounted noble." [64]

The physician Hippocrates at the turn of the fifth century BCE was more explicit in his account of the physiology of mating. About the female emotional experience, however, he was a male guessing and conjecturing. He compared the meeting of the male sperm and the womb to wine poured on a flame, the excitement flaring up but dying away quickly. [65]

Once, the oracle of Delphi advised a husband to use moderation, not for the purpose of preventing but of fostering conception. In his play *Medea*, Euripides told the story of king Aegeus of Athens who inquired about his inability to have children. The implication was that his wife remained barren because he attempted too often to create a new life with her. The oracle's advice was cryptic, as usual, yet leaving no doubt about its general meaning. The English translators have been hard pressed to give it a clear wording: They all say to loosen or untie the wineskin's neck or foot. David Kovacs is as reliable as any other: "Do not the wineskin's salient foot untie". [66] The message is clearly one of moderation in the frequency of intercourse. This understanding is indirectly confirmed by the chorus of Corinthian women whose following words just preceded Aegeus' revelation of the oracle's advice:

> Loves that come to us in excess bring no good name or goodness to man. If Aphrodite comes in moderation, no other goddess brings such happiness. Never, O goddess, may you smear with desire one of your ineluctable arrows and let it fly against my heart from your golden bow! May moderation attend me, fairest gift of the gods! [67]

---

[64] Sophocles, *Ajax*, 520-524: Loeb 20, 78.
[65] *On the Generation Seed and the Nature of the Child*, 4: M.R. Lefkowitz and M.B. Fant, *Women's Life in Greece and Rome*, 86.
[66] Euripides, *Medea*, 679-681: Loeb 12, 342-345.
[67] *Ibid.*, 629-636: Loeb 12, 338.

The Athenian men had no other standard of behavior but moderation which applied directly in the preceding passage to extramarital excesses of husbands who did not always refrain from them in their public conduct. Their ideal was moderation in all behavior, including their management of sexual behavior in their private lives as well. [68]

The fact is that the husband had another short-coming about sexual intercourse with his wife: he did not pay attention to the speed. Sometimes it could be he who was slow and cool when he was "preoccupied with troubles" but more often it was she who was slow reaching orgasm. He wrote:

> For if it is true that the wife too contributes to the seed and the generation, plainly there is need of equal speed on both sides. Therefore if he has completed quickly while she has hardly done so (for in most things women are slower), this is an impediment. [69]

The impediment is to the pleasure of copulation and its effect in pregnancy. In another instance, Aristotle referred again to the testimony of women – "If women are telling the truth" – women's dreams affect their success in sexual intercourse with their husbands, psychologically in predisposing their minds and stirring up their emotions, and biologically by producing in the uterus some moistering emission that facilitates the aspiration of the semen and, as a result, favors the desired pregnancy. [70]

Pregnancy

In the absence of effective contraceptive medicine, pregnancy was indeed frequent. Besides, the desire to perpetuate the family and strengthen the state was always present in the husbands' minds. Inasmuch as no record was kept about the fertility of Athenian women, it would be only guesswork to attempt giving more information on this

---

[68] Plato, *Laws*, 8, 839: Loeb 192, 158-163.
[69] *History of Animals*, 10, 636b, 16-19: Loeb 439, 508.
[70] *Ibid.*, 10, 636b, 24; 637b, 27 & 638a, 6: Loeb 439, 508; 524 & 528.

subject. The scent of garlic inserted in the womb was recommended by physicians to test a woman's fertility. [71]

Aristotle commented about women's pains of pregnancy, from the discomfort of carrying the weight to severe suffering from headaches, nausea and vomiting, "swellings about the legs and eruption of the flesh." Then he added:

> It is usual for pregnant women to develop all kinds of desires and to change them sharply – what some call jay-sickness [*kissan*]; in the case of female embryos, (*embruon*), the desires are sharper but they are less able to enjoy them when achieved. [72]

This translation of *kissan* as "jay-sickness" seems to refer to the image of jaywalking, the erratic and careless behavior of pedestrian crossing the streets. About the fertility of women, Aristotle suggested also that a healthy uterus, which meant strong, well positioned and moist, and menses at regular intervals were important to fertility. [73] She could then not only receive and suction well the man's seed but also provide her own and thus contribute actively to the production of an embryo. [74]

Here and in other places of his gynological observations, one wonders how extensive was Aristotle's validating survey. For sure, he used other observers frequently, keenly and judiciously, including some women, but, of course, never any of the instrumentation improving the quality required today in scientific research. For his time, however, his biological work was a remarkable achievement.

The ideal age for a woman to be childbearing was about twenty-one years old, when she has fully grown to maturity. [75] At any age, however, the lack of prenatal care prevalent nowadays made pregnancy and childbirth subject to more complications. No records have been kept about

---

[71] Hippocrates, *Diseases of Women*, 3, 214: J. Longrigg, *Greek Medicine*, 16, 15, p. 197.

[72] *History of Animals*, 9, 584a, 2-22: Loeb 439, 438-441. *Kissan* is also translated as ivy-sickness.

[73] *Ibid.*, 10, 633b, 30-636a, 9: Loeb 439, 478-501.

[74] *Ibid.*, 10, 637b, 31-34: Loeb 439, 526.

[75] *Ibid.*, 9, 582a, 26-29: Loeb 439, 424.

infant and mother's mortality. It must have been high. One indication, detected by Ian Morris in Attic cemeteries, may be the large number of children burials, amounting to fifty percent of all burials. [76] Also, the tradition of offering the garments of mothers who died in childbirth to Artemis in her temple at Brauron, east of Athens, suggests that such deaths were not rare. The intent was to placate the virgin goddess. [77]

The Hippocratic physicians, almost all male, were able to provide only limited assistance to women with gynecological problems. Not only did they have to compete with religious healers who appealed to Artemis or Asclepius in this matter but also with women themselves, either patients or advisors. The physicians had to seek the assistance of these women in order to diagnose and prescribe accurately. In the treatise *On the Diseases of Women*, Hippocrates was aware of his limitations:

> Doctors are in error in not ascertaining accurately the cause of a [woman's] disease and treating it as if they were dealing with men's diseases. I have already seen many women destroyed by such experiences. It is necessary straightway to inquire into the precise cause. For the treatment of women's diseases differs greatly from that of men's. [78]

According to Geoffrey Lloyd, [79] it is not clear whether male physicians ever performed gynecological examinations. They performed some gynecological surgery such as removing a dead fetus from the womb. Otherwise, they relied entirely on their female patients' and other female assistants to elicit answers, only to their questions related to gynecology. Unfortunately, women did not always know the answers to the physician's inquiry, especially about the cause of their ailments, and, furthermore, they were usually ashamed to speak about it to a man even when they knew

---

[76] *Burial and Ancient Society*, App. 1, 218-221.
[77] Euripides, *Iphigenia Among the Taurians*, 1465-1466: Loeb 10, 308.
[78] 1, 62: J. Longrigg, *Greek Medicine*, 16, 3, p. 192.
[79] *Science, Folklore and Ideology*, 62-86.

the answers.[80] For the rest of the human condition, the physicians did not perceive any significant difference between men and women.

M.R. Lefkowitz and M.B. Fant refer to a memorial tablet found in Athens and dated of the fourth century. The inscription reads as follows: "Phanostrate, a midwife and physician, lies here. She caused pain to none, and all lamented her death." [81] On the tablet, Phanostrate is seated and honored by one of her female patients, surrounded by infants of both sexes. She is the sole female physician that we know of the Classical period.

Childbirth

Women complained about the pains of childbirth. Addressing the chorus of Corinthian women, Medea made a statement written by a man, Euripides, about a subject that only mothers could fully understand:

> Men say that we live a life free from danger at home while they fight with the spear. How wrong they are! I would rather stand three times with a shield in battle than give birth once. [82]

In his *Iliad*, Homer compared the pain of Agamemnon when he was wounded in battle to the pain "when the sharp dart strikes a woman in labor." [83] Nicole Loraux commented that the pain (*ponos*) in childhirth is an attribute of women, so much so that men like warriors and peasants, who are afflicted by enduring pain, not sorrow, are said to suffer like women in the labor of childbirth. Men artisans and women housekeepers do not experience such pain and, for this reason, their efforts are not especially meritorious. But, through the pains of childbirth, women produce citizens for the state. So, also, Heracles harvested glory from his labors, equated to women's pains, because they contributed to the creation of civilization. [84]

---

[80] Hippocrates, *On the Diseases of Women*, 126, 12 ff.: G. Lloyd, *Science, Folklore and Ideology*, 75.

[81] *Women's Life in Greece and Rome*, 376, p. 266-267.

[82] *Medea*, 248-251: Loeb 12, 306.

[83] *Iliad*, 11, 269: Loeb 170, 512.

[84] N. Loraux, *The Experiences of Tiresias*, 23-58.

Women helped women in the pains of childbirth. Especially those who had borne a child and had passed bearing age were sought as midwives. They helped women in need during pregnancy and were assisting at the crucial moment of delivery which took place normally after ten lunar months. They were known, like Socrates' mother Phaenarete, for their skills in assisting, not only with drugs and incantations, but mainly with their quick-witted skills in dealing with contingencies, especially in cutting and tying the baby's navel-cord. If not done right, the baby may die and, on the other hand, if skillfully done, it may even revive a baby that appeared to be dead. A normal baby first cries, then brings his hands up to his mouth and voids excrements. [85]

Midwives were never equal to physicians who were men almost to the last. [86] They intervened in child delivery only in cases of complications, usually caused by disease. Then, their lack of diagnostic devices and personal experience placed their patients at a disadvantage. They seemed to expect their female patients to tell them the cause and kind of pain, which their gender prevented them to know. Women themselves were often at a loss to know the cause and explain the kind, as we pointed out about the difficulties of pregnancy.

Poisonous plants like mandrake and belladonna, the source of atropine, were used to alleviate pains, including those of menstrual cramps and childbirth. Recent analyses of residues found in small vases dating back to the Mycenaean period, between 1450 and 1200 BCE have revealed that opium and hashish were also used as painkillers.

The mother probably adopted a squatting or sitting position to deliver her baby who was at once bathed in warm water, anointed with oil and completely swaddled in woolen cloth.

According to Aristotle's observation, "women who have intercourse with their husbands before the birth have a quicker delivery." [87] The safety of the mother and the child was never addressed in these matters.

---

[85] Aristotle, *History of Animals*, 9, 587a, 9-32: Loeb 439, 464-467.
[86] Plato, *Theaetetus*, 149A & C and 151C: Loeb 123, 30-33 and 38.
[87] *History of Animals*, 9, 584a, 29-31: Loeb 439, 440.

The joy of delivering a child, especially a boy, remained hidden behind the pains until the following third day when the mother performed a rite of purification and, with her husband, watched the nurse carrying the baby around the family hearth and the father decided whether to raise it or expose it to die. If this ritual, called *amphidromia*, ended unfavorably and the baby did not pass inspection the ritual and the ensuing action were kept quiet and secret. If, on the contrary, as it was the more common case, the decision was favorable and the baby was to be brought up, the members of the larger family (*anchisteia*) gathered for a dinner feast. They gathered again at the house on the tenth day, this time with the members of the phratrie, for another ritualistic purification of the mother and the official and joyful introduction of the child as the offspring of Athenian parents.

Population Control

Although badly structured, a passage of Aristotle's *Politics* can help us at this point summarize the subjects previously discussed and bring us to the delicate subject of infanticide. In this passage, he referred to raising children including those who are deformed, exposing them to die, aborting them and not exceeding the number of children allowed by customs and the law. He wrote:

> As to the exposing and rearing the children born, let there be a law that no deformed child shall be reared, but on the ground of number of children, if the regular customs hinder any of those born being exposed there must be a limit fixed to the procreation of offspring, and if any people have a child as a result of intercourse in contravention of these regulations, abortion must be practiced on it before it has developed sensation and life; for the line between lawful and unlawful abortion will be marked by the fact of having sensation and being alive. [88]

[88] Aristotle, *Politics*, 7, 14, 1336b, 19-27: Loeb 264, 622-625.

After the post-war crisis at the beginning of the fourth century, It seems that a limit was prescribed in Athens on the number of children a couple was allowed to have, probably one son to continue the family line and one daughter for marriage. The reason for such a limit was the inability of the land of Attica to support any increase in population without endangering the quality of life the residents desired to have. Attica was small in size, about 1,560 sq. miles: about the same size as the State of Rhode Island at 1,545 sq. miles, the smallest of all U.S. states. It was also poor in resources after the disastrous Peloponnesian war -- the mines of silver and quarries of marble were exhausted and the agriculture forced into specialty farming. Worst of all, it was unstable politically and unable to rely on colonies for support. Every increase in population was exacting a toll on the residents who, therefore, considered population control an obligation which could be fulfilled in three ways: by preventing conception, by aborting the fetus, or by being rid of the babies in one way or another.

The Hippocratic physicians were concerned with the fertility of women, not the prevention of conception. So, they remained silent about it. Aristotle had the same concern when he advised pregnant women to "take care of their bodies, not avoiding exercise nor adopting a low diet" and also to worship the goddesses of childbirth and have a quiet mind, "for children before birth are evidently affected by the mother just as growing plants are by the earth." [89]

The male writers did not discuss contraception because of their lack of knowledge and interest. This matter was left to women. Besides, men who had their outlet for sexual satisfaction outside married life, tended to neglect their wives and, as a result, contributed by omission to birth control in the citizen class.

The Athenian population was also kept under control by frequent miscarriages and infant mortality. But these natural mishaps were not sufficient to keep the population at the same level. Other means needed to be taken. Aristotle recommended abortion and exposure, considering, however, that abortion was preferable to exposure. If an excess in number of children needed to be corrected, he

---

[89] *Politics*, 7, 14, 1336b, 13-19: Loeb 264, 622.

estimated furthermore that abortion should not be used after life and sensation had begun in the womb, which meant after the third month of pregnancy when the foetus is articulated. Aristotle estimated that most abortions took place during the first seven days after conception and miscarriages up to forty days. [90]

The means to know were totally left to the mother through the cessation of her menses and especially the feeling she had of the fetus growing and moving inside her womb. General customs neither encouraged nor prohibited contraception and abortion. In reality, they were not widely attempted because the techniques were ineffective. For example, from the Hippocratic physicians:

> If a woman does not want to become pregnant, make as thick a mixture of [vicia] beans and water as you can, make her drink it, and she will not become pregnant for a year. [91]

Hippocrates expected his disciples to "not give to a woman a pessary [vaginal shield] to produce abortion." [92] In one case, he suggested a method which may have succeeded in aborting the fetus but could have also caused serious harm to the mother: he advised a danseuse who wanted an abortion in order to salvage her career, "to jump up and down, touching her buttocks with her heels at each leap". Thank god, the method succeeded after "no more than seven times"! [93] If she needed to terminate her pregnancy by miscarriage without the assistance of any physician, the pregnant woman usually resorted to bleeding herself. [94]

Abortion was never induced because childbirth was expected to be difficult -- the caesarian section being unknown to Greek physicians before the Roman times -- or

---

[90] *History of Animals*, 9, 583b, 10-24: Loeb 439, 434-437.
[91] *Nature of Woman*, 98: M.R. Lefkowitz and M.B. Fant, *Women's Life in Greece and Rome*, 94, p. 88.
[92] Id., *Oath*: Loeb 147, xiii.
[93] Id., *On the Generation Seed and the Nature of the Child*, 13: M.R. Lefkowitz and M.B. Fant, *Women's Life in Greece and Rome*, 93, p. 88.
[94] Id., *Aphorisms*, 5, 31: Loeb 150, 166.

because the baby was expected to be deformed or retarded -- the techniques of discovery being totally unknown.

In view of this, was infanticide used to get rid of an unwanted child, if contraception and abortion were not widely used to prevent or interrupt a pregnancy? This question has been raised and debated, but has not yet been answered satisfactorily. Some comments can be made, however, with a fair measure of certainty. Ancient Athens never had the kind of mass sacrifices like those that probably took place in Ancient Carthage (Modern Tunis). Also, the private procedure did not commonly involve a violent assault that resulted in murder. The Greeks loved all their children and attempted to be compassionate even when they felt the need to resort to such an extreme measure.

The exposure of an infant seemed to have been the method of choice. The fact is that it was a cruel choice, yet more humane than murder, from the viewpoint of the parents. They inflicted no direct violence upon their baby. On the contrary, they seemed to hope it would survive when they left a little food with it and a silent prayer that it will be kept alive by the gods' will and be found and adopted by a compassionate passer-by. For sure, the Greeks never resorted to exposure lightly and without some qualms. The father made the decision, not always with the mother's concurrence, as Socrates once pointed out. [95] In the passage at hand, Aristotle recommended a law to forbid raising a deformed child because there were enough well-formed children being born. Nevertheless, for the purpose of controlling the birth rate, he also recommended to use abortion rather than exposure. Did he infer then that, if a couple had decided before the birth of their child to let it live, a deformity would not justify letting it die by exposure after birth, in the absence of a law which he wished would allow it? The answer is not clear.

Inasmuch as the father had full power over his children, he was free to raise his babies or abandon them, like Oedipus and Ion, perhaps to starve to death or be killed by beasts, if it was the gods' will. In spite of the scarce information, we may reasonably believe that infanticide was practiced in Athens by the fathers and done to baby girls

---

[95] Plato, *Theaetetus*, 151C: Loeb 123, 38.

more often than to baby boys, because of some deformity or defect. The prospect of giving a girl in marriage was ever present in the father's mind: her physical attributes were important for her future roles as wife and mother. The same rigidity did not exist about the baby boys. The Greeks conceived their god Hephaistos as being born lame and yet let to live. Mark Golden estimated that some twenty percent of the baby girls in Ancient Athens were victims of some form of infanticide. [96] At any rate, the high incidence of infant mortality probably restrained any wider practice of infanticide in any form.

In the dialogue *Theaetetus*, Plato related a conversation between Socrates, Theodorus and Theaetetus. Socrates had led his disciples to the idea that "knowledge is only perception". This idea, he continued, is like a child that came into the world with his help as a midwife. Then he developed a simile using a real situation that had to be well known and widely accepted, if he used it to clarify the point he intended to make. This passage is worth reading with care:

> Well, we have at last managed to bring this forth [idea compared to a child], whatever it turns out to be; and now that it is born, we must in very truth perform the rite of running round with it in a circle [referring to *amphidromia*] – the circle of our argument – and see whether it may not turn out to be after all not worth rearing, but only a wind-egg, an imposture. But, perhaps, you think that any offspring of yours ought to be cared for and not put away; or will you bear to see it examined and not get angry if it is taken away from you, though it is your first-born? [97]

Socrates implied that, at the birth of a child or shortly thereafter, a father had the right to decide whether the child was going to be reared or put away. This passage was an indirect recognition of infanticide as a practice, not a crime if the father ordered it for a justifiable reason such as some physical or mental defect.

---

[96] *The Exposure of Girls in Athens*, in Phoenix 35 (1981) 316-331.
[97] Plato, *Theaetetus*, 160E-161A: Loeb 123, 72-75.

In his dialogue *Republic*, Plato recognized explicitly
that "the purity of the guardians' breed required that

The offspring of the inferior, and any of those of the
other sort who are born defective, they will properly
dispose of in secret, so that no one will know what
has become of them. [98]

The cases of Oedipus and Ion were abnormal, first
because they were boys, also because god Apollo was
guiding the action. Oedipus' parents, Laius and Jocasta,
exposed him in order to prevent him from committing
crimes against nature, namely to kill his father and marry
his mother. Such crimes were abhorrent to the Greeks.
Therefore, for such a good reason and by the father's
decision, infanticide was not a crime. The exposure of Ion
was executed by a woman, his mother Creusa, but at the
command of his divine father, Apollo, who wanted to hide
the rape he committed.

Medea killed her two sons, not by exposure, but with
the sword, against the will of their father, Jason. But she was
not Greek, and in the Greek mentality, not civilized. When
she placed the blame on Jason's shoulders, she was trying
to exculpate herself like a mad woman who makes no
sense: "The gods know", she declared, "who struck the first
blow", implying it was her husband, Jason. [99] After her
crime, Medea saved her own life by the intervention of the
sun-god Helios, her grandfather, who provided her with a
dragon-driven chariot. Her liberation was clearly farfetched
and not taken realistically by the Greek audience.

Euripides knew how revolting infanticide was in the
minds of his Greek audience. In the same play, he used his
chorus of Corinthian women to bring up the memory of Ino,
Phrixus' stepmother, in order to suggest a remedy:

One woman, only one, of all that have been, have I
heard of who put her hand to her own children: Ino
driven mad by the gods when Hera sent her forth
from the house to wander in madness. The unhappy
woman fell into the sea, impiously murdering her

[98] Plato, *Republic*, 5, 460C: Loeb 237, 462.
[99] Euripides, *Medea*, 1372: Loeb 12, 408.

sons. Stepping over the sea's edge, she perished with her children. [100]

The implication is clear: like the Greek Ino, Medea should have committed suicide, like Jason told her: "No Greek woman would have dared to do this", [101] thus explaining, if not justifying, her survival by returning to her barbarian upbringing.

Euripides ignored Althaea's myth that weakened Jason's argument about Greek women killing their progeny but confirmed the suicide anyway. When Meleager was born of Althaea and her husband Oeneus, king of Calydon, the Fates declared that he would die when the brand on the hearth was consumed. In order to prevent the death of her son, Althaea took the brand and hid it in a chest. Later, when Meleager was grown up, he had an argument with two of his maternal uncles and killed them. Then Althaea, a Greek woman, retrieved the brand and threw it into the fire, thus causing her son to die suddenly. Her feeling of guilt led her, like the Greek Ino, to commit suicide. In any event, this son was grown-up when he was killed by his mother, like Pentheus was when he was killed unintentionally by his mother Agave in a frenzy on Mount Cithaeron. For it, she went into exile, which was almost as bad as committing suicide.

No doubt, Euripides knew that the citizen class sometimes used infanticide for the purpose of upgrading their family in the Athenian society of his time. Nevertheless, even if fathers had absolute rights and power over their children, such killings were always done quietly, without public recognition of approval or disapproval and without any records.

Were the gods partners in the killing of these children? How could Medea escape unpunished? The Chorus of Corinthian women probed the depth of the mysterious ways of the gods and sang the final verses, perhaps added to Euripides' play at a later date:

Zeus on Olympus has many things in his treasure house, and many are the things the gods accomplish

---

[100] *Medea*, 1282-1289: Loeb 12, 398.
[101] *Ibid.*, 1339: Loeb 12, 404.

against our expectation. What men look for is not brought to pass, but a god finds a way to achieve the unexpected. Such is the outcome of this story. [102]

Another practice, probably dominant only about young girls was to sell them into slavery. It must have been done in the sixth century if Solon saw fit to forbid it by law unless they were found deflowered before getting married. [103] It probably continued quietly and unrecorded, without being widespread, during the Classical period of the fifth and fourth centuries. Substitution was similar to selling into slavery. Both were cruel to the girls but substitution was more humane. The kinsman Mnesilochus listed it among the evil deeds Athenian women committed and covered up. He claimed:

> How your slave girl had a baby boy and you passed it off as your own, and gave your own baby girl to the slave. [104]

This substitution was deceitful and insolent but more humane because the illegitimate boy and the legitimate girl were raised together in the same household, yet the girl was becoming a slave for life and the boy a citizen for life and an heir. This kind of rejection was unfair to the girl. It was a symptom of the subverted desire of women to have a son. This instance brought up in a comedy was probably representing an occurrence the audience could recognize, but surely exaggerating it if anyone thought it was a common practice.

The assortment of control factors from the use of contraceptives to infanticide resulted in making the average Athenian family quite small, barely large enough to maintain the population at its same level. Aristotle believed that too large a state was not good for its citizens. Therefore, he advocated deliberate population control if nature failed to do it:

---

[102] *Medea*, 1415-1419: Loeb 12, 412.
[103] Plutarch, *Parallel Lives, Solon*, 23, 2: Loeb 46, 466.
[104] Aristophanes, *Women at the Thesmophoria*, 564-565: Loeb 179, 522.

A great state is not the same as a state with a large population. But certainly experience also shows that it is difficult and perhaps impossible for a state with too large a population to have good legal government. At all events we see that none of the states reputed to be well governed is without some restriction in regards to numbers. The evidence of theory proves the same point. Law is a form of order, and good law must necessarily mean good order; but an excessively large number cannot participate in order. [105]

The best estimates are from two to four children per family, depending on the times. In percentages, it appears that twenty percent of all couples were infertile. Assuming that boys and girls were evenly distributed in the fertile families, only forty percent of the children, which amounted to the number of boys in sixty percent of the families, were responsible for the survival of the patriline. In order to avoid extinction, especially of the forty percent of families without a son, adoption, even a suppositious one on rare occasions, was the last resort. [106] Inasmuch as the adopted sons had to come from Athenian families, most of them probably came from the twenty percent of families with two sons or more. The ideal was also to keep the adoptions within the larger family (anchisteia). But the ideal was sometimes out of reach. So, as the orator Isaeus stated, a man should be allowed to adopt whomever he wished. More than ninety percent of all adoptions were of boys from either side of the parents' families. [107] Nevertheless, Euripides seemed to question the advantage of adoption in all cases, unless it was absolutely necessary, and to discourage it entirely when the husband was childless. [108]

Infant mortality was a reality bearing on the frequency of adoptions. If as many as fifty percent of all children did not reach maturity, the need for distributing

---

[105] Politics, 7, 4, 1326a, 25-32: Loeb 264, 554.
[106] Aristophanes, Women at the Thesmophoria, 502 ff.: Loeb 179, 516.
[107] On the Estate of Menecles, 13: Loeb 202, 46-49.
[108] Fr., Erechtheus, 359 & Melanippe Captive, 491: Loeb 504, 374 & 592.

the male descendants within the larger family was quite important and consequently quite frequent.

In addition to giving birth, the women of Ancient Athens had two other major responsibilities: the management of the household and the rearing of children.

*

*

*

CHAPTER FIVE

HOUSEWIVES

The House

The men and women of Attica belonged to a partnership on three levels: the lowest and smallest was the house (*oikos* or *oikia*) where the family resided, the middle was the village (*kômê*) filled with a few or many houses, depending on the size, and the highest and largest was the city-state (*polis*).[1] Now, following the principle that "the male is by nature superior and the female inferior, the male ruler and the female subject",[2] women were submitted to men at all three levels, yet differently. At the upper two levels of the village and the city-state, she had no participation in the life of the community except through her husband (*anêr*) or guardian (*kurios*), At the lowest level, namely the household, although she was still under the supervision and direction of her husband, she had the distinct responsibility of managing it, members and things.

The house was the place where the wife and her children spent most of their time. Euripides' statement was categorical about it:

A wife who stays at home is certain to be a good one, and one who spends time out of doors is certain to be worthless.[3]

The first house the newlyweds occupied was usually very simple, with no more than four rooms. Demosthenes attempted to explain, if not justify, the humble conditions of the common houses:

---

[1] Aristotle, *Politics*, 1, 1252b, 9-1253a, 6: Loeb 264, 6-9.
[2] *Ibid.*, 1, 1254b, 13-15: Loeb 264, 20.
[3] *Fr.*, *Meleager*, 521: Loeb 504, 622.

Out of the wealth of the state they [the leaders] set up for our delight so many fair buildings and things of beauty, temples and offerings to the gods, that we who come after must despair of outsurpassing them; yet in private they were so modest, so careful to obey the spirit of the Constitution, that the houses of their famous men, of Aristides or of Miltiades, as any of you can see that knows them, are not a whit more splendid than those of their neighours.[4]

A fifth-century house excavated on the north slope of the Acropolis shows two separate rooms, one (*andrôn*) with the hearth for the men and male guests on the north side and the other (*gunaikônitis*) for the women on the south side, with separate entrances. Two-storied houses had the women's quarters, especially for sleeping, on the upper level. [5]

In the city of Athens, the houses were usually modest in size and decorations. They were also in a crowded neighborhood with little space between houses and narrow streets for circulation. [6] The better houses were built to open onto a courtyard. For protection, the entrance was inconspicuous and the windows were placed high. Even the most luxurious houses were discreet. The focus was always the interior rather than the exterior appearance. The culture of democracy invaded even this aspect of daily living.

The partitioning of the interior is not clear because both archaeology and literature remain almost completely silent about it. Some houses were two-storied, but most of them were of only one story. "Unburnt brick on a low stone socle may be taken to be the usual technique" of construction. [7] Wooden pillars reinforced the walls and helped support the roof structure and the terra cotta tiles. The houses usually faced southward, so that the cold northerly wind would be at their back. Attica, however, was blessed with a Mediterranean climate, generally sunny and mild. The floor was usually the earth itself, leveled and hard-packed. The rooms were hardly distinguishable,

[4] Demoshenes, *Olynthiacs*, 3, 25-26: Loeb 238, 56.
[5] Lysias, *On the Murder of Erastosthenes*, 9: Loeb 244, 8.
[6] Thucydides, Peloponnesian War, 2, 3, 3: Loeb 108, 262.
[7] R.E. Wycherley, *How the Greeks Built Cities*, 187.

although men and women had separate quarters, as indicated above. [8]

The basic family needs were the same then as they are today, so the available space had to provide for a kitchen, a dining area, a bedroom, a work-room, a store-room, a guest room and a bathroom. Depending on the size of the house, one room served more than one function. The only toilet facility of most houses consisted of chamber pots and a nearby cesspool where a female slave emptied them. For the majority of people, the living arrangements were harsh and uninviting. It appeats that the house of the wealthy had another chamber of dressed stone where the gold was laid out and the seal for the door remained in the care of the wife. [9] Wherever they lived, however, all the residents of Attica enjoyed equally the splendor of their public buildings, such as temples, theatres and agoras.

Financial Support

Most Athenian women of all ages stayed home and never worked in public places. Women who acquired a tan by working outdoor, either in the fields or at the market, were considered inferior, even if free. The Athenian women worked only indoor and never for a salary or a fee. Only extreme poverty could force them to work for financial gain.

In the Athenian culture, the guardian was the financial provider. He was the husband or, if he was absent or incapacitated, a substitute, always a male and usually a relative or close friend of the family. A son would be first to take charge, if he was of adult age, or the closest adult relative in the larger family (*anchisteia*). According to the bleak ideas of Hesiod and his followers, especially Simonedes of Amorgos, most women were considered drones who live off the busy bees. They were content to stay in the hive and do their mischief.

And as in thatched hives bees feed the drones whose nature is to do mischief -- by day and throughout the day until the sun goes down the bees are busy and lay the white combs, while the drones stay at home in

[8] Lysias, *On the Murder of Eratosthenes*, 1, 9-10: Loeb 244, 8 and
    Xenophon, *Oeconomicus*, 9, 5: Loeb 168, 440.
[9] Euripides, *Fr., Phaethon*, 781, 222-223: Loeb 506, 352.

the covered skeps and reap the toil of others into their own bellies -- even so Zeus who thunders on high made women to be an evil to mortal men, with a nature to do evil. [10]

When men do not work, they are like drones "eating without working" and living off the products of the working men who are the bees, explained Hesiod. [11] As for women, whether they work or not, they always receive support from their guardians. More than once already, we have recognized the misogynist attitude of Hesiod.

On several occasions, Aristophanes made the point that the husband provided for his family. For example, in *Wasps*, the old Lovecleon was eager to attend the court as juror in order to collect his pittance of three obols a day and then give them generously to his happy family. For this, his daughter and wife gave him a warm welcome. His wife,

the little woman fusses over me and brings me a puff pastry, and then sits by and coaxes me, "Eat this, eat this up!" I love all that, and I don't have to look to you and your steward to see when he'll get around to serving my lunch with his usual curses and grumbles. [12]

The financial arrangements, however, were not always so congenial. In *Clouds*, also of Aristophanes, the countrified Strepsiades was being bled by his high-society wife and his extravagant son. The bill collectors were after him for their payments. He sought an idiotic solution: to turn to Argument, personified in the play, instead of using earnings. Either way, he made the point that he felt responsible for the debts incurred by the members of his family. [13]

In another play, *Wealth* of 388 BCE, Aristophanes repeated the same point. The subject was wealth of which,

---

[10] *Theogony*, 595-601: Loeb 57, 122.

[11] *Works and Days*, 302-306: Loeb 57, 24; see Simonides, *On Women*: H. Lloyd-Jones, *Females of the Species*, 83-93, trans, p. 52.

[12] *Wasps*, 610-613: Loeb 488, 298; see also *Peace*, 119-123: Loeb 488, 442.

[13] *Clouds*, 739: Loeb 488, 108.

declared the leading character Chremylus, "no one ever gets their fill of you." [14] After god Wealth, also known as Plutus, was cured of his blindness and happy to share his wealth, not only Chremylus but also his wife wanted their portion. [15]

Another of Aristophanes' characters, Mnesilochus, was one of the most colorful tricksters. He proved himself not only by displaying a female appearance and befooling for a while the women at the *Thesmophoria* but also, more obviously, by snatching the alleged baby from a woman's arms and drinking the wine to the last drop, and by playing several roles to fit the rescue attempts made by Euripides. So Mnesilochus was not the kind of characters whose deeds and words could be trusted without giving them a second thought. On the other hand, his creator Aristophanes used him often to express serious ideas about and provide penetrating insights into the lives of his contemporary Athenians. When Mnesilochus first entered the assembly of women he fretted upon his deceptive intrusion. Then he inserted the following comments that gave a resonance of reality. The Greek text has a subtlety that seems to be best rendered by the translation of Jeffrey Henderson:

> And may my daughter Pussy meet a man who's rich but also childishly stupid, and may little Dick have brains and sense! [16]

In addition to the double entendres, the following points emerge from this quotation. First, a father thinks highly of his daughter but not more highly than he thinks of money. He wished that her beauty and charm can be used to lure the right husband who should be wealthy but not too bright. Otherwise, he will supervise, control and dominate her to the point of letting her have no free access to his wealth. No doubt, fathers thought their daughters were bright enough to take advantage of dull husbands but they did not realize, so it seems, that husbands were sons also and they could be their own. Did they appreciate their daughters more than they did their sons? Certainly not. This is where comedy branches off from reality. On stage,

---

[14] *Wealth*, 187: Loeb 180, 450.

[15] *Ibid.*, 828 ff.: Loeb 180, 540; see also Hesiod, *Works and Days*, 373-374: Loeb 57, 30.

[16] *Women at the Thesmophoria*, 289-291: Loeb 179, 498.

however, it made the contrast amusing for the male audience.

Management

The wife had the total care and responsibility of the home under the supervision of her husband. Early in the sixth century, Solon advised the new husband to start his married life in a spirit of cooperation, by fostering discussions with his wife. Keeping in mind the age difference between the wedded partners and the mutual acceptance of male superiority, such discussions, no doubt, tended to be dominated by the husband. Yet, Solon wanted the wife to be heard in order to avoid festering misunderstandings between the two, especially in financial matters. The law read as follows:

> The husband of an heiress shall approach her thrice a month without fail. For even though they have no children, still, this is a mark of esteem and affection which a man should pay to a chaste wife; it removes many of the annoyances which develop in all such cases and prevents their being altogether estranged by their differences. [17]

Euripides pointed out later that "weak masters have outspoken wives. [18] He believed it was wrong for the husbands to be weak and the wives to be unrestrained in their advice. When the right balance was respected, the wives' "proper sphere of knowledge" was brought out and utilized, so they became the greatest help to their husbands, especially when they were confronted with troubles outside the home, otherwise they were his greatest harm. [19]

The wives' primary role was to produce heirs and then to nurse and educate them as infants. This role implied several responsibilities related to the management of the household (oikonomia). The same Euripides stated:

---

[17] Plutarch, *Parallel Lives, Solon*, 20, 3: Loeb 46, 458.
[18] Euripides, *Fr., Aegeus*, 3: Loeb 504, 6.
[19] Id., *Fr., Meleager*, 522 & *Alcmeon*, 78: Loeb 504, 622 & 94,
   Phrixus, 822, 34-36 & 823: Loeb 506, 446 & 452 and
   Unidentified Play, 1055-1060: Loeb 506, 594-597.

Women manage the household and preserve its valuable property. ... No house is clean and prosperous without a wife. ... There is nothing worse than a bad woman, and nothing better than a good one. [20]

In his later years, Xenophon (445-355 BCE) told that his friend Socrates, who died in 399, once met Ischomachos in the portico (*stoa*) of Zeus the Deliverer (*Eleutherius*). There he sat with him and asked whether his wife needed to be educated when he married her. Ischomachos replied:

What knowledge could she have had, Socrates, when I took her for my wife? She was not yet fifteen years old when she came to me, and up to that time she had lived in leading-strings, seeing, hearing and saying as little as possible. If when she came she knew no more than how, when given wool, to turn out a cloak, and had seen only how the spinning is given out to the maids, is not that as much as could be expected? [21]

The wife needed to be educated further because

as God made them partners in their children, so the law appoints them partners in the home. ... To the woman it is more honorouble to stay indoors than to abide in the fields, but to the man it is umseemly rather to stay indoors than to attend to the work outside. [22]

Husband and wife must share equally in memory, diligence and self-control, but differently. Ischomachos explained while thinking, no doubt, that his wife was in her teens and he was twice her age:

Just because both have not the same aptitudes, they have the more need of each other, and each member

---

[20] Euripides, *Fr.*, 13: Fantham, E. et al., *Women in the Classical World*, 95-96.
[21] Xenophon, *Oeconomicus*, 7, 5-6: Loeb 168, 414.
[22] *Ibid.*, 7, 30: Loeb 168, 422.

of the pair is the more useful to the other, the one being competent where the other is deficient. [23]

Euripides had already pointed at the "artful ways" women take to accomplish a task while their husbands "achieve their aim better with the spear." [24] This is clear enough, but we must continue listening to Ischomachos for a moment: he encouraged his wife to "stand before the loom and be ready to instruct those who know less than you, and to learn from those who know more." [25] If the husband could afford servants, his wife ruled over them. Otherwise, she did all the work herself until a daughter would be old enough to help and learn. She prepared the meals, kept the house clean and weaved for all the members of the household. Euripides said it well, in one of his better moments:

> Vainly does censure from men twang an idle bowshot at women and denounce them. In fact they are better than men, as I shall demonstrate ... contracts without witnesses ... and not reneging ... They manage households, and save what is brought by sea within the home, and no house deprived of a woman can be tidy and prosperous. [26]

What kind of contracts could an Athenian woman make? She was not allowed to make any that amounted to more than the equivalent of a few days' supply for the household. She could also make agreements concerning things which may have had some monetary value but involved no monetary compensation, for example her contribution to a shrine or her testimony in a court case involving money but without any return to her. In this latter situation, she could be completely trusted, her word alone being enough to guarantee her telling the truth. In the most serious and official cases, her testimony was covered by an

---

[23] Xenophon, *Oeconomicus* 7, 28: Loeb 168, 422.
[24] *Fr., Danae,* 321: Loeb 504, 330.
[25] Xenophon, *Oeconomicus,* 10, 10: Loeb 168, 450.
[26] *Melanippe Captive,* 494: Loeb 504, 594.

oath to goddesses such as Demeter, Persephone or Aphrodite. [27]

Demosthenes once stated that any male citizen may dispose of his property unless, among other things, he is "under the influence of a woman", especially a bad one. [28] Such a statement reveals men's disparaging view not only about women's rights but also about women's ability to transact business. Some women thought differently, as Aristophanes implied when he let Lysistrata claim that women better than men could handle the public treasury of Athens. So they occupied the Acropolis where the treasury was stored. [29] He stated elsewhere that women were moneymakers, [30] to mean that they were thrifty in managing the small provisions given to them or gained by them for the household. His male audience must have agreed with him since he was always eager to please them.

Aristotle offered later a summary of the managerial responsibilities of both, husband and wife:

> The household functions of a man and of a woman are different – his business is to get and hers to keep. [31]

This distribution of duties and responsibilities was not equal, as if the contribution of one was equal to that of the other, because the purpose of wives in life was always to supply their husbands' all everyday needs. Husbands were only guardians and providers.

The wife knew little of the real world when she married as a teenager. She needed to learn how to manage her new home and grow up, which probably came quickly about her domestic chores but more slowly about her relationship with her new husband, his family and friends. Her reputation was important to her but more so to her husband.

---

[27] Aristophanes, *Assemblywomen*, 156-159 & 189: Loeb 180, 264 & 268.
[28] *Against Stephanus II*, 46, 14: Loeb 155, 254; also Isaeus, *On the Estate of Menecles*, 19 & *On the Estate of Philoctemon* 48: Loeb 202, 50 & 230.
[29] *Lysistrata*, 176: Loeb 179, 290.
[30] *Assemblywomen*, 442: Loeb 180, 298.
[31] *Politics*, 3, 4, 1227b, 24-25: Loeb 264, 194.

The point was made above that a wife's major virtue was fidelity to her husband. As Euripides commented: "It is better to have in the house a wife of low rank who is chaste than one who is high borne." [32] For this reason, the Greek husband was very protective of his wife when she was at home. In fact, his trust in her expired on the threshold of jealousy. Aristophanes caricatured him when he came home from the theatre giving "suspicious looks and searching the house for a hidden lover." [33]

For the same reason, before he left for Troy, king Agamemnon gave strict orders to a minstrel to guard his wife and watch over her in his absence. [34] Why a minstrel and not a regular guard? Because the danger of betrayal, if it were to occur, would be more easily observed by a minstrel acquainted with the social life inside the palace.

The privacy of the home was respected. For example, break-ins, even by public officials for public reasons, were not acceptable. [35] Debt collectors were blamed for bursting into a house when the husband was away. Demosthenes who reported one incident added that a neighbor who came to investigate satisfied himself by observing from the threshold. [36] The *oikos* meant the house and the persons living in it. Both had a legal right to privacy.

Returning home from the fields, Electra's peasant husband found his wife conversing at the door with two male strangers. He was puzzled at first but, after realizing their friendly intent, he invited them to spend the night. They accepted and entered the house. [37]

A husband was fortunate when he married a young girl coming from a family in which the mother had imparted to her daughters all the domestic skills she had. Still the husband felt his bride needed some additional education in family management, like sharing with him as a partner. The husband had no interest or desire to do anything in the home, except comment either favorably or unfavorably

---

[32] *Electra*, 1098-1099: Loeb 9, 270.

[33] *Women at the Thesmophoria*, 395-397: Loeb 179, 506.

[34] Homer, *Odyssey*, 3, 268: Loeb 104, 98.

[35] Demosthenes, *Against Timocrates*, 24, 197: Loeb 299, 498; also Lysias, *Against Eratosthenes*, 30-31: Loeb 244, 240.

[36] *Against Evergus*, 47, 52-61: Loeb 155 and *Mnesibulus*, 47, 57 & 60: Loeb 155, 310 & 313.

[37] Euripides, *Electra*, 341 ff.: Loeb 9, 188-191.

about the outcome. He could praise his wife for a special dish or a new tunic (*chitôn*), or complain about her use of cosmetics or excessive babbling. Sometimes, like Ischomachos of Xenophon's treatise, he could advise her on how to arrange things the way he thought was most convenient. [38] In other words, he expected of her a fair degree of self-discipline, as Euripides said: "Ordinary unions, and ordinary wives with self-discipline, are best for mortals to find" [39]

This partnership, which did not consist of sharing in the same activities, rarely involved a close friendship. In his *Nicomachean Ethics*, Aristotle wrote a long dissertation about friendship among men. It covers two entire books: eight and nine. [40] But he remained silent about any kind of friendship that may exist between husband and wife. The subject begged for some comments but he ignored it, leaving us to discover it only through anecdotes.

On the wedding day, love was present only in a beautiful dream. Real love may grow later in married life, if the couple was compatible. First to remember, however, is that the love between husband and wife was always between a superior and an inferior, never between two equals. Nevertheless, it was not the same as the love between a father and his child or a master and his slave. The child and the slave were totally dependent like any other object of ownership: the slave forever but the child only for the period of time before its maturity or wedding. The wife was an inferior, yet a real partner, allowed to discuss and expected to cooperate wilfully. In cases of conflict of opinions, her role was to obey. Such was household justice. [41]

Plato reported in his Dialogue *Phaedo* the incident that became a classic example of the relationship between husband and wife. It showed not only consideration and some degree of love with discretion for a wife but also the place of friends in a man's interests and affections. Socrates was in jail, on the day he was due to die at the age of seventy. His wife, Xantippe, came to pay him a final visit with their son in her arms. She was first admitted by a guard

---

[38] *Oeconomicus*, 9, 1: Loeb 168, 438.
[39] *Fr., Melanippe Wise*, 503: Loeb 504, 606.
[40] Aristotle, *Nicomachean Ethics*, 1155a-1172a: Loeb 73, 450-575.
[41] *Ibid.*, Chapters 7 & 8: Loeb 73, 374-515.

who guided her to the room of his incarceration. There, she sat and conversed with him. Then, realizing that his friends were waiting, she remarked that it was the last time they could converse with each other. Her remark was a kind anticipation of his wish. So, immediately,

> Socrates glanced at Crito and said: "Crito, let somebody take her home." And some of Crito's people took her away, wailing and beating her breast. [42]

When Xantippe left the room, she was gone also from Socrates' mind. A wife and some friends were two separate necessities: a wife for procreation and management of the household, some friends for intellectual stimulation and camaraderie.

Greek men intended to treat their wives with justice, if not with love. Household justice was real justice, but different and, to a certain extent, independent from public justice. Aristotle differentiated the husband's justice administered within his household from the magistrate's justice administered in the courts. He explained that the kind of justice practiced by a magistrate was a postulate of equality in the treatment of others. In the practice of household justice, the husband did not use equality as the norm because the relationship between husband and wife did not include equality, like

> persons who share equally in ruling and being ruled. Hence Justice exists in a fuller degree between husband and wife than between father and children, or master and slaves; in fact, justice between husband and wife is Domestic Justice in the real sense, though this too is different from Political Justice. [43]

The orator Isaeus of the fourth century reported a law that allowed women to handle values up to one bushel (*medimnos*) of barley [44] which amounted to about 1.85 cu. ft. (0.0523 cu. meter), probably the portion required to feed

---

[42] *Phaedo*, 60A: Loeb 36, 208.

[43] Aristotle, *Nicomachean Ethics*, 5, 6, 1134b, 12-16: Loeb 73, 292-295.

[44] *On the Estate of Aristarchus*, 10, 10: Loeb 202, 366.

a family of four for five or six days, which represented in
normal times the equivalent of between three and six
drachmas, according to D.M. Schaps. [45] This minimum
allowance was made into law because some men, including
those for whom opulence was the product of avarice,
neglected to provide their wives with a modest living. [46]

Such a restriction, however, did not prevent some
women to find a way to use their dowry or their inheritance
to make occasional gifts, loans, purchases or sales of much
larger amounts, certainly with the approval of their
guardian, although the records do not usually mention it.

Occasionally, some men were unable to support the
women in their charge, like this Aristarchus who once
confided to Socrates that, after the enemy had taken all his
properties, fourteen of his female relatives took refuge with
him in his new residence. He had no financial resources.
Socrates suggested putting the women to work at weaving
clothes that he, Aristarchus, could sell for profit. He did it
and made enough money to support them all. [47]

Most husbands seemed to care well for their wives,
especially if they had borne them children. Some husbands
even shared their financial activities with their wives, setting
shops with them or making loans jointly. Archippe, the wife
of the banker Pasio and adoptive mother of Phormio whom
she married after Pasio's death [48] and the unnamed wife of
Diodotus, his niece, [49] were cognizant of the large financial
dealings made by their husbands and probably influenced
them in the process. At least, until the fourth century,
women had no right to ownership of property and assets,
except as dowry, and no right to manage them, but it seems
that a good measure of tolerance was granted in practice
not only to Athenian women but to other freewomen as
well, the rich among them because of their prosperity and
the poor because of their needs. Some women were known
to lend money and charge interest. Aristophanes referred to
such a practice in an aside (*parabasis*) of the year 411 [50]

---

[45] *Economic Rights of women in Ancient Athens*, 61.
[46] Euripides, *Fr., Melanippe Wise*, 504: Loeb 405, 606.
[47] Xenophon, *Memorabilia*, 2, 7, 10-12: Loeb 168, 152-155.
[48] Demosthenes, *For Phormio*, 36, 14: Loeb 318, 332 & passim.
[49] Lysias, *Against Diogeiton*, 5-7 & 14-18: Loeb 244, 662 & 666-
671.
[50] *Women at the Thesmophoria*, 839-845: Loeb 179, 560.

and, at a later date, Demosthenes in a court presentation. [51] No doubt, such a practice remained rare and in every case under the control of a guardian.

Finally, it is worth mentioning that all adult men, married or not, had a responsibility to their elderly parents, especially their mothers in need. The sons had to provide for their subsistence. The law was clear about disqualying anyone who attempted to speak before the people if "he beats his father or mother, or fails to support them or to provide a home for them." [52] Witnesses could be called upon to verify the facts, according to Aristotle [53] who knew, for sure, that Solon, in the early sixth century, also made the son's obligation contingent upon the father having taught him his means of subsistence. In an agrarian society, as it was then in Attica, teaching meant simply for parents sharing the chores and pointing out observations with their children, thus assuring "the very best of support in old age". [54]

As a general perspective, it appears that the respect due to one's own parents was a religious as well as a civic duty. For example, Euthyphro's accusation of impiety (*asebeia*) by his kin for prosecuting his father for homicide shows that respect for parents was a matter related to the gods. [55] Therefore, the conduct of children toward their parents was a part of the religious rituals offered to the gods and not only a domestic or civic responsibility.

Athens was a man's world of privileges and responsibilities in the public arena and in the family where his parents, his wife, and his children by any woman expected his unfailing support. Even the needy orphans within his larger family (*anchisteia*) could come under his care if he had the means and was the nearest of kin. He did not perform the duties of daily care at home but left it to his wife to do it under his supervision.

---

[51] *Against Spudias*, 41. 9 & 21: Loeb 155, 10 & 18.
[52] Aeschines, *Against Timarchus*. 1, 28: Loeb 106, 26 and Xenophon, *Memorabilia*, 2, 2, 13-14: Loeb 168, 110-113..
[53] *Athenian Constitution*, 55, 3: Loeb 285, 150.
[54] Plutarch, *Parallel Lives, Solon*, 22, 1: Loeb 46, 464 and Xenophon, *Oeconomicus*, 7, 12: Loeb 168, 416.
[55] Hesiod, *Works and Days*, 376-380: Loeb 57, 30 and Plato, *Euthyphro*, 4: Loeb 36, 12-17.

Water

Water was the most important resource for all the household tasks. The wife or one of her servant-slave filled a pitcher with fresh water every day. Wealthy families controlled the water supply and sold it by the jar called *hudria*, until the time of Peisistratus in mid-sixth century. Then, as ruler of Athens, he socialized this practice by making the water a public commodity accessible to all, including the poor. [56] In about 520 BCE, his son Hippias built a nine-pipe fountain-house (*enneakrounos*) in the Athenian Agora, with easy access from the residential district.

Black-figured paintings on water jars of the sixth century illustrate how women in their working clothes fetched the water at a public fountain-house or cistern. [57] By underground conduits, through terra cotta pipes embedded in inclined channels, the water supply came from natural springs, tapped from underground streams or a river, if one was in the proximity, and conveyed it to fountain-houses conveniently located for the community. The semi-arid condition of Attica did not favor the use of cisterns for collecting the little amount of rainwater.

The first task of the morning was to make sure that a supply of water for the day be brought home. After Electra married a peasant farmer and moved to a hut in the Argive hills, she had to "look after the indoors", while her husband was going to the field and a slave woman of hers was "carrying her burden of water on her close-cropped head." [58]

Herodotus of the fifth century BCE told a charming story about fetching the water; unfortunately, it had a sad ending. Two Paeonians who intended to resist their people's displacement ordered by the Persian king Darius, went to meet him at Sardis, in Asia Minor. Herodotus described how they used their attractive and skillful sister to get his attention. She was

a woman tall and fair, there, waiting till Darius should be sitting in the suburb of the Lydian city [Sardis].

---

[56] Thucydides, *Peloponnesian War*, 2, 15, 5: Loeb 108, 290.
[57] See Fantham, E. et al., *Women in the Classical World*, 108.
[58] Euripides, *Electra*, 74 & 107-108: Loeb 9, 158-161.

They put on their sister the best adornment they had, and sent her to draw water, bearing a vessel on her head and leading a horse by the bridle on her arm and spinning flax the while.

Of course, the king could not miss noticing her because he had never seen any women in all of Asia that could do so much and be so attractive, all at one time. So, he sent at once his bodyguard to see what she would do with the horse at the river. Herodotus continued:

She, coming to the river, watered the horse; then, having so done, and filled her vessel with the water, she passed back again by the same way, bearing the water on her head and leading the horse on her arm and plying her distaff. [59]

The rest of the story was sad and, although not pertaining to our subject, is well worth summarizing: Darius interrogated the girl in the presence of her two brothers, then ordered all the Paeonians to be brought to him from the region of the Hellespont where they lived. The Paeonians tried to escape, but were caught and transferred to Asia while their towns were destroyed.

Fetching water from the fountain or the river was an arduous task, left to a slave girl, if one was available in the family. In Aristophanes' play *Lysistrata*, the women complained when they had to do it in order to extinguish the flames on the Acropolis:

I could hardly fill it [pitcher] in the dim light of dawn,
In the throng and crash and clatter of pots,
Fighting the elbows of housemaids
And branded slaves; zealously
I hoisted it onto my head, and to aid the women,
My fellow citizens faced with fire
Here I am with water! [60]

These women were compelled by an emergency. The fetching of water, however, was the same struggle every day

---

[59] *Histories*, 5, 12: Loeb 119, 10-13.
[60] *Lysistrata*, 328-335: Loeb 179, 310.

when a throng of women came to fill their jars at the
fountain at about the same time. Some male predators were
also harassing them, thus making the task not only arduous
but also hazardous.

Adding to the traffic and confusion, some women
would also wash clothes at the fountain or the stream.
Euripides reported this activity in his play *Hippolytus*. The
women of the chorus are speaking:

> There is a cliff dripping water whose source, men
> say, is the river Oceanus; it pours forth over its
> beetling edge a flowing stream into which pitchers
> are dipped. It was there that I found a friend soaking
> her brightly colored clothes in the river water and
> laying them out on the warm rock's broad back in the
> sun. [61]

Women used water and oil mixed with fine sand to
scrub cooking and serving ware, and clean stand-like tables.
They heated water over an open fire to prepare warm baths
for their husbands and the members of their family,
including themselves. [62] The practice of bathing was neither
a daily nor an easy exercise. Washing and bathing in the sea
or a river, if nearby, was a favorite place, like Nausicaa and
her entourage did while Odysseus was asleep. Homer
described the scene when the maidens

> took in their arms the clothes from the wagon, and
> bore them into the dark water, and trampled them in
> the trenches, busily vying each with one another.
> Now when they had washed the garments, and had
> cleansed them of all stains, they spread them out in
> rows on the shore of the sea where the waves
> dashing against the land washed the pebbles
> cleanest; and they after they had bathed and
> anointed themselves richly with oil, took their meal
> on the river's banks, and waited for the clothes to dry
> in the bright sunshine. [63]

---

[61] *Hippolytus*, 121-129: Loeb 484, 136.
[62] Homer, *Iliad*, 22, 442-446: Loeb 171, 486.
[63] Id., *Odyssey*, 6, 90-98: Loeb 104, 226.

Men could also use bathtubs at the palestra and women the water flow at the fountain. Otherwise, bathing was usually done at home, using a washing basin in the shape of a margarita drinking glass: a stem on a flat base supporting a wide and shallow basin, high enough to allow the bather to hand-scoop the water while standing.

Soap did not become widely known before the period of the Roman Empire, at the turn of the millennium and beyond. Galen (c. 130-200 CE) mentioned soap as medication as well as cleansing product. It was made of animal fat mixed with plant ashes. It may have been invented by the Phoenicians as early as about 600 BCE and later exported to the Gauls who introduced it to the Romans, since their Latin word *sapo* came from the Celtic word *saipo*. The Greeks did not know the cleansing soap. For cleaning their skin they used a less effective mixture of oil and fine sand, then scraped it with a strigil before rinsing and applying oil. Such a bathing exercise took place probably late in the day, before dinner, like Socrates did before attending a symposium. [64]

Other familiar tasks of women were to sweep the floor, "shake and fold cloaks and bedclothes" [65] and care for the sick, when necessary. Farmers' wives helped also with lighter tasks in the fields, like weeding and clearing.

Food and Drink

Planning and preparing the meals kept the wife riveted to the home everyday. In the courtyard, she cooked in an oven but more commonly on an open hearth, either on a grill or in a cauldron. Utensils were rudimentary. They consisted of pincers, knives, ladles and spoons, mallets, and vases of various shapes from flat bowls to tall amphorae. Pans were greased with olive or sesame oil for cooking.

Baking bread in the oven was a daily chore that involved several steps. The common grain came from a husky wheat, called spelt, grown in northern Greece; the finer one came by ship from the Crimea hugged by the Black Sea. [66] After it was separated from the chaff either by

---

[64] Plato, *Symposium*, 174A: Loeb 166, 86.
[65] Xenophon, *Oeconomicus*, 10, 11: Loeb 168, 450.
[66] Demosthenes, *Against Leptines*, 20, 31: Loeb 238, 512.

winnowing or by using a millstone and a sieve, the grain
was cleaned by hand, then ground into flour with a pestle
and a mortar. The flour was changed into dough, kneaded,
rolled into paste and baked. Bread, mostly pita, was also
available at bread shops where women cooked. [67] Butter and
cheese were introduced into Ancient Greece only after the
fourth century BCE.

Barley could be eaten as a poor substitute for wheat.
It did not require baking but only roasting in a shallow pan
called *phrugetron* and kneading with water, milk or oil to
make a barley-cake (*maza*).

The Athenians had a frugal diet about which only
tidbits of information can be garnered from the Hippocratic
physicians and from authors such as Herodotus and
Aristophanes. The earliest major source of information
came late, in the early years of the Hellenistic Period, in the
Inquiry into Plants and *Growth into Plants* written by
Theophrastus (372-287 BCE) who succeeded Aristotle as
director of the Lyceum at Athens. A few hundred years later,
Pliny the Elder (23-79 CE) must have borrowed from him
extensively for his own encyclopedic *Natural History*.

It must have been for a reason that Comedy
presented the Athenians as abstemious, eating little in
comparison with the Thebans who were known to eat a lot.
It was a habit probably imposed upon them by the poverty
of the land. Nevertheless, the Athenians were gourmet on
the rare occasions of feasts and banquets, best of all at
weddings, when they enjoyed the delectable tastes of food,
especially the eel, and wine, especially from Lesbos. Those
who indulged in food delicacies (*opsophago*i) were
considered addicts like the alcoholics. [68]

Balance according to the seasons was considered
more important to good health than abundance –
"proportion is best in all things." [69] One should eat much
and drink little of undiluted wine in winter but, eat lightly
and drink plenty of very diluted wine in summer. [70] The
Hippocratic physicians did not fail to discern the effect of
diet combined with exercise on the maintenance of good

---

[67] Aristophanes, *Wasps*, 238: Loeb 488, 252.
[68] Hippocrates. *On Sound Diet*: H.E. Sigerist, *A History of Medicine*,
2, p. 24.
[69] Hesiod, *Works and Days*, 694: Loeb 57, 52.
[70] Hippocrates, *Regimen in Health*, 1, 1-39: Loeb 150, 44-47.

health but did not elaborate on the subject like dietitians do. [71]

Concerned with the well-being of their families, mothers determined the most appropriate diet which they learned to plan and prepare according to their best knowledge and experience. The major impediment to their success was in not being allowed to do the shopping themselves, except in special circumstances, for example when the husbands were away or the maidservants were not available. So the urban wives rarely went to the marketplace to buy foodstuff. About their culinary needs, they normally informed their husbands who fulfilled their task according to the family budget and taste. Husbands did not want their wives to be seen and did not trust them with accounting.

In the common household, three meals a day were customary: breakfast (arista), dinner (deipna) and supper (dorpa). [72] Breakfast was a private snack. The other two meals carried a social quality: dinner at mid-day and supper shortly before sunset. Being the main meal, dinner included as staple (sitos) bread or bread-like cakes or tortillas, beans, lentils, and some millet or barleycorn porridge. The evening meal included also vegetables and fruits, usually good but unvaried. Olives, grapes, quinces and figs were sufficiently plentiful in most regions. Some berries, pears, apples and nuts were also available locally, as well as some vegetables like lettuce, artichoke, asparagus, broccoli, celery, garlic, leaf beet, onion, parsley, chickpeas and carob, but none in abundance, and in hard times only mallow and apshodel.

Other native trees and plants grew well in the better soil, mostly outside Attica. The known fruits were the olive, lemon, pear, plum, pomegranate, cherry and fig. Among the vegetables, the following grew well also: cabbage, kohlrabi, spinach and cucumber, and were eaten cold or hot.

Before proceeding further, we should be reminded that most so-called Athenians did not live in the city proper but in small villages and homestead farmhouses. Those who lived isolated on their small farms, near their fields, had all they needed for a humble and comfortable existence. They satisfied themselves with their own variety of produce and some occasional barter with their neighbors. So the farmer's

---

[71] Diocles, Fr.: J. Longrigg, Greek Medicine, 12, 14, p. 151.
[72] Aeschylus, Fr., Palamedes, 96: Loeb 146, 442.

wife fed her family mostly with produce from the farm. T.W. Gallant estimated that the dietary regime of the ancient peasant consisted of approximately 65-70 percent cereal products, 20-25 percent fruits, pulses and vegetables, 5-15 percent oils, meat and wine. [73] They lived like Odysseus' father Laërtes, of times past, who grew his own food, made his own wine, and was

> attended by an aged woman as his handmaid, who sets before him food and drink, after weariness has laid hold of his limbs, as he creeps along the slope of his vineyard plot. [74]

These farmers' wives, assisted by male and female servants, were also involved in the husbandry of animals, as small as chicken and as large as oxen. They catered to dogs, not for their meat, but for protection against robbers and poachers.

Meat was served only on special days. Cows and goats were fattened for meat. They produced little milk, of which only a portion was converted into cheese. Hens laid few eggs and were kept mostly for their meat: "chicken is wholesome", wrote Aristotle. [75] Lamb was the most important course because the sheep had abundant grazing.

Already in the eight century, Homer revealed that pork was also part of the diet, not only on the island of Ithaca. The loyal swineherd Eumaeus of the *Odyssey* certified to the raising of pigs for food. He described in great detail the slaughtering and cooking process. He first told his men:

> 'Bring in the best of the boars, that I may slaughter him for this stranger [Odysseus] who comes from afar, and we too shall have some profit from it, who have long borne toil and suffering for the sake of the white-tusked swine, while others devour our labor without atonement.' So saying he split wood with the pitiless bronze, and the others brought in a fatted boar five years old, and set him by the hearth. [76]

---

[73] *Risk and Survival in Ancient Greece*, 68.
[74] *Odyssey*, 1, 190-193: Loeb 104, 26.
[75] *Nicomachean Ethics*, 6, 7, 1141b, 21: Loeb 71, 346.
[76] *Odyssey*, 14, 414-420: Loeb 105, 66.

Eumaeus lit a fire and offered to the gods "bristles from the head" which he threw into the fire, praying to all the gods. [77] It must be noted that the sacrifice of animals to the gods had in Greece a long tradition born in the myth of the dispute between Zeus and Prometheus, in which Man propitiated the God by sacrificing animals and dividing their parts for consumption. [78]

Eumaeus continued the preparation of the dinner feast:

> Then he raised himself up, and struck the boar with a billet of oak ... and the boar's life left him. And the others cut the boar's throat, and singed him, and quickly cut him up, and the swineherd took as first offerings bits of raw flesh from all the limbs, and laid them in the rich fat. These he cast into the fire, when he had sprinkled them with barley meal, and the rest they cut up and spitted, and roasted it carefully, and drew it all off the spits, and threw it in a heap on platters. Then the swineherd stood up to carve, for well did his heart know what was fair, and he cut up the meat. [79]

Eumaeus made seven portions, one for god Hermes, the other six for the men. "And Odysseus he honored with the long chine of the white-tusked boar." [80]

Aeschylus confirmed that pork was still part of the diet in the fifth century and, better still, as a delicacy: "for what daintier dish could a man get than this?" he asked. [81] Later in the century, Aristophanes told the story of a Megarian who came to Athens to trade a delicious piggy for some garlic and salt. [82] When a pig was served for an Athenian feast, the wife probably followed Eumaeus' cooking instructions.

Dog and horse meats were probably served also, but only rarely when they were needed and available, never for a feast. Birds, like chicken, were scarce on the menu. Fish

---

[77] *Odyssey*, 14, 424: Loeb 105, 66.
[78] See J. Wilkins, *Food in Antiquity*, 172-174.
[79] *Odyssey*, 14, 426-434: Loeb 105, 66-69.
[80] *Ibid.*, 14, 437: Loeb 105, 68.
[81] *Fr.*, Uncertain Play, 169: Loeb 146, 482-483.
[82] *Acharnians*, esp. 795 & 830: Loeb 178, 154 & 160;

was seldom mentioned in Homer's writings, although the Achaeans were either at sea or near the sea [83] and the Aegean Sea was rich in fish, especially tunny. Between about 700 and 525 BCE, a change took place: fish was more frequently served for dinner and the eel gained the respectability of a delicacy to the point that Aristophanes called a fine girl "an eel from Boeotia," [84] in a more sexual manner than we call someone a peach, in today's slang. The word *opson* which meant a seasoning for taste came to mean fish as the best of seasoning. Salt was used for preserving rather than seasoning foods.

When Electra's peasant husband invited the two strangers, Orestes and Pylades, to stay with them, she became quite embarrassed by her meager resources. She enjoined her husband to fetch the old servant who took care of her as a young princess and ask him to help honor their guests. Before going, her husband expressed some embarrassment: "Surely a woman who wants to can find something to add to the feast." [85] Nicely put to urge a wife's ingenuity!

The sunny and moderate climate of Greece favored grape growing. The Greeks used their grapes mostly to make wine which they drank diluted with spring water, except on special occasions like a festival or a symposium, when they served the first round undiluted and the others diluted with water. The ratio of alcohol content was 15-16 percent, higher than the common 12.5 percent today. The quality varied depending on the grapes and other factors such as aging, container, and added condiments like herbs. Local wine was cheap, yet not everywhere in sufficient quantity. Therefore, some wines had to be imported from other places, like the island of Chios, and were for this reason more expensive. Cheap wine was also used to make vinegar.

One more responsibility of the wives was to take care of the beehives and collect the honey. A satirist of about 650 BCE, Simonedes of Amorgos in the Cyclades, had very little to say that was good about women. In spite of his bleak and deprecating attitude about women, however, he dedicated a few lines to a good woman whom he compared

---

[83] *Odyssey*, 4, 367-369: Loeb 104, 144.

[84] *Lysistrata*, 702: Loeb 179, 362.

[85] Euripides, *Electra*, 422-423: Loeb 9, 196.

to the industrious bee. [86] This passage serves for us the peripheral purpose of finding honey on the Greek menu. In addition to honey, some small amounts of raw sugar may have been made as sweetener from the starch content of cereals such as barleycorn.

Did the ancient Greeks have any practice similar to lent or ramadan when they fasted or abstained from meat? They did not, although they fasted on occasions, for example for one day when the votaries gathered at Eleusis to celebrate the *Mysteries of Demeter* or in Athens, near the Pnyx, for the *Thesmophoria*. On both occasions, the fast preceded a feast. Also, in certain circumstances of extreme distress, fasting seemed to be a normal reaction. Achilles did so after the loss of his dear friend Patroclus [87] and Phaedra after the loss of her dream-lover Hippolytus. [88] In these two instances, the common emotion was the passion for making the slate clean, in the first through revenge and in the second through suicide. A form of purification was the underlying process.

Men seemed to believe that women, including their wives, tended to exceed in their consumption of food and drink. The husbands spent so much time away from their house and the wives were naturally so secretive about their disorders at home that their binges with drink and food could remain unknown for a long time, even to this day. Therefore, only indirect evidence is available to us about gluttony and drunkenness at home. Aristophanes' stories in *Lysistrata* and *Women at the Thesmophoria*, to be reviewed later, seem to address the problems women had in their social life.

Heavy drinking and eating at home were not punished, like adulterous affairs, unless they disturbed the peace, yet they were frowned upon as offensive to the norms of moderation and respectability. Besides, they often resulted in obesity and endangered the moral education of the children and the efficient management of the household.

In spite of the black clouds that covered this subject of table habits, we should guard ourselves against every

---

[86] Simonides, *On Women*: H. Lloyd-Jones, *Females of the Species*, 83-93, trans, p. 52.

[87] Homer, *Iliad*, 19, 205-210: Loeb 171, 348.

[88] Euripides, *Hippolytus*, 135-140: Loeb 484, 136.

generalization. The majority of women were not addicted to binging on food or drink. That they enjoyed their wine and their food is perfectly natural and that they liked them sometimes to excess is nothing to make a big fuss about. They accomplished so many physical tasks around the house that they could not have been frequently intoxicated or bulging at the waist.

<u>Weaving</u>

Like the art of cooking, the art of weaving was learned and practiced at home. All garments were made at home by the mother with the help of daughters and slaves. So, the girls learned at home first how to interlace manually two sets of flexible reeds, canes or other rigid vegetable fibers to make baskets. The art of basket weaving was one of the most primitive in the history of Greece and in the development of young girls. It probably inspired the geometric style of vase painting, as early as the eighth century BCE.

Basketry led to the discovery of weaving other fibers, such as wool and flax, and, also cotton and silk during the Hellenistic period starting with the third century BCE. After the wool was cleansed in hot water and shaped into balls on a distaff, it was spun into yarn by spinning, to mean pulling a filament and twisting it by hand or more efficiently with the spindle. Then on a vertical loom for large pieces, the yarn was hand-woven into cloth by interlacing the warp and the weft, over and under in an alternating fashion. It was done standing, as represented on a sixth-century flask for oil (*lêkuthos*) attributed to Amasis Painter. [89] Women made dresses, coats, blankets, carpets and shrouds with large rectangular pieces of cloth, of which none has been preserved because, like the baskets, they disintegrated with time. This work was done indoor, but preferably in the courtyard on sunny days.

In his *Lysistrata*, Aristophanes presented a rough description of the process of weaving and applied it to making a democratic government. By extracting the description, we obtain the following:

---

[89] See S.B. Pomeroy, *Xenophon, Oeconomicus*, 307.

First, put it in a bath and wash out all the sheep
dung, spread it on a bed and beat out the riff-raff
with a stick, and pluck out the thorns; as for those
who clump and knot themselves together to snag ...
Next card the wool into a sewing basket ... joining
[the flocks later] and making one big bobbin. And
from this weave a fine new cloak for the people. [90]

The use of flax was less frequent because the initial
process was difficult and time-consuming. First, the plants
had to be gathered and the stalks combed, soaked and
beaten to soften the fibers; only then could the finer ones
be used to make large pieces of cloth as garments to wrap
the body or blankets for the beds or smaller pieces for small
clothing, aprons or cleaning rags.

The garments could be decorated with needlework.
The use of dye extracted from plants and trees was not
frequent because it was more expensive as an operation
added to the making of the garments. Also, because the
acid smells required an environment other than a home,
dying and fulling the cloth were usually done commercially.

These female tasks were so respected that the
invention of needlework and weaving, according to Hesiod,
was attributed to goddess Athena. [91] Athenian girls learned
to weave by doing it with their mothers for the family and
for Athena's "saffron-colored gown" presented to her every
four years at the *Greater Panathenaea*. [92] For four years,
selected girls and women weaved this new robe for Athena's
statue. On the quadrennial, a seven-year-old girl carried the
Basket (*arrêphoros*) containing the robe (*peplos*). [93] Because
of the heavy weight, several girls must have carried it in
relays. Lysistrata was chosen at seven for this high honor.
On the Acropolis, the precious robe was spread like a sail
above the image of Athena.

Girls learned to weave and also to enjoy doing it.
Homer said of Calypso: "She within was singing with a sweet
voice as she went to and fro before the loom, weaving with

---

[90] *Lysistrata*, 574-582: Loeb 179, 348.
[91] *Works and Days*, 63-64: Loeb 57, 6.
[92] Euripides, *Hecuba*, 467-468: Loeb 484, 440; see EWA 11, Pl. 125
showing the east frieze of the Parthenon of Athens.
[93] Aristophanes, *Lysistrata*, 641: Loeb 179, 356.

a golden shuttle." [94] The same Homer represented Andromache, the wife of the Trojan warrior Hector, "weaving a tapestry in the innermost part of the lofty house, a purple tapestry of double fold, and in it she was weaving flowers of varied hue." [95] He described also the mythical city of the Phaeacians where

> the women are cunning workers at the loom; for Athena has given to them above all others knowledge of beautiful handiwork and excellent character. [96]

The wives provided all members of her family not only with clothes but also shoes, mostly sandals, they needed for all seasons. These were made of animal hide soaked and scraped to remove the layer of hair and glands, then some oil was applied to the rawhide which was soaked again for several weeks in order to obtain a waterproof leather resistant enough and yet solft enough to be cut and shaped into sandals.

The Athenian women cherished their weaving, needleworking and shoemaking tasks. They found in them a sense of independence and self-expression, more than they did in cooking and cleaning. They used ingenuity in making panels of cloth attractive to the eyes and distinctive of their own lineage. The shapes were standard but the selection of colors, the coordination of lines, the design of embroideries and the decorations with beads called upon their artistic creativity and individuality.

The wife was the one who gave the final touches to the pieces to be used by their family as clothing, blankets or shoes. Obviously, some wives were more skillful than others and ready to help their relatives and neighbors, probably for some compensation. The more skillful among them produced more than they needed for their own household and, therefore, could make them available to their husbands for sale or barter. With the help of slaves, some wives may have turned their homes into small domestic factories.

---

[94] *Odyssey*, 5, 61-63: Loeb 104, 186.
[95] *Iliad*, 22, 440-442: Loeb 171, 484.
[96] *Odyssey*, 7, 109-111: Loeb 104, 254.

Poverty

The wives who could claim to be rich were few in Ancient Athens, and they seemed to have followed the impulse to claim it in words and actions. Aristotle remarked that "the wives of oligarchic rulers are luxurious." [97] Aristophanes is lending the same complaint to Strepsiades about his wife, typical of the aristocracy: "From town, haughty, spoiled, thoroughly Coesyrized" by her rich family. [98]

The majority of Athenian families were of small means. To make things worse, certain husbands were unable to provide for the subsistence of their family for a variety of reasons, such as absence, illness or laziness and, as a result, their wives had to resort to gainful activities inside the house, especially weaving clothes and carpets, or painting pictures which could be sold to relatives or friends without setting up shop.

A good number of other gainful activities, however, brought the wives outside the house, depending on their status in society. Some women worked in the fields, pulling weeds or harvesting, especially in the vineyards, and some city women worked as vendors in the marketplace. [99] Atistophanes' disparaging reference to Euripides as the "son of that herb-selling woman" must be taken with skepticism, yet it confirms the fact that some women were selling pot-herbs and other produce in public places. [100] Other women sold chaplets and trinkets to worshippers at shrines and temples. [101] Some women worked as innkeepers and bakers and the best of them as midwives, like Socrates' mother, [102] or as nurses if they had the bearing age. [103] One epitaph of mid-fourth century referred to Phanostrate as "midwife and physician," [104] the only one known with this latter title.

---

[97] *Politics*, 4, 12, 1300a, 8: Loeb 264, 360.
[98] *Clouds*, 47-48: Loeb 488, 14.
[99] Aristophanes, *Peace*, 535: Loeb 488, 496 & Demosthenes, *Against Eubulides*, 30-31 & 45: Loeb 351, 252-255 & 264.
[100] *Women at the Thesmophoria*, 387 & 455-456: Loeb 179, 506 & 512.
[101] *Ibid.*, 448-449: Loeb 179, 510.
[102] Plato, *Theaetetus*, 149A & 151C: Loeb 123, 30 & 38.
[103] Demosthenes, *Against Eubulides*, 57, 35-45: Loeb 351, 257.
[104] Clairmont, C., *Classical Attic Tombstones*, 2, 890.

The absence of the husband on military campaigns, especially during the Peloponnesian War, was a frequent cause of poverty for the family left behind without resources available from parents or relatives. This unfortunate situation explains Aristophanes' frequent comments about women working in public places, one selling "ten obols' worth of bread ... plus four loaves more" [105] and others spawning of the marketplace soup, vegetables, garlic and bread. [106] Being thus exposed to the sun, the more tanned was a woman's face the poorer she appeared to be.

Later, in the fourth century, Aristotle admitted that the Superintendent of women cannot in a democracy "prevent the wives of the poor from going out of doors." [107] At about the same time, Demosthenes referred to the bad times when Athenian women were forced to be "nurses and labourers at the loom or in the vineyards." [108] Also, on Athenian epitaphs of the fourth century, Melita was called "a nurse ... a good nurse" and Melinna was praised:

> By her handiwork and skill, and with righteous courage, Melinna raised her children and set up this memorial to you, Athena, goddess of handiwork, a share of the possessions she has won, in honor of your kindness. [109]

The same source offers a list of occupations, gathered from inscriptions of the fourth century and filled then by some destitute women: washerwomen, sesame-seed seller, wet-nurse, woodworker, groceress, horse tender, pulse vendor, flute player, perfume vendor, honey-seller, frankincense-seller, cloak-seller, unguent-boiler, salt-vendor, tumbler. [110] If needs be, they could also partake with their husbands in lending money at interest and, as widows, succeed them in the business. [111]

---

[105] *Wasps*, 1390-1391: Loeb 488, 396.
[106] Arstophanes, *Lysistrata*, 457-459: Loeb 179, 326.
[107] *Politics*, 4, 12, 1300a, 8-9: Loeb, 264, 360.
[108] *Against Eubulides*, 57, 45: Loeb 351, 265.
[109] M.R. Lefkowitz and M.B. Fant, *Women's Life in Greece and Rome*, 54-55, p. 28.
[110] *Ibid.*, 50-51 & 57-60, p. 27 & 29.
[111] See E.E. Cohen, *Athenian Economy and Society*, 80.

Ménage à Trois

As manager of the household, the wife had such an important role, as she was contributing the major effort toward making it a home for her husband and children, that she considered it an injustice to share her house with another woman as companion (*hetaira*) or concubine (*pallakê*) of her husband. She was jealous of her special relationship as wife and abhorred sharing the marital bed with any other woman, although she ignored and tolerated the sexual affairs of her husband outside the house. She probably did not like them, as nature commands some exclusivity, but she had no choice against the common practice of men. Men, however, were careful to avoid adultery and have their affairs only with women of non-citizen status.

Medea wished that jealousy would not enter her heart when her husband Jason left her for a younger woman, princess Glauce of Corinth. The chorus of Corinthian women sang to the same tune:

> May dread Aphrodite (*kupris*) never cast contentious wrath and insatiate quarreling upon me and madden my heart with love for a stranger's bed! But may she honor marriages that are peaceful and wisely determine whom we are to wed! [112]

Neoptolemus, the son of Achilles, brought home his concubine Andromache, after the war, and had a son by her. [113] He later took a wife, Hermione, who found the arrangement intolerable by Greek custom:

> For it is also not right for one man to hold the reins of two women. Rather, everyone who wants to live decently is content to look for a single mate for his bed. [114]

In her distress, Hermione accused Andromache not only of sharing with her the marriage bed but of using a

---

[112] Euripides, *Medea*, 639-643: Loeb 12, 338.
[113] Id., *Andromache*, 25: Loeb 484, 276.
[114] *Ibid.*, 177-180: Loeb 484, 288.

love-drug (*pharmakoisi*) to seduce her husband away from her and keep her barren. The kind of drug is not clear but it seems to be more than the pure enchantment of her beauty and personality. [115] In similar instances, for example when Helen used drugs brought from Egypt, *pharmakon* was a word used for real drug extracted from herbs, [116] which makes C.A. Faraone believe correctly that "Andromache was using magic, including drugs, to make her [Hermione] hateful to her own husband." [117]

So, one day, Neoptolemus went away on a pilgrimage to Delphi, probably to seek the oracle's advice about his wife's infertility. Knowing that she had no right to divorce her husband, [118] Hermione took advantage of his absence to seek the assistance of her cousin, Orestes, and her father, Menelaus, in a plot to slay both Andromache and her son, Molossus. [119]

In fear, Andromache took refuge at the small shrine of Thetis, divine mother of Achilles, next to the house where she lived with Neoptolemus in Phthia, Achaia Phthiotis. However, when she met with Hermione, the young and free princess, she spoke like a fearless queen with maturity and experience, though a slave. Her language was bold, with even a sprinkling of arrogance, in the face of death. As soon as Hermione left, Andromache reflected Euripides' misogynic bias:

> It is strange that some god has given man remedies against snakes of the wild, yet where something worse than snake or fire is concerned, no one has yet found the specific against a woman, a bad one; such a great bane we are to mankind. [120]

At the end, the victor became the victim when Neoptolemus fell slain at Delphi and Molossus, his young son by a concubine, was cast by the goddess Themis to continue the Phthian race of Peleus and Achilles. As for

---

[115] *Andromache,,* 155-158: Loeb 484, 288; also 32, 205 & 355: Loeb 484, 276, 290 & 306.
[116] Homer, *Odyssey*, 4, 220: Loeb 104, 134.
[117] *Ancient Greek Love Magic*, 13.
[118] Euripides, *Andromache*, 213-214: Loeb 484, 292.
[119] *Ibid.*, 911-912: Loeb 484, 356; see 510-512: Loeb 484, 320.
[120] *Ibid.*, 269-273: Loeb 484, 300.

Andromache, she faded off the history chart while Hermione was given in marriage to Orestes of the Atreid family.

A similar situation occurred in Deianeira's house in Trachis. She bitterly described how much she despised the young princess Iole, a competitor Heracles brought back into her bedroom from Oechalia, on the island of Euboea:

> For I have taken in the maiden – but I think she is no maiden, but taken by him – as a captain takes on a cargo, a merchandise that does outrage to my feelings, and now the two of us remain beneath one blanket for him to embrace; such is the reward that Heracles, he who is called true and noble, has sent me for having kept the house so long. I do not know how to be angry with my husband now that he is suffering severely from this malady [love]; yet what woman could live together with this girl, sharing a marriage with the same man? For I see her youth advancing, and mine perishing; and the desiring eye turns away from those whose bloom it snatches. [121]

When Agamemnon returned home from the war against the Trojans, he also brought with him a concubine, Priam's daughter Cassandra. Nothing was unusual in this exercise of a victor's privilege. His fault was to flaunt his capture with great insensitivity and arrogance. Homer was seldom kind to him for his leadership during the war, showing him pretentious and pompous while weak and indecisive, especially in comparison to Achilles. Now that he was returning triumphant, Agamemnon ignored completely his wife's feelings and rode in with Cassandra at his side on the chariot. His approach did not endear him to his wife Clytemnestra who had already planned his assassination. He ordered her:

> Yon stranger damsel do thou receive into the house with kindness. God from afar looks graciously upon a gentle master; for of free choice no one takes upon him the yoke of slavery. But she, the choicest flower

---

[121] Sophocles, *Women of Trachis*, 536-549: Loeb 21, 182.

of rich treasure, has followed in my train, my army's gift. [122]

The Achaean warrior Phoenix, the tutor of Achilles, came to Phthia when he had a quarrel with his father, Amyntor, "because of his fair-haired concubine." [123] The affliction it brought to his mother was so great that he wanted to kill his father, but the gods prevented him. Then he decided to flee but his cousins and clansmen kept him under guard for nine nights. On the tenth night, he broke out of his room and escaped to Achilles' father, Peleus, who made him ruler over the Dolopians.

Murder would not have been part of these incidents about concubines sharing the home with the wife if these Greek heroes had only remembered the example of another hero of their ancient past, Laërtes, the father-in-law of queen Penelope of Ithaca and father of Odysseus. He had bought a slave, true-hearted Euryclea, when she was young and desirable, but, as Homer said,

> He honored her even as he honored his faithful wife in his halls, but he never lay with her in love, for he avoided the wrath of his wife. [124]

If a wife became unable to bear a child, her husband had one option other than divorce. He could take a concubine into his house and treat the child born of this union like his son, regardless of his wife's resentment. The case of king Menelaus is one in point, although his wife Helen had little leverage to bear upon his decisions after he took her back home in Sparta. Homer tells us that

> for his son he was bringing to his home from Sparta the daughter of Alector, to wed the stalwart Megapenthes, who was his son well-beloved, born of a slave woman; for to Helen the gods vouchsafed issue no more after she had at the first borne her lovely child, Hermione, who had the beauty of golden Aphrodite. [125]

---

[122] Aeschylus, *Agamemnon*, 950-955: Loeb 146, 80.
[123] Homer, *Iliad*, 9, 449: Loeb 170, 426.
[124] Id., *Odyssey*, 1, 433-436: Loeb 104, 44.
[125] *Ibid.*, 4, 10-14: Loeb 104, 118.

The ménage à trois never blended with the customs of Ancient Greece because of the resentment it caused with the wife, not only in bed which certainly was the most awkward situation but also in the kitchen and the parlor room they had to share. The wife and the concubine were trapped together inside four walls for all that women do. The concubine must have appeared to the wife as an adopted daughter who competed with her in every way as an equal, including in the most intimate and privileged activities of married life. The wife would raised without complaint the illegitimate children generated by her husband outside the home, as we shall see later, but never welcomed graciously, as her husband sometimes expected in his folly, the foreign lover who could become in her home the mother of these children.

*

*

*

CHAPTER SIX

PARENTS

Child Introduction

The newborn was first introduced to the family and admitted to the cult of the household gods when, three days after birth, it was carried by the nurse or the father around the hearth (*amphidromia*), usually located in the courtyard of the house. Either on this day or on the tenth day after birth (*dekatê*), dedicated to the mother's purification, the baby was given a name. Girls' names were often feminine forms of boys' names, like Apolloniê from Apollonios, but also abstract names, for example Philia (love) or neutral names, like Lysion. Names were frequently passed down from generation to generation with a view to signifying the children's lineage: the first son by the name of his paternal grandfather and the second son by that of his maternal grandfather. Sometimes, the names were only semantically similar, although still affirming the family unity. Girls' names were not as closely related to the lineage.

The tenth-day purification was required because the mother had acquired from giving birth a taint (*miasma*) which had kept her away from having intercourse with her husband and any close contact with all people. The ritual of purification consisted of a sacrifice to Artemis, the goddess of childbirth, and to other domestic goddesses. Since the mother was considered still too weak and too busy nursing her baby, the planning of this event was left to the grandmother and the midwife who was still the handy woman around the house. [1]

Sometime later, every Athenian child was officially and publicly introduced by the father. Here, the grandson of Ciron is speaking:

[1] Euripides, *Electra*, 654 & 1128: Loeb 9, 224 & 274.

> Our father at our birth introduced us to the members
> of his ward, having declared on oath, in accordance
> with the established laws, that he was introducing the
> children of an Athenian mother [Ciron's daughter]
> duly married; and none of the wardsmen made any
> objection or disputed the truth of his statements,
> though they were present in large numbers and
> always look carefully into such matters. [2]

Isaeus of the fourth century, who made the previous
statement referring to his own parents, concluded that his
father's action proved that not only his mother was a
legitimate Athenian wife but that he was himself a
legitimate Athenian citizen. This conclusion was pertinent to
his court case.

Such was the law that the father introduced his
babies, always the boys and sometimes the girls, to citizen
witnesses and identified them as Athenians with all the
rights and obligations to be devolved unto them later in life.
Following this introduction, the name of the baby boy was
added to the deme's list of citizens. The name of a baby girl
was not listed. She needed only to be introduced as the
daughter of a listed Athenian father and, when legally
married by him to a listed Athenian citizen, she became
capable of producing Athenian children. The introduction
was one of the father's most sacred obligations in order to
establish the right to inheritance and the Athenian status. [3]

The exact time of this official introduction was
dictated by tradition, not by any written law. Because of the
high infant mortality and depending on the father's decision
to raise the child, it was not done shortly after birth for a
baby girl but later, sometimes as late as a year or more
later. When the time came, he attached a fillet of wool to the
outside of the main door, offered a sacrifice to the gods and
held a reception for some witnesses. Financial affordability
was also a factor, at least about the timing, yet the most
humble of Athenian fathers never failed to hold this event.

---

[2] Isaeus, *On the Estate if Ciron*, 19-20: Loeb 202, 300.
[3] Id., *On the Estate of Pyrrhus*, 71: Loeb 202, 116-119.

Family Ties

The bond with her child started already very strong in the mother's womb, while a similar bond between father and child tended to grow only after birth with parenting. Euripides put it well: "A mother always loves her children more than a father does, for she knows they are hers, while he only thinks so. [4]

Inasmuch as the parents' conduct of the household was not expected to be harsh, the ties between parents and children were extremely warm and firm. Several examples reveal the tender and caring relationship between them and their children. One of Aristotle's disciples, Theophrastus, described how a father comported himself with his children, including his daughters, at a certain feast where his wife was also probably present. He wrote: "If he go visiting a friend of his he will run ahead and tell him he is coming, and then face round and say 'I have announced you'." [5]

When Iphigenia begged her father Agamemnon to spare her life, she spoke of the loving attention he gave her:

> I was the first to call you father and you called me your daughter first of all. I was the first to be dandled on your knees and to give and receive that dear joy. You used to say, "Shall I see you happy in your husband's house, living a flourishing life worthy of me?" And I used to say as I hung about your chin, the chin I now grasp in my hand, "And how shall I see you faring, father? Shall I lovingly receive you into my house as an old man, father, repaying you for the toil of my nurture?" [6]

In his play *The Wasps*, Aristophanes introduced two characters, Lovecleon and his son Loathecleon, arguing about the worth of working in the court as jurors. The father liked it and one argument he used to make his point was the good feelings he had when he came home after a day's work. He told his son:

---

[4] *Fr.*, Unidentified Play, 1015: Loeb 506, 576.
[5] *Characters*, 2, 8-9: Loeb 225, 44.
[6] Euripides, *Iphigenia at Aulis*, 1220-1230: Loeb 495, 296-299.

But the nicest part of all, which slipped my mind, is when I come home with my pay. That's when everyone gives me a warm welcome at the door because of the money. First my daughter washes me and oils my feet and bends down to kiss me, calling me "daddy" while she tries to fish out the three obol piece with her tongue. And the little woman fusses over me and brings me a puff pastry, and then sits by and coaxes me, "Eat this, eat this up!" I love all that. [7]

For the sake of comedy, Aristophanes made the snatching of the three-obol piece the outcome of the warm reception. The father, however, did not seem to resent it at all. On the contrary, it was the nicest and pleasantest part of his day.

In spite of these examples of close relationship between father and daughters, most fathers seemed to prefer their sons for the perpetuation of their seeds and their similar lifestyle as guardians, citizens and warriors. Mothers tended to be more even-handed with their love, although they gave more attention to their daughters in the management of their household and spent more time with them.

Mothers probably prayed often to Hestia, the goddess of the hearth, like Alcestis did before she offered herself to Death and entrusted her children to her husband:

As my last entreaty I ask you to care for my orphaned children: marry my son to a loving wife and give my daughter to a noble husband. And may they not, like their mother, perish untimely but live out their lives in happiness in their ancestral land! [8]

A mother expressed love for her children more openly, generously and tenderly than their father did. In return, all children, even those who turned out to be misogynist as adults, could take the words of Euripides as their own: "Except for my mother I hate all womankind." [9]

The relationship between mother and daughter was especially close. The boys started going to school when they

---

[7] Aristophanes, *Wasps*, 605-612: Loeb 488, 298.
[8] Euripides, *Alcestis*, 163-169: Loeb 12, 170.
[9] Id., *Fr.*, *Melanippe Wise*, 498: Loeb 504, 604.

were toddlers and then left home for military school when they were young teenagers. The girls stayed home until they were given to a man in marriage at about the age of fifteen. The adjustments made at this time were traumatic for both the daughter who moved away from home and the mother who lost the child she had prepared for this moment. In most cases, mother and daughter tried to remain in contact because they continued to feel a need for each other, for family love and occasional assistance. Sons loved their mother very dearly but bonded more closely with their father, especially from the age of six when they turned to his immediate tutelage, and loved him also very much. Euripides added wisely: mothers "are not to grudge it". [10]

Mythology has preserved the memory of goddess Demeter and her daughter Persephone, how close the bond of love was between them. Persephone was reluctant to marry Hades "because she yearned for her mother." Then, "Aidoneus, ruler of the dead", at the behest of Zeus, urged her to go to her "dark-robed mother [and] be not so exceedingly cast down." Hearing this, "wise Persephone was filled with joy and hastily sprang up for gladness." Nevertheless, Aidoneus gave her some pomegranate seed so "that she might not remain continually with grace, dark-robed Demeter." He took upon himself to drive her in a chariot to the temple of Demeter where mother and daughter rushed forth to each other and hugged each other in a warm embrace. [11]

Hecuba was the Trojan queen of the late thirteenth century BCE, taken by the victorious Achaean warriors as their hostage and war prize. She was to them a barbarian woman and yet when Euripides, a Greek dramatist of the fifth century, brought her character to the Athenian stage she appeared endowed with the best of all the Greek qualities of maternal love and courage. When her daughter Polyxena was chosen to die in sacrifice for the killing of Achilles she turned to the wise Odysseus, grasped his hand and cheek in supplication and begged him by his beard: "Do not tear my child from my arms, do not kill her!" And then, after she realized that her plea was ignored, she pleaded to die with her: "No matter: I shall cling to her like ivy to the

---

[10] Id., *Fr.*, Unidentified Play, 1064: Loeb 506, 600.
[11] *Homeric Hymns, To Demeter*, 2, 343-436: Loeb 57, 312-321.

oak." This plea of hers was not granted either. When her daughter was taken away, she cried for her pain and, lying on the ground, covered her head with her garment. [12] The sacrifice of Polyxena was represented on an Ionic marble sarcophagus of about 520-500 BCE, thus attesting of the widespread knowledge of her sacrifice in the Greek world. [13]

Hecuba was not inspired by a patriotic motive since her city of Troy had been burned to the ground and she was a captive of the victors, but another mother, Praxithea, was thus inspired when she lost her daughter for the salvation of her homeland, because she loved her homeland more than she did her daughter. [14]

Wives had the responsibility to nurse and raise all their husbands' children. They must have done it with all the natural instincts, because children responded with great affection to the care given to them not only by their mother but also by their grandmother. After the Trojan boy, Astyanax, was sentenced to die by the Greeks, who feared revenge from him for the destruction of Troy and the slaughter and enslavement of her people, his mother, Andromache, cried her lamentation for all Ages:

> O child that my arms have held when young, so dear to your mother, O sweet fragrance of your flesh! It was for nothing, it seems, that this breast of mine suckled you when you were in swaddling clothes. And all in vain were my labor and the pain of my toil! Now, and never again, kiss your mother, fall into my embrace, put your arms around me and press your lips against mine! [15]

When the grandmother, Hecuba, was given the boy's body for burial, she remembered

> Those curls upon your head which I so often tended, so often smothered with kisses! ... O hands, how sweet is your resemblance to your father's [Hector's]

---

[12] *Hecuba*, 277, 398 & 438: Loeb 484, 422, 432 & 438; see also 197-215: Loeb 484, 416.

[13] See J. Neils and J.H. Oakley, *Coming of Age in Ancient Greece*, 121.

[14] Euripides, *Fr.*, *Erechtheus*, 360, 360a: Loeb 504, 374-381.

[15] Id., *Trojan Women*, 756-763: Loeb 10, 90.

hands, ... You often uttered grand promises, dear lips, ... when you used to fling yourself into my bed and say, "Grandmother, I shall cut a great lock of curls for you and bring gatherings of my agemates to your tomb and speak loving words of farewell!" ,,, Ah me, those countless kisses, my care for you, the slumbers we shared. [16]

If they were alive and well, the grandparents contributed to the care of their grandchildren. They usually pampered them and, no doubt, taught them much about the values that made their family strong and respected. The older daughters also took care of their younger siblings, as is still the case to this day. In the process, they nurtured their maternal feelings and learned to make them serve for good purpose.

Helen, whom Hecuba blamed for her miseries after the defeat of her people at Troy, recognized that she was accused of being responsible for the war and that she was hated by all men. She knew also that her mother Leda committed suicide by hanging because of her disgrace, but she denied being a traitor to her family and attributed the war to "the gods' contrivances". That Helen's mother was so distressed is a sign of her wounded love for her daughter. [17]

Viewed in context, a scene of Euripides' play *Orestes* is also very significant about the family relationships. Summarily, the context is as follows: Tyndareus and Leda had two daughters, Helen who married Menelaus of Sparta and Clytemnestra who married Agamemnon of Argos. Helen eloped with Paris of Troy. A ten-year war ensued between the Greeks and the Trojans. The Greek leader Agamemnon sacrificed his daughter Iphigenia in order to get the gods' favors and sail to Troy. When he returned home after the war, Clytemnestra murdered him because the daughter he sacrificed was not only his, but hers also. Then, in complicity with his sister Electra, Orestes avenged his father and murdered his mother Clytemnestra. Now he expected to be sentenced to die for his crime. While he was asking his uncle Menelaus for help, his maternal grandfather Tyndareus joined them. The old king was deeply hurt by the

---

[16] *Trojan Women*, 1175-1188: Loeb 10, 124-127.
[17] Euripides, *Helen*, 200, 280, 686, & 926-835: Loeb 11, 34, 42, 90 & 118.

evil deeds of his daughters and, now furthermore, by the revenge taken by his grandson Orestes.

Orestes' memories from his most tender years were not about his mother because his sister Electra smuggled him out of Mycenae to be raised in Phocis by his maternal grandparents, king Tyndareus and Leda, and by his paternal aunt, Anaxibia, who probably resided with them. [18] It may have been during these short years that his paternal grandfather Atreus was slain by his brother Thyestes with the help of his son Aegisthus who became Clytemnestra's paramour and consort. It appears that the only fond memories Orestes had in addition to those of his sister Electra and his aunt Anaxilia, were of Tyndareus and Leda, the only grandparents he knew.

For a short time, when Orestes was still an infant growing up in the Argive palace where his mother Clytemnestra was venting her outrage toward his father Agamemnon, his sister Electra, probably more than their grandparents and mother, gave him day after day the close and affectionate care he needed. When Electra later heard of his death -- a deception he used to test her feelings -- she lamented, holding the faked urn of his ashes:

> O remaining memorial of the life of the dearest of men to me, Orestes, how far from the hopes with which I sent you off do I receive you back! ... I stole you with these hands, saving you from murder, and sent you to a foreign land. ... The care I often rendered [you], delighting in my labour! You were never your mother's more than you were mine, and the women in the house were not your nurses, but always you called me nurse and called me sister! [19]

Later, Orestes himself recalled in shame for his matricide that his grandfather Tyndareus

> took care of me when I was a child, showing me much affection and carrying "Agamemnon's boy" around in his arms. So did Leda, and the two of them

[18] Sophocles, *Electra*, 297: Loeb 20, 190.
[19] *Ibid.*, 1126-1148: Loeb 20, 272-275.

honored me equally with the Dioscuri [Castor and Pollux, their own sons]. [20]

Now, at the time of his trial for murder, Orestes came to understand that love, although founded on blood relations, should be never totally blind and never unjust. He understood that his grandfather Tyndareus had nothing but contempt for him because the old king still loved the law more than his grandson and, therefore, could not condone his crime. [21]

The story in another Euripides' play, *Heracles Mad*, involves with great insight and tender details the roles of fathers and mothers in caring for their children, especially in times of danger. Heracles' wife, Macaria, had been left alone at home with their children while her husband was travelling and accomplishing famous labors. In his absence, a usurper named Lycus was threatening to execute his entire family in order to acquire the Theban throne. Macaria told her anguish to her father-in-law, Amphitryon:

> You and I, sir, will soon be killed, and Heracles' children as well, children I shelter like a bird her brood, nestling under my wings. They fall to questioning me, one from this direction, another from that, saying, "Mother, where in the world has father gone off to, what is he doing, when will he come back?" In their youthful confusion they look for their father. I tell them stories to put them off. Whenever the door creaks, they all in wonder jump up in order to hurl themselves at their father's knees. [22]

When Heracles came home, with "light of rescue shining on" him, [23] he found his wife and children in mortal danger. He pledged to protect them in words that defy time and place:

> Well, I will take these tow boats in by the hand and like a ship drag them after me. I do not refuse to tend my children. Men's lot is everywhere the same.

---

[20] Euripides, *Orestes*, 462-465: Loeb 11, 464.
[21] *Ibid.*, 479-481: Loeb11, 466.
[22] *Heracles Mad*, 70-79: Loeb 9, 316.
[23] *Ibid.*, 531: Loeb 9, 356.

High and low alike love their children; they differ in
wealth, and some are rich, others poor, but the whole
human race is fond of its young. [24]

Shortly before he died in 399 BCE, Socrates had a
long conversation with his friend Ischomachus who was
thinking of his wife and God's plan for women when he
said:

Knowing that he [god] had created in the woman and
had imposed on her the nourishment of the infants,
he meted out to her a larger portion of affection for
new-born babes than to the man. [25]

In moments of depression, Euripides questioned the
benefits of having children. For the mother, childbirth had
its pains and, for both parents, the growth of their children
had its anxieties: if they turned out well, they neverteless
brought out fears of evil befalling them, including death,
and if they turned out bad they caused their parents "a most
hateful affliction". [26] These were only passing moments
because the Ancient Greeks never avoided on these grounds
their obligations of having children for the pride of their
family and the benefit of their State.

Mothers shared with their husbands the
responsibility of rearing all their children, yet they carried
the lion's share because they were constantly at home with
them and the fathers were out all day and, in times of war,
for months at a time. Also, since wives tolerated by force of
nature and customs the affairs their husbands had with
other women, usually free aliens or slaves, they tolerated
also the consequences ensuing the birth of illegitimate
babies. These babies were accepted in the home and
nurtured without discrimination, although they did not
enjoy later in life the same rights as the legitimate children.
The example of the marriage of Hector and Andromache of
Troy is significant for her devotion and his expectations, as
viewed by a Greek observer. Euripides lent these generous
words to Andromache:

---

[24] *Heracles Mad*, 631-636: Loeb 9, 368.
[25] Xenophon, *Oeconomicus*, 7, 24: Loeb 168, 420.
[26] Euripides, *Fr., Oenomaus*, 571: Loeb 506, 42 and *Fr.*,
Unidentified Play, 908 & 908a: Loeb 506, 504.

Dearest Hector, I even went so far as to help you in
your amours, if Aphrodite ever tripped you up, and I
often gave the breast to your bastards in order that I
might show you no bitterness. By doing this I won my
husband's love with my goodness. [27]

Like Andromache, Theano, wife of Antenor, reared
his illegitimate son, Pedaeus, "carefully like her own
children". [28] But Odysseus was the most famous of all
illegitimate sons. He was Cretan by birth, and the Cretans,
unlike the Trojans, were considered the ancestors of the
Greeks. He was an illegitimate son of a rich father and his
slave-concubine. yet he became king of Ithaca, an island of
the Ionian Sea, and was a warrior nine times before he
joined the Achaeans in the Trojan War. When he returned
home stealthily, disguised as a beggar, and revealed his
identity to his loyal servant, the swineherd Eumaeus, he
started with these words:

From broad Crete I claim my lineage, the son of a
wealthy man. And many other sons too were born
and bred in his halls, true sons of a lawful wife; but
the mother that bore me was bought, a concubine.
Yet Castor, [29] son of Hylax, of whom I declare that I
am sprung, honored me even as his true-born sons.
He was at that time honored as a god among the
Cretans in the land for his good estate and his
wealth, and his glorious sons. But the Fates of
death bore him away to the house of Hades, and his
proud sons divided among them his property, and
cast lots for it. To me they gave a very small
portion, and allotted a dwelling. But I took to me a
wife [Penelope] from a house that had wide
possessions, winning her by my valor, for I was no
weakling, nor a coward in battle. [30]

---

[27] Euripides, *Andromache*, 222-226: Loeb 484, 292.
[28] Homer, *Iliad*, 5, 68-71: Loeb 170, 210.
[29] Castor was a fictitious name; the father who raised him was
   Laërtes but his real father was Sisyphus who seduced his mother
   Anticleia, the wife of Laërtes.
[30] Homer, *Odyssey*, 14, 199-213: Loeb 105, 50-53.

This passage is significant for showing the equal treatment given in the family to both legitimate and illegitimate children, except for the inheritance. This kind of equal treatment was extended even to the slave children who were entitled to no inheritance at all. For this reason, Euripides discouraged husbands from having illegitimate sons: "Though in no way inferior to legitimate ones, they are handicapped by convention (*nomos*)." [31]

A short time later, Homer reported the words of Eumaeus, the servant, about Anticleia, the queen mother of Ithaca, mother of Odysseus:

> She herself had brought me up with long-robed Ctimene, her noble daughter, whom she bore as her youngest child. With her was I brought up, and the mother honored me little less than her own children. But when we both reached the lovely prime of youth they sent her to Same [another island of the Ionian Sea] to be married, and got themselves countless bridal gifts, but as for me, my lady clad me in a cloak and tunic, very handsome ones, and gave me sandals for my feet and sent me forth to the field, but in her heart she loved me the more. [32]

Eumaeus became the swineherd of Penelope, with enough to eat and drink and to welcome strangers. As for Penelope, the faithful wife of Odysseus, she was made of the same mold as her mother, Periboea: she treated the pretty and ungrateful Melantho, a maidservant, with the same attention as her own child, Telemachus.

> Melantho, whom Dolius begot, but whom Penelope had reared and cherished as her own child, and gave her playthings to her heart's desire. [33]

These cases of children, one noble and the other humble, made two points: One, all the children of the husband and of a resident slave father were raised together like equals in the same household and, second, the distribution of benefits was unequal after they grew up.

---

[31] *Fr., Andromeda*, 141: Loeb 504, 148.
[32] Homer, *Odyssey*, 15, 363-370: Loeb 105, 102.
[33] Ibid., 18, 321-323: Loeb 105, 224.

Furthermore, these cases told a lot about the liberal sexual habits of men and even more about the expectations they had of their wives' unselfish devotion to their entire family. To be a mother was not only to be for her husband a procreator of children but also a nurturer of all his children equally from birth to maturity.

One case is not yet included here, namely the case of a stepmother having to raise the children of her husband's first wife, either dead or divorced. Then she feels insecure because her husband may show a preference for his first wife's children and deprive her own children of the inheritance she feels they deserve. Euripides who went through such an experience in his own life did not fail to observe it:

> A woman is naturally somewhat hostile towards the children of a previous marriage when she is their father's second wife. [34]

Parents at different times had some help in rearing their children from the grandparents or the older sisters in the family. The slaves also could be very effective in rearing their master's children but it was for them a task more than an instinct since they did not have the same blood relation. If they were married and had children of their own they tended to favor them with their attention.

The funeral reliefs known to be of the late fifth and fourth centuries borrow often from the closeness of the Greek family. For example, one of a grandmother and grandson buried together shows the grandmother, Amphirete, holding with one hand her grandson closely on her knees, and with the other hand a bird symbolizing his departure. [35]

The immediate family (oikos) was the haven where the little children were sheltered and reared. Around it, however, was the larger family from grandparents to second cousins (anchisteia), with whom contacts were frequent and relaxed. In time of need, the members of the oikos found shelter with their relatives [36] who formed a clan or village (kômê) [37] that found in sharing of blood and ancestral origin

---

[34] Fr., Aegeus, 4: Loeb 504, 6.
[35] See C.M. Bowra, Classical Greece, 79.
[36] Plato, Laws, 6, 754B: Loeb 187, 402.
[37] Aristotle, Politics, 1, 1252b, 17-18: Loeb 264, 6.

the reason for sharing in social, religious and funerary activities. For example, they tended to offer sacrifices to the same deities, partake in the same family feasts, marry among themselves and bury their dead in the same burial ground.

During the Classical Age, the clan was the foundation of the government structure: thirty clans formed a phratry, three phratries a tribe, and four tribes the city-state of Athens. Late in the sixth century, Cleisthenes had used territory instead of kinship to restructure Attica, dividing it into ten tribes, each subdivided into districts (*demoi*) selected equally from the Plain, the Coast and the City.

According to Plutarch, Solon of the early sixth century enacted a controversial law: if an heiress lost her husband by death or divorce, she was to marry his nearest kinsman. Solon's obvious purpose was to keep the wealth within the clan. Plutarch approved that the wealth, but more so that the children "may be of his family and lineage". [38] By the same token, the rearing of all the husband's children was made easier for the second wife. The Athenians believed that it took a village to raise a family. The bonds binding the larger family (*anchisteia*) were tight for reasons of nature and economic interests.

The evidence is clear that parents of Ancient Athens loved and nurtured their children very dearly. Most children responded in kind to their parents' love by practicing, according to Euripides' advice, one of three virtues, namely to honor "the parents who begot you", the other two being the gods and the common laws of Greece. [39]

Early Training

Education (*Paideia*) started the moment the child was born and was at once the primary responsibility of the mother, usually with the help of a maid. At first, it consisted of teaching the rudimentary social manners by responding to the infant's needs, such as eating, first at the breast, toilet training and keeping its linen clean, [40] also how to

---

[38] *Parallel Lives, Solon*, 20, 3: Loeb 46, 458.
[39] *Fr.*, Unidentified Play, 853: Loeb 506, 478.
[40] Aeschylus, *Libation-Bearers*, 756-760: Loeb 146, 230.

walk, speak and behave. The stages in the development of children were the same as they are today.

Children in their infancy were like tablets of wax that take every imprint easily and tend to keep it for a long time, unless corrected with effort in later years. These were the years when children learned also to love their mother because there was no greater "joy than their mother, ... no other joy brings more joy than this." [41]

After his divorce, Euripides must have recalled some personnal experience about a bad wife's influence on her children when he wrote that an inferior wife, even if she was married to a man of worth, "would not get good children", although it can happen that a handsome child is the offspring of an unattractive mother, but a noble and virtuous child cannot be produced from money or by a mother without "nobility and virtue." And about physical strength, he wrote: "A father and mother who toil at strenuous activities will have children who are stronger." [42]

Most mothers breast-fed their babies until they were about two years old. [43] Some wet-nurses were available when required. Babies wore diapers (*spargana*) until they were potty trained, also at about two years old. Mothers, or nurses in their stead, kept the babies in swaddling clothes until the age of two and carried them until the age of three. [44] To put their babies to sleep, they used a combination of dance and song: "they rock them constantly in their arms; and instead of silence, they use a kind of crooning noise." [45]

The early years were of paramount importance for nurturing in a child the habits of goodness and honor, as the dramatist Euripides described in the following choral words:

> The nurture of the well educated
> contributes much to goodness. ...
> To seek after goodness is something great;
> for women it is in the hidden sphere
> of love, while among men

---

[41] Euripides, *Fr., Erechtheus*, 358: Loeb 504, 374.
[42] *Fr., Meleager*, 520, 525 & 527: Loeb 504, 622-627,
[43] Euripides, *Hecuba*, 424: Loeb 484, 436.
[44] Plato, *Laws*, 7, 789E: Loeb 192, 6.
[45] *Ibid.*, 7, 790D-E: Loeb 192, 10.

when good order in its fullness is present,
it makes the city greater.[46]

The same Euripides wrote also that

Good nurturing teaches noble behavior,
and if a man learns this lesson well.
he knows what is base,
measuring it by the standard of the honorable. [47]

Euripides again is emphatic about the importance of
a good and early education of children:

Every man who is trained in good deeds
is prevented by shame from becoming base.
Courage is teachable; even a babe learns to say
and to hear things he does not yet understand.
And what a man learns he tends to keep
until he is old. Therefore raise your children well! [48]

For the philosopher Plato the accent was different
and typical of the fourth century. Nurture in a child, he said,
is to make the soul "more bright and cheerful." [49]

A child's early education was a mother's best form of
caring. Mothers not only taught their infants the
rudimentary social and physical manners according to
customs, but also disciplined them all, boys and girls, when
they felt the need was present. They punished them at
times, but never in a degrading way, according to Plato. [50]
Lysis admitted to Socrates that his mother would have
beaten him if he had touched "her batten, or her comb, or
any other of her wool-work implements." [51]

In the Dialogue *Protagoras*, Plato explained that
parents tell their children

To do this and not to do that. And if he readily obeys,
-- so, ; but if not, they treat him as a bent and twisted

---

[46] *Iphigenia at Aulis*, 561-572: Loeb 495, 222.
[47] *Hecuba*, 600-602: Loeb 484, 450-453.
[48] *Suppliant Women*, 912-917: Loeb 9, 102-105
[49] Plato, *Laws*, 7, 792B-793E: Loeb 192, 16-21.
[50] *Ibid.*, 7, 793B: Loeb 192, 20.
[51] Id., *Lysis*, 208D: Loeb 166, 24.

piece of wood and straighten him with threats and blows. [52]

In this instance, Plato is thinking, or at least framing all his thoughts, about a boy's education. If a beating was good enough for a boy, it was probably good enough for a girl also. Related to this harsh practice of physical punishment is the subject of justice discussed by Aristotle in his *Nicomachean Ethics*, He declared that justice does not really apply to children:

> Justice between master and slave and between father and child is not the same as absolute and political justice, but only analogous to them. For there is no such thing as injustice in the absolute sense towards what is one's own; and a chattel, or a child till it reaches a certain age and becomes independent, is, as it were, a part of oneself, and no one chooses to harm himself; hence there can be no injustice towards them, and therefore nothing just or unjust in the political sense. [53]

There is a form of domestic justice between husband and wife, different from the court justice that is based on equality. If there is some degree of domestic justice also between parents and their children, it is in the sense of fairness, and it must exist in the application of punishments. Fairness, if not Justice, toward children consists primarily of making them obey without recourse and learn by sharing in household and occupational chores. In fact, there is no doubt that it existed in the household of most Ancient Athenians.

All mothers attempted to impart their children as much knowledge as they were privileged to have. Some of them were able to teach their children to read, write and count, at least to the extent that they could recognize the difference between obols, drachmas, minas and talents. Several paintings on vases of the fifth and fourth centuries show women holding book rolls. In literature, the only woman who could write was Phaedra of Euripides' play

---

[52] *Protagoras*, 325D: Loeb 165, 142.
[53] *Nicomachean Ethics*, 5, 6, 1134b, 8-14: Loeb 73, 292.

Hippolytus. [54] Undoubtedly, she could read also, as well as her husband Theseus who read her letter. The assumption is that some exceptional mothers read to their children and thus taught them to do the same. Such was probably the case of Deianeira, the wife of Heracles who gave her an oracle written on a tablet. [55]

All mothers guided their children to play (*paidia*) with toys, dolls and pets, and made them share fun games with other children, as early as the age of three. [56] The toys and games were simple, yet plentiful: for example, wooden horse, roller or cart, rattle, hoop, balancing stick, swing, see-saw, knucklebones, balls, spinning tops. Girls had an inclination to jewelry boxes. Jointed dolls were a favorite, especially in puppet shows. [57] Cats and dogs were pets of choice, but goats, piglets and birds, including fighting cocks, were also well liked. Children enjoyed riding on adults' shoulders, running, playing tag or hide-and-seek and, best or all, dancing.

As a sport, dance was one of the first skills mothers taught their children, girls as well as boys, as early as the age of three. It was a technique used toward developing physical and social graces while releasing the pent-up energy of their young limbs. It was a form of discipline and control in a social setting. The interaction among children in chorus dancing was monitored, measured, and stylized. Early on, they learned to imitate animals, such as snakes, lions, and especially bears in honor of Artemis Brauronia. Dance was a great activity not only for channeling energy but also for acquiring the skills of social and moral conduct.

These activities were supervised by a committee of twelve women elected by the women charged with the supervision of marriage and appointed by the law-warden in order to give them a legal status, like police officers. [58] The order of a society in which each member fills a role in coordination with compeers was perceived and pursued through the choreography and harmonized rhythms of steps appropriate to each dancer. [59]

---

[54] *Hippolytus*, 856: Loeb 484, 206.
[55] Sophocles, *Women of Trachis*, 47 & 157: Loeb 21, 134 & 144.
[56] Plato, *Laws*, 7, 793B & 794A: Loeb 192, 20-23.
[57] *Ibid.*, 2, 658C: Loeb 187, 106.
[58] *Ibid.*, 7, 794B: Loeb 192, 22.
[59] *Ibid.*, 2, 653E ff.: Loeb 187, 90 ff.

Music was an integral part of dancing, even when it was reduced, as it often was in the household, to percussion beats made with any available objects such as a ladle and a pot. The practice of dance was for the masses while the practice of music was restricted to those with special talents such as acute sense of rhythm, ear for pitch and timbre, coordination of lips or fingers with tunes, keen memory of melody and oftentimes words. The Greeks used the cymbal and the tambourine for percussion, the lyre and probably the harp as string instruments, and the single or double-reed flute, called *aulos*, as wind instrument.

The musical fragments preserved from Ancient Greece are rare and poor, although we know from literary sources that music was important in the social life of the Greek people. Parchments, especially of oracles, were often inscribed with songs. [60] Some of their gods, such Apollo and Orpheus, were intimately associated with music. As early as the sixth century BCE, Pythagoras of Crotona discovered the musical scale. Therefore, we can assume that the children who displayed at an early age some special talent for music, either as instrumentalists or singers, were encouraged to pursue the development of their skills. The iconography represented women as well as men singing in chorus or singly, or playing singly some musical instruments, like the male *aulos* player and the female dancer holding rattles (*krotala*) painted inside a drinking cup (*kulix*) signed by Epictetos between 520 and 510 BCE. [61]

In spite of the popularity of music and dance as well as the respect and admiration for the performers of these dynamic arts in Ancient Greece, the Greeks did not claim its origin but gave it a mythological origin on the island of Crete, thus making it even more important in their culture. Homer is our witness in the following incomparable description:

On it furthermore the famed god of the two lame legs [Hephaestus] cunningly inlaid a dancing floor like the one which in wide Cnossus Daedalus fashioned of old for fair-tressed Ariadne. There were youths dancing; and maidens of the price of many cattle, holding

[60] Euripides, *Fr., Pleisthenes*, 627: Loeb 506, 84; Thucydides, *Peloponnesian War*, 2, 8, 2: Loeb 108, 272.
[61] EWA 10, Pl. 227.

their hands on one another's wrists. Of these the maidens were clad in fine linen, while the youths wore well-woven tunics softly glistening with oil; and the maidens had fair chaplets, and the youths had daggers of gold hanging from silver baldrics. Now would they run round with cunning feet very nimbly, as when a potter sits by his wheel that is fitted between his hands and makes trial of it will run in rows toward each other. And a great company stood around the lovely dance taking joy in it; and two tumblers whirled up and down among them, leading the dance. [62]

The same Homer, this time in the *Odyssey*, told us that the Phaeacians, probably of the island of Crete, surpassed all others "in fleetness of foot, and in the dance and in song." So, they fetched the blind Demodocus, the lyre player, and "leveled a place for the dance, and marked out a fair wide ring." When Demodocus arrived,

he then moved into the midst, and around him stood boys in the first loom of youth, well skilled in the dance, and they struck the sacred dancing floor with their feet. [63]

On this subject of dance and music, Plato's *Laws* is frequently quoted. He wrote this Dialogue in the last years of his life and could not even finish it. It was not a work of history but a projection of his vision about a State of his liking. He may have exaggerated the role played by music and dance but did not depart from his own experience when he described the general practice in Athens of the fourth century.

At first, the infant learned to dance only as a playful activity, called gymnastic [64] The word *paizô* meant both to play and to dance. Then, as the child grew up, it became an activity controlled by rules. Between the ages of three and six, the children could meet, of course under supervision, at the village temple to play and learn to socialize. [65] The

---

[62] *Iliad*, 18, 590-605: Loeb 171, 330-333.
[63] *Odyssey*, 8, 258-264: Loeb 104, 290.
[64] Plato, *Laws*, 2, 673A: Loeb 187, 156.
[65] *Laws*, 7, 794A: Loeb 192, 22.

second day of the festival *Anthesteria*, celebrating god Hermes of the Underworld, featured the transition from infancy to childhood. Then, past the age of six, dance and music could develop separately for boys and girls into performances either at a wedding, [66] a festival or a theatrical production under the direction of male and female public teachers paid, probably at some times, by the state. When the event was public, the parents and other spectators took pride and joy in watching the young men's and maidens' limber feet glide on the earth floor in unison and harmony. Plato reserved his comments to young male dancers and elderly men enjoying the sight but, inasmuch as young girls danced in chorus also at festivals and were seen indiscriminately by men and women, the enjoyment may have been equal for both. [67]

From Plato we learn also that children's dances, including the weapon dance, were competitive exercises for both boys and girls. For the girls, the symbolism of the pyrrhic dances was to childbirth instead of combat on the battlefield, in the context of the cults of Artemis and Athena instead of Ares. In either situation, hiding and emerging was a strategy replete with danger.[68]

To dance the bear (*arktos*) at the festival of Artemis Brauronia was a prominent practice in Attica because it served as an initiation rite for girls, marking their transition into womanhood after the age of ten. [69] Families and other citizens could easily travel the twenty miles between Athens and Brauron on the east coast. The public festival itself presented some dangers to the girls who performed nude, according to the iconography discovered at Brauron. The exhilaration of the initiation rites was tempered with a good measure of fear, similar to Iphigenia's feelings "when she shed to earth her safron robe" [70] before her sacrifice as a maiden dedicated to the will of Artemis. In the girls' initiation ritual, the bear symbolized the husband who, like the bear, ought to be tamed and always handled with caution lest he scratched her face with his paw. The young

---

[66] Euripides, *Trojan Women*, 325-341: Loeb 10, 48-51,
[67] Plato, *Laws*, 2, 655C-657E: Loeb, 187, 96-105.
[68] *Ibid.*, 7, 796B-D & 815-816: Loeb 192, 28-31 & 90-97.
[69] Aristophanes, *Lysistrata*, 643: Loeb 179, 356.
[70] Aeschylus, *Agamemnon*, 239: Loeb 146, 22.

girls needed to prepare their minds to handling cautiously their future husbands, twice their age.

Girls' Education

Girls remained with their mother until they were given in marriage to a man, at about the age of fifteen. Boys remained under their mother's care only until about the age of six when they started playing games separately from girlrs [71] and gradually passed on to the supervision of their father. Most parents were attentive to the task of raising their children, not only for the pride of one and the good of the other, but for the ultimate public purpose of producing worthy citizens of the state which counted so much on it as to hold the parents responsible for providing proper education according to the rules and practices dictated by nature and instituted by customs and the laws.

Girls learned early in life the place they held in the social structure of Athens and the role they were called to perform later for their family and the city. They were not given any public education, unlike boys who were required to be trained in physical exercise and war practices and, if they were wealthy enough, would also receive a liberal education in poetry, the arts, philosophy, mathematics and the sciences. The so-called girls' school of Sappho was an anomaly, especially in the Archaic Period of the seventh century. It was a club rather than a school as we understand it.

Girls were educated at home in the domestic arts of cooking, weaving and cleaning and, in the process, as Xenophon pointed out, in self-control. [72] Perhaps they occasionally gathered together within a phratry to receive from a more competent woman advanced instructions in a special art, such as weaving. Girls would also learn to sing and dance, since it was required of them to perform at the various festivals and weddings. A few women in the fifth century like Phaedra, king Theseus' wife, had the opportunity and intelligence to learn in their young age how to read and write. [73] Xenophon gives us a clue that, at least

---

[71] Plato, *Laws*, 7, 794C: Loeb 192, 22.
[72] *Oeconomicus*, 7, 6: Loeb 168, 414.
[73] Euripides, *Hippolytus*, 877-880: Loeb 484, 198; see Id., *Fr.*, *Melanippe Wise*. 482: Loeb 504, 580..

starting in the late fifth century, it became more common for girls to acquire a rudimentary ability to read and write, since they were "counting and making a written list of all the items" in the household. [74] Euripides probably echoed the general belief when he attributed the invention of writing to Palamedes, son of the Argonaut Nauplius and a warrior at Troy. His expectation was that it "prevents the telling of lies". It may have been true, but not for Phaedra who lied when she wrote her final message. [75]

One other indication of the ability of many women to write and read appears in the inscriptions found on vases expressly used by women. The water-jar (*hudria*) had a general purpose, but was used mostly for women's chores. Other containers were also specifically made for her personal usage: the *puxis*, round box for holding cosmetics or other small objects, the *lekanis*, basin-shaped vessel or large bowl with a lid and two handles for mixing cosmetics, and the *alabastron*, narrow-necked perfume vase. Anthony Snodgrass made an important point concerning the inscriptions on these vases directed at women. He wrote:

> "It is a fact well known to the small group of scholars who have worked on this subject that, among the scenes in vase painting which show a mortal person (as distinct from, say, a Muse) holding up or reading from a book-roll, a remarkably high proportion -- about half -- show women doing so. From this, it is a reasonable inference that the wives and daughters of educated Athenians could often read and write. I infer therefore that Athenian women quite often read aloud to their children, servants and men-folk; and this makes it less surprising that the short messages painted on hudriai or puxides should have been normally designed for female customers. [76]

In view of this evidence, the home schooling of girls by their mothers in the fourth century must have frequently

---

[74] *Oeconomicus*, 9, 10: Loeb 168, 442.
[75] *Fr., Palamedes*, 578: Loeb 506, 52; see Euripides, *Hippolytus*, 856 ff.: Loeb 484, 206-209.
[76] A. Snodgrass, *The Uses of Writing on Early Greek Painted Pottery*, in *Word and Image in Ancient Greece*, ed. By N.K. Rutter and B.A. Sparkes, 29.

included writing and reading and the daughters who displayed the interest and the ability to learn must have acquired this knowledge well. The mothers who were unable to write and read could have resorted to a female relative or neighbor to teach these skills to their daughters. So, the inscriptions provided us with the opportunity to peek through a special window into the private education of the Athenian girls. Already in 412 BCE, when Aristophanes' *The Frogs* was produced, the audience was ready to hear that god Dionysus was reading Euripides' *Andromeda* to himself. [77]

What role had the mother in pursuing a suitable life partner for her children? She had no legal role since her husband or his male substitute alone had the responsibility of finding husbands for their daughters and of executing the contract. Yet she cared naturally for daughters she had prepared since infancy for their role as mothers. She wished them to be the happy mates of considerate and responsible husbands and satisfied mothers of bright and healthy children. Behind the scene, she probably watched every move, commented on every suitor, advised on every decision. She cared also about her sons although they legally belonged to her husband since early age and were emancipated while teenagers. If she had anything to do in the choice of her sons' bride, it was because sons still loved their mothers even after they left home and mothers never ceased to wish for them success and happiness.

All feelings of mothers being equal, regardless of status in society, Megara's dream for her three sons must be typical. It started early, long before they were of age to marry. She already wished for them wives who would be dutiful mothers and managers of their households, having been raised by families of good reputation and, in her case, with power and wealth. Her husband and hero, Heracles, had planned for each of them three cities: Argos, Thebes and Oechalia. But, in his absence, Megara dreamt of a brighter future for them. As she told her three young sons:

> While I was choosing the finest of brides for you and was making marriage alliances with Athens, Sparta

---

[77] *Frogs*, 52: Loeb 180:22.

and Thebes so that with your stern cables fastened to firm anchorage you might have a happy life. [78]

Megara's choice of these three cities was a far better choice than the one made by Heracles: Sparta of the fifth century was better than Argos and Athens infinitely better than Oechalia. She retained Thebes because it was the city of her home. Greek mothers and fathers wished a happy future for all their children. The marriage contract and the dowry were only the legal expression of their hopes and good wishes.

Every mother often thought, long before the marriage contract was made for her daughter, that she would one day lose her to a man who would take her away to a new home but, at the same time, she knew that her daughter would remain for a lifetime her closest friend and ally, closer than her husband could be in personal matters of female experiences, especially the birth of her children, and then she wished to have a role as a loving and caring grandmother.

Fathers' Role

Most wives were either pleased with the status quo of being under the tutelage of her husbands or too weak to change a tradition so deeply rooted in the Greek culture. Some mothers, like Medea, may have hurt the sons they loved in order to hurt the father and husband they detested. Most women, however, did not go this far, yet may have used their sons to complain against their husbands, saying that they lacked in political or financial ambition, or were selfish or indifferent. In one case, reported by Plato, a mother told "the boy that his father is too slack and no kind of a man, with all the other complaints with which women nag in such cases." [79]

The Achaean Phoenix, warrior in the Trojan War, related once how enraged his father, Amyntor, was with him:

[78] Euripides, *Heracles Mad*, 476-479: Loeb 9, 350-353.
[79] *Republic*, 8, 549D-E: Loeb 276, 258.

Because of his fair-haired concubine, whom he
himself ever loved, and scorned his wife, my mother.
So she begged me by my knees continually, to sleep
with his concubine first myself, so that the old man
might be hateful in her eyes. I obeyed her and did the
deed, but my father learned of this immediately and
cursed me mightily. [80]

Now the feud which originated with the resentment
of Phoenix' mother extended to her son who fled home with
hatred in his heart. Such attempts by a wife to use her son
in order to alienate her husband from a competitor in her
bed was one   way of venting resentment for a loveless
marriage or of reaching the husband with whom direct
communication was impossible. Whatever the motives for
these complaints, they always jeopardized the proper
rearing of children, even if they did not result in the total
destruction of the marriage. Clytemnestra's loveless
marriage to Agamemnon was a case in point. How could she
forget that he had killed her former husband and two sons
in order to claim her as his wife? And when the life of her
daughter Iphigenia depended on her husband's decision,
she argued and pleaded with him: "Do not kill your daughter
and mine – and you will show good sense." [81]
        Iphigenia's sister, Electra, did not espouse her
mother's hatred for Agamemnon. For seven years after
Clytemnestra murdered him, Electra agonized over the loss
of her father and her deep resentment surged into an
unbridled hatred for her mother. [82]
        Children were fond of their fathers, especially the
girls who depended on them for their future marriage. It
seems natural for a girl to be close to her father for
protection and to resent the competition with her mother
for his attention and love. In times of crisis, she is often first
to be there for him. Antigone was the eyes of her father
Oedipus after he blinded himself in shame for his
incestuous marriage. On the other hand, Evadne opted to
die with her husband rather than live to continue supporting
her father, Iphis, in old age. Nevertheless, In his

---

[80] Homer, *Iliad*, 9, 449-454: Loeb 170, 426.
[81] Euripides, *Iphigenia at Aulis*, 1207-1208: Loeb 495, 206.
[82] Sophocles, *Electra*, 579 ff.: Loeb 20, 216 ff.

disappointment, he remembered the loving care she gave him:

> She who always used to draw my cheek to her lips and hold my head in her hands, Nothing is sweeter to an aged father than a daughter. Sons are more spirited but not as endearing. [83]

Regardless of the children's preference, there is no doubt that both parents loved their children very dearly and were well compensated in return by their children. This love created a bond so strong between parents and children that, when pushed to extreme, they were identified as Freudian complexes with Greek names: the Oedipus complex and its analogue, the Electra complex, to signify the love of a child for the parent of the opposite sex.

Homer wrote that, after the Trojan leader Hector was killed on the battlefield, his dear wife Andromache reminisced about their son,

> Astyanax, who once on his father's knees ate only marrow and the rich fat of sheep; and when sleep came on him and he ceased from his childish play, then would he slumber in a bed in the arms of his nurse, in his soft bed, his heart filled with good things. [84]

One of the most endearing pages of Homer's *Iliad* is dedicated to the farewell the same Hector gave his dear wife Andromache and his infant son Astyanax, before his anticipated death on the battlefield. Here, the tender traits of love glisten from the page as a reflection of Hector's warm relationship with his wife and infant son. This page must be read in its entirety in order to understand how tender was his affection for them when he found them at the Scaean gates of the city, on his way to the battlefield:

> There came running to meet him, his wife ... and with her came a handmaid holding to her bosom the tender boy, a mere babe, the well-loved son of

---

[83] Euripides, *Suppliant Women*, 1099-1103: Loeb 9, 124.
[84] *Iliad*, 22, 500-504: Loeb 171, 488.

Hector, like a fair star. Him Hector was used to call Scamandrius, but other men Astyanax, for only Hector guarded Ilios. Then Hector smiled as he glanced at his boy in silence, but Andromache came close to his side weeping, and clasped his hand and spoke to him, saying: "Ah, my husband, this might of yours will be your doom, and you have no pity for your infant child or for unfortunate me, who soon will be your widow; for soon will the Achaeans all set on you and slay you. But for me it would be better to go down to the grave if I lose you, for never more will any comfort be mine, when you have met your fate, but only woes. [85]

Hector explained that the pain of leaving his wife, perhaps destined to become the slave and concubine of an Achaean lord, and his son, so young and vulnerable, cannot keep him away from his duty as a Trojan warrior. The emotions had reached the highest point when a scene broke the tension, unexpectedly and yet so revealing of this heartbreaking moment of a father with his child.

Glorious Hector stretched out his arms to his boy, but back into the bosom of his fair-belted nurse shrank the child crying, frightened at the sight of his dear father, and seized with fear of the bronze and the crest of horse-hair, as he caught sight of it waving terribly from the top of the helmet. Aloud then laughed his dear father and queenly mother; and immediately glorious Hector took the helmet from his head and laid it all gleaming on the ground. And he kissed his dear son and fondled him in his arms, and spoke in prayer to Zeus and the other gods. [86]

Hector prayed that posterity will say of his son that he was far better than his father. So saying, he placed his child in his dear wife's arms, and she took him to her fragrant bosom, smiling through her tears. [87] Then, Hector caressed his dear wife fondly, comforted and directed her

---

[85] Homer, *Iliad*, 6, 394-411: Loeb 170, 304.
[86] *Ibid.*, 6, 466-475: Loeb 170, 308.
[87] *Ibid.*, 6, 482-484: Loeb 170, 308.

gently. As she left to return to the house, she was "often turning back, and shedding large tears." [88] He turned around and left for battle.

No poet could have ever described a scene with such touching details without having experienced it in real life, like many other fathers in the history of our world.

An observation which applies in this case and in all other cases of relationship between a father and his children, a young father can usually be more effective in rearing his children than an older one. Euripides wrote:

> And now I advise all younger men not to delay until old age and be leisurely in fathering children. ... For rearing children is really good, and a son who shares his youth with a young father is a pleasing thing. [89]

The man who was the father was also a husband whose responsibilities included not only to contribute to the education of his children but also to supervise his wife on her handling of his children. Most mothers needed little advice about the rearing of their children but some may have had faults that needed corrections. A good measure of collaboration was required between husband and wife. If it did not exist and the wife was incorrigible, a more drastic action, like a divorce, may have had to be taken. Such an important decision was never taken lightly and, in all cases, involved the consideration of the children's welfare and the connections inside and outside the home. [90] A man alone being worthy of raising good children could hardly succeed in a culture where the mother had a predominant role inside the home [91] and a man being a single parent was impossible in a dichotomous culture where the man's role was primarily outside the home.

Incest

Mothers and fathers were the closest relatives of their children, yet a distance between them was never crossed without shame and impunity. Incest was absolutely

---

[88] *Iliad*, 6, 496: Loeb 170, 310.
[89] *Fr., Danae*, 317: Loeb 405, 328.
[90] Euripides, *Fr., Melanippe Wise*, 497: Loeb 504, 604.
[91] Id., *Fr., Meleager*, 520: Loeb 504, 622.

unacceptable. Being prohibited by nature and custom, it was not an issue for a special prohibition by law. [92] In his *Memorabilia*, Xenophon expressed this norm of conduct that "parents shall not have sexual intercourse with their children nor children with their parents." [93]

Every foul relation between mother and son of any age was considered repulsive. This made for the anguish of Oedipus when he faced the truth of his marriage to his mother, Jocasta, whose shame prompted to commit suicide. The case of Oedipus' marriage with his mother Jocasta made this point emphatically clear because, although it was totally innocent, it brought extreme shame on both of them: "After she had borne me she brought forth children for me to my shame!" [94]

In 428 BCE, Euripides told the story of Hippolytus who could not contain his anger when he heard of the infatuation his stepmother Phaedra had for him. He was horrified that any woman would so blatantly desire a man, especially one in her family. Why has Zeus created women as a snare for men! Why is there no other way of having a family! His anguish was so real, his language almost delirious. He could not contain his anger when he heard that his stepmother Phaedra had fallen in love with him, especially because it was without his advances or consent. He came out of the palace spilling his feelings of horror that any woman, and more so his father's wife, would think of blatantly propositioning her stepson. To the nurse who pleaded for his understanding, he replied:

> O Zeus, why have you settled women, this bane to cheat mankind, in the light of the sun? If you wished to propagate the human race, it was not from women that you should have provided this. Rather, men should put down in the temples either bronze or iron or a mass of gold and buy offspring, each for a price appropriate to his means, and then dwell in houses free from the female sex. [95]

---

[92] Euripides, *Andromache*, 173-177: Loeb 484, 288.
[93] *Memorabilia*, 4, 4, 21: Loeb 168, 320; also, Plato, *Republic*, 5, 461C: Loeb 237, 466.
[94] Sophocles, *Oedipus at Colonus*, 982-984: Loeb 21, 524.
[95] Euripides, *Hippolytus*, 616-624: Loeb 484, 184.

Such sexual desire, let alone sexual intercourse, between a wife and her stepson was so repugnant to the Athenian sense of morality and decorum, and surely men's pride also, that Euripides was forced to delete from his original version of *Hippolytus* the passage in which Phaedra directly propositioned her stepson. [96]

In the present situation of incest in the heart, the sensitivity of the public took into account the fear of the father's anger. The characters on stage reflected the audience's feelings: Phaedra lied to cover up the affair when she wrote her final words on a tablet [97] and Hippolytus took exile to forget it. Phaedra's duplicity had led to his banishment and death.

Also, writers of the fourth century, more permissive about sexual relations, expressed their minds clearly on this subject, for example Plato who stated that incest was "by no means holy, but hated of God, and most shamefully shameful" [98] and Aristotle who described it as unseemly and improper. [99] They were in this matter more exacting than the Egyptians and other barbarian peoples of the East. For example, the Egyptian pharaoh Akhenaten of the fourteenth century BCE had children by three of his daughters. Also the other pharaohs, including the Macedonian Greeks who ruled over Egypt after Alexander's conquest, did freely entertain marriages between brothers and sisters. The Greeks in their homeland considered this behavior barbarian.

If true, strange things happened even among the Ancient Greeks, for example in the family of Pelops, father of Atreus and Thyestes. The latter impregnated his daughter Pelopia who became the wife of her uncle Atreus after he killed his first wife Aërope, the mother of Agamemnon and Menelaus. This Pelopia became the mother of Aegisthus, thought to be the biological son of Atreus when he was of Thyestes and became the lover of Clytemnestra in the absence of her husband Agamemnon, his half-cousin.

At the end of his life, Heracles forced upon his son another kind of union repugnant to the Greeks. Burned to the core, his body was in excruciating pain and his mind

---

[96] See T.B.L. Webster, *Tragedies of Euripides*, 64 ff.
[97] Euripides, *Hippolytus*, 856 ff.: Loeb 484, 206-209.
[98] *Laws*, 8, 838C: Loeb 192, 156.
[99] *Politics*, 2, 4, 1262b, 29-30: Loeb 264, 82.

obviously deranged when he requested his son Hyllus to marry Iole, the concubine he had chosen for himself:

> Make her your wife and do not disobey me; and let no other man but you take her, who has lain by my side, but make this marriage yourself! [100]

Hyllus yielded to his father's request, like Phoenix did to his mother's who wanted to spite her husband Amyntor for keeping a concubine with her in his bed: both did an impious act. [101] Hyllus thus continued the Heraclean bloodline but Phoenix was less fortunate when he was forced into exile. In the Greek mentality, the forbidden limits of incest extended beyond the parents to the stepparents and the concubines.

Among all the peoples in their world, the Athenian Greeks were unique and supreme for their mental acumen and productivity and for their moral sense of justice and mutual respect, in a culture still wanting in its treatment of women, as it is still today in many parts of our much larger world.

Philosophy of Education

The philosophers of the fourth century were more explicit about certain aspects of the education of children and, for this reason, deserve a closer attention.

Plato (427-357 BCE) dealt with the education and nurture of children in Book 7 of his Dialogue entitled *Laws*, dated among the last of his writings. It is a subject, he warned, "treated more suitably by way of precept and exhortation than by legislation." [102]

At the age of six, the boys were separated from the girls. [103] The boys went to teachers for learning gymnastic and music -- the kind of music that is "noble and of a manly tendency", to mean loud and boisterous, while girls' music was said to be inclined "rather to decorum and sedateness." [104] Girls learned gymnastic also from their own female

---

[100] Sophocles, *Women of Trachis*, 1224-1227: Loeb 21, 244.
[101] Homer, *Iliad*, 9, 448-456: Loeb 170, 426.
[102] Plato, Laws, 7, 788A: Loeb 192, 2.
[103] Ibid., 7, 794C: Loeb 192, 22.
[104] Ibid., 7, 802E: Loeb 192, 52.

instructors in the gymnasium open to both boys and girls, separately. Plato stated: "I will unhesitatingly affirm that neither riding nor gymnastics, which are proper for men, are improper for women." [105]

Plato knew this for a fact because the practice took place elsewhere, for example near the Black Sea. So he did not agree with the custom in Athens to refuse the women the privilege to be trained in these skills, thus reducing the strength of the State to a half. Therefore, "the female sex must share with the male, to the greatest extent possible, both in education and in all else." [106]

Plato was utterly avant-garde in his views when he declared:

> In regard both to military operations and to freedom of poetic speech I state that the same rules shall apply equally to both men and women. [107]

When the people of Athens were called en masse to attend games and sacrificial feasts, women and their children were included. [108] Concerning their participation in the games, Plato explained that women should be allowed to participate in the equestrian contests, except those that require fighting with armor, and in other games, only "up to the age of marriage" and if from previous training they have acquired the habit and are strong enough and like to take part. [109] He boldly recommended:

> In the case of females, we shall ordain races of a furlong, a quarter-mile, a half-mile, and a three-quarters for girls under the age of puberty, who shall be stripped, and shall race on the course itself; and girls over thirteen shall continue to take part until married, up to the age of twenty at most, or at least eighteen; but these, when they come forward and compete in these races, must be clad in decent apparel. [110]

---

[105] *Laws*, 7, 804E: Loeb 192, 58.
[106] *Ibid.*, 7, 805C: Loeb 192, 60; also, 806C; Loeb 192, 62.
[107] *Ibid.*, 8, 829E: Loeb 192, 128.
[108] *Ibid.*, 8, 829B: Loeb 192, 128.
[109] *Ibid.*, 8, 834A & D: Loeb 192, 142 &145.
[110] *Ibid.*, 8, 833C-D: Loeb 192, 140-143.

Judges will determine, he added, who was victorious and who was defeated among these women.

In spite of Plato's advocacy for equal education of girls and boys, it did not seem to carry over to the reality of life in Athens. In Sparta, only the unmarried girls shared with the boys the education in gymnastic and music; the married women were busying themselves with the household duties. Plato's real motive for wanting women to share in the same education as men was not for any appreciation of the female character and ability. Women's liberation for purely humanitarian reasons never entered his mind. He revealed his true motive when he scolded the legislator to be whole-hearted about

> letting the female sex indulge in luxury and expenses and disorderly ways of life, while supervising the male sex; for thus he is bequeathing to the State the half only, instead of the whole, of a life of complete prosperity. [111]

In Plato's mind, the contribution of women to the welfare of the State was only a matter of efficiency, not one of human rights. The details of his prescriptions concerning the education of girls substantiate this assertion. First, "both girls and boys must learn both dancing and gymnastics", the girls under mistresses. [112] It is worthy to note at this point that military exercises fell under gymnastics. Plato explained that for these military exercises under public instructors

> Their pupils should be not only the boys and men in the State, but also the girls and women who understand all these matters – being practised in military drill and fighting while still girls and, when grown to womanhood, taking part in evolutions and rank-forming and the piling and shouldering of arms. [113]

Such training would serve at least two purposes: either the women could assist in the orderly evacuation of the city in case of a foreign invasion or even "do as do the

---

[111] *Laws*, 7, 806C: Loeb 192, 62.
[112] *Ibid.*, 7, 813B: Loeb 192, 84.
[113] *Ibid.*, 7, 813E: Loeb 192, 86.

mother-birds, which fight the strongest beasts in defence of their broods." [114]

Plato acknowledged, however, that such an education that places boys and girls in close proximity at sacrifices, feasts and dances may create problems he called wantonness (*hubris*), [115] to mean the condition in which the passions are not yet under control in the youths. He asked:

> How will the young abstain from those desires which frequently plunge many into ruin, -- all those desires from which reason, in its endeavour to be law, enjoins abstinence?

His answer was:

> That the laws previously ordained serve to repress the majority of desires is not surprising; thus, for example, the proscription of excessive wealth is of no small benefit for promoting temperance, and the whole of our education-system contains laws useful for the same purpose; in addition to this, there is the watchful eye of the magistrates, trained to fix its gaze always on this point and to keep constant watch on the young people. These means, then, are sufficient (so far as any human means suffice) to deal with the other desires. [116]

These desires are the amorous passions between boys and girls, men and women, and of both sexes for one of the same sex. Any law, even one that is based on nature, is not enough to prevent the reprehensible practices caused by such passions. Plato believed that the understanding of what friendship is about, namely soul for soul (*philia*) rather than body for body (*erôs*), and acceptance of its benefits will be most helpful. Nevertheless, it is indeed difficult to guard against the perils of letting the two sexes associate freely, albeit in public places. [117]

The philosopher Aristotle's approach to the subject of education was systematic and consistent with the

---

[114] *Laws*, 7, 814B: Loeb 192, 88.
[115] *Ibid.*, 8, 835E: Loeb 192, 148.
[116] *Ibid.*, 8, 835E-836A: Loeb 192, 148.
[117] *Ibid.*, 8, 836-837: Loeb 192, 148-155.

structure of his general philosophy. A simile could be used to illustrate it: like water impregnates clay, lime and gravel, and makes them boil and turns the whole into concrete, so also his fundamental theory of change and the four causes impregnates every part of his system, makes them coalesce and develop into an articulate view of the world as he knew it. The four causes – formal, material, efficient and final -- direct and produce the passage from potentiality to actuality that is education.

Aristotle first agreed that the education of boys and girls should be conducted in the same manner. The path to skill and virtue is the same for both. All children had in their bodies and souls (material and formal causes) the potential to develop certain skills and virtues. Ancient writers had attributed to nature such traits as courage to men and fear to women. But some men are cowards and some women without fear. Some predispositions favored one or the other, for example the difference in physical strength but, as he argued against most writers of the past, it is not in the nature of man to be courageous and of woman to be fearful. In both there is a potentiality that can be actualized either way by education.

The tool of education is habituation in the exercise of skills as well as virtues. A girl can learn weaving and dancing by practicing and acquiring the habit; she can also learn to be virtuous, for example brave and just, by repeating such virtuous actions that create the habit. He declared:

> The virtues therefore are engendered in us neither by nature nor yet in violation of nature; nature gives us the capacity to receive them, and this capacity is brought to maturity by habit. ... we acquire [virtues] by first having actually practiced them, just as we do the arts. We learn an art or craft by doing the things that we shall have to do when we have learnt it: for instance, men become builders by building houses, harpers by playing on the harp. Similarly we become just by doing just acts, temperate by doing temperate acts, brave by doing brave acts. [118]

---

[118] *Nicomachean Ethics*, 2, 1103a, 24-1103b, 4: Loeb 73, 70-73.

On the one hand, inasmuch as the goal (final cause) pursued in every human activity is the acquisition of pleasure and the avoidance of pain, and, on the other hand, the mind has the potentiality for either good or bad, the purpose of education is to make the good pleasurable. This is the role of the educator (efficient cause). He explained:

> For pleasure is thought to be especially congenial to mankind; and this is why pleasure and pain are employed in the education of the young, as means whereby to steer their course. [119]

By using pleasure as a goal (final cause), children can learn how to be brave, truthful, just and, in general, virtuous, and can acquire the habit of behaving accordingly. So it is also with the skills, like weaving and dancing. The word *aretê* meant excellence applied to both virtue and skills as it consists of doing a certain action well, repeatedly and consistently, according to its intent. Aristotle recognized in humans not only the ability but also the freedom to choose consistently the right action. He explained further:

> Virtue then is a settled disposition of the mind determining the choice of actions and emotions, consisting essentially in the observance of the mean relative to us, this being determined by principle, that is, as the prudent man would determine it. And it is a mean state between two vices, one of excess and one of defect. [120]

For example, the mean of courage lies between being brash and coward. Aristotle explained, however, that certain actions are not good by applying a mean, but are intrinsically bad, regardless of the circumstances and degrees, like adultery - sexual intercourse between a man and an Athenian married woman other than his wife -- which has no middle between two extremes for such a man.

Children ought to acquire the right habits through education and, for this reason, parents and other educators

---

[119] *Nicomachean Ethics*, 10, 1, 1172a, 20-22: Loeb 73, 576.
[120] *Ibid.*, 2, 6, 1106b, 36-1107a, 3: Loeb 73, 94.

of boys and girls should be intent on teaching them and not frown on it. Aristotle said it well with a twist of humor:

> It is therefore not of small moment whether we are trained from childhood in one set of habits or another, on the contrary it is of very great, or rather of supreme, importance. [121]

In a passage of his *Rhetoric*, Aristotle recognized again that happiness is the goal of every human life.

> Men [including women], individually and in common, nearly all have some aim, in the attainment of which they choose or avoid certain things, This aim, briefly stated, is happiness and its component parts. [122]

When it came to listing the component parts of happiness, Aristotle became long-winded and yet probably incomplete. Everyone has a notion of what happiness is for himself or herself and when he or she has it or not. Besides, what may constitute happiness for one individual may not be included at all on another's list. The only truth that is sure is that the purpose of education should be the happiness of the educated person. About women, he stated:

> The bodily excellences are beauty and stature, their moral excellences self-control and industrious habits, Free from servility. [123]

In conclusion, according to Aristotle, although the process and the ultimate goal of education as well as the need to provide it are equally important for girls and boys, every emphasis on the respective functions of women and men at home and in society is also very important. Boys and girls must learn to be good but not in the same way, since for the boys it is to become rulers and the girls subjects in the household and in the city. [124] For example, quoting in part Sophocles' *Ajax*, [125] "silence gives grace to

---

[121] *Nicomachean Ethics*, 2, 1, 1103b, 23-25: Loeb 73, 74.
[122] *Rhetoric*, 1, 5, 1360b, 1: Loeb 193, 46.
[123] *Ibid.*, 1, 5, 1331a, 6: Loeb 193, 50.
[124] *Politics*, 1, 1260a, 6 ff.: Loeb 264, 62.
[125] *Ajax*, 293: Loeb 20, 58.

woman – though that is not the case likewise with a man."
[126]

One can imagine the different treatment mothers ought to give their sons and daughters and the relationship they ought to nurture with them. In this respect, the writers of the fourth century, especially Aristotle, conveyed in the clearest terms how important the educational role of a mother was in the family and the city.

*

*

*

[126] Aristotle, *Politics*, 1, 5, 1289a, 31-32: Loeb 264, 64.

CHAPTER SEVEN

UNMARRIED WOMEN

If not legally married to and living with an Athenian husband, the Athenian woman could live an unmarried life in five different manners: first, as spinster, remaining without a husband for a lifetime; second, as widow, a wife whose husband is deceased; third, as divorcée, a wife divorced from her husband; fourth, as grass widow, a wife separated from her husband but not divorced and, fifth, as eloper, a wife who left her husband to marry another man. An Athenian woman could be a partner in adultery or fornication but never a concubine or a prostitute, as a general rule.

Spinster

Women who never married annoyed their guardians and disappointed their families. For theses reasons, they disappeared and soon died without mention. Nothing is known of them because nothing worthy could be said about them, since the only worth of women in the Athenian culture was in the procreation of children for the family and the state. Is it not, however, an anomaly in the Athenian men's mind that they retained Athena for their mythological model although she turned away the advances of god Hephaestus in order to preserve her virginity? [1] Surely, they liked her for her virility, not her virginity.

In spite of her marriage at the time of death, Antigone remains for all ages the model of a generous and courageous spinster. Her sister Ismene also lived an unmarried life and cared for her father, yet in a more discreet and distant way. Born of their father Oedipus and his mother Jocasta they were by birth implicated in a shameful union. Their mother committed suicide and their

---

[1] Euripides, *Fr.*, Unidentified Play, 925: Loeb 506, 516.

father not only blinded himself but sought exile as a rejected man. Then, for the years that her miserable father lived, Antigone dedicated her own life to accompanying him, supporting him in all his physical needs and with all the tender love a daughter can provide. She traveled with him probably with many zigzags from Thebes, in Boeotia, to Colonus, near Athens, where he died a mysterious death. Later, being left alone with her sister Ismene, she adopted the noble cause of a decent burial for her brother Polynices and sacrificed her life for it. Sentenced to die by King Creon of Thebes, although promised by him to marry his son Haemon, the couple died a suicidal death in a cave, she by hanging and he by the sword.

The two phases in the life of Antigone, first as care giver and second as activist, show that she remained in character throughout her life: strong, not in physical strength but in mental fortitude, devoted to family with love for everyone, yet independent in her thinking about everyone. In the first phase when she chose to remain a spinster and a virgin in order to dedicate all her time and energy to care for her father Oedipus, her life was mostly private and, for this reason, will be considered in this chapter. The second phase, when she moved to the public stage as an activist confronting king Creon of Thebes in her defense of the right to a decent burial for her brother Polynices, will be considered later in chapter ten.

Ismene also lived the life of a spinster and virgin, near her sister and, like her, remaining in character, different from her as she was the quiet one, dedicated to help her father but unwilling to share later the public fight for a decent burial of their brother. For this reason, she never received from history the same fame bestowed on her sister Antigone.

As it was the case in the life of Helen of Sparta, two versions of the life of Oedipus appeared in Antiquity. One version, based on Homer's report of the late eight century, kept Oedipus as king of Thebes after the discovery of his incestuous marriage, and placed his death and burial there. [2] The second version surfaced later in the fifth century, first in 410 BCE when Euripides briefly alluded to his exile [3] and

---

[2] *Iliad*, 23, 679: Loeb 171, 542 & *Odyssey*, 11, 271-280: Loeb 104, 420.

[3] *Phoenician Women*, 1758-1763: Loeb 11, 394.

second, two years later, when Sophocles produced a full-blown story of his exile and death in one of his best plays, *Oedipus at Colonus*. This last version may be a folktale. Nevertheless, because it was told to an Athenian audience in terms that would resonate with such an audience, not only did it prevail in popularity down the ages, but it also revealed an aspect, probably real in some cases, in which the life of a spinster was spent caring for a parent. This is the version presented in the following pages. [4]

Accompanied by his daughter Antigone, the blind king Oedipus traveled on foot in his exile from Thebes to Colonus, a present suburb of Athens, where he was seeking refuge and an exchange of mutual protection with king Theseus of Athens. Oedipus recognized that Antigone shared with him in the pain of his exile:

> The one has wandered, poor creature, with me, ever since she seized to be cared for as a child and attained her strength, guiding an aged man. Straying often through the wild jungle without food or footwear, and vexed often by the rain and by the scorching sun, the unhappy one gives second place to her home comforts, if her father can be cared for. [5]

At Colonus, Antigone helped her father sit and rest on a rock and took hold of him and led him when he had to move, as she suggested, "leaning your aged body upon my loving arm." [6] She warned him about the arrival of a peasant and later of elders; also, when they were ready to leave, she warned him again about the arrival of her sister, Ismene, after her arduous search for the place where they were. Oedipus acknowledged the good services of this younger daughter as faithful guardian at the beginning of his exile and now as news deliverer about the war taking place in Thebes. [7]

When Oedipus was asked to perform the rite of purification to the Eumenides, Ismene volunteered to do it

---

[4] For a review of the entire play, see the author's book *Heracles and Oedipus in Greek Classical Drama*.

[5] Sophocles, *Oedipus at Colonus*, 345-352: Loeb 21, 452.

[6] *Ibid.*, 200: Loeb 21, 434.

[7] *Ibid.*, 324 ff.: Loeb 21, 448 ff.

in his stead. [8] While she was away, Antigone again warned her father of the arrival of Creon of Thebes with an escort. [9] When, after capturing Ismene, he attempted to take Antigone away from Oedipus, knowing full well how much she was needed for his survival, she resisted but did not have the strength and was captured also. But "the sufferings of the girls who have endured grievous things, and have had grievous treatment from their kindred, will soon abate" [10] when king Theseus of Athens and his retainers brought them back by force to their desperate and now overjoyed father:

> I have what is dearest to me, and now I shall not be entirely miserable if I died when you two stand by me! Grow one with your father, daughter, each of you pressing to a side of me, and give repose to one who was made desolate by that unhappy wandering! [11]

Again, Antigone announced the arrival of her brother Polynices to her suspicious father who, after hearing his son's plea for support, cursed him for planning to attack his native city of Thebes. Antigone joined her father trying to dissuade her brother, but to no avail. "Then woe is me indeed," she cried, "if I am to be deprived of you!" [12] She will fight later and die defending his right to a decent burial.

For the moment, Oedipus was ready to respond to the summons of Zeus and go to his death. Although blind, he took the lead for his daughters and, further on the path near a verdant hill, he asked them to fetch the water for a bath and libation. Then hearing Zeus' thunder, they all shuddered. "Falling by their father's knees, they wept, and did not cease to beat their breasts and to cry out at length." But the frail Oedipus brought them to their feet, embraced them and said to them:

> It was hard, I know, my daughter; but a single word dissolves all these hardships. For from none did you

---

[8] Sophocles, *Oedipus at Colonus*, 503-504: Loeb 21, 468.
[9] *Ibid.*, 722-723: Loeb 21, 496.
[10] *Ibid.*, 1076-1079: Loeb 21, 530-533.
[11] *Ibid.*, 1110-1114: Loeb 21, 534-537.
[12] *Ibid.*, 1443: Loeb 21, 564.

have love more than from this man, without whom you will now spend the remainder of your lives. [13]

Before going to his mysterious death, Oedipus dismissed his daughters and called upon king Theseus of Athens alone to accompany him. He was the only one who witnessed how this once impetuous, now peaceful old king faded away, without a burial. Antigone, who believed so strongly in providing a decent burial, not only as an obligation to the deceased but also as a closing ritual for the loved ones left behind, was now left with this additional grief for the rest of her life. She lamented:

> He died in the foreign land as he desired; and he occupies a bed shady for ever, nor did he fail to leave behind mourning with tears. For this eye of mine, Father, laments for you with weeping, nor do I know how I can make away with such great grief, unhappy one! Alas, you wished to die in a foreign land, but you died thus, far from me! [14]

The only closing of this present phase in Antigone"s life was now in wishing to join her father in death for herself, but her wish was not granted and she resigned herself to return to Thebes with her sister Ismene and to "prevent the slaughter that is coming to our brothers", [15] Eteocles and Polynices.

Widow

The household (*oikos*), created on wedding day, could end by the death of one of the partners. If the wife died first, the husband was free and, if he had young children, was bound to make either temporary arrangements for their care until a new wife would restore his family or their permanent adoption in the family of one of his close relatives or friends. If the husband died first, the wife and her young children returned under the tutelage of her original guardian or his substitute, except when she had a mature son capable of providing for them. If neither her

---

[13] Sophocles, *Oedipus at Colonus*, 1606-1619: Loeb 21, 580.
[14] *Ibid.*, 1705-1714: Loeb 21, 588.
[15] *Ibid.*, 1770-1772: Loeb 21, 598.

original guardian, usually her father, nor her son were available, then her guardianship devolved to the closest relative in the patrilineal line. In some cases, like that of the garland seller in Aristophanes' *Women at the Thesmophoria*, she had to provide for herself and her children, as she explained:

> My husband died in Cyprus, leaving me with five small children that I've had to struggle to feed by weaving garlands in the myrtle market. So until recently I managed to feed them only half badly. But now this guy [Euripides] who composes in the tragedy market has persuaded the men that gods don't exist, so my sales aren't even half what they were. ... I've got an order to plait garlands for a group of twenty men. [16]

In the winter following the first campaign of the Peloponnesian War, in 431/430 BCE, Pericles delivered the funeral oration in honor of the fallen soldiers. Addressing the widows, he used words of advice instead of sympathy, knowing how difficult it will be for their guardians to find new husbands for them. He declared:

> If I am to speak also of womanly virtues, referring to those of you who still will henceforth be in widowhood, I will sum up all in a brief admonition: Great is your glory if you fall not below the standard which nature has set for your sex, and great also is hers of whom there is least talk among men whether in praise or in blame. [17]

Such an exhortation was neither fair nor compassionate. How could a widow be given to a new husband if men never talked about her? How could she ever hope to have a husband and provider again if all her ambition was to be ignored? Perhaps the subliminal message of Pericles' exhortation included a warning: do not set your hopes too high, men are in short supply and many younger girls are coming of age, fend for yourselves and

---

[16] Aristophanes, *Women at the Thesmophoria*, 446-458: Loeb 179, 510-513.

[17] Thucydides, *Peloponnesian War*, 2, 45, 2: Loeb 108, 340.

accept widowhood if this is your fate in life. Furthermore, it should be noted that the Classical playwrights of Tragedy challenged the validity of Pericles' advice when they assigned so many speaking roles to women, especially widows, for example queen mother Atossa in Aeschylus' *The Persians*, Tecmessa in Sophocles' *Ajax*, Aethra and Evadne in *Suppliant Women*, by Euripides, and Hecuba and Andromache in the plays named after them, also by Euripides.

Before his death, the naturalized banker Pasio made two decisions affecting his wife as a widow: first, his elder son, Apollodorus, will become her guardian as well as the guardian of her other sons, Archippe and the younger Pasicles; second, his employee Phormio will become later her husband and thus replace his elder son as guardian. But, when the time came, this Phormio could not wait, so he dared marry her in the absence of Apollodorus. The son was so offended by it that he suggested that they already had been living in adultery while his father was still alive and that his brother Pasicles was the natural offspring of their affair. [18] He also instituted legal action to correct the advantage his mother showed in her inheritance in favor of her two sons by Phormio against the two sons she had had by Pasio. The court agreed to divide it equally among the four sons. [19]

Pregnant widows were also provided special protection by the state because they could produce a male descendant who would perpetuate the family and sustain the state with new male citizens. It was, nevertheless, in the interest of the state that the guardian seek a husband for each widow under his tutelage.

According to T.W. Gallant's calculations based on forensic speeches of the fourth century, thirty-five percent of the widows married again, the majority of them having either no children or only infants. Most widows who had grown-up children had passed the attractive age for a remarriage. So they spent their remaining years living with one of their children, preferably a son. [20]

---

[18] Demosthenes, *Against Stephanus I*, 45, 79 & 84: Loeb 155, 230 & 234.

[19] *Id.*, *For Phormio*, 36, 15, 32 & 38: Loeb 318, 332, 344 & 348-351.

[20] *Risks and Survival in Ancient Greece*, 26-27.

Divorcée

The household could end also by divorce, Then, the wife automatically returned to her original guardian. Divorces were rare and rarely happened because the wife was a pest and the husband a bully, but because of the couple's inability to have children, and this condition was also rare.

Menecles thought he was responsible for his childless marriage, so he returned his wife to her family before she would grow too old to remarry and bear children. [21] Also, after the birth of Ion, his mother Creusa could not have children with her husband Xuthus, so they sought the counsel of Apollo's oracle at Delphi. [22] In this case, short of a favorable solution, divorce would have been mandatory, especially because she was the only child of king Erechtheus of Athens, therefore the only descendant who could carry the dynastic line. King Aegeus of Athens had a similar problem of infertility. When he encountered Medea in Corinth, he was returning from Delphi where he had also sought Apollo's oracle that gave him a cryptic answer. [23]

A major responsibility of the committee of women overseeing the couples for the first ten years of their married life was to make sure that children would be born from their union. If none was born, although through no fault of their own, Plato's advice was to

> take counsel in common to decide what terms are advantageous for both parties, in conjunction with their kindred and the women-officials, and be divorced. [24]

Divorce was legally easy, but socially difficult in Ancient Athens. It required only the agreement between two guardians: the present husband and the original father or the new husband. Nevertheless, it sometimes left bitter feelings of failure, like the fifth-century orator Antiphon suggested. [25] The city did not intervene, yet could exert a

---

[21] Isaeus, *On the Estate of Menecles*, 2, 6-9: Loeb 202, 44.
[22] Euripides, *Ion*, 304: Loeb 10, 354.
[23] Id., *Medea*, 669ff: Loeb 12, 342.
[24] *Laws*, 6, 784B: Loeb 187, 496-499.
[25] *Fr.*, 49: H.P. Foley, *Female Acts in Greek Tragedy*, 80.

considerable influence on the decision. When the purpose was to produce citizens for the city, all other considerations were ignored. The head of the original family in which the wife was born and raised could reclaim her, if she were the only one capable of producing an heir-citizen.

Furthermore, if the husband was tied to his wife's dowry as an additional asset, he could hardly separate himself from her by divorcing her. On the other hand, a wife could initiate a divorce if her husband did not do it, but the procedure was awkward, inasmuch as she had to appear in person with the head of her original family and register her claim with the leader (archôn) of the city. Such an undertaking was extremely rare. Hipparete is the only wife we know who attempted to do it. But she was stopped by her husband, Alcibiades, and forcibly carried back home, which shows that the husband still controlled his wife's private and public activities. [26] The loss of Hipparete's dowry -- a total of twenty talents, an enormous sum for the time -- was more than Alcibiades could part with in order to continue his extravagant life style. Hipparete died a short time later, while he was gone to Ephesus, in Asia Minor. The thought of a suicide is not too far-fetched a speculation.

If only they were free from the bedroom competition that plagued Hipparete's married life, most Greek wives were happy to have children, manage the household and stay away from the affairs of state. They interfered with their husband's business or assumed some of his responsibilities only in times of crisis, as was the case during the Trojan War and the Peloponnesian War.

Euripides complained about the rarity of divorces in Ancient Athens:

> Some men do not get rid of a woman when they find she is bad, either considering their children or for the sake of a family connection; then her wrongdoing overflows to many others and progresses, so their virtue vanishes entirely. [27]

---

[26] Plutarch, *Parallel Lives, Alcibiades*, 8, 3-4: Loeb 80, 20.
[27] *Fr.*, *Melanippe Wise*, 497: Loeb 504, 604.

Grass Widow

In 411 BCE, Aristophanes used Lysistrata as the voice shouting the plight of women when husbands and sons were away at war and many not returning home.

> We bear more than our fair share, in the first place by giving birth to sons and sending them off to the army. ... Then, when we ought to be having fun and enjoying our bloom of youth, we sleep alone because of the campaigns. ... But a woman's prime is brief; if she doesn't seize it, no one wants to marry her, and she sits at home looking for good omens. [28]

Not only were the husbands and sons sacrificed to the Peloponnesian War—the estimate is about 12,000 -- but the city of Athens was in ruin. The countryside of Attica had been so completely devastated -- land fallowed, trees uprooted and mines closed -- that the local production became more specialized and insufficient to sustain the population. When the Spartan troops invaded Attica in 413,

> more than twenty thousand slaves had already deserted, a large portion of these being artisans, and all their small cattle and beasts of burden were lost. [29]

Most wives were left alone with their children in utter misery. This desperate situation prompted the few families of farmers left behind and the families living in the countryside without a breadwinner to flock to the city. In the last ten years of the war until the turn of the century, starvation was everywhere. The voices of widows and mothers were crying for relief and pressuring their men to alleviate the needs of their domestic life. The transplanted women from the countryside to the city were prepared by the dire circumstances of extreme poverty to follow their habits of moving about quite freely for survival. Their behavior, no doubt, tended to liberalize the behavior of the city-women and thus created a different network of communications in Athens. Some relief came only in 393,

[28] *Lysistrata*, 588-597: Loeb 179, 350.
[29] Thucydides, *Peloponnesian War*, 7, 27, 5: Loeb 169, 48.

some twenty years later, after the Athenians rebuilt the Long Walls between Athens and Piraeus, thus assuring the import of grain.

The plight inflicted on the survivors of the war led them to seek some measure of happiness in pleasures that affected the life of women. For example, the Cynic school of thought created by Antisthenes (c. 444-365 BCE) and popularized by Diogenes (412?-323 BCE) involved women as men's sexual pleasure. The Cynics professed to share women without any restriction from marriage or social modesty. It contributed to the attitude, if not the reality, of a freer life style beginning to grow in the last years of the fifth century BCE.

The common sexual access to women, ridiculed by Aristophanes who produced in 392 his comedy *Assembly-women* in which he ridiculed the theory of sexual communism and in 388 another comedy, *Wealth*, in which he analyzed the broader concept of communism and its dire consequences for women as one object of men's sharing in common. It is worthy of note, however, that the shared women in these plays were not Athenian women but alien women, with loose morals to boot.

In about 348 in his *Law* and 367 in his *Republic*, the philosopher Plato gave prestige to the theory of common sharing of women for sex and procreation and thus provided one more indication of the views men entertained about women and of the freedom of both sexes from the constraints of bondage. The fact that such ideas started being debated in Athens at the turn of the century was a symptom not only of the uncertainties of the time, after the lengthy and devastating Peloponnesian War, but also of the expectation men had about choosing a bride, as previously discussed in Chapter Two, and about their grass widows while they were away from home for long periods of time.

The fact that such a theory was debated is enough evidence of a change in men's mood and attitude toward women. The sensuality brought to the stage with the discussion of mores was probably no more than a reflection of the new, more openly permissive manners in salons and symposia. Plato acknowledged Aristophanes' attendance at a symposium on love. [30] They were friends in spite of some

---

[30] *Symposium*, 185C ff.: Loeb 166, 122 ff.

difference in age, Aristophanes being Plato's elder by about twenty years.

The more sedate society of Athens in the fifth century, after the Persian War (479 BCE) and before the Peloponnesian War (431 BCE) would not have allowed such libertine activities. As a society more controlled by laws, it would not have also witnessed a behavior like the one of Penelope in Ithaca. In his *Odyssey* of about 700 BCE, Homer represented Penelope, the wife of Odysseus, as the paragon of women in Ancient Greece.

> She kept before her the image of Odysseus, her wedded husband, therefore the fame of her excellence shall never perish, but the immortals shall make among men on earth a song full of delight in honor of her, constant Penelope. [31]

Penelope's story was encrusted in the minds of all women and men of Athens since it was read to them, young and old, every four years at the festival of *Panathenaea*. In 411 BCE, Aristophanes praised her as "a woman noted for her virtue." [32]

Married to Odysseus, Icarius' daughter Penelope bore him a son, Telemachus. Then, her husband left for the protracted Trojan War: ten years besieging the city of Troy and nearly ten more years returning home, tossed by the winds and threatened by strange women. Calypso offered him sensual pleasure, [33] Circe made him a passionate lover, [34] Nausicaa provided him with romance; [35] the Sirens enchanted him with their song. [36] All these years, Penelope stayed home, managing the household, as she had been given charge by her husband when he left for the war, [37] and raising their son to adulthood, telling him of his father in such glowing terms that prompted him to travel from home on the island of Ithaca, off northwest Greece, to Sparta, in southern Peloponnesus, in search of information about him.

---

[31] Homer, *Odyssey*, 24, 195-198: Loeb 105, 426.
[32] *Women at the Thesmophoria*, 547-548: Loeb 179, 520.
[33] Homer, *Odyssey*, 5, 192 ff. & 9, 29-30: Loeb 104, 196 & 318.
[34] *Ibid.*, 9, 31-32 & 10, 467-472: Loeb 104, 318 & 392.
[35] *Ibid.*, 6, 127 ff.: Loeb 104, 228 ff.
[36] *Ibid.*, 12, 41 ff.: Loeb 104, 450 ff.
[37] *Ibid.*, 18, 266: Loeb 105, 220.

[38] While Odysseus was yielding to female seductions, she was resisting the advances of many suitors who wanted to marry her. She was the opposite of Clytemnestra who took a lover, Aegisthus, while her husband, Agamemnon, was engaged in this faraway war alongside Odysseus.

Penelope was tested and found to be a diamond of the first water. When her son, Telemachus, was growing up, she considered no other option for herself but being a good mother and manager of the palace. One day, when the bard Phemius was singing downstairs the sad tale of "the woeful return from Troy", she heard his wonderful song from her upper chamber. She could not resist coming down, yet she did it with great caution against every misinterpretation by the suitors who were in attendance.

> She went down the high stairway from her chamber, not alone, for two handmaids attended her. Now when the fair lady had come to the suitors, she stood by the doorpost of the well-built hall, holding before her face her shining veil; and a faithful handmaid stood on either side of her. Then, the tears filled her eyes. [39]

When she asked the bard to sing of other feats of gods and heroes, she was signifying to every one of the suitors present how much her heart was grieving for the loss of her husband: "so dear a face do I always remember with longing, my husband's, whose fame is wide through Hellas and mid-Argos." [40]

Penelope knew that her place as a woman was inside the palace. Still, she was its sole manager in her husband's absence and the mother of a son who was growing up into adulthood. She accepted his acid words, insulting and cruel if they were meant to being heard by the suitors. Let the bard sing what he wishes, he admonished, and do not writhe so much about your husband since there are many other men not returning from Troy. His last words sounded like a command:

---

[38] Homer, *Odyssey*, 4, 20 ff. & 15, 1 ff.: Loeb 104, 118 ff. & 105, 76 ff.

[39] *Ibid.*,1, 325-335: Loeb 104, 36.

[40] *Ibid.*, 1, 343-344: Loeb 104, 36-39; see 13, 339-341: Loeb 105, 26.

Now go to your chamber, and busy yourself with your own tasks, the loom and the distaff, and bid your handmaids be about their tasks; but speech shall be men's care, for all, but most of all for me; since mine is the authority in this house. [41]

Penelope did not argue with her son. She simply "went back to her chamber, for she laid to her heart the wise saying of her son." [42] With the strength of a lioness training her cub for the battle of life, she endured the hardship of raising an adolescent son, arrogant as he was because of his confusion and frustration about his father's absence and now his fear of the suitors' vengeance. Besides, he was suspicious of his mother, whether she told the truth about his real father, [43] worse yet, whether she would abandon him, take away the family fortune and marry one of the suitors. [44] Penelope knew her place was inside the house, yet she knew also her role, especially as a grass widow and the single parent of a teen-age son running wild with conceit and self-assurance. So she tolerated the brash tone of his statements expressed out of sadness more than male superiority.

The old servant Eumaeus also understood Telemachus' frustrations. When Odysseus returned as a disguised stranger, he told him:

But now it is for his son that I grieve exceedingly, for Telemachus, whom Odysseus begot. When the gods had made him grow like a sapling, and I thought that he would be among men no whit worse than his staunch father, glorious in form and looks, then someone of the immortals injured the wise spirit within him, or some man, and he went to sacred Pylos after tidings of his father. [45]

Penelope was clever avoiding the suitors' advances, not as much for the sake of her husband Odysseus, of whom she knew not whether he was alive or dead after

[41] Homer, *Odyssey*, 1, 356-359: Loeb 104, 38.

[42] *Ibid.*, 1, 360-361: Loeb 104, 38.

[43] *Ibid.*, 1, 215-216: Loeb 104, 28.

[44] *Ibid.*, 15, 16-23 & 16, 32-36: Loeb 105, 76 & 120.

[45] *Ibid.*, 14, 174-180: Loeb 105, 48.

almost twenty years away from home, but for the sake of her son Telemachus who would have resented the presence of another man as guardian of the household before he could assume the role himself as an adult man. The suitors admitted to him that of all the women of old, "not one was like Penelope in shrewd device." [46]

Penelope was buying time with the suitors by working late in the night for up to four years at "a shroud for the hero Laërtes", her father-in-law, in which he could be buried according to his noble rank. But this was more than a tender duty; it was also an excuse for keeping the suitors at bay. They understood her stratagem when they heard from one of her maids that she was undoing her work and redoing it, again and again, without ever finishing it. [47] Women used to admire her skill at weaving and needlework. [48] Now they could praise her for using the skill of deceit (*metis*) of which Odysseus would have been very proud.

Before Telemachus reached his maturity, probably at twenty years of age, he could not act as guardian and, therefore, could not give his mother away in marriage. He would have had to let her return to her father, Icarius of Sparta, and bring back with her the dowry he had paid when she married his father, Odysseus. [49] He was reluctant to let her do it, probably more for the money than the imposition on his mother. [50] So Penelope stayed and resisted the suitors' wooing, also her father's and brothers' urging, in deference to her son's wishes. [51]

But when Telemachus saw the day of his adulthood approaching -- when "him it does not escape if any of the women in the halls are sinning; he is no longer the child he was" [52] -- he will replace his father as guardian of the palace. First, however, he needed to be sure that his father was not to return. So he decided to journey to Pylos and Sparta in southern Peloponnesus, and inquire about him. In keeping with his character, he did it without consulting, even informing his mother, moved by a god or his own heart, as

---

[46] Homer, *Odyssey*, 2, 121: Loeb 104, 54.
[47] *Ibid.*, 2, 87 ff.: Loeb 104, 52 ff.
[48] *Ibid.*, 19, 235: Loeb 105, 250.
[49] *Ibid.*, 1, 275: Loeb 104, 32.
[50] *Ibid.*, 2, 132-133: Loeb 104, 56.
[51] *Ibid.*, 15, 16 ff.: Loeb 105, 76.
[52] *Ibid.*, 19, 87-88: Loeb 105, 240.

the herald Medon said. [53] He may have feared her objecting to his journey. The motive for his silence is not clear but cannot be far from his feelings as an independent, and sometimes arrogant, young man. In any case, Penelope was dumbstruck when Medon told her about his departure.

> Her knees were loosened where she sat, and her heart melted, For long she was speechless, and both her eyes were filled with tears, and the flow of her voice was checked. But at last she made answer and said to him: "Herald, why is my son gone? He had no need to go ... " [54]

Penelope cared for her son without being weak and tolerated his whims without being lax. She worried about him, like all mothers do when danger looms ahead for their child. She said a prayer to goddess Athena. [55] She feared for him away from home but, when he returned, she feared even more the suitors who vowed to cut him down with their swords. [56]

Telemachus returned in haste with the thought that his father had probably drowned at sea. He then was entitled to take the reins of command and assume from him the role of guardian of the palace. He resented the presence of the suitors who continued to make havoc of his property. [57] Their plot only confirmed the enmity between them and the young prince.

When Telemachus was a teenager and Penelope a single mother, her greatness came not only from her wisdom and wit, which are different forms of reasoning, but also from her patience and self-control (*sôphrosunê*), which involve emotions and call for virtue (*aretê*). She had to make choices. Some were purely about the best means to achieve a goal, but others were between good and bad in the light of the values of loyalty, fairness and self-respect she had learned to uphold, probably from her own parents in Sparta. Penelope was the prototype of the reputable women of the Classical Age in the fifth and fourth centuries. She lived in a

---

[53] Homer, *Odyssey*, 4, 711-714: Loeb 104, 170.
[54] *Ibid.*, 4, 703-710: Loeb 104, 170.
[55] *Ibid.*, 4, 762 ff.: Loeb 104, 174.
[56] *Ibid.*, 4, 771 & 789: Loeb 104, 174-177.
[57] *Ibid.*, 1, 250: Loeb 104, 30.

past long gone and yet well known, and admired by the women of Ancient Athens. She had more freedom than they had to make decisions of her own either about raising her son or dealing with the suitors. She had the freedom to choose when and whom she would marry if she were to remarry at all. All her choices were made with a view to making her son a worthy heir to his father. Women of a later age were more dominated by their husbands or, in their absence, by their guardians. Such domination already existed but was not as severe in the Archaic Age as it was in the Classical one. Helen and Clytemnestra, her cousins, were cases in point, although with more detrimental results. For almost twenty years, Penelope showed the highest standards of devotion to her task and loyalty to her family, primarily for the good of her son.

When Telemachus reached maturity, Penelope's status changed and with it her feelings. She realized that it was time for her to go on with her life. Besides, her son was now encouraging her to make the move he had feared and she had resisted in prior years. He was even begging her to be married again because, as he said, he was "vexed for his property that the Achaeans devour to his cost," [58] being now more reckless and insistent than ever. The time had come for his mother to marry again, take her inheritance and personal belongings, and move to a new husband's house under a new tutelage. Besides, Odysseus himself had advised her before leaving: "When you shall see my son a bearded man, wed whom you will, and leave your house." [59]

When Telemachus returned from Sparta to Ithaca, he enquired from the swineherd Eumaeus, as he said, "whether my mother still stays in the halls, or whether by now some other man has wedded her." [60] Athena had warned him to watch closely such a change of family because when a mother engages in a new marriage she tends to favor her new children over those of her previous family. [61]

Penelope still hesitated before making up her mind about marrying another man because several rumors had come to her that Odysseus was still alive and on his way

---

[58] Homer, *Odyssey*, 19, 533-534: Loeb 105, 272.
[59] *Ibid.*, 18, 269-270: Loeb 105, 220.
[60] *Ibid.*, 16, 32-34: Loeb 105, 120.
[61] *Ibid.*, 15, 20-23: Loeb 105, 76-79.

home. She was hesitant to make a change before she knew for sure. [62] She explained:

> When night comes and sleep lays hold of all, I lie upon my bed, and sharp cares, crowding close about my throbbing heart, disquiet me, as I mourn. ... My heart is stirred to and fro in doubt, whether to remain with my son and keep all things safe, my possessions, my slaves, and my great, high-roofed house, respecting the bed of my husband and the voice of the people, or to go now with him whoever is best of the Achaeans, who woos me in the halls and offers bride-gifts past counting. [63]

Then, if Penelope's mind was assailed by so much doubt, why did she decide at this moment of uncertainty to marry a suitor and move out of the house? Scholars are at odds to explain her decision. Some have gone as far as theorizing that she had already recognized Odysseus when he returned in disguise and together she and her husband, both masters of cunning, had devised the test of shooting the arrow through the twelve axes. This interpretation is very unlikely in view of her initial refusal to recognize the identity of the disguised Odysseus because she had not yet seen, she said, "the signs which we two alone know, signs hidden from others." [64]

The timing, which required a change of guardian from her son to a new husband, made her situation untenable because of the enormous pressures from all sides. Such a change entailed the painful loss not only of her husband but also of her son. Nevertheless, regardless of her fragile state of mind, Penelope decided to remarry but only the man who could be a protector as able as Odysseus. [65] First, she prepared to appear before the suitors. The attending maids received some help from goddess Athena who sent "sweet sleep" on her [66] and made her radiant with stature and beauty. Then, accompanied by two of her maidens, Penelope descended from her chamber. When they

---

[62] Homer, *Odyssey*, 14, 121 ff. & 17, 114: Loeb 105, 44 & 162.
[63] *Ibid.*, 19, 515-529: Loeb 105, 272.
[64] *Ibid.*, 23, 109-110: Loeb 105, 392.
[65] *Ibid.*, 20, 80-82: Loeb 105, 286.
[66] *Ibid.*, 18, 188: Loeb 105, 214.

saw her, the suitors became passionately enamoured of her [67] and, one of them, Eurymachus, expressed their admiration, saying: "You excel all women in beauty and stature and in good sense." [68]

The suitors gave her beautiful gifts, each hoping to be chosen by her as husband, unaware that her true husband was already in their midst. She withdrew to her upper room, her maids carrying the presents after her and leaving the suitors dancing and singing in the hall, late into the night. [69]

Perhaps it was the next day when she was told of a beggar who had just joined the company of the suitors. No doubt, she was intrigued by him, yet, not knowing who he was, she ventured to meet with him in the hall, only in the presence of her maids and other servants. She questioned him, but he refused to reveal his identity. He questioned her and she answered guardedly. They were testing each other, he about her fidelity and she about his identity. [70] Anyway, she accepted him as a guest (*xenos*) in the palace.

Penelope devised the test that would make the best man rise above all others, the one who could string Odysseus' bow and shoot an arrow through twelve axes. She was saved from committing evil, although unwittingly, when Odysseus alone succeeded [71] and then massacred the suitors assembled in the hall. [72] He was now the only one remaining, yet she was still hesitant to recognize him for the same Odysseus she had known and was now told he was.

Odysseus, however, had already recognized her as his dear wife. He gave her the greatest of tribute when he praised her for having been a queen worthy to be compared to a blameless king:

> Lady, no one among mortals upon the boundless earth could find fault with you, for your fame goes up to the broad heaven, as does the fame of some blameless king, who, with the fear of the gods in his

---

[67] Homer, *Odyssey*, 18, 212-214: Loeb 105, 216.
[68] *Ibid.*, 18, 248-249: Loeb 105, 218.
[69] *Ibid.*, 18, 303 ff.: Loeb 105, 222.
[70] *Ibid.*, 19, 215 ff.: Loeb 105, 250.
[71] *Ibid.*, 21, 414 ff.: Loeb 105, 340.
[72] *Ibid.*, 22, 1-389: Loeb 105, 344-374.

heart, is lord over many valiant men, upholding justice; and the black earth bears wheat and barley, and the trees are laden with fruit, the flocks bring forth young unceasingly, and the sea yields fish, all from his good leading, and the people prosper under him. [73]

Penelope's response to such a praise, before she had recognized Odysseus, was humble, as a grass widow's response should be. She Lost much of her strength and youthful beauty after her husband joined the Achaeans and sailed to Troy. His return will make her a respected wife and a fulfilled woman again:

Stranger, all excellence of mine, both of beauty and of form, the immortals destroyed on the day when the Argives embarked for Ilium, and with them went my husband, Odysseus. If he might but come, and tend this life of mine, greater would be my fame and fairer. [74]

For the moment, Penelope continued to take with equanimity the harsh treatment by her son who was still accusing her that her heart was cruel and unyielding. [75] Indeed, she was careful, circumspect and patient before becoming intimate again with Odysseus, a man who needed to be proven to be her husband after an absence of some twenty years. But she knew her son well and remained a mother to him, scolding him firmly when he deserved it. As part of the scene when she descended to meet the suitors is how even there she remained a mother unhampered by age and legal status. She rebuked him for letting the suitors abuse the stranger, Odysseus. She did it in truth perhaps only to protect her son from the suitors' hostility – guile was never far from her intentions. She publicly scolded him:

Telemachus, your mind and your thoughts are no longer steadfast as heretofore. Even when you were still a child you behaved more intelligently; but now that you are grown and have reached the bounds of

---

[73] Homer, *Odyssey*, 19, 107-114: Loeb 105, 242.
[74] *Ibid.*, 19, 124-128: Loeb 105, 242.
[75] *Ibid.*, 23, 97: Loeb 105, 390.

manhood, ... your mind and your thoughts are no longer right as before. [76]

Telemachus yielded to her reprimand, probably because he already suspected what the outcome would be. When Penelope met again with Odysseus, she challenged him to describe their marital bed, the only secret they shared only with each other. [77] Indeed, as she confessed:

> The heart in my breast was full of fear that some man would come and beguile me with his words; for there are many who scheme for their own profit. [78]

Odysseus complied and described their marital bed as he built it with his own hands, so heavy that no man alone could move it. From an olive tree that grew within the precinct of the house, he cut off the top boughs, smoothed the trunk "well and cunningly" and made the bedpost inlaid with gold, silver and ivory. Then, he stretched "on it a thong of oxide, bright with purple." When Penelope heard the description in her husband's own words, "bursting into tears, she ran straight toward him, and flung her arms about his neck, and kissed his face." [79]

Now she went back to her husband without reluctance. Her fear had dissipated and her heart had found relief in tears, melting like snow on the mountains when the summer sun shines upon it.

> [Odysseus] wept, holding in his arms his beloved true-hearted wife. ... so welcome to her was her husband, as she gazed upon him, and from his neck still did not loosen her white arms at all. [80]

Goddess Athena was so moved by the sight of this man and his wife reunited in love, as if nothing had happened during their long years of separation, that

---

[76] Homer, *Odyssey*, 18, 215-223: Loeb 105, 216.
[77] *Ibid.*, 23, 177 ff.: Loeb 105, 396 ff.
[78] *Ibid.*, 23, 215-217: Loeb 105, 400.
[79] *Ibid.*, 23, 195-209: Loeb 105, 398.
[80] *Ibid.*, 23, 232-240: Loeb 105, 400.

The long night she held back at the end of its course,
and likewise stayed golden-throne Dawn at the
streams of Oceanus, and would not let her yoke her
swift-footed horses that bring light to men. [81]

This passage is one of the loftiest in all Homeric
poetry, but loftier still is the drama of love between these
two persons, a man and a woman, both equally strong, now
crushed in sorrow for the time lost and in joy for the happy
years to come.

We have witnessed Penelope's hardships of twenty
years without her husband, managing the palace of a king
without ever claiming his title, unlike Clytemnestra who did.
We have seen her caring to raise alone a son from infancy,
through the difficult years of adolescence until he became a
mature man and the pride of his father, then deciding for
his good to make the belated move to remarry, with all the
risks it entailed and, finally, welcoming the embrace of her
husband after so many life-altering experiences they both
had while being away from each other for so long. The
adjustment to their new life together demanded from her
more effort than from her husband, but she was
conditioned to it by custom and culture.

As a final trial, Odysseus was returning home with his
war-prize and concubine, Hecuba, the former queen of the
great city of Troy. He was expecting his wife, queen also but
of a small kingdom, to overcome her feelings and treat well
this new comer in her house. Once, the messenger
Talthybius had encouraged Hecuba to follow Odysseus:

And you, when the son of Laërtes wants to take you
away, follow him. You will be the servant of a
virtuous woman [Penelope]: so say those who have
come to Troy. [82]

In spite of this encouragement, Hecuba avoided the
journey to Ithaca as Odysseus' concubine, [83] and Penelope
was spared this final trial. Neverthless, the praise of her
virtue in courage and loyalty remained for all times.

---

[81] Homer, *Odyssey*, 23, 243-245: Loeb 105, 402.
[82] Euripides, *Trojan Women*, 421-423: Loeb 10, 56.
[83] Id., *Hecuba*, 1271: Loeb 484, 514.

Happy son of Laërtes, Odysseus of many devices, truly full of all excellence was the wife you won. How good of understanding was flawless Penelope, daughter of Icarius! How well she kept before her the image of Odysseus, her wedded husband! Therefore the fame of her excellence will never perish, but the immortals shall make among men on earth a song full of delight in honor of constant Penelope. [84]

Military campaigns were the most frequent cause of separation that could strain a marriage without breaking it, as Penelope had shown in the Homeric Age. Incalculable was the number of Greek women who were forced through the same experience from the Trojan War of about 1200 BCE to the conquest of Asia by Alexander the Great during the second half of the fourth century BCE.

Penelope's picture was drawn in about 700 BCE according to memories of the Bronze Age, older by some 500 years. At once, the Homeric poem captured the imagination of the Athenian people. Every four years, the stories of the Trojan War and of Odysseus' return home were read to audiences of men, women and children who treasured them in their memories as inspirations in courage for men and of marital fidelity for women. They became their delight at festivals, the essence of their teaching to children and the inspiration of the best in their lives as men and women. No other poem ever stood like a lighthouse in the stormy sea they valiantly crossed, creating a society of law and democratic engagement, repulsing the Persian invaders in the early fifth century and extending their own influence into an empire of city-states, until Aeschylus, with the mind and style of Homer, produced on stage in 458 his trilogy of Tragedies about the Atreid family: *Agamemnon, Libation-Bearers* and *Eumenides*.

The Periclean Age of the fifth century was one of great glory for the men of Athens but of inferior service and silent submission for the women. How could the common men of Athens ignore the noble and most capable figure of Penelope in some aspects of her life? Her story, couched in the most beautiful poetic lines, was recited to them from their most tender age. They saw in her the image of their

---

[84] Homer, Odyssey, 24, 192-198: Loeb 105, 426.

own mothers. Their thoughts of harsh misogyny were softened, yet not rejected, by those of admiration for their mothers' dedication and attentive nurturing in the home. Penelope was relevant to the views men had about their women and women about themselves and these views were of seclusion of women in the home and exclusion from all public functions of government.

It is indeed unfortunate that the Ancient Athenians ignored how capable Penelope had been, not only in administering her household and raising a son as a grass widow, but also in governing a state for some twenty years. Plato rerminded them in the fourth century that they thus missed the contribution of half the population. But his effort was to no avail, except for a few rare exceptions, until our recent centuries. To the men and women of our age, a complete view of Penelope is still relevant as an inspiration of incomparable value.

Eloper

The women of Ancient Athens had no opportunity to elope, guarded as they were against it by everyone around them. So the cases are either nonexisting or kept a secret to history, except for the elopement of Helen of Sparta with Paris of Troy in the early age of the late thirteenth century BCE. The epic poems of Homer had much to do with the disastrous consequences of this illicit love affair. Paris' love for Helen, a married woman, and her elopement with him caused the Trojan War. The rare and long history of this tragic event deserves some scrutiny since it was so well known in Classical Athens.

As a reward from goddess Aphrodite, Paris chose Helen, a married woman, and made her his wife because of her beauty and also her availability. They took advantage that Helen's husband Menelaus was absent on a voyage to Crete. [85] It was her radiant beauty, however, that caused all her troubles in life. The seventh century poetess Sappho admired her "lovely walk and the bright sparkle of her face." [86]

---

[85] Euripides, *Trojan Women*, 944: Loeb 10, 104.
[86] *Fr.* 16: Loeb, *Greek Lyric*, 142, 66.

Helen's adult life spanned over three phases. The first one was in Sparta, as the wife of prince Menelaus and the mother of a daughter, Hermione. No direct testimony has revealed the condition of her married life, but indirectly, thanks to some evidence she provided later, it appeared to have been a happy and peaceful life. There is no evidence also that she was raped or abducted by Paris. Why then did she succumb to his persuasion? Holding her to be bright and stable, yet culpable of such an outrageous deed, the Greek writers who followed Homer's tradition made her doomed to it by the goddess of Love, Aphrodite. So, the surfeit argument that Aphrodite forced love upon her and that she could not resist because Love (*Erôs*) is a god seemed to have been generally accepted.

Nevertheless, in the *Iliad*, Homer placed the blame for the war on "Helen, for whose sake many Achaeans have perished in Troy, far from their dear native land." [87] Yet, he added in the *Odyssey*:

Even Argive Helen, daughter of Zeus, would not have lain in love with a foreigner [Paris of Troy], had she known that the warlike sons of the Achaeans were to bring her home again to her own native land. [88]

Homer's blame for the war was mitigated by his knowledge of the myth of the Golden Apple -- how Paris gave it to Aphrodite who rewarded him in return with the love of Helen -- so he was never so harsh on her. His judgment of her was ambivalent: the goddess Iris, he wrote,

Put into her heart sweet longing for her former husband [Menelaus] and her city and parents; and immediately she veiled herself with shining linen, and started out of her chamber, letting fall round tears. ... When they [the elders] saw Helen coming on to the wall, softly they spoke winged words to one another: 'Small blame that Trojans and well-greaved Achaeans would for such a woman long suffer woes; she is dreadfully like immortal goddesses to look on. But even so, though she is like them, let her go home on

[87] *Iliad*, 2, 161-162: Loeb 170, 72.
[88] *Odyssey*, 23, 218-221: Loeb 105, 400.

the ships, and not be left here to be a bane to us and to our children after us.' [89]

Homer continued by relating Helen's conversation with the good king Priam who blamed the gods, not her, for the war. Then, facing the king, she made a statement most revealing of her former life In Sparta:

> I wish that evil death had been pleasing to me when I followed your son here, and left my bridal chamber and my kinspeople and my daughter, well-beloved, and the lovely companions of my girlhood. But that was not to be; so I pine away with weeping. [90]

The dramatist Aeschylus' language was sharper than Homer's in his blame of Helen when, in his play *Agamemnon* (458 BCE), he made the chorus of elders address Agamemnon himself:

> When thou didst marshal the armament in Helen's cause, thou wert depicted in my eyes (for I will not hide it from thee) in most ungracious lineaments and as not guiding aright the helm of thy mind in seeking through thy sacrifices to bring courage to dying men. [91]

The king replied:

> Touching thy sentiments – the which I heard and still bear in memory – I both agree and thou hast in me an advocate therein. [92].

Euripides repeated the indictment of Helen initiated by Homer and carried by Aeschylus. In *The Trojan Women* of 415 BCE, he lent these words to Cassandra, the Trojan princess endowed with the gift of prophecy:

> In their quest for Helen the Greeks lost countless lives for the sake of one woman and one passion. ...

---

[89] *Iliad*, 3, 139-160: Loeb 170, 138-141.
[90] *Ibid.*, 3, 173-176: Loeb 170, 140.
[91] *Agamemnon.*, 799-805: Loeb 146, 66.
[92] *Ibid.*, 830-833: Loeb 146, 68.

a woman who was abducted of her own fee will, not forcibly. [93]

The Greeks felt more comfortable blaming Paris of Troy for the elopement and its enormous consequences than blaming their own Helen of Sparta. After all, Paris abused his host's hospitality and sinned against the gods when he breached the rules of friendship as a guest in Menelaus' palace. [94] Besides, he was one of their barbarian enemies always seeking wars while she always remained one of their own people. [95]

The first phase in Helen's Life was normal and without blemish until she fell for Paris and eloped with him. Then the track in her history bifurcated, one in the direction of Egypt and the other in the direction of Troy.

A few years after Homer blamed Helen for the war, the poet Stesichorus (c. 640-555 BCE) suggested a way out of blaming Helen, by creating the story of a mysterious woman who would have impersonated her. He was one of the bucolic poets who reacted against the epic poetry of Homer. He lived in Himera, Sicily, and was praised by Horace (65-8 BCE) and Quintillian (40-118 CE) for his songs of love in verses of which only a few fragments have been preserved. The legend is that he lost his sight as punishment for repeating Homer's story of Helen's infidelity. He then recanted in a second poetic song, called *Palinodes*, in which he told the story of Helen's sojourn in Egypt, while an impersonator posed as Helen in Troy. [96]

In his *Histories*, Herodotus added some useful links of information. From the palace of Menelaus in Sparta where he was a guest, Paris abducted Helen and took some treasures. Sailing through the Aegean sea, his vessel was pushed by the winds to the east end of the Mediterranean Sea, as far as Sidon in Phoenicia, then, hugging the coast southwardly toward Egypt, he landed at Canobis in the Nile Delta. There, Paris was arrested, interrogated and finally released to continue his voyage to Troy while his new wife Helen and the treasures remained in Egypt. Later, Menelaus

---

[93] Euripides, *Trojan Women*, 367-373: Loeb 10, 52.
[94] Homer, *Iliad*, 13, 626-627: Loeb 171, 48.
[95] *Ibid.*,13, 634-635: Loeb 171, 48.
[96] Stesichorus, *Palinodes*: Loeb, *Greek Lyric*, 476, 19, 43, 93-97 & 192-195.

found her there and returned her to Greece. [97] Herodotus
added:

> To my thinking, Homer too knew this story; but
> seeing that it suited not so well with epic poetry as
> the tale of which he made use, he rejected it of set
> purpose, showing withal that he knew it. [98]

In any event, Herodotus quoted two other passages
as evidence that Homer knew about this story and ignored
it. First, in Egypt where she was treated well, Helen was
given herbs that made a drug potent enough "to quiet all
pain and strife, and bring forgetfulness of every ill." [99] The
second passage quoted by Herodotus was attributed to
Menelaus who stated, according to Homer, that the gods
detained him in Egypt until he had satisfactorily sacrificed
to them. Then he could sail from the harbor of Pharos. [100]

In 413 BCE, Euripides brought up this version of
Helen's story at the end of his play *Electra*, in reference to
Clytemnestra's burial at Nauplia by Menelaus and Helen:

> Helen has left Egypt and the house of Proteus behind
> and come home. She never went to Troy. Rather, in
> order to cause strife and the slaying of mortals, Zeus
> sent an image of Helen to Troy. [101]

The next year, 412 BCE, Menelaus' search for the real
Helen served as the theme of one of Euripides' patriotic
plays. Produced at one of the most tragic moments of the
Peloponnesian war, his play *Helen* exposed the futility of the
Trojan War which could have been avoided by arbitration, as
the choral women suggested. [102] It was fought in vain for the
mirage of the real Helen as the symbol of the present
Peloponnesian War fought for the mirage of an Athenian
empire. Returning the real Helen home was the symbol of

---

[97] Herodotus, *Histories*, 2, 113: Loeb 117, 402.
[98] *Ibid.*, 2, 116: Loeb 117, 406; see Homer, *Iliad*, 6, 290-292: Loeb
    170, 290-297.
[99] *Odyssey*, 4, 220-221: Loeb 104, 134.
[100] *Ibid.*, 4, 351-356: Loeb 104, 144.
[101] *Electra*, 1280-1283: Loeb 9, 290.
[102] Id., *Helen*, 1151-1162: Loeb 11, 138.

returning to peace, prosperity and a civilized way of life. Helen admitted that goddess Hera

> made Alexandros' [Paris] union with me [Helen] as vain as the wind: she gave to kind Priam's son not me but a breathing image she fashioned from the heavens to resemble me. He imagines – vain imagination – that he has me, though he does not. [103]

The real Helen, secluded in Egypt, remained faithful to her husband, Menelaus, for at least seventeen years. When she finally heard from Teucer, an Achaean warrior in the Trojan War, that her husband Menelaus had died at sea while returning to Sparta and her mother Leda had committed suicide in shame, [104] she was so devastated by this news that she contemplated committing suicide, having lost all hopes for a happy future, [105] but Menelaus, saved from drowning at sea, came to her rescue. They met and recognized each other. She declared again: "That was an image: I never went to Troy, ... Hera [made me], as a substitute, so that Paris would not get me." [106]

The reunion of husband and wife was full of joy and love, surely without any sign of deep friction between the two. They devised some escape and succeeded in sailing the Mediterranean Sea from Egypt to the port of Nauplia in Greece.

Homer may have rejected this entire story if he really knew it completely, not only because it was less suited to epic poetry but also because it was humiliating to the Greeks to have their most beautiful woman abducted by a barbarian prince and then have a war of great magnitude fought only for the return of a phantom of her. In the second phase of her life, either in reality or imposture, the Helen of Egypt remained faithful and the other of Troy, the one we traditionally know because of the influence of Homer, lived the life of a good woman, spending time

> In the hall, where she was weaving a great purple web of double fold on which she was embroidering

---

[103] Euripides, *Helen*, 32-35: Loeb 11, 14.
[104] *Ibid.*, 132-136: Loeb 11, 28.
[105] *Ibid.*, 293 ff.: Loeb 11, 42 ff.
[106] *Ibid.*, 582-586: Loeb 11, 74-77.

many battles of the horse-taming Trojans and the bronze-clad Achaeans, which for her sake they had endured at the hands of Ares. [107]

Helen made every effort to blend with the other women of Troy. After the death of their great hero Hector and of her Trojan husband Paris, she was given a new husband, their brother Deiphobus. However, in the disarray of the Trojan defeat, she was captured with the other Trojan women and taken away. She joined them in their lamentations. Ten years had passed since she had come and entangled herself in a web of controversy. Some of the Trojan men and women resented her as the cause of this horrible war, but neither king Priam nor his son Hector blamed her for it. Addressing Hector as if he were still alive, she wept and eulogized him:

> Hector, far dearest to my heart of all my husband's brothers! ... Never yet have I yet heard evil or spiteful word from you, but if any other spoke reproachfully of me in the halls, a brother of yours or a sister, or brother's fair-robed wife, or your mother – but your father was ever gentle as if he had been my own – yet you would turn them with speech and restrain them by your gentleness and your gentle words. So I wail alike for you and for my unlucky self with grief at heart; for no longer have I anyone else in broad Troy who is gentle to me or kind; but all men shudder at me. [108]

Helen could have stopped the war if she had returned to her legal husband Menelaus. She loved Paris, had affection for his father, Priam, and respect for her brother-in-law, Hector, but she had no bond with the Trojan people. She wished to return home but could not escape. She was well guarded inside the walls of Troy because everyone knew how she fled from Sparta in the absence of her husband. Having no chance to escape, she tied her feelings to both sides. She enjoyed the life at Priam's palace and yet, in her heart, wished to return to Sparta.

---

[107] Homer, *Iliad*, 3, 125-128: Loeb 170, 136-139.
[108] *Ibid.*, 24, 767-775L Loeb 171, 620.

Homer pictured Helen as a double agent, spying for the Trojans and the Achaeans. A model of deceit and stealth, she found a way to conspire with her compatriots, the Achaeans, in order to give them the advantage in the war, because their victory would bring her back home. But, in the manner of a double agent, she argued in her debate with Menelaus about his death sentence against her, that he should place a garland of victory on her head rather than give her a death sentence. [109] The fact is that she dared commit treason against the Trojans in order to achieve their defeat, as she revealed many years later at a gathering of guests in Sparta. While they were at supper in the palace, entertaining Telemachus, Odysseus' son.

First, she cast into the wine of which they were drinking a drug to quiet all pain and strife, and bring forgetfulness of every ill. [110] Then, as the altered wine took its effect, she spoke among men in a manner self-serving, yet allowed to women only in the Heroic Age. She revealed the following war story about Odysseus and herself.

Marring his own body with cruel blows, and flinging a wretched garment about his shoulders, in the fashion of a slave he entered the broad-wayed city of the foe, and he hid himself under the likeness of another, a beggar, he who was not al all such at the ships of the Achaeans. In this likeness he entered the city of the Trojans, and all of them were deceived. I alone recognized him in this disguise, and questioned him, but he in his cunning sought to avoid me. But when I was bathing him and anointing him with oil, and had put clothes upon him, and sworn a mighty oath not to make him known among the Trojans as Odysseus before he reached the swift ships and the huts, then at last he told me all the purpose of the Achaeans. And when he had slain many of the Trojans with the long sword, he returned to the company of the Argives and brought back plentiful tidings. [111]

Helen could have betrayed Odysseus at this time but, if she had, the Achaeans may have lost the war and she

---

[109] Euripides, *Trojan Women*, 937: Loeb 10, 104.
[110] Homer, *Odyssey*, 4, 220-221: Loeb 104, 134.
[111] *Ibid.*, 4, 244-256: Loeb 104, 136.

would not have returned to her homeland where she wanted to be. Now, years later and back home, she is enjoying a certain measure of honor in her husband's palace. Still remaining the same selfish Helen she always was, she could not miss, however, the opportunity to ingratiate herself with the guests by telling this story, albeit when they were intoxicated and no threat to her. She exploited them for sympathy and lied to them, not in what she said which was true, but in what she omitted to say about her learning the whole Achaean strategy which, no doubt, included the wooden horse being built to be offered as a gift and introduced inside the walls with the Greek warriors in its belly.

Helen's husband, Menelaus, was there, in the horse's belly. He remembered an incident that displayed either her stupidity or her betrayal, and the courage of quick-witted Odysseus. With the poise of a royal host, he revealed to his guests the exploitive and duplicitous character of his wife when she came to the horse:

> You came there then, and it must be that you were bidden by some god who wished to grant glory to the Trojans; and godlike Deiphobus [her new husband] followed you on your way. Three times did you circle the hollow ambush, trying it with your touch, and you named aloud the chieftains of the Danaans by their names, likening your voice to the voices of the wives of all the Argives. Now I and the son of Tydeus and noble Odysseus sat there in the midst and heard how you called, and we two were eager to rise up and come out, or else to answer at once from inside, but Odysseus held us back and stopped us, in spite of our eagerness. Then all the other sons of the Achaeans kept quiet, but Anticlus alone wished to speak and answer you; but Odysseus firmly closed his mouth with strong hands, and saved all the Achaeans, and held him thus until Pallas Athena led you away. [112]

For her own self-preservation, Helen was helping both sides in the conflict, but only to a point. First, she

---

[112] Homer, *Odyssey*, 4, 274-289: Loeb 104, 138.

assisted Odysseus, letting him leave unharmed, yet extracting from him information about the Achaeans' strategy. Then, she used this information to betray them by coming to the wooden horse. She was aware of the danger she was causing the warriors inside this horse when she approached it, not alone but with her new Trojan husband. Odysseus saved the day for an Achaean victory when he physically silenced Anticlus. In Menelaus' assessment, Athena alone was responsible for Helen's change of mind. She would not have done it on her own. Stupidity never was one of Helen's weaknesses, but duplicity and connivance certainly were from the day she eloped with Paris to this day back in Sparta when, for purely self-serving reasons, she praised Odysseus in front of the assembly.

While in Troy, Helen used both sides to her advantage. If the Trojans lost the war, she would become a slave to the victors with the other women of Troy. She would continue to be despised by the Trojans for losing the war and by the Greeks for causing it, but she would return to her homeland and her lawful husband, king Menelaus of Sparta. If the Achaeans lost the war, she would be forever reviled by them and would never return to Sparta. At the end, she was better off favoring the Achaeans and let the stratagem of the wooden horse win the war.

Before his production of *Helen* in which Menelaus and Helen meet again in Egypt, Euripides produced another play in 415 BCE, *Trojan Women*, in which he introduced Menelaus in search of his wife, Helen, among the slave women of Troy. Incidentally, this contradiction about history by the same dramatist is the most blatant sign that theater is not history, although it must not offend history as the audience knows it. Theater is drama and can exploit any material, historical or fictitious, in order to make the audience feel, in this case of tragedy, the emotions of pity and fear.

At this time near Troy, Helen knew of her death sentence, yet she dared offer a last summation in self-defense. She pleaded for Menelaus' pardon by questioning herself:

> What was I thinking of that I left the house in company with a stranger [Paris of Troy], abandoning

my country and my home? Discipline the goddess
[Aphrodite] ... so it is pardonable in me. [113]

More than any other words of defense, her beauty
saved her life when Menelaus should have killed her. [114] The
same Euripides lent this explanation to Peleus, the father of
Achilles:

You did not kill your wife when you had her in your
power, but when you saw her breasts, you threw
away your sword and kissed the traitorous bitch and
fawned on her, proving no match, coward that you
are, for Aphrodite's power. [115]

Euripides never held much respect for Menelaus'
behavior, but surely recognized the alluring power of
Helen's beauty and sensuality, even in her middle age. He
once wrote that "It is unsafe to have beauty beyond the
average", [116] yet true about Helen eloping with Paris, his
statement does not apply now because her beauty saved her
life for a safe return home.

To this point, our dissertation has served our
purpose in two ways: one, by showing that Homer was
deliberately responsible for the bad press Helen received
during the following centuries and, second, that the
interpreters of legends have to choose either one of the two
tracts, that of Homer charging the real Helen for the
elopement to Troy and the ensuing war or that of
Stesichorus who first followed Homer's version but later
recanted, according to Plato [117] and placed the blame on an
impostor impersonating Helen in Troy while the real Helen
was in Egypt.

One other reason why Homer prevailed in assuring
the survival of his story may lie in the language: Homer
wrote in the Ionic dialect that prevailed over the Doric
dialect used by Stesichorus. In any case, both stories,
legendary as they are, serve our purpose well because in

---

[113] Euripides, *Trojan Women*, 946-950: Loeb 10, 104-107.
[114] *Ibid.*, 936: Loeb 10, 104
[115] Euripides, *Andromache*. 628-631: Loeb 484, 330; see
Aristophanes, *Lysistrata*, 155-156: Loeb 179, 288.
[116] Euripides, *Fr.*, Unidentified Play, 928: Loeb 506, 518.
[117] *Phaedrus*, 243A: Loeb 36, 460-463.

both situations Helen appears as a loving wife while in Sparta. Whoever eloped with Paris, the Helen of Egypt or the other of Troy, did it because of some transient infatuation planted in her heart by Aphrodite, not because of some dark feelings of sorrow, dissatisfaction or rebellion while living in Sparta.

In the third phase of Helen's life, after she was spared death near Troy or rescued from Egypt, in both cases by her husband Menelaus, she was back home in Greece and allowed to live again the life of a Greek wife of nobility. She remained, however, the curse of Hellas. Euripides used Iphigenia to call her aunt Helen a "hateful creature in Greece's eyes". [118] When Electra called her "god-detested", she heard Helen's self-serving explanation: "My unfortunate voyage to Ilium – a voyage caused by god-sent madness." [119]

The following exchange between Helen and Electra revealed Helen's state of mind after her return home. The occasion was her visit to the tomb of her sister, Clytemnestra:

> Helen -- Shame prevents me from showing myself to the Argives.
> Electra – Your good sense comes late; previously you left your home disgracefully.
> Helen -- Your words are true but unkindly spoken.
> Electra – But what inhibition do you feel toward the Myceneans?
> Helen -- I am afraid of the fathers of those who died at Troy.
> Electra -- Yes; in Argos your name is fearsomely shouted out. [120]

As soon as Helen left her, Electra snapped:

> See how she cut off just the ends of her hair, trying to keep her beauty unchanged! She is the old Helen still. May the gods' hatred fall upon you for ruining me and him [Orestes] and all of Greece. [121]

---

[118] *Iphigenia Among the Taurians*, 525: Loeb 10, 200.
[119] *Orestes*, 19 & 78-79: Loeb 11, 414 & 418.
[120] *Ibid.*, 98-103: Loeb 11, 422.
[121] *Ibid.*, 128-131: Loeb 11, 424.

Helen suffered all her life opprobrium and shame for her infidelity, in Troy or Egypt where she felt unwelcome and in Greece where she felt despised. When Electra told her brother, Orestes, that Menelaus had returned from Troy and brought his wife, Helen, along with him, the young man remarked:

> Had he survived alone, his fate would have been more enviable: if he brings his wife, he has come home bringing a great bane. [122]

At the end of the play, Orestes was sentenced to die. To save him, his friend Pylades suggested: "Let us kill Helen." [123] Then he added:

> If we were to take the sword to a woman of greater virtue, the bloodletting would bring disgrace on us. As things are, she'll be paying for her crimes against all of Hellas, those whose fathers she slew and whose sons she destroyed while depriving brides of their husbands. [124]

Euripides explained that, when Helen was attacked and about to be killed, she was saved by some mysterious intervention. [125]

In the *Odyssey*, Homer offered a different version and clearly showed Helen's better dispositions as she greeted Telemachus in search for his father Odysseus. [126] She appeared to be calmer, wiser and more content with her life, yet withdrawn behind her sad life experiences, either in Troy or in Egypt. After the death of Menelaus, she went to the island of Rhodes to be with her friend, Polyxo, the widow of Tlepolemus, little that she knew that this friend would take revenge against her for treason and called the Furies, also known as Erinyes, to do the deed. They hanged Helen from a tree and for this reason her death was later

---

[122] Euripides, *Orestes*, 247-248: Loeb 11, 438.
[123] *Ibid.*, 1105: Loeb 11, 534.
[124] *Ibid.*, 1132-1136: Loeb 11, 538.
[125] *Ibid.*, 1491 ff.: Loeb 11, 576.
[126] *Odyssey*, 4, 138 ff.: Loeb 104, 128.

memorialized as a cult to Helen Dendritis. [127] In the end, the Greeks harbored mixed feelings about her, good more than bad, since they made her a goddess after she died, and offered sacrifices to her at Therapnê in Laconia, as well as to her husband Menelaus whom she had made a god. [128]

*

*

*

---

[127] Pausanias, *Description of Greece*, *Laconia*, 3, 19, 9-11: Loeb 188, 123-125.

[128] Herodotus, *Histories*, 6, 61: Loeb 119, 208 and Isocrates, *Helen*, 10, 63: Loeb 373, 94.

CHAPTER EIGHT

RELATIVES

Women and children belonged to their immediate family (*oikia*) and also to their larger family of relatives (*anchisteia*) from their grandparents down to their second cousins. The larger family of relatives was like a flowering tree with two major branches, paternal and maternal, covered with members like flowers, each contributing by association to a large and beautiful cluster.

Every member of the larger family, especially the mothers and their children, could associate freely with their relatives, visit or welcome each other in their home, celebrate together the birth and introduction of a newborn child, attend festivals together in Athens or as far as Brauron and Eleusis, dance together at weddings and lament together at funerals. Relatives helped each other, sharing tasks, advice and entertainment, as they wished, and also assume certain obligations, especially toward widows and orphans. In the society of Ancient Athens, the larger family of relatives was a recognized level above the family unit, where its influence as a clan reached as far as the commercial and political activities of the city-state.

Mothers and their children received their subsistence from their male guardian and may inherit from any of their deceased relatives, depending on the closeness of their relation.

Rules of Inheritance

From Solon in the sixth century to the court orators of the fourth century the laws, often obscure and incomplete, remained substantially the same. According to the Constitution of the fourth century BCE, when the law is obscure and disputed for whatever reason, "the jury-court is the umpire in all business both public and private." [1] In the interest of clarity, the heiress (*epiklêros*) as daughter, wife or mother will be the hub of our review. Inasmuch as all the relatives she had in her larger family may have a right to inheritance, the following chart may help visualize the family connections:

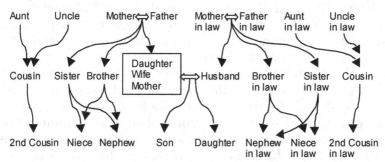

Before Solon's time, only the close relatives inherited, to an extent and according to a rank determined by their blood relation and their gender, not obvious to us today. Then, in the sixth century BCE, Solon promulgated a law in which a man could bequeath his property (*klêros*) in a will not only to close relatives but also to other persons, like close friends. [2]

During the Classical Period of the fifth and fourth century BCE, a will could be contested in court, according to Demosthenes, under any one of the following counts, namely lack of sound mind, madness, disease, drugs, old age or the influence of a woman. [3] She could not influence the dictates of a man's will, yet she could herself inherit furniture, jewelry, money, slaves and probably real estate, until her son reached maturity at the age of twenty, when he took precedence.

The situation of a woman differed whether her father or husband died with or without a will. In general, if a man died intestate, all the members in his larger family, as shown above graphically, could inherit from him, but not equally.

---

[1] Aristotle, *Athenian Constitution*, 9, 2: Loeb 285, 32.
[2] Plutarch, *Parallel Lives, Solon*, 21, 2: Loeb 46, 462.
[3] Demosthenes, *Against Stephanus II*, 16: Loeb 155, 254.

Males and the sons of males shall take precedence, if they are of the same ancestors [grandparents] even though they be more remote of kin. [4]

The titles for the inheritance depended on the closeness of their family relationship (*genos*), not further than "the children of cousins", namely second cousins.

If no male relative -- brother, uncle or cousin -- was surviving or claiming priority and a father died intestate, his daughter came first to inherit from his estate as she could from the estate of any of her male relatives. The inheritance was added to the dowry she was promised for her marriage. When married, she was restricted by law about disposing of her possessions without the consent of her husband or, in his absence and with cause, of a close male relative. On the other hand, the husband or every other close male relative carried the obligation to preserve her property as dowry and managed it according to the deceased's wishes, if they were known, or his good judgment in consultation with the heiress. Upon her death, the property had to be handed down to her children and, if she did not have any, turned over to her guardian (*kurios*).

A daughter, whether natural or adopted, who became the heiress of an intestate father or grandfather was to be married to the nearest of the father's male relatives who was available. Such endogamic rule did not exist before Solon, except for Hesiod's advice to farmers to marry a woman who lived nearby, probably from his clan. [5] If the daughter was already married at the time she became the only available heiress, she was in the awkward obligation of divorcing her husband in order to marry her closest relative unless her present husband was already fairly close either by blood or adoption. Brother and sister were allowed to marry each other, unless they had the same mother. [6]

If a wife became her husband's heiress, she was to be married to her closest available relative either as bachelor or widower. If she was rich because of her inheritance, he had usually no reluctance to marrying her and, if he was a younger man, his motives may be only financial. As a result, the success of such a marriage may be in jeopardy, so it

---

[4] Demosthenes, *Against Macartatus*, 43, 51: Loeb 155, 94.
[5] Hesiod, *Works and Days*, 700: Loeb 57, 54.
[6] Demosthenes, *Against Spudias*, 41, 3-5: Loeb 155, 6.

should probably be avoided. [7] On the other hand, if the widow was poor and still able to have children and her closest relative refused to marry her, he, instead of her guardian, had the obligation to provide her with a dowry so that she could find a husband. This law was an implicit recognition that the natural condition of an Athenian woman was to be married and have children. [8]

This law about a wealthy heiress encouraged financial graft. Such a union being purely for financial gain tended to degenerate into total neglect of the wife by her husband after she had given him an heir. Solon's law prescribed in this situation that he will have sexual relation with her at least three times a month. [9] This corrective measure was an implicit recognition that every wife had a right to sexual attention from her husband and have more babies. Otherwise, contrary to her husband, she had no other choices but to resort to unnatural abstinence, illicit adultery or disreputable lesbianism, and none of these choices were acceptable. Nevertheless, the intent of the law was to insure the stability of the home and family through the unity of husband and wife, not the sexual satisfaction of the wife.

When seriously ill, a father or husband frequently arranged the marriage of his wife and daughter, to take place after his death, thus showing that he cared for them. [10] A friendly divorce could also include such an arrangement, [11] not without some political considerations, as it was probably the case between Pericles and his wife. All marriage arrangements, however, were not so considerate. For example, Nicodemus made one in his own financial interests when he bartered his sister in marriage to a man who pledged in exchange to give in court some false evidence in his favor. [12]

As a matter of priority, a wife fell under the guardianship of any man appointed by her husband, when he died, and for as long as she remained a widow. If none had been appointed and she had a young son, they fell

---

[7] Euripides, *Fr.*, Unidentified Play, 914: Loeb 506, 512.
[8] Demosthenes, *Against Macartatus*, 43, 54: Loeb 155, 96.
[9] Plutarch, *Parallel Lives, Solon*, 20, 3: Loeb 46, 458.
[10] Demosthenes, *Against Onetor I*, 30, 7: Loeb 238, 132 & *Against Eubulides*, 57, 41: Loeb 351, 260-263.
[11] Isaeus, *On the Estate of Menecles*, 2, 7-9: Loeb 202, 44.
[12] Id., *On the Estate of Pyrrhus*, 3, 39: Loeb 202, 98.

under the patrilineal guardianship; otherwise, if she had only unmarried daughters, she returned with them to her original guardian or his substitute. In all cases, she may continue to live in the same house. The dowry brought into her marriage remained with her intact as a security her guardian could use to support her and her children.

Unless barred by his father's will, a son by his legal wife was first in line to inherit from him. An adopted son also preempted his adoptive mother for the inheritance, although he had to relinquish all rights of inheritance from his biological family. [13]

If a son was too young to assume control of his inheritance from a deceased father or grandfather, his mother would hold it in trust and have it controlled by her own guardian, but not beyond her son's second year past the age of manhood, namely twenty years old. At the same age of twenty, he became also entitled to control his mother's inheritance, if she received any and was still a widow. In both cases, however, he was obligated to assure her sustenance for the rest of her life. [14]

If there was no son or other male relative capable to inherit, the mother and her unmarried daughters inherited, but the control was with their guardian, as it was in the case of Arete, queen of the Phaeacians, who inherited from the estate of her father, Rhexenor, only through her uncle, Alcinous, whom she married. He had control over her inheritance while keeping the wealth within the family. [15]

A legally adopted daughter could inherit equally with the natural daughter but not from the mother's dowry. [16] The illegitimate children had a right to some inheritance but, if they were sons, less than the legitimate sons. Odysseus who was the bastard of a well-to-do Cretan man, Laërtes, and his concubine was raised equally with the legitimate sons but, when their father died, they cast lots for their shares in the inheritance and to him "they gave a very small portion, and allotted a dwelling." [17]

A legitimate child in Athens was one who was born of an Athenian mother and an Athenian father duly married by

---

[13] Isaeus, *On the Estate of Pyrrhus*, 3, 68 ff.: Loeb 202, 116.
[14] Demosthenes, *Against Stephanus II*, 46, 20: Loeb 155, 258.
[15] Homer, *Odyssey*, 7, 63-66: Loeb 104, 250.
[16] Isaeus, *On the Estate of Hagnias*, 11, 41-42: Loeb 202, 418.
[17] Homer, *Odyssey*, 14, 199-210: Loeb 105, 50.

public contract (enguê), albeit oral, between the mother's prior guardian and her husband. This determination was made by the Periclean law of 451/0 but not always followed rigorously, especially during the war. When the descent as citizen needed to be proven, members of the phratry who had witnessed the introduction of the child at the gathering called gamelia, shortly after birth, could testify to it either in court or privately, and therefore ascertain the right to some inheritance, even if the girl's name had not been placed on the register. [18]

If the parents divorced and the wife remarried, her child living with her had a right to the stepfather's inheritance but only up to a certain amount, lesser than the amount given to his own legitimate children, introduced and registered with all the formalities. [19]

In the context of the gods and demigods, Aristophanes made a similar point with a margin of legal error. Heracles was the son of Zeus and his human paramour Alcmena, therefore an illegitimate son. Zeus' brother Poseidon and his daughter Athena, in that sequence, had the first right to his inheritance. As a bastard son, Heracles received nothing, not even a portion of his father's property. Peisetaerus explained:

> The law won't let him. Poseidon here, who's now getting your hopes up, will be the first to dispute your claim to your father's property, declaring himself the legitimate brother. I'll even quote you the law of Solon. "A bastard shall not qualify as next of kin, if there are legitimate children; if there are no legitimate children, the next of kin shall share the property." [20]

If there were no legitimate children alive but only illegitimate ones, these would have a right to inherit together with the legal wife, but the concubine mother had no right to any inheritance.

---

[18] Isaeus, On the Estate of Pyrrhus, 3, 76: Loeb 202, 121.

[19] Id., On the Estate of Apollodorus, 7, 16: Loeb 202, 258 & On the Estate of Ciron, 8, 19-20: Loeb 202, 298-301.

[20] Birds, 1656-1666: Loeb 179, 238.

Court Cases

Matters of inheritance created legal problems that
often appeared on the court's docket. The fourth century
orators provided some of the details, more often about the
cases than about the verdicts and always from the
viewpoints of the male litigants. For example, Isaeus once
represented the family of a certain Euctemon who had one
legitimate son, Philoctemon, and several daughters.
Euctemon lived a prosperous life for many years with his
wife and children. But, in his old age, he went to live with a
mistress, Alce, who managed a tenement-house for him at
the Piraeus. Then, after much wrangling and threats, he
succeeded convincing his son Philoctemon to let him adopt
the eldest son of his mistress whom she had had with
another man, Dion, who raised him. The final agreement
was that he may adopt him but bequeath only "a single
farm" to him. [21] At about the time the old man Euctemon
died at the old age of 96, the legitimate son Philoctemon
died also. So the adopted son of Alce claimed a larger share
of the inheritance. In these circumstances, the eldest
legitimate daughter, Philoctemon's sister, who had only her
husband's voice in court, felt justified to claim priority over
the adopted son of Alce to the inheritance of her deceased
father. Isaeus pleaded her case against the adopted son. As
we previously pointed out, the adopted son preempted his
stepmother, in this case Euctemon's wife who was probably
deceased, but not a legitimate daughter, his stepsister,
especially when the adopted son's mother was only a
concubine. Besides, an agreement had already specified for
him the inheritance of a single farm. Therefore, it is likely
that the jury let it stand and refused to grant Alce's son a
larger share of his adoptive father's inheritance. [22]

A will did not always assure a clear and fair
succession. The orator Demosthenes revealed that his
father, the Elder Demosthenes, appointed three guardians:
one for his wife, Cleobule, and the other two for their two
children, Demosthenes himself and his sister. The guardians
Aphobus and Demophon were the Elder Demosthenes'

---

[21] Isaeus, *On the Estate of Philoctemon*, 6, 24: Loeb 202, 216.
[22] *Ibid*, 6, 18-24: Loeb 202, 214-219.

nephews but the third one, Therippides of Paeania, was only his lifelong friend.

Publicly, the Elder Demosthenes bequeathed a generous dowry of two talents (12,000 drachmas) to his daughter and 8,000 drachmas to his wife, in addition to her original dowry of 5,000 drachmas, for a total of 13,000 drachmas. Both were also promised by him in marriage to the two related guardians, his wife to Aphobus of about the same age and his daughter to Demophon. With this arrangement, the Elder Demosthenes was providing well for his widow and his orphaned daughter, while keeping the wealth within the family. He also secretly circumvented the rules of inheritance when he hid four talents in the ground and revealed it only to his wife Cleobule with the understanding that she could use this stash at her discretion. This clandestine action may not have been an unusual practice.

The bulk of the inheritance, some fourteen talents (84,000 drachmas), went to his son Demosthenes, still a minor. His guardian, Therippides, was to receive the usufruct of 70 minas (8.3 percent at one mina per 100 drachmas) for managing these funds until Demosthenes reached maturity. The outcome of this elaborate will turned out to be less clean than anticipated because the weddings never took place and the nephews and the friend squandered the inheritance they controlled. If he ever thought that friendship was "a stronger tie than kindred, and affection than necessity", he was indeed mistaken, although it can often be true. [23]

So, soon after he reached his majority at the age of twenty, Demosthenes prosecuted the three guardians for misappropriation of funds and demanded restitution of ten talents from each of them. He won his case against his mother's guardian, Aphobus, but received for her only the portion that was left of his father's estate. Then, he probably settled for an undisclosed amount from the other two guardians, namely Therippides, his own, and Demophon, his younger sister's guardian. At this point, he had become the rightful guardian (*kurios*) of his mother and sister, until they married, and it appears that he provided for them in the best way he could, which meant without any

---

[23] Plutarch, *Parallel Lives*, *Solon*, 21, 2: Loeb 46, 462.

luxury, because his family had been fleeced by the unscrupulous guardians whom his father had appointed executors of his will. [24]

Perhaps Plato had such cases in mind when he lent these words of advice to his Athenian Stranger addressing the Cretan Clinias:

> What I think, Clinias, is this – that the old lawgivers were cowardly ... It was through fear, my dear sir, of that angry speech that they made the law allowing the man unconditionally to dispose by will of his goods exactly how he pleases. [25]

What did Demosthenes and Plato have better to say? They disagreed with the cowardly lawgivers, like most Greek people did everywhere. First, earthly possessions do not belong to an individual man but to his entire family and, ultimately, to the State. Therefore, the legislator will prevent every undue influence upon a father in the disposition of his testament: the son who will take care of the paternal lot will be the first heir, then will come the other sons as he pleases and finally the daughters who have not yet been betrothed.

Demosthenes cared considerably about the daughters and their marriages, as well as about the appointment of guardians for the orphaned children, but not at all about the widow's fate because direct line descendants had the priority. In their absence, other relatives could become legal heirs: the closest males among them being first, down to the second cousins.

The same Demosthenes who had learned early in life the intrigues of inheritance pleaded another court case which affirmed not only the right of inheritance and the bond of agreement but also the extent to which a women's plight can be relevant, if not to the case itself, at least to its narrative to the jury. The case was about Callistratus versus his brother-in-law, Olympiodorus, who kept for himself with the court's consent the entire inheritance of a relative, thus breaking his agreement to share it with his wife. So her brother, Callistratus, retained Demosthenes to demonstrate the injustice inflicted upon his family. Doing so,

---

[24] *Against Aphobus*: Loeb 318, 6-123.
[25] *Laws*, 11, 922E: Loeb 192, 420.

Demosthenes went beyond the legal argument and revealed that Olympiodorus was not honorable in other matters:

> He keeps in his house a mistress whose freedom he had purchased, and it is she who is the ruin of us all and who drives the man on to a higher pitch of madness. [26]

Demosthenes called it "madness" when an Athenian citizen, such as Olympiodorus, accepted the influence of a woman, worse still an ex-slave. Having no children, this Opympiodorus made his mistress, who flaunted her jewelry and fancy clothes, the beneficiary of his inherited wealth. By thus bringing life style into the case, Demosthenes used the contestant's madness in order to demonstrate the injustice he committed against his client's sister, Olympiodorus' wife, as well as his own wife and daughter, therefore against him as head of the family. The legal case took place between two men, Callistratus and Olympiodorus, but the court allowed introducing in the narrative the sister as a plaintiff against her husband. The inferior status of a woman was not so low that it could not be used to appeal emotionally to the feelings of the male jury: Callistratus pleaded that the three women, his sister (Opympiodorus' wife), his wife and daughter were "wronged not less than I, but even more. ... They are themselves too poor to enjoy such things [as] going abroad in splendid state", like the arrogant mistress. [27]

The prosecution for the benefits of the case belonged legally to the man only, although they involved all the members of his family. They did not include directly any woman, wife or daughter, even if they were living with him, but only indirectly as an argument used in the presentation of the case.

The case of another ex-slave and courtesan, Neaera, can be viewed from the various angles of adultery, public deception and fraud. She had been made a free woman by her former Athenian lover, Phrynion, and was now living with a new one, Stephanus. She committed a crime by posing as an Athenian wife. Our concern here is only with

---

[26] Demosthenes, *Against Olympiodorus*, 48, 53: Loeb 155, 364-367.

[27] *Ibid.*, 48, 55: Loeb 155, 366.

I

276Rel

her illegal intent shared persuasively with her husband. She wanted their daughter to be recognized as an Athenian woman with the privilege of participation in the religious rites and the rights of marriage and inheritance. Stephanus was prosecuted by Apollodorus and found guilty as charged, together with his mistress. She was severely punished by being not only forbidden to attend public sacrifices but also to cohabit with her alleged husband. Their daughter received none of the privileges and rights of an Athenian woman. [28]

Aristotle's will is informative also in several ways about details. He appointed Antipater the executor and Nicanor the guardian (*kurios*) of his female companion (*hetaira*) or second wife, Herpyllis, also of his children and property. This Nicanor will be given his daughter in marriage when she is of age. He will also be assigned the guardianship of his son Nicomachus until he is of age. Should Nicanor be unable to fulfill this assignment, Theophratus shall have the same rights as Nicanor, if he is willing. Both Antipater and Nicanor shall take good care of Herpyllis who has shown a "steady affection" towards him, Aristotle. Then, he continued with specific instructions about the other members of his household, eight in all. As for the servants, none

> shall be sold but they shall continue to be employed; and when they arrive at the proper age they shall have their freedom if they deserve it. [29]

Aristotle made sure also that the images he had commissioned be finished. Finally, he expressed his wish to be buried with his first wife, Pythias, "according with her own instructions." [30] Aristotle's will was so detailed that it included also the amounts of money to the beneficiaries and the caring provisions for their future in life. In general, Aristotle was democratically fair and aristocratically conservative in his views. He observed that the disparity of wealth should preferably be in favor of the husband and added:

[28] Id., *Against Neaera*, 59, 13, 30-40, 45-48 & 86: Loeb, 351, 360, 372-381, 384-387 & 416.
[29] Diogenes Laërtius, *Aristotle*, 5, 13-15: Loeb 184, 456-459.
[30] *Ibid.*, 5, 16: Loeb 184, 458.

Sometimes when the wife is an heiress, it is she who rules. In these cases then authority goes not by virtue but wealth and power, as in an oligarchy. [31]

Husbands had no greater ambition than to have a son with whom they could share their manly life style in society and politics and, when the time came, their fortune as an heir. This ambition was so important to a marriage alliance that the absence of a son could by itself be a cause for divorce. The city government encouraged it because of its interest in filling the ranks of citizens. Such a divorce was friendly since the motive suggested no character flaw and society accepted it without any stigma. It was only an unfortunate event, like the loss of a friend. As reported by Isaeus, Menecles married one of his friend's daughters when his wife died childless. As a result, this friend, Eponymus of Acharnae, entered his family as a relative. But this new union remained also childless probably because of his sterility. Nevertheless, the overwhelming desire of having an heir prevailed and Menecles divorced this second wife, no doubt with the approval of her father, Eponymus, who remained his close friend. The overwhelming desire, however, to have a male heir prompted Menecles to negotiate further, adopt one of his friend's two sons and make him his heir. [32] Men who succeeded in gathering a fortune, no matter how large or small, had no greater ambition than to keep it in the family and to bequeath it to a son.

On the other hand, if the husband died without leaving any inheritance and the dowry was either nonexisting or insufficient and, furthermore, no other member of the family could provide for the widow and her orphaned children, the *Archôn Eponumos*, so called because his name was used to designate the year, had, according to the Athenian Constitution as mentioned above, even if he was not one of Menecles' friends, the responsibility to supervise the orphans, heiresses and pregnant women. [33]

The interest of the state was not in the women's welfare but in the children's, up to the age of fourteen when

---

[31] Aristotle, *Nicomachean Ethics*, 8, 10, 1161a, 1-3: Loeb 73, 492.

[32] Isaeus, *On the Estate of Menecles*, 2, 5: Loeb 202, 43.

[33] Aristotle, *The Athenian Constitution*, 56, 7: Loeb 285, 156.

the girls could marry and the boys would begin military training. After this time, the mother received no further allowance from the state.

*

*

*

CHAPTER NINE

SOCIAL LIFE

Women were segregated in public, kept unseen behind their veil, and excluded from political meetings, yet they were not secluded inside their houses as if they were in jail. In fact, they were neither prevented from nor afraid of visiting their relatives who were kept in real jails, like Xantippe who took her child to visit Socrates in jail. [1] Women and children appeared also in court, not to speak but to arouse the judges' sympathy by their presence. [2]

Women spent the major part of their time inside their house or in their courtyard surrounded by walls, occupied at their chores of managing the household and raising their family. We understand that "women's conversations should be indoors and with the members of their household". [3] Nevertheless, after their home duties were fulfilled, wives vsited each other, especially in the neighborhood, to chat and play games. They helped each other when one was in need, especially during pregnancy and childbirth. [4] With female companions, they went to the marketplace, fetched water and did their laundry at the nearby stream. They had on occasions, such as preparing for a wedding or grieving for the loss of a dear one, the opportunity and sometimes the obligation to leave their premises for short times and mix with relatives, friends, neighbors and occasional strangers. These occasions could be more frequent after they had passed child-bearing age.

---

[1] Plato, *Phaedo*, 60A: Loeb 36, 208; see Lysias, *Against Agoratus*, 13, 39-41: Loeb 244, 300, about a similar case.
[2] Plato, *Apology*, 34C: Loeb 36, 122.
[3] Euripides, *Fr.*, Unidentified Play, 927: Loeb 506, 518.
[4] Aristophanes, *Assemblywomen*, 528: Loeb 180, 310; also Demosthenes, *Against Callicles*, 55, 23-24: Loeb 351, 178-181.

Feelings and Attitudes

First coming to mind among the feelings commanding the attitudes of women in their social life outside the home, none is more important than inferiority and, as a result, fear of men and manly duties.

Inferiority

The feeling of inferiority that permeated the private life of women carried over, albeit amplified, in their public activities. The women and men of Athens conducted their lives separately, mostly confined to the home for women but extended over all aspects of private and public activities for men. Therefore, the social life of men in the public arena was free, natural and expected, while the social life of women outside the home was restricted, exceptional and often awkward.

Such was the life style during the Homeric and Archaic periods of Greek history. The Democratic movement of the fifth century reinforced it because all the Athenian men participated in the political discussions on the agora, at the gymnasium and in the Assembly where all the important decisions were debated and taken. Their involvement in political affairs boosted their self-assurance and sense of power in their public meetings as well as in the privacy of their homes where wives and daughters were their possessions.

Early in the fifth century, in 467 BCE, Aeschylus lent these words to his brash character, Eteocles, addressing the Theban maidens: "Thy task is to hold thy peace and bide within the house." [5]

Pericles, the leader of Athens at the peak of her glory, was blatant in 430 BCE about the place of women in public affairs when he associated a woman's glory to her natural character of seeking to remain unknown. [6] Such a view, no doubt, reflected the condescending expectations of the Athenian men of his time who excluded all women from the community of male citizens. On the other hand, the dramatists contemporary to Pericles assigned many major

---

[5] *The Seven Against Thebes*, 232: Loeb 145, 338.
[6] Thucydides, *Peloponnesian War*, 2, 45, 2: Loeb 108, 340.

speaking roles to women, albeit played on stage by men for a largely male audience. Men did not mind to hear women in fictional dramas. It is in life that they expected them to remain silent.

Before offering herself in sacrifice for the salvation of her family, Macaria, daughter of the hero Heracles, recognized her obligation to silence. Euripides lent her the following words of inquiry as she came out of the temple:

> Strangers, please do not consider my coming out to be overbold; this is the first indulgence I shall ask. I know that for a woman silence is best, and modest behavior, and staying quietly within doors. [7]

Ajax to his wife Tecmessa, repeated that "silence makes woman beautiful." [8] This was the voice of Sophocles in 447 BCE.

Men were responsible for women's welfare and safety. They filled the role of providers and also of protectors against robbers, adulterers and murderers. In order to fulfill this role easily and effectively, they locked them inside their bedrooms at night and made sure that no intruder would invade their quarters in the daytime. In the words of a woman of the aggrieved party at the *Thesmophoria*:

> They install locks and bolts on the women's doors to guard them, and not only that, they raise Molossic hounds to spook lovers. [9]

The speaker is Mica, a woman, blaming Euripides for encouraging the husbands in their practice of secluding women behind locked doors. The same Euripides seemed to think that such close guarding of women was not serving its purpose of keeping them always virtuous and safe, unless they cooperated:

> We waste our effort keeping guard on the female sex; when a woman is herself not naturally law-abiding,

---

[7] Euripides, *Children of Heracles*, 474-477: Loeb 484, 54.
[8] Sophocles, *Ajax*, 293: Loeb 20, 58.
[9] Aristophanes, *Women at the Thesmophoria*, 414-417: Loeb 179, 508.

what use is there in guarding her, and compounding our error? [10]

As for Aristophanes, he always caricatured the condition of women for the purpose of comedy, yet could not exaggerate his depictions so much that the audience, mostly male, could not recognize in them a substantial core of reality. He even went one step further when he related in *Assemblywomen* of the year 392 an incident which must have had little or no ring of reality, yet made a real point. He used a woman dressed like a good-looking young man to suggest to the Assembly to place the State in the hands of women; "the people from the country made deep rumbles," because it sounded so unreal and outrageous. [11]

Men set the division of labor and responsibilities in the city-state. Women were expected to remain outside the public arena where the conduct of government and war was the affair of men. The Athenian men expected their women to play no political role at any level, therefore to have no part in the government of their deme or city. This role was reserved to male citizens, normally of twenty years of age and older -- never before they were eighteen -- registered as born of two Athenian parents married by contract (*enguê*) and after having completed their military patrol for two years. [12] Such was the law adopted under Pericles in 451 BCE and reinstated by Euklides in 403, the year after the Peloponnesian War ended. [13] Even at home, where women had the role of mother of a family and manager of a household, they acted always under the supervision and direction of their husband or guardian, therefore, "in second place, always at a distance from men." [14]

The orators of the fourth century were made of the same cloth. In one of his speeches, Isaeus (c. 420-350 BCE) declared that no one

would dare to serenade a married woman, nor do married women accompany their husbands to

[10] *Fr.*, Unidentified Play, 1061: Loeb 506, 596; also *Ibid.*, 1063: Loeb 598..
[11] *Assemblywomen*, 432-433: Loeb 180, 296.
[12] Aristotle, *Athenian Constitution*, 42, 2-5: Loeb 285, 118-121.
[13] Id., *Politics*, 3, 1, 1275b, 22-24: Loeb 264, 178.
[14] Euripides, *Fr.*, *Danae*, 319: Loeb 504, 330.

banquets or think of feasting in the company of strangers, especially mere chance comers. [15]

Hyperides, an orator who died the same year as Aristotle in 322 BCE, wished young women, probably of the age corresponding to men's bachelorhood until about the age of 35, be excluded physically from public appearances, except at funerals, weddings and religious festivals. He wished that

> A woman who travels outside the house must be of such an age, that onlookers might ask, not whose wife she is, but whose mother. [16]

The ancient Greeks had a long way to go before they could reach a semblance of equality between men and women. When Antigone discussed with her sister Ismene her plan to bury her brother Polynices, against king Creon's edict, she heard her sister say:

> We must remember that we are women, who cannot fight against men; and then we are ruled by those whose power is greater, so that we must consent to this and to other things even more painful! [17]

Fear

In the Greek mind, fear was the opposite of courage: like weights on a scale, the heavier the fear, the lighter the courage. The Athenian men associated courage only with the "mighty" branch of physical strength. Therefore, because women could not compete with men in this kind of physical strength, they were viewed by men as having less courage (*andreia*) than they had. The word itself borrowed from *anêr*, a great man. So, they thought bravery was a trait of men, fear a trait of women. Aristotle who viewed humans as the highest form of life observed in animals the same traits he observed in humans. He gave the following example: the male

---

[15] Isaeus, *On the Estate of Pyrrhus*, 3, 14: Loeb 202, 84.
[16] Hyperides, *Fr.*, 205: Fantham, E. et al., *Women in the Classical World*, 79.
[17] Sophocles, *Antigone*, 61-64: Loeb 21, 10.

is a readier ally and is braver than the female, since even among the cephalopods when the cuttle-fish has been struck by the trident the male comes to the female's help, whereas the female runs away when the male has been struck. [18]

In this respect, the Amazons fascinated the male artists of ancient Greece because they displayed the happy combination of women's beautiful bodies with men's courage in combat.

Aeschylus began his play *The Seven Against Thebes* of 467 BCE by exposing his perception of a typical female reaction. The Theban War of pretenders to the throne gave him the opportunity to make this point on the Athenian stage. As Polynices' forces from Argos were besieging the gates of Thebes, the young king Eteocles who was defending them went into a fit when he saw the women running around in panic. He stood up and ordered everyone to obey his command. In such a military confrontation he would be naturally expected to validate his order by his position as a king and commander-in-chief. On the contrary, he appealed only to his status as a man.

Hearing the roar of the army, the clashing shields, the clatter of spears, the Theban maidens were stricken with terror. [19] They appealed to the gods for help. [20] Eteocles ignored their prayers since he believed the gods were already on his side. Their panic, however, did not set well with him because he needed to ensure their loyalty by not interfering with his struggle. In his exasperation he struck hard at their weakness and fear, venting his contempt in demeaning terms:

> You, I ask, insufferable creatures that ye are! ...
> Neither in evil days nor in gladsome prosperity may I
> have to house with womankind. Has she the upper
> hand, -- 'tis insolence past living with; but, if seized
> with fear, to home and city she is a still greater bane.
> So now, by thus hurrying to and fro in flight, in your

---

[18] *History of Animals*, 8, 608b, 15-19: Loeb 439, 218-221.
[19] Aeschylus, *The Seven Against Thebes*, 100-104 & 204: Loeb 145, 330 & 336.
[20] See Euripides, *Fr., Erechtheus*, 351: Loeb 504, 370.

clamour ye have spread craven cowardice among the townsfolk. [21]

Indeed, their obedience was important to his success, but he was unsure of it. So, while he was commanding them to hold their "peace and bide within the house", he cried in exasperation: "O Zeus, what a breed thou hast given us in womankind!" [22]

The same Aeschylus in his play *Eumenides* of 458 BCE carried the same observation about women in fear: "An aged woman, overcome with fright, is a thing of naught – nay rather, she is but as a child." [23]

Another instance described by Euripides made the same point in 415 BCE. While conversing with Argive women, Electra spotted strangers identified later as her brother Orestes and his friend Pylades. They were approaching her house. She could confront them like a man. On the contrary, she told the women around her: "Let's flee these criminals, you along the path and I into the house!" [24]

Again in 408 BCE, Euripides described Electra's anguish and fear for her own life after the Argive council sentenced her brother Orestes to die. When he returned home, she could hardly bear the sight of him, her last before his execution. He then delivered this curt reply: "Stop these womanish laments and endure in silence what has been ordained!" When she continued to cry, he pleaded with her: "Don't cover me with cowardice by making me weep with the recitation of my woes!" [25]

Women had good reasons to fear when their men were to die or were gone to war on the battlefield or at sea. Women were left behind at home with scarce resources and the constant fear that the men they relied on may never return. Maidens and mothers feared death in war for a son or for a present or future husband, as Lysistrata did when she retorted angrily to the magistrate's comment that women "share none of the war's burdens":

---

[21] Aeschylus, *The Seven Against Thebes*, 183-192: Loeb 145, 334.
[22] *Ibid.*, 224, 232 & 256: Loeb 145, 338 & 342.
[23] Id., *Eumenides*, 37-38: Loeb 146, 274.
[24] Euripides, *Electra*, 218-219: Loeb 9, 170.
[25] Id., *Orestes*, 1022 & 1031-1032: Loeb 11, 524-527.

None? You monster! We bear more than our fair
share, in the first place by giving birth to sons and
sending them off to the army. ... Then, when we
ought to be having fun and enjoying our bloom of
youth, we sleep alone because of the campaign. And
to say no more about our own case, it pains me to
think of the maidens growing old in their rooms. [26]

The most manly of all Greek heroes, the mythical
Heracles, who destroyed the nine-headed Hydra, captured
the cattle of Geryon, diverted two rivers and held the earth
for Atlas, was consumed by a burning flame hidden in a gift
from his wife, Deianeira. In agony, he was carried to Mount
Oeta, probably in east Malis, south of Thermopulae. When
he arrived, he cried a long complaint because, while nothing
in the past had been able to destroy him, "but a woman, a
female and unmanly in her nature, alone has brought me
down without a sword." [27] Then, ashamed of his "crying out,
weeping like a girl", he confessed that "such a thing has
shown me as a womanish creature." [28]

A strong man (anêr) such as Odysseus wept like a
woman, unable to control his emotions, when he listened to
the sad stories of the Trojan War. [29] He behaved like a
woman who, as the foreign Medea once admitted, "is by
nature soft and prone to tears." [30]

Aristophanes associated women with the lack of
strength and courage when he alluded to the effeminate
Cleonymus' cowardice on the battlefield, throwing away his
shield to run faster and escape the enemy's pursuit. [31]

In The Clouds, about Socrates' pedantic school,
Aristophanes brought up the master's teaching that the
masculine names are different from the feminine ones. The
joke began when Strepsiades used the word "mortar"
(kardopos). Socrates corrected him at once:

---

[26] Aristophanes, Lysistrata, 588-593: Loeb 179, 350.
[27] Sophocles, Women of Trachis, 1062-1063: Loeb 21, 226.
[28] Ibid., 1071-1074: Loeb 21, 228.
[29] Homer, Odyssey, 8, 521 ff.: Loeb 104, 310.
[30] Euripides, Medea, 928: Loeb 12, 366.
[31] Birds, 289: Loeb 179, 54; Clouds, 254 & Peace, 678: Loeb 488,
58 & 510.

There, you did it again; this is another example. You refer to a masculine mortar, though it's a feminine noun. ... Absolutely, just like "Cleonymus."... Morté, just as you say Sostraté. [Then Strepsiades exclaimed:] I can handle that: Morté, Cleonymé. [32]

The audience understood the joke since women were perceived as lacking the strength and courage needed on the battlefield. Inasmuch as women were thus considered inferior to men, the misogynist view that women must be subservient to men reared its arrogant head as a consequence.

The same point was made by King Creon of Thebes demanding Antigone's obedience in the following terms:

In this way [obedience] we have to protect discipline, and we must never allow a woman to vanquish us. If we must perish, it is better to do so by the hand of a man, and then we cannot be called inferior to women. [33]

These were in fifth-century Athens the feelings and attitudes of women and of men about them, namely that women were by nature inferior to men in strength and courage and, therefore, prone to fear, especially outside their homes. Because of such feelings, women tended to support each other, especially in times of danger, as Euripides said: "A woman is a woman's natural ally." [34] Then a woman can display an invincible courage about persons like a family member or situations like love and peace, with sheer determination of the kind Antigone and Lysistrata used for good without physical strength or like Medea for bad and admitted it:

In all other things a woman is full of fear, incapable of looking on battle or cold steel; but when she is injured in love, no mind is more murderous than hers. [35]

---

[32] Aristophanes, *Peace*, 669-680: Loeb 488, 96-99.
[33] Sophocles, *Antigone*, 677-680: Loeb 21, 66.
[34] *Fr., Alope*, 108: Loeb 504, 122.
[35] Euripides, *Medea*, 263-266: Loeb 12, 306.

For one of his less known female characters, probably Auge, Euripides wrote: "We are women. In some things, timidity overcomes us, but in others no one could exceed our courage," [36] as we shall see in our next chapter.

Philosophers' Views

In the following fourth century, the philosophers Plato and Aristotle scrutinized and sorted out some of these views expressed by the dramatists in fifth-century Athens about women' inferiority and fear in their social life.

Plato

No women had a role in any of Plato's Dialogues, except Diotima of Mantineia who did not appear in person but was quoted extensively by him, through Socrates, on the subject of love (erôs). He thought of her as higly skilled in the subject of love "and in many others too." [37] He had learned so much from her that he dared introducing her to his male friends. Really, the pertinent question is not why Diotima was a woman competent in the art of love but why a woman of any name appeared as Socrates' teacher, unless the learning came to him not in words but in the practice of love. On the other hand, He may have recognized Diotima's expertise in love only as an advocate of the noblest ideals of knowledge and beauty, identified during the Renaissance of the fifteenth century CE as the concept of Platonic Love. In this context, women meant to men little more than manipulating their behavior and Diotima was invented and Socrates, the most respectable of teachers, was charged to use her for one purpose, namely to teach that sex ought to be primarily for procreation and not for pleasure. In the Greek mind, this was a feminine view because, as he explained elsewhere, woman "is an indwelling creature desirous of child-bearing." [38]

Plato carried further the destabilization of women's status in society. On the one hand, he allowed women to have some sense of identity, albeit as inferior to men,

---

[36] Fr., Auge, 271a: Loeb 504, 272.
[37] Plato, Symposium, 201D: Loeb 166, 172.
[38] Id., Timaeus, 91C: Loeb 234, 250.

through their unique relationship as wives, each to one husband and, on the other hand, he made this relationship only a lifeline he threw to women when he drowned them all in the large pool of the city. Furthermore, such a lifeline was flimsy at best because the family that was women's realm was deprived of its unique role and absorbed into the city. The center of a woman's life -- the woman as wife and manager of the household – did not belong to her any more but to the city. As a result, she was left with no distinct responsibility, but only with some illusive opportunities resulting in unrealistic roles.

Although Plato's standards of sexual ethics were idealistic, they reflected a real change in the Athenian mentality from the Classical time of Pericles, male dominated and conservative in the fifth century, to his own Late Classical time in the fourth century. The thirty-year Peloponnesian War that intervened between the two periods resulted in the humiliation and devastation of Athens and changed men's views on women at the turn of the century. Men still wanted their women to be subservient because they were physically weaker, but they could not stop them from gaining power because their male roster had shrunk so much. When Plato suggested that women could offer more than only babies to replace the thousands of men lost in the war, he was an opportunist and a dreamer. His idealistic promotion of women was well connected to neither his heart nor the conservative attitudes of the masses.

Plato's steps were unstable, as if he were walking down a slippery slope. His direction was not clear and his positions sometimes contradictory. On the one hand, he granted the Athenian women the equal opportunity to education and leadership as guardians, if they so desired and had the ability, but, on the other hand, he took away from them piecemeal every important role in public affairs beyond the care of children. His underlying fear may have been that the dual access to power would create disunity in the state. There is no greater good, he declared, than the bond of unity, which he found in his utopian theory of community of all goods, including women. [39]

---

[39] Plato, *Republic*, 5, 462A-B: Loeb 237, 468.

In his *Republic*, Plato proposed a division of the
Athenian society into three classes, the highest class being
that of the guardians. In this class, men and women would
share equally in the same education, privileges and
obligations, and all families and properties would be in
common under the regulation of the state. The difference
between men and women, he explained, "consists only in
women bearing and men begetting children", otherwise they
have the same nature. Inasmuch as this sole difference has
no impact on the sort of education women would receive,
both men and women ought to have the same pursuit of
occupations.

> It appears that they differ only in just this respect
> that the female bears and the male begets, we shall
> say that no proof has yet been produced that the
> woman differs from the man for our purposes [such
> as education], but we shall continue to think that our
> guardians and their wives ought to follow the same
> pursuits [in society]. [40]

From this premise, Plato concluded: "There is no
pursuit connected with the administration of a state that is
peculiar to women." [41] Indeed, he explained, some men and
some women are more gifted than others. Therefore, some
women are more gifted than some men, although women in
general are inferior to men. But gender as such has nothing
to do with ability because it varies as much among men as it
does among women. As for the responsibility of being
guardians of the State,

> The women and the men, then, have the same nature
> in respect to the guardianship of the state, save in so
> far as the one is weaker, the other stronger
> [physically]. [42]

But when Plato addressed the subject of women's
nature, he invalidated this simplistic assertion in the
previous centuries, by advocating that females and males
"have all things in common ... except that we treat the

---

[40] Plato, *Republic*, 5, 454E: Loeb 237, 444.
[41] *Ibid.*, 5, 455A: Loeb 237, 444.
[42] *Ibid.*, 5, 456A: Loeb 237, 448.

females as weaker and the males as stronger", and, as a result, as having less courage. [43] About strength and courage, he recognized that certan females have more of these than some males.

Also, Plato admitted that certain activities were more suitable to women, like weaving and cooking. Therefore, cerain women can be superior to men in these activities, although inferior to men in strength. [44] Furthermore, certain women may have special gifts, like being healers, musicians or athletes. Furthermore, Plato was flexible enough to recognize that, like individual men, individual women were unequal not only in skills but also in virtue. So, the more perfect among them, regardless of their gender, could become guardians of the state, if given the same education and nurture. Functions and responsibilities depend not on gender but on ability. Women can have such ability. This consideration is more generous than any other ever expressed about women in Antiquity, except indirectly and in a limited way on the theater stage by Aristophanes in his *Lysistrata*.

In view of this and within the framework of Plato's political theory, some outstanding women should be included as guardians of the state because, if they can become philosophers, they can also become kings. [45] Plato did not dare saying it. Obviously, some loose ends could unravel his tapestry of men and women intertwined. Still, the general view of his utopia is one of respect for women, especially in their unique function of motherhood and in equality of individual opportunities to some public functions, hence to schooling for girls as well as for boys. [46]

Plato proposed that men and women share in all occupations, including military service, yet

> in the distribution of labours the lighter are to be assigned to the women, who are the weaker natures, but in other respects their duties are to be the same.

Then, he immediately added a remark of pure idealistic Plato:

---

[43] Plato, *Republic*, 5, 451E: Loeb 237, 434.

[44] *Ibid.*,5, 455C-D: Loeb 237, 446.

[45] *Ibid.*, 5, 473C-D: Loeb 237, 508.

[46] *Laws*, 6, 765D-E: Loeb 187, 438.

But the man who ridicules unclad women, exercising because it is best that they should, 'plucks the unripe fruit' of laughter and does not know, it appears, the end of his laughter nor what he would be at. For the fairest thing that is said or ever will be said is this, that the helpful is fair and the harmful foul. [47]

Nobody would disagree that "the helpful is fair" and that "women exercising" is useful, ergo that women exercising is fair. But can the fair in some activities be at times laughable? Yes; not because they are foul but because they are either unexpected or suggestive. Plato did not really address the issue in his response and we may laugh at unclad women – or men -- exercising if, like many other things in life, it appears to be laughable.

Plato further recommended that wives and children be held in common, without licentiousness. Such a dream, worthy of Socrates' clouds, loses credibility in the details. His political theories interest us only for the recognition of the natural similarity of men and women, except in the role of procreation. Plato appears to be the most modern of all the writers of Antiquity!

As for the public sharing of women by men, it never went beyond being the theory of a dreaming philosopher. Even in Plato's days, it received no favors. As already noted (p. 74 and 239), Aristophanes made every effort to ridicule it to death in two of his plays.

In *Assemblywomen* of 392 BCE, Aristophanes reduced it to the absurd. Near the end of his play, when Praxagora was preparing a banquet to celebrate her victory at the pnyx, he introduced a hilarious and bawdy situation resulting from the theory of sexual communism. He brought out two women, one old and the other young, under the age of twenty. When a young man, Epigenes, came along courting the young woman, the old one claimed him, according to the new democratic law. He wanted the girl. "That was true," replied the old hag, "under the old system, my sweet; but under current law you've got to enter us first." [48]

---

[47] Plato, *Republic*, 5, 457B: Loeb 237, 450-453.
[48] Aristophanes, *Assemblywomen*, 985-986: Loeb 180, 384.

Unfortunately, an older hag, more repulsive than the first one, intervened making a claim of her own, then a third one "another horror, and much more revolting than the last", came along to make a similar claim. [49] The young man was finally rescued from this impasse when a maidservant entered to call everyone again to Praxagora's dinner feast. [50]

In *Wealth*, produced only four years later, in 388 BCE, Aristophanes destroyed Plato's theory by raising in several ways the fear of its inexorable consequences. As one of the ways, he introduced an old woman who complained that the new system of equal distribution of wealth had made her life not worth living. [51] When she was rich, she could afford a young gigolo who needed her money, but now that he is equally rich he can ignore her, an old hag, and go for the young and pretty girl. [52] Therefore, the consequences of equal wealth are not equally distributed!

Plato's theory of equal access to women gave them no advantage in society. It did not also give them any significant role in the government of the city. If they became guardians, it could not be of men. They could not be magistrates or archons. Procreate and care for children were their unique role, which they fulfilled often without the affection of a partner. In the end, Plato's views on the new role he assigned to women degraded them to a level lower than the one they were given in the society of his time.

Isolated as a group which meant about half of the population and without regulations from the state, women retrenched and gave each other support. Aware of this situation, Plato brought up the aspect of secrecy related to it when he, still a misogynist, wrote of

> the female sex, that very section of humanity which, owing to its frailty, is in other respects most secretive and intriguing. [53]

Plato was not a friend of women. He did not like them as a group and probably never cared to be married to one. He must have recognized, however, the importance of the

---

[49] *Assemblywomen*, 1053 & 1070: Loeb 180, 394 & 396.
[50] *Ibid.*, 1112 ff.: Loeb 180, 404.
[51] *Ibid.*, 967-969: Loeb 180, 560.
[52] Aristophanes, *Wealth*, 975 ff.: Loeb 180, 562 ff.
[53] *Laws*, 6, 781A: Loeb 187, 486.

family structure for the perpetuation of the race when, in
the *Laws*, he advocated that the father should leave his
property to his favorite son, give the others for adoption to
husbands who do not have any, and "marry off the females
according to the law that is to be ordained." [54] He
formulated this law about dowries and inheritance later in
Book Eleven, [55] in a manner consistent with his other
appeals to male priority over female right. For example, of
the three conditions he set up for marrying a daughter, the
least important and the one worthy of forgiveness if omitted
was the "character and disposition" of the husband. The
only sine qua non was "nearness of kinship and the security
of the lot." [56] Every consideration of the woman as a person
was ignored completely, except in a negative way when he
dealt with disputes and adultery for which he applied the
same penalties equally to husband and wife. [57]

The orators turned jurists, like Lysias, Demosthenes
and Isaeus, who were Plato's contemporaries, painted a
more realistic picture of women's life in Athens as one that
was still secluded in the home and controlled by one
guardian or another. Of course, court cases are only one
indicator of a society's standards. They show the darker side
of reality, like the case of Euphiletus' wife seduced by
Eratosthenes who was murdered by her husband, as Lysias
reported. Court orators had little opportunity to speak
about the capable and virtuous women and, when they did,
they could be very unreliable because they did it to win a
case. Through all the cases handled by the jurists, the view
is clear that the double standards remained as traditionally
applied to men and women from time immemorial.

Plato's views on the public role of women were not
realistic, yet were true in some aspects, such as the
qualifications of certain women, equal to those of men, for
the functions of guardians of the state, but the Athenian
culture was not ready for it in his fourth century and even
less in the fifth century. The dramatist Euripides
summarized in only a few words the enduring position
taken by men of both centuries about their women:

---

[54] *Laws*, 5, 740C: Loeb 187, 364.
[55] *Ibid.*, 11, 922E-926: Loeb 192, 420-433 and 5, 742C: Loeb 187, 372.
[56] *Ibid.*, 11, 924D: Loeb 192, 426.
[57] *Ibid.*, 6, 784D-E: Loeb 187, 498.

> A wife who stays At home is certain to be a good one,
> and one who spends time out of doors is certain to
> be worthless. [58]

Aristotle

Aristotle spent some twenty years in daily contact
with Plato at his Academy where, as a disciple, he learned
about all of his master's theories including this one about
women sharing with men in the same ability, education,
privileges and responsibilities. He subjected it to a kind of
analysis consistent with his general methodology which
consisted of, first, observing the facts about the subject at
hand; second, raising questions about them; third, listing
and reviewing the common opinions about the answers and,
finally, assuming these steps well taken, among these
opinions,

> If the discrepancies can be solved, and a residuum of
> current opinion left standing, the true view will have
> been sufficiently established. [59]

Aristotle was more realistic than Plato as an observer
of his society of the fourth century, not only because he
knew both Plato and the orators and could stand on their
shoulders but also because of his interests as a man of
science who sought to be more accurate in his observations
and more moderate in his interpretations than they were.

Aristotle applied his methodology first to arguing
against Plato's abolition of the family, as theorized in his
Dialogue *The Republic.* [60] Then, he rejected his master's
subsequent ideas about women, such as their common use
for procreation and their equal opportunities for education.
His major contribution concerning women's education
appeared in one of his latest writings, his *Nicomachean
Ethics*, so-called because his son Nicomachus edited it.

In his view, women were by nature similar but inferior
to men, therefore gender equality was an impossible dream,
unfounded and unworkable in practice. In positive terms:
women should fulfill their private role in the family under

---

[58] Euripides, *Fr., Meleager*, 521: Loeb 504, 623.
[59] Aristotle, *Nicomachean Ethics*, 7, 1145b, 5: Loeb 73, 376.
[60] *Politics*, 2, 1, 1261a, 1 ff.: Loeb 264, 68 ff.

the leadership of men. And he stated clearly the principle upon which this traditional position was based:

> As between the sexes, the male is by nature superior, and the female inferior, the male ruler and the female subject. And the same must necessarily apply in the case of mankind generally. [61]

After explaining that the freeman should have the ability to rule and be ruled, he added that

> Temperance and courage are different in a man and in a woman (for a man would be thought a coward if he were only as brave as a brave woman, and a woman a chatterer if she were only as modest as a good man. [62]

Aristotle explained further that a man who showed self-indulgence – the opposite of self-restraint -- in his pursuit of pleasures or his endurance of pains was not really a man. He explained with some candor:

> But we are surprised when a man is overcome by pleasures and pains which most men are able to withstand, except when its failure to resist is due to some innate tendency [such as hereditary effeminacy], or to disease [such as low energy]. [63]

Therefore, Aristotle remained loyal to the Greek tradition of placing women inferior to men, physically and emotionally. Due to this long tradition of women's inferiority to men, it is no surprise that women had little self-esteem in the face of a perceived threat or injustice, and found some release in disreputable actions which men considered major pitfalls in their social life.

Both men and women were essential to the State in their respective roles: men as rulers and women as ruled, but not like masters and slaves, because slaves, either men or women, were not persons but things, without any

---

[61] *Politics*, 1, 2, 1254b, 13-16: Loeb 264, 20.
[62] *Ibid.*, 3, 2, 1277b, 20-23: Loeb 264, 192-195.
[63] *Nicomachean Ethics*, 7, 7, 1150b, 11-16: Loeb 73, 414-417.

freedom. [64] So, according to the common belief among Athenians, the Barbarians made no distinction between women and slaves, but the Greeks did because their women were born free and as mothers contributed to providing the City (*Polis*) with the citizens it needed. Politically, the difference between women and slaves was negligible because neither had a role in government since they were both, in one way or another, subjects of the citizen-rulers. The difference was purely social, inasmuch as they belonged to different levels of society, women being superior to slaves and, for this reason, granted special privileges and treated with more respect. Therefore, as free persons, women were situated between the male citizens and the slaves. Aristotle commented further, thinking for sure of the slaves: "It is true that not all the persons indispensable for the existence of a state are to be deemed citizens." [65]

Men were the guardians (*kurioi*) of their daughters and wives but not like they were the masters of their slaves. Aristotle explained that slaves performed only menial tasks that would be degrading for a master to execute. Women performed menial tasks as well, especially in the absence of slaves, but they performed also other tasks that placed them on the level of co-masters in the private management of the household. In view of this, the virtues equired of women who managed their households were different from those required of the slaves whom they ruled and of their husbands who ruled over them all.

Aristotle knew the status and roles of women in the society of his time, for example that women were necessary to the state but were not citizens themselves because men, who had all the power, were allowing them no role in society, except for the procreation and nurturing of male citizens and other female procreators. Marriage, therefore, had not only a private value in the institution of the family but a public value in the structure of the State. Plato had already adopted this viewpoint. He wrote:

> Regarding marriage as a whole there shall be one
> general rule: each man must seek to form such a

---

[64] *Politics*, 1, 1259a, 5: Loeb 264, 56 ff.
[65] *Ibid.*, 3, 1278a, 3, 1: Loeb 264, 194.

marriage as shall benefit the State, rather than such as best pleases himself. [66]

Not only Athenian women, resident aliens and slaves of all ages, but also all boys to the age of twenty, had no role in the public affairs of the city. As a result, only ten percent of the residents of Attica, some 30,000 citizens out of the estimated 300,000 residents, had a right to participate in democracy after 451 BCE, when the dual parentage law was enacted, and only 9.26% -- some 23,500 citizens from the estimated population of 253,500 -- after the end of the Peloponnesian War in 404 BCE. The large majority of the residents were disfranchised politically.

Aristotle knew also that women's access to the courts of justice was restricted. Like other non-citizens, they could not instigate any action, plead any case, even testify in court. They could be brought to a court session as silent witnesses when their sad appearance, usually accompanied with tears, could mollify the jury's sentence. They had a voice in the family council and could speak to arbitrators retained by their husbands. But such a situation was private and often used only to avoid the public display and scrutiny that the appearance in court always entailed. Slaves had no rights, even to private justice and, of course, no access to public justice in the courts. Men made all the decisions about procedures. We can surmise, however, that they seldom made them without the opinion of the women interested in the case.

Also, the silence of our sources should not prevent us from assuming that widows and wives with absentee husbands had special privileges with the courts, not by right but by force majeure. Such a thought gives credit to men of sound common sense and too old to serve in the armed forces.

In favor of the playwrights, Aristotle pointed out in his *Poetics* four aims regarding the characters presented on the Athenian stage of Tragedy. For our present purpose, his third aim should be brought up first, namely that the characters should be like reality, "which is distinct from making the character good and appropriate." [67] Being good

---

[66] *Laws*, 6, 773B: Loeb 187, 462.
[67] *Poetics*, 15, 1454a, 23-25: Loeb 199, 78.

and appropriate were his first two points, different from the third point because true Tragedy cannot extol, although it can include, evil purpose and inappropriate behavior as part of reality. In reference to women, he admitted that they can be morally good even if they are, and should appear on stage, in a status inferior to men's. But if the character ought to appear "courageous or clever", women cannot rise to the occasion because it is not appropriate.

Two misogynic points are made here about the representation of women "like reality": first, they can appear morally good, yet in a manner inferior to men's and, second, they cannot appear courageous or clever because it is not befitting their nature. [68] Even Antigone, who was very strong in her moral purpose, was neither completely courageous nor entirely clever in her political demonstration, as we shall see later.

In his *Politics*, Aristotle made a similar point when he declared that both men and women should use practical wisdom in their respective role as rulers of the households, but not to the same extent because women are subjected to men's rule: "wisdom assuredly is not a subject's virtue, but only right opinion." [69] Women may have a right opinion about certain decisions, including those regarding the good of the state, but they do not have the wisdom that considers all aspects of a situation and provides the courage to make those decisions, like men do.

Better than Plato, Aristotle understood the Athenian women's plight in society and men's appreciation for their moral excellence, especially when he deplored the liberties taken by the Spartan women. He explained that, Inasmuch as they constitute half the population, when they are bad,

> one half of the state must be deemed to have been neglected in framing the law. And this has taken place in the state under consideration [Sparta], for the lawgiver wishing the whole community to be hardy displays his intention clearly in relation to the men, but in the case of the women has entirely neglected the matter for they live without restraint in

[68] Aristotle, *Poetics*, 15, 1454a, 16-22: Loeb 199, 78.
[69] Id., *Politics*, 3, 1277b, 4, 28-29: Loeb 264, 194; see Xenophon, *Agesilaus*, 11, 5: Loeb 183, 129 & Demosthenes, *Against Meidias*, 21, 31-35: Loeb 299, 26-29.

respect to every sort of dissoluteness, and luxuriously. [70]

Aristotle was a man of science who saw in man and woman no more than a superior form of animals. "Man's (*anthrôpos*) nature", he wrote in his *History of Animals*, "is the most complete" of all animals. Humans and animals share in the same dispositions, but they "are more evident in humans." [71] From this starting point, he described women's good and bad qualities by which he stereotyped them all as compared to men's qualities. He stated first some of the good qualities of the females as he saw them from his male point of view:

> The character of the females is softer, and quicker to be tamed, and more receptive of handling, and readier to learn. [72]

In a longer passage, Aristotle contrasted women with men in character traits that, he admitted, were found more clearly detectable in women:

> A wife is more compassionate than a husband and more given to tears, but also more jealous and complaining and more apt to scold and fight. The female is also more dispirited and despondent than the male, more shameless and lying, is readier to deceive and has a longer memory; furthermore she is more wakeful, more afraid of action, and in general is less inclined to move than the male, and takes less nourishment. [73]

This was not a pretty picture of women and, by our modern standards, not even a fair one, but it was probably an accurate picture in the view of most men of Ancient Athens, even in the fourth century when some amelioration in the condition of women had taken place in the aftermath of the Peloponnesian War because of the social necessities of the time. From Pericles in the fifth century to Aristotle in

---

[70] *Politics*, 2, 6, 1269b, 18-23: Loeb 264, 134.
[71] Aristotle, *History of Animals*, 8, 608b, 7: Loeb 439, 218.
[72] *Ibid.*, 8, 608a, 26-28: Loeb 439, 216.
[73] *Ibid.*, 8, 608b, 9-17: Loeb 439, 218.

the fourth, the consciousness of male superiority endured, even through the disastrous years of war and unrest caused by men alone. When Aristotle continued his dissertation contrasting male and female qualities, he spoke only of men's courage and of their willingness to help the weak female -- another way of putting them down -- and said not a word of men's wisdom as guardians of women or leaders of the State. Was he then humble, cautious or careless? In keeping with the general culture of Ancient Athens, he certainly cared about the welfare of the State but not in any clear way whether the guardianship of women was fair and wise as long as it remained unchanged.

Aristotle concluded his dissertation with a view on education:

> It is necessary that the education both of the children and of the women should be carried on with a regard to the form of the Constitution, if it makes any difference as regards the goodness of the state for the children and the women to be good. And it must necessarily make a difference; for the women are a half of the free population, and [male] children grow up to be the partners in the government or the state. [74]

Influence

In Aristotle's view, quoted above, a woman can have "right opinion" and, therefore, some private influence on a man, even in the affairs of State. Tied to the previous statement in the *Poetics*, we can understand that the female influence can be real, because a woman's "speech or action reveals the nature of a moral choice", [75] still always subordinate to man's wisdom. She does not have man's wisdom because it is not in her nature to be clever and courageous. Aristotle does not reject entirely a woman's advice, however, but restrict it to the boundaries set by her inferiority.

The politics of government, the administration of justice and the strategies of war were the affairs of men.

---

[74] *Politics*, 1, 1260b, 5, 12: Loeb 264, 66.
[75] *Poetics*, 15, 1454a, 18: Loeb 199, 78.

Xenophon of the early fourth century carved the position of women in society when he placed them by nature inside the house, while the men conducted their activities outside. [76] He explained that every male citizen had full responsibility for the public domain. If married, he also had the responsibility of directing and supervising his wife whose vicarious responsibility was to manage the private domain of the family. Furthermore, every husband was personally involved in the education of his wife and children and in the financial support and expenditures required for the family welfare. Therefore, men had a dual responsibility, public and private, while women had only one, in the private domain and, furthermore, with some limitations imposed upon her by her inferior status and her husband's character.

Tecmessa realized to her great distress how limited her influence was on her warrior lord, Ajax. [77] After learning from her the carnage he had caused in his fit of madness, he fell into despair and wanted to die. In her own tender way, Tecmessa pleaded with her husband to take heart and go on living: "I have nothing to look to except you", she told him. [78] She also brought in their son, Eurysaces. Moved by her plea and the sight of their son, Ajax yielded a promise to bury his sword. But later, away from them, he changed his mind and, in the manly way of a warrior, bid farewell to his troops and thrusted himself upon his sword. When Tecmessa heard about his suicide, she exclaimed: "For I see that he has deceived me and cast me out from the favour I once enjoyed." [79] She was crushed, yet shared with her son in the funeral rites of her husband, recognizing that he remained a great hero.

The women of Thebes failed in their effort to influence Eteocles in his battle against his brother Polynices, yet they dared speak up: "Be ruled by women although thou likest it not." He replied: "Say aught that's possible; nor need ye speak at length." Their advice was: "Go thou not forth on this mission to defend the seventh gate!" [80] He refused to yield to their advice and the end is known, as

---

[76] *Oeconomicus*, 7, 2-30: Loeb 168, 412-421.
[77] Sophocles, *Ajax*, 368-371: Loeb 20, 64-67.
[78] *Ibid.*, 514: Loeb 20, 78.
[79] *Ibid.*, 807-808: Loeb 20, 104.
[80] Aeschylus, *The Seven Against Thebes*, 712-714: Loeb 145, 380.

tragic as it was: Eteocles was killed in single combat with his brother Polynices at the seventh gate.

Nevertheless, most wives exerted a real influence on their husbands' decisions and underestimated it, perhaps because they simply wanted to display their discretion rather than their effectiveness, like Andromache did in Euripides' *Trojan Women*. She affirmed the submissiveness which she intended to show toward her husband -- "I kept my tongue quiet and my gaze tranquil before my husband" -- and affirmed also the sharing of her own mind with him in making decisions about their lives -- "I knew where I ought to be the winner over my husband and where I should yield the victory to him." [81]

In order to achieve success, the wives' influence had to be always discreet, tactful and within bounds. Nevertheless, the typical wives and daughters were curious and eager to know what their husbands or fathers were doing on the outside. We may assume that the juror Philocleon had to answer a few questions after he gave his three obols and received his supper at home. [82] What case did you have at the court today? Who was prosecuted? What was the defense? How did you vote? If we now let Demosthenes provide some answers in his own words as prosecutor in one of his most famous cases some seventy-five years later, it would sound like this:

> Against Neaera. She was accused of illegally marrying an Athenian, and of getting one of her daughters -- a prostitute -- married to Theogenes the archon. [83]

No doubt, this and other cases and verdicts were discussed in detail and the opinions of the women heard. Husbands and fathers could not but be permeable to some influence from their family at home.

For their own good, the children knew well how effective their mother's influence could be on their father. When the young girl Nausicaa brought back a stranger, Odysseus, to the palace, she advised him in this fashion:

---

[81] *Trojan Women*, 654-656: Loeb 10, 80.
[82] Aristophanes, *Wasps*, 605 ff.: Loeb 488, 298.
[83] *Against Neaera*, 59, 13 ff.: Loeb 351, 360 ff.

When the house and the court enclose you, pass quickly through the great hall, till you come to my mother, who sits at the hearth in the light of the fire, spinning the purple yarn. ... There, too, leaning against the selfsame pillar, is set the throne of my father, whereon he sits and quaffs his wine, like an immortal. Pass him by, and throw your arms about my mother's knees, that you may quickly see with rejoicing the day of your return, though you have come from ever so far. If in her sight you win favor, then there is hope that you will see your people, and return to your well-built house and to your native land. [84]

Nausicaa's mother, Arete, was highly respected not only by her husband under whose authority she directed the household, but by all the people in the realm, as Homer explained:

So heartily is she honored, and has ever been, by her children and by Alcinous himself and by the people, who look upon her as upon a goddess, and greet her as she goes through the city. For she of herself is in no way lacking in good understanding, and settles the quarrels of those to whom she has good will, even if they are men.

Then, addressing Odysseus, Nausicaa repeated her advice:

If in her sight you win favor, then there is hope that you will see your own people, and will return to your high-roofed house and to your native land. [85]

Did Adrastus, king of Argos, and his suppliant mothers not do the same when they came to Thebes at festival time to claim and bury the bodies of their sons killed in the war? They needed the support of king Theseus of Athens in order to bear on Creon, the king of Thebes, and make him change the law forbidding the burial of

---

[84] Homer, *Odyssey*, 6, 303-315: Loeb 104, 242.
[85] *Ibid.*, 7, 69-77: Loeb 104, 250-253.

enemy soldiers. Euripides tells us that they first approached Theseus' mother, Aethra, and pleaded with her:

> Prevail on your son, I beg you. ... My plea is just, and you have some power to relieve my misfortune by the noble son you bore. [86]

As we can see, a woman was not kept out of every avenue of influence in the affairs concerning the state. Her influence was never direct by command, but only indirect by assistance and persuasion. Married so young to a man twice her age and well groomed in worldly affairs, she needed to be educated by him out of her totally sheltered life as a young girl. But, as she matured in her role as housewife, she acquired more personal power over her husband, as well as over her relatives and friends.

Xenophon reported that Socrates was once scolding his friend Critobulus for not speaking enough with his wife. Socrates asked him first, before making his point: "Is there anyone to whom you commit more affairs of importance than you commit to your wife?" and the reply was "There is not." Socrates continued: "Is there anyone with whom you talk less?" Critobulus replied: "There are few or none, I confess". Socrates asked further: "And you married her when she was a mere child who had seen and heard almost nothing?" [87]

This exchange was leading toward establishing the need for the wives to be educated by their husbands. Such an education focused primarily on the wives' household duties, but it is hard to believe that men kept them completely ignorant and that they wanted to remain ignorant of these public affairs which affected their lives so deeply, like war and peace. So, it is probable that most men discussed politics in the privacy of their homes and some wives probably expressed their views that later were reflected in the public positions taken by their husbands.

Xenophon complained that some mothers had a vile temper that caused them to be abusive, without being for that malicious or uncaring. [88] Such domineering mothers were also wives with the same dispositions. They must have

---

[86] *Suppliant Women*, 60-64: Loeb 9, 18.
[87] *Oeconomicus*, 3, 12-13: Loeb 168, 386-389.
[88] *Memorabilia*, 2, 2, 7 ff.: Loeb 168, 106 ff.

had their own ideas about politics. Aristophanes could not have presented the political activists Lysistrata and Praxagora on stage unless some women were like them in life. They certainly did not appreciate their husbands' decisions about war and they dared take drastic measures to change them. [89]

When a quarrel broke out in Athens between the factions of Megacles and Cylon, in mid-sixth century, the followers of Megacles slaughtered the Cylonians and, among them, only those "were spared who made supplication to the wives of the archons." They were later hated for it, probably because they yielded to the counsel of their wives. [90]

War was the affair of men. Women were not expected to fight on the battlefield or at sea. Yet, when the occasion appeared favorable, they did not shun giving their men military assistance in their own feminine way. Thucydides reported several instances of such assistance given by women. When the Athenians needed to hurry building the Long Walls, five miles long, between Athens and Piraeus in 479 BCE, the entire population contributed, including the wives and children of Athens. [91] In the summer of 431, when the war started at Plataea, the women, screaming and yelling, pelted the assailants from the rooftops with stones and tiles. Also one woman gave an axe to some trapped Thebans who used it to cut through the bar of a deserted gate. A few of them succeeded in escaping and were saved. [92] Later, in the summer of 429, 480 infantry men who encamped at Plataea were fed with the cooking of 110 women who remained with them until the Spartans defeated them. Then, the men were executed and the women taken as slaves. [93] In the summer of 427, the women of Corcyra (Corfu) repeated the feat of the women of Plataea, pelting their assailants with tiles from the houses. In this case, Thucydides commented that their valiant intervention was

---

[89] Aristophanes, *Lysistrata*, 507 ff.: Loeb 179, 336 ff.
[90] Plutarch, *Parallel Lives, Solon*, 11, 1-2: Loeb 46, 430.
[91] *Peloponnesian War*, 1, 90, 3: Loeb 108, 152.
[92] *Ibid.*, 2, 4, 1-5: Loeb 108, 262-265.
[93] *Ibid.*, 2, 78, 3-4 & 3, 68: Loeb 108, 402 & 3, 68, 3: Loeb 109, 122.

worthy of praise since they acted "with a courage beyond their sex" (*para phusin*). [94]

Strong-willed wives were likely to have ideas also about their husbands' inheritance because it was bound to affect them personally in the future. A law, quoted by Demosthenes, is being reported here in the part that serves our purpose:

> Any citizen ... shall have the right to dispose of his own property by will as he shall see fit ... unless [among other things] he be under the influence of a woman, or under constraint, or deprived of his liberty. [95]

Such female influence was declared illegal. Regardless of the law, children resented their mothers' interference, when they were old enough to realize that their benefit was on the balance and their mothers could tip it on one side or the other. Their resentment was aggravated when they feared the influence of stepmothers or concubines.

It was this kind of situation that prompted Sophocles' legitimate son, Iophon, to take his father to court about his inheritance. In his old age, Sophocles probably enjoyed a considerable wealth in properties and assets, since he was known to have been a miser all his life: "To make a profit he would go to sea on a wicker mat." [96] But he took a companion (*hetaira*), Theoris, when he was in his eighties and even had by her a son called Ariston. We can easily suspect her whispering in his ear some self-serving assignments to be written in his will which would be implemented, for sure, in only a few years. The fact is that Sophocles' legitimate son, Iophon, had the same suspicion. So he took his father to court and tried to have him declared incompetent from senility, so that every undue influence to change his will would be rendered invalid.

Iophon lost his case because he made it rest upon the argument of senility. Sophocles appeared in court and, in response to the claim, recited the first choral ode (*stasimon*) of *Oedipus at Colonus* which he had recently

---

[94] *Peloponnesian War*, 3, 74, 1: Loeb 109, 130.
[95] *Against Stephanus II*, 46, 14: Loeb 155, 252-255.
[96] Aristophanes, *Peace*, 699: Loeb 488, 514.

written in 402 about his beautiful Colonus. [97] The judges dismissed the case and, out of respect, escorted him back to his home. [98]

This incident in the life of a famous man reveals the conflicts that the influence of a new woman can bring into a family. The balance between a strong-willed Theoris and an old Sophocles, at least in practical matters, is unclear to us, yet it was clear enough to Iophon. At the end, he lost not only his court case but also his inheritance for a reason unrelated to the case, in spite of the impression it made on the judges.

One other aspect of women's personal influence has little to do with politics and finance, and is more favorable to her. It pertains to her wisdom, a quality the Ancient Greeks understood to be the ability to invade the mystery of the human condition and appreciate its greatness and limitations, under the inscrutable power of the gods. The playwrights of the fifth century were the philosophers (philosophoi: lovers of wisdom) as well as the entertainers of the masses. Some of their most insightful expressions of wisdom were attributed to women. They would have avoided lending them such expressions if the audience, composed mostly of men, had resented women saying them. The dramatists respected the sensitivities of their audience. They would not have dared jeopardizing the impact of their sayings and, more importantly, the success of their career by offending the feelings of their audience. This indicates to us that the Athenian public had no prejudice against attributing some wisdom to women. Only a few examples will make this important point. It is worth mentioning at the outset that the use of the word "man" in the English translation should generally be taken in its generic sense.

Confronted with the most profound of man's search for answers about divine power and human will, Aeschylus seemed to confess at the end that his mind was overwhelmed by the mystery, not only about god but also about the course of our own lives. In The Suppliant Maidens of about 489 BCE, a play about the psychology of women, he used the voices of women, the Danaids, to declare:

---

[97] Oedipus at Colonus, 668-719: Loeb 21, 492-495.
[98] J.A. Symonds, Studies of the Greek Poets, 278.

Whereon Zeus hath set his desire, that is hard to trace; verily it flareth everywhere, even in the gloom, howbeit attended by events obscure to mortal man. Secure it falleth, and not upon its back, whatsoever is decreed unto fulfillment by the nod of Zeus; for the pathway of his understanding stretch dark and tangled, beyond ken to scan. [99]

Born also of experience as well as of motherly love was the admonition the fateful queen Jocasta gave her son Eteocles. She was old and he was already an adult man aspiring to be king of Thebes. The matter was not of private but of public concern, unlike Penelope who admonished her son Telemachus when he endangered the life of a guest in the palace at Ithaca. [100] Jocasta was attempting to stop a bloody war between her two sons competing for the throne. She spoke like a mother and a queen, with authority and wisdom:

My son, Eteocles, not all that attends old age is bad; the old have experience, which can speak more wisely than youth. Why, do you strive for Ambition, the basest of divinities, my son? Do not do so: she is an unjust goddess! Often she goes in and out of prosperous cities and houses and ruins those who have dealings with her! Yet for her you have lost your senses. Far finer, my son, to honor Equality, which binds friends to friends, cities to cities, and allies to allies. For Equality, men find, conduces to lawfulness, whereas the lesser is always hostile to the greater and making war against it. [101]

Jocasta continued commenting on the value of Equality and the dangers of Ambition, especially the kind that couples with greed. As a mother, she warned her son:

A sufficiency is enough for the self-controlled. Mortals do not own wealth as their own property; we merely hold what is the gods' and look after it. When

---

[99] Aeschylus, *Suppliant Maidens*, 87-95: Loeb 145, 10.

[100] Homer, *Odyssey*, 18, 221-225: Loeb 105, 216.

[101] Euripides, *Phoenician Women*, 528-540: Loeb 11, 264.

they want it, they take it away again. Wealth is not secure but fleeting. [102]

The men who wrote such words of profound wisdom did not shun attributing them to women. Furthermore, the men who heard the same words did not find them out of place on women's lips and did not take offense for the firm admonitions they were giving.

After the surrender to Sparta in 404 BCE and the reign of terror in Athens, the Athenians adopted their eleventh Constitution, preserved later among the writings of Aristotle. [103] None of this legislation applied to women directly. Some of it, however, affected them indirectly, for example;

1. The dual parentage requirement for citizenship; [104]
2. The posts of Market Commissioners, Commissioners of Weights and Measures, Corn Commissioners and Superintendent of the Mart to which they were elected by lot to see that the produce were pure and unadulterated, and in sufficient quantities; [105]
3. The function of Introducers of Cases to the law-courts, such as "for non-payment of dowry"; [106]
4. The point that, in order to be selected as magistrate, the candidate has to establish that, among other things, he has family shrines and tombs, and treats his parents well; [107]
5. The points that, among other suits and indictments, the Archon handles ill-usage of parents, orphans and heiresses by their guardians; [108]
6. The case of legal justification of homicide when a man takes an adulterer in the act. [109]
7. Whatever the Archon does for the citizens, the War-lord does for resident aliens"; [110]

The political insecurity and instability throughout the fourth century contributed also to some degree of

---

[102] *Phoenician Women*, 555-558: Loeb 11, 266.
[103] *Athenian Constitution*, 41, 1-2: Loeb 285, 114.
[104] *Ibid.*, 42, 1: Loeb 285, 118.
[105] *Ibid.*, 51, 1-4: Loeb 285, 138-141.
[106] *Ibid.*, 52, 2: Loeb 285, 142.
[107] *Ibid.*, 55, 3: Loeb 285, 150.
[108] *Ibid.*, 56, 6: Loeb 285, 156.
[109] *Ibid.*, 57, 3: Loeb 285, 158.
[110] *Ibid.*, 58, 3: Loeb 285, 160.

emancipation for women, not in the law but in the practice and application of the law in their social life that seemed to become more relaxed.

Advice is more commonly given in private and on personal matters, and it is always like banking on the assumptions that the present is now well understood and the future anticipated as it will develop. Such banking is never secure; therefore the advice may be good and helpful or bad and harmful. When Hermione was caught in the web of planning the murder of Andromache and her son, she complained:

> My undoing was bad women coming into the house.They puffed me up in folly by speaking in this vein: "Will you put up with this wretched captive in your house sharing in your marriage bed? By the goddess [Hera], in my house she would not have taken her pleasure of my husband and live to see the light!" I listened to these Siren's words, these clever, knavish, deceitful chatterers, and became inflated with foolish thoughts. [111]

Pitfalls

The most natural feelings and commanding attitudes in the social life of women were inferiority and fear. Other traits were more or less common, yet appearing frequently enough to create pitfalls for all women. They were the result of both nature and nurture. The one Greek word *phusis* applied to both. [112]

Aristotle tended to attribute all the women's traits to nature. No doubt, they were all rooted in nature, but certain traits grew faster in women because of the nurture they received, being sheltered, secluded in the home, dominated by men and imbued with the idea of their inferiority from the most tender age. The result in a low self-esteem was pervasive among women.

---

[111] Euripides, *Andromache*, 930-942: Loeb 484, 358.
[112] See Aristophanes, *Wasps*, 1457: Loeb 488, 404 and Plato, *Laws*, 8, 834D: Loeb 192, 144 & *Republic*, 4, 424A: Loeb 237, 330.

Low Self-esteem

Homer extolled the exploits of war where women had no opportunity to shine. Nevertheless, when he introduced them in his story, he did it with respect, even admiration, for example for Penelope's virtue and loyalty. Hesiod wrote his poems at about the same time or shortly before Homer wrote the *Iliad* and the *Odyssey* in the late eighth century. His tone, however, was very different. He disliked women and accepted them in the life of men only as a necessary evil for the good purpose of procreation. He was suspicious of their virtue and of any contribution they could make to the economy of the household.

A satirist of about 650 BCE, Simonedes of Amorgos in the Cyclades, had very little to say that was good about women. He estimated that most of them were deceptive, stubborn, whining and altogether bad. He would have been a friend of Hesiod if he had lived a hundred years earlier. Yet, in spite of his bleak and deprecating attitude about women, he introduced a virtuous woman, Melissa, whom he compared to the industrious and sexless bee. These are his words of praise:

> The man who gets her is fortunate, for on her alone blame does not settle. She causes his property to grow and increase, and she grows old with a husband whom she loves and who loves her, the mother of a handsome and reputable family. She stands out among all women, and a godlike beauty plays about her. She takes no pleasure in sitting among women in places where they tell stories about love. Women like her are the best and most sensible whom Zeus bestows on men. [113]

In the context of the entire poem, these lines were no panegyric of women. Besides, he praised her only for what she did for her husband in managing the household. Indeed, this passage emphasizes only that some women can be trusted as good managers and, therefore, benefit their husbands mostly in their property and well-being. All in all,

---

[113] Simonedes, *Fr.*, 83-93: H. Lloyd-Jones, *Females of the Species*, 52.

in spite of this flicker of praise, silent to boot about the wives' sexual engagement except for procreation, the attitude of men during the seventh and sixth centuries remained one of virulent and destructive misogyny.

Such dark colors on the picture of women created a trend of misogyny that restricted women's role to the household, albeit under the supervision of men, father or husband, and reflected on the low esteem they held of themselves and the attitudes they adopted to correct it even during the Classical Period of the late fifth century.

For example, women's words of complaints, which are a natural reaction of defense against their lot, cannot be interpreted as being always excessive. Complaints were prompted by the circumstances. For example, Medea was abandoned by her husband, Creusa was seduced when still unmarried, then married to an old impotent man, Megara was left at home when her husband Heracles was roaming the world; Deianeira was invaded in her home by her husband's young concubine, Iole; the Trojan women were made the slaves of their Greek victors. Another woman, Alcestis, was forced to give up her life in order to let her husband live. The male chorus in Euripides' *Alcestis* did not make a big fuss about the loss of a wife when its leader commented: "A wife. Different misfortunes arise to press on different mortals." [114] Most women had little appreciation of their worth. Iphigenia recognized that "when the house loses a male, his loss is felt, but a woman's loss is of little effect." [115]

From Hesiod of the eight century to the end of the Fifth century the attitude of men toward women was generally demeaning, with the resulting feeling among women that their worth in society was not held in high esteem. Then, as already pointed out several times, the miseries and loses caused by the Peloponnesian War boosted women's role at the turn of the century and carried over in a greater consideration for their contribution to society during the fourth century.

The turn of the century was a landmark of progress for women's self-esteem and freedom, especially through the quiet opportunity to reach a higher level of education.

---

[114] *Alcestis*, 893-894: Loeb 12, 246.
[115] Euripides, *Iphigenia Among the Taurians*, 1005-1006: Loeb 10, 256.

Diogenes Laërtius of the third century CE informed us that two female students attended the Academy of Plato: among his disciples were "two women Lastheneia of Mantineia and Axiothea of Phlius ... who have worn men's clothes." [116] This tidbit of information at the end ought to be interpreted in the sense that they needed to remain incognito rather than wanted to be transvestite.

When Aristophanes made the statement in 414 that the Athenians, like the birds at the crack of dawn, "all fly the coop together, just like us [men], to root for writs; then they flock to the archives and there sharpen their bills", [117] and in 405 that Dionysus was reading Euripides' *Andromeda*, staged in 411, [118] the seed was planted for a change in the manner of learning from listening to reading. Dramatic as it was, this change came about neither by the exclusion of the oral tradition nor as a rapid instead of a gradual transformation.

In the first half of the fourth century, when Plato was preserving in writing the words of Socrates, reading had made progress but had not yet supplanted listening to rhapsodies, theater productions and teachers' instructions. Plato's Dialogues may have been read to students but were not widely read by students during his lifetime.

Later in the century, Aristotle's writings received greater acceptance because students needed more time to delve carefully into his lecture notes and his more sophisticated writings.

Women were excluded from higher education. However, their commingling in the family circle with brothers and male cousins who were included could not but have some influence on them. They may have seen a brother, as represented on vases, concentrating on a scroll held in his hand. [119] Then, their interest was aroused. Furthermore, because of their seclusion and especially if they had a craving for poetry, they had a personal incentive to learn reading books. A man they trusted, either a relative or an educated slave, could obtain the books for them.

---

[116] *Lives of Eminent Philosophers, Plato*, 3, 46 & *Speusippus*, 4, 2: Loeb 184, 316 & 374.

[117] *Birds*, 1288-1289: Loeb 179, 190.

[118] *Frogs*, 52-53: Loeb 180, 22.

[119] K. Robb, *Literacy and Paideia in Ancient Greece*, 185-188; also 190-191 & 221.

Furthermore, inasmuch as the fourth century witnessed a steady increase in public inscriptions and written documents, the common people were encouraged to learn reading. Literacy was not yet widespread. However, before the end of the century, reading was widely sought in the upper classes of the Athenian society.

Alexander's conquests from 334 to 323 when he prematurely died and the subsequent removal of Athens as the pivotal point of all Greek cultural life did in practice open to women opportunities they never had before. One Hipparchia delved in philosophy and another, Laia of Cyzicus, turned to the art of painting. Even obstetrics, a subject of woman's personal interest, attracted women, for example Hagnodice of Athens, for the first time. Female poets also made their entrance. Poetry was probably never far from women's minds but the fact that several short poems and epigrams were preserved starting with the end of the fourth century is significant of a trend and of the respectability given to female poets known by names such as Erinna of Teos, Nossis of Locri, Anyte of Tegea and Corinne of Tanagra. The lack of direct evidence should not prevent us from thinking that reading had crossed the threshold into women's lives.

The events of the turn of the century marked the transition from the serene beauty and segregated status of women in the fifth century to a more relaxed, inquisitive, venturesome and self-assured life style in the fourth century, leading to the more flamboyant Hellenistic period.

Emotions

Women felt vulnerable because of their physical weakness and sense of inferiority, also because of their emotional proclivity. Especially for this reason, they tended to stick together in order to compensate for their difficulties coping with crises in a rational way. In her second stage of life, Iphigenia could rely only on her brother Orestes and his friend Pylades to return home to Argos from the land of the Taurians in northwest Asia. She began her plea, however, with this reference to the Argive women around her: "We are women, and our sex wish each other well and are most firm in defending our common interests." [120]

Emotions are varied, yet the most powerful of all and most difficult to steer in a good direction is the emotion of love. Love has two hands to hold the heart of people, one is sexual love (erôs) that can be good or bad according to the circumstances, the other is affection (philia) that binds parents to their children and friends to friends, for instance in mothers and fathers, like Penelope and Odysseus toward their son Telemachus. The Ancient Greek women were sometimes the victims of erôs, like Helen, for disastrous consequences like war, but were often the masters of philia, caring for dear ones, like Antigone did for her vagrant father Oedipus.

The emotions naturally floating between men and women were reinforced in women by the aggressive emotions of men toward them. In spite of the barriers of segregation that kept women separated from men in public places, there were probably exchanges of looks and words, perhaps even quick encounters in more private places outside the home, inasmuch as such a practice was noticed already in the prior Archaic Age. [121]

As a rule, flirting was in every way condemned and rejected. Nevertheless, like Xanthus said, some women were in their manners a little bit too free. [122] Men preferred to blame their women for luring them to sexual advances, but men are the only ones we hear! Any understanding of the way men and women tended to relate when the restraints were relaxed would lead to the assumption that such not-so-innocent contacts did really take place. A short paragraph of a choral ode in Birds, one of Aristophanes' comedies, seems to confirm it while blowing it up as usual:

> And if there's anyone among you who happens to be an adulterer, and sees the lady's husband in the Councillors' seats, he'd have used his wings to launch himself out of the audience, gone and fucked

---

[120] Euripides, Iphigenia Among the Taurians, 1061-1062: Loeb 10, 264.

[121] Homer, Iliad, 22, 128-129: Loeb 171, 460.

[122] Aristophanes, Wasps, 495-499: Loeb 488, 284; also, about Andromache speaking too freely to men: Euripides, Andromache, 363-365: Loeb 484, 306.

her, and then flown back here again. So isn't getting wings worth any price? [123]

In his dialogue *Symposium*, Plato described the gathering of seven to fifteen friends to partake in food and wine while reclining on couches, and to share in a discussion of some social or philosophical subject, like love. It carried on with quite a sopihistication until it often ended up in complete inebriation. Women were included in this symposium of men, not as participants in the feast and discussion, but as entertainers. Some of them were flute-girls, others prostitutes, most of them alien or slave, but some of them known to be wives of Athenian men. Their services made up for a lucrative business because they were not free of charge and the men were willing to pay for them.

As a result of women's presumed romantic disposition, men perceived women as falling in love more easily than men and as more erotic than they were. Several conflicting legends about the seer Tiresias, who had a prominent role in the Oedipus saga, include the story of his transformation into a woman and of his return to be a man after a few years. He then reported that women enjoy love-making more than men, which goddess Hera flatly denied. [124]

Mythology has preserved the story of Stheneboea burning with sexual desire for the suppliant Bellerophon who had found refuge in her husband Proteus' palace at Tiryns. She propositioned him and, when he refused, she accused him of trying to seduce her. Proteus believed his wife and chased the young suppliant from the palace, [125] not unliked king Theseus of Athens did to Hippolytus in Euripides' play.

Irritability and madness also were attributed to the physical nature of women as baneful coordinates of their propensity to love. If the blood their bodies absorbed more abundantly than men's bodies does not find its release, it causes some affliction in the mind, a condition that is either temporary or pathological. Therefore, healthy women experience such mental distress only moderately. However,

---

[123] Aristophanes, *Birds*, 792-796: Loeb 179, 126.

[124] See N. Loraux, *The Experiences of Tiresias*, 11.

[125] Euripides, *Fr.*, *Stheneboea*, 661: Loeb 506, 130-135; see Id., *Fr.*, *Hippolytus Veiled*, 429: Loeb 504, 478.

when the distress was severe, for example in the case of Medea, it was much more severe in women than it could ever be in men, short of a fit of insanity, as was the case with Heracles and Ajax.

In Plato's Dialogue *Symposium*, Socrates explained that sexual love (*erôs*) is honorable provided it is done honorably, like between husband and wife. [126] On the other hand, the kind of love Phaedra entertained for Hippolytus, her stepson, was illicit not only because she was his father's wife, as previously covered under the subject of incest, but because he was not interested in it or attracted to her at all. For her disgrace, she became "a thing all men hate", [127] except Theseus who still believed her rather than his son, especially after she committed suicide and, albeit falsely, accused the young man of having seduced her. The king banished his son and justified his action by asking: "But will you say that folly is not to be found in men but is native to women?" His answer was a reflection of the memories he had, more of his own life than of his son's behavior:

> I know young men who are no more stable than women when Cypris [Aphrodite] stirs their young hearts to confusion. But their standing as males serves them well. [128]

Theseus implied also in this statement that women are like immature young men who have little control over their sexual emotions but cannot get away with them as easily as young men do in the Greek culture. In this regard, the comedy playwright Aristophanes provided his support not only in the wild wedding feast (*gamos*) ending his plays but also in major scenes always enwrapped in lurid bawdiness.

The high emotional charge in women's heart coupled with the culture of superstition and magic gave also to some of them the ability to become psychics. For example, young girls were preferred as media for oracles, because of their greater suggestibility. The pythia of Delphi claimed to be the voice of Apollo when she was in fact a medium used by another clever person. However, possession by a god or

---

[126] *Symposium*, 183D: Loeb 166, 116.
[127] Euripides, *Hippolytus*, 404: Loeb 484, 264.
[128] *Ibid.*, 966-970: Loeb 484, 216-219.

a devil and its counterpart, exorcism, were foreign to the Classical Greeks.

Cassandra was not a medium in the strict sense when she delivered her famous prophesy in Aeschylus' play *Agamemnon*. [129] She was under the spell of a prophetic trance. She called on Apollo but spoke in her own name because she had been left on her own after the god had given her the gift of prophesy. What she saw in her mad vision was what she told. It included the past and the future: the past crimes of Thyestes and Atreus, and also the future murder of Agamemnon and her own by Clytemnestra and Aegisthus who will be slain by Orestes. Her trance was beyond every explanation by normal techniques. It belonged to the realm of psychic knowledge, like out-of-body experiences that escape rational explanations, yet resemble minor experiences of the same kind, true or false, that most people think they have at one time or another in their lives. Cassandra was a woman with a special gift, like the seers Calchas and Tiresias who could see the unknown past and predict the elusive future.

The frenzy of the women devotees at the end of Euripides' play *The Bacchae* had the quality of trance or madness, not as much for the words as for the deeds of wild ecstasy and cruelty which grew among them like an infectious disease induced by dance and music. Herodotus said that Dionysus was "a god who leads men on to madness." [130] Agave's "mouth dripped foam and her eyes rolled: she was not in her right mind." [131] She hallucinated when she carried her son's head, thinking it was that of a lion's whelp. Her state was one of divine possession or, more accurately, of schizophrenic madness. Such a state of demented emotions was not peculiar to women. Strong men like Heracles [132] and Ajax [133] had similar fits of madness, but women, being known to be more emotional than men, seemed to have had a greater share of such madness in real life.

Women felt vulnerable by their physical weakness, their sense of inferiority and their emotional proclivity. They

[129] *Agamemnon*, 1072-1330: Loeb 146, 90-119.
[130] *Histories*, 4, 79: Loeb 118, 280.
[131] Euripides, *Bacchae*, 11222-1123: Loeb 495, 120.
[132] Id., *Heracles Mad*, 858 ff,: Loeb 9, 300.
[133] Sophocles, *Ajax*, 51 ff.: Loeb 20, 34.

tended to stick together in order to compensate for their individual vulnerability. One pitfall that could ensue and threaten not only their virtue but also their survival as wives was lesbianism.

This subject cannot be ignored, considering the variety in sexual orientation and the condition of wives in Ancient Athens. They had no choice about their husbands, their marital relationship was often without any sexual love, their social interactions were mainly with women and they felt the normal desires for love not only as friends but also as sexual partners, so lesbianism was bound to be present, although in hiding.

As a practice without a specific name, homosexuality was recognized and accepted for men for at least two hundred and fifty years when the Classical Age began in 480 BCE. The relationship of Achilles and Patroclus, first related in Homer's *Iliad*, served as prototype for the innumerable homosexual relationships, especially between men and boys, throughout the fifth and fourth centuries. To engage in the pursuit of a fair boy (*erômenos*) out of erotic love was not at all shameful as long as the lover's pride and the beloved's self-esteem were respected. [134] Wives knew about it and, without having any choice to be contrary, condoned it silently. Needless to say that effeminacy was accepted as a fact of life, as it was the case for Cleisthenes and Cleonymus in Aristophanes' plays, but carried very little respect from men and attention from women. [135]

When Plato considered the desires for a partner of the same sex to be contrary to nature and virtue and yet confessed his inability to recommend any remedy, he was then thinking only of male homosexuality since it seemed that lesbianism was simply unthinkable, at least by a man whose pride would never allow female love to be for any other but a man.

This Greek view of sexual intercourse between two partners, in which the male is active without domination and the female passive without submission, applied as well to the homosexual relation. The beloved boy (*erômenos*) impersonated a woman and tended to be sexually passive. However, the conditions of homosexual intercourse

---

[134] Plato, *Lysis*, 205B & 206A: Loeb 166, 12-15.
[135] *Clouds*, 355-356: Loeb 488, 58 and *Birds*, 289: Loeb 179, 54.

required that he be more active than a woman. Otherwise, The Athenians feared that he would make himself unsuitable to become a full-fledged citizen, ready to assume an active role in governing the city. Therefore, it was paramount among the responsibilities of the adult lover (*erastês*) to foster in the youth the male dominant traits of decisiveness, courage and cooperation. In order to be honorable, their relationship had to contribute to building a strong and happy society. [136]

Therefore, if the order of nature in sexual relations is to take place in a dominant versus subordinate relationship between a man and a woman or a man and a womanly boy, it is not the order of nature between two adult men who should both be dominant. [137]

Most men were bisexual, holding firm to a wife for procreation and, intermittently, having sexual encounters for pleasure with women of inferior status and with men or boys of any status, high or low.

The artistic productions, in sculpture and painting, can be an indication of the comfort men had with the male body. The nude *kouros* (young man) appeared in public display long before the female nude. As early as about 600 BCE, the *kouros* of Sounion was represented in the nude, with little sensuality. [138] The same comfort appeared in the pederastic scenes painted on vases after 550 BCE. [139] The nude *Kourê* (young woman) did not appear in a standing position before the end of the fifth century. Then, gradually during the fourth century and more aggressively during the following Hellenistic period, the female body became a subject of choice, especially in sculpture.

In his discourse reported in Plato's *Symposium*, Aristophanes recognized two categories of men: one desiring women and the other only men. Since only the first category is naturally inclined to produce children for the state, the other category has to do it only "under stress of customs". [140] Civic duty included male-female relations, even when a homosexual proclivity made it repugnant.

---

[136] Aristotle, *Eudemian Ethics*, 7, 12, 1245a, 25: Loeb 285, 440.
[137] Plato, *Laws*, 1, 636C & 8, 836C: Loeb 187, 40 & 192, 150.
[138] EWA 1, Pl. 346.
[139] J. Bremmer, *From Sappho to De Sade*, 7-10.
[140] Plato, *Symposium*, 192B: Loeb 166, 142.

What did the male homosexual culture do to the perception women had of men, including their husbands? Nothing that seemed to be disturbing them. They knew that male homosexuality was pervasive and had no choice but to live with it. Did they do the same as men? Were they the lovers of fair girls like men were of fair boys? Since wives had frequent and free contacts with other women, did they and their husbands accept lesbianism as a natural form of sexuality? The answer is bound to come from men since women had no voice and no interest in telling.

Men never spoke about such activities that hurt their manly pride by suggesting their inability to satisfy their women and, furthermore, women could easily hide their amours, if they had them, since they always took place in the privacy of a home under the bland cover-up of friendship. Lesbianism probably existed among women but the extent and the form it had in a man's world are almost entirely unknown to us.

Unlike Sparta, Athens had no public sympathy for lesbian women. Out of 106 illustrations of homosexual relations, K.J. Dover showed women together only in two, neither from Athens. [141] Furthermore, the only reference to them appeared in the context of Aristophanes' myth about the origin of women, previously quoted. He divided the original human race into three groups: male, female and androgynous. When Zeus split them in halves, he created in them the desire to be reunited and be one again. Then,

> All the women who are sections of the woman [second group] have no great fancy for men; they are inclined rather to women and of this stock are the she-minions [hetairistriai]. [142]

Such a late statement, only in the fourth century, recognized the existence of a group of women characterized by a sexual preference for women. They may belong to every level of society, from the highest of the Athenian women to the lowest of the slaves. The details are lacking. The Athenian sources are silent.

---

[141] *Greek Homosexuality*, CE 34 & R 207.
[142] Plato, *Symposium*, 191E: Loeb 166, 140.

We may reasonably assume, however, that married women who were often neglected by their husbands and did not have or dared not encourage any inclination toward men, resorted to clandestine love affairs with other married women. It is also reasonable to assume that lesbian affairs took place between married women and young girls, on a more limited range than between men and boys, because the girls of the same age as boys growing their first beards were getting married and given to a man who educated and supervised them according to his own expectations. These are reasonable assumptions made without hard evidence.

Nevertheless, one early document, made of poems referring to the passionate, tender and probably more-than-Platonic love of one woman for another, was well known in Athens, although it had been produced on the island of Lesbos. The author was Sappho who appeared to be anachronistic in the early sixth century BCE when she wrote about love. [143] She was in her lifetime a recognized poet, an influential leader, the first liberated woman in history. She recited or sang some of her poems to groups of friends of both sexes, at occasions like banquets and weddings. She allegedly ran a school or club for girls where she became deeply disturbed when a love affair she had with a young girl, named Atthis, was interrupted by the advances of a young man of Mytilene or by her transfer to another mistress, perhaps Andromeda.

The Roman critic Longinus of the third century CE preserved the following fragment of one of Sappho's poems, the first poem known about the jealous love for another woman, a young girl with a "sweet speech and lovely laughter":

> It's this that makes my heart flutter in my breast. If I see you but for a little, my voice comes no more and my tongue is broken. At once a delicate flame runs through my limbs; I see nothing with my eyes and my ears thunder. The sweat pours down: shivers grip me all over. I am grown paler than grass, and seem to myself to be very near to death. But all must be endured. [144]

---

[143] 16: Sappho: Loeb, *Greek Lyric*, 142, 66.
[144] *On The Sublime*, 10, 2: Loeb 199, 198.

It is wishful thinking to believe that we can learn more in the future about the practice of lesbianism in ancient Athens. The subject was too sensitive, especially in the Classical Age, for men to dare tell about it or depict it in graphic images and for women to dare tell about anything, especially about their clandestine love affairs with women or girls. [145]

Restricted as they were by life style and customs, women had to contend not only with their men's attraction to boys but also with their transient desires to satisfy their libidinous appetites with women of dubious repute. Prostitution was not criminalized. On the outskirt of Athens and especially at Piraeus, in houses of prostitution, free alien and slave women offered their services for a price. [146] They lured their customers by street walking or standing in the windows. The most attractive among them were invited to visit the symposia where they served wine and entertained the male guests. Even after the men had become husbands, the same activities tended to continue, since their habits were well established and their desires not always completely satisfied at home.

Venereal diseases may have been rampant in such a permissive society. We do not know about them because of the lack of records and such a lack exists because the Athenian men, even the Hippocratic physicians, probably did not identify them.

One occasion was especially propitious to uncharted sexual experiences. It was the festival of Dionysus that took place in the early spring and brought together female Maenads and male Satyrs who danced and sang their way to the countryside with sexual interludes in the bushes. When Xuthus thought Ion was his natural son, he attributed his birth to one of his youthful exuberances at the *Great Dionysia*. [147]

In his play *Bacchae*, Euripides introduced king Pentheus worrying that orgies were the norm at such a festival. Even allowing for some exaggeration, it seems fair to believe that some married Athenian women frolicked

---

[145] See Laurin, J.R., *Homosexuality in Ancient Athens*, cover and p. 110-116.

[146] See Attic red-figured paintings on drinking cup (*kulix*) by Phintias, c. 510 BCE, at the J. Paul Getty Museum, Malibu, CA..

[147] Euripides, *Ion*, 545-553: Loeb 10, 388-391.

quite freely on this occasion. Vase paintings show little discretion in their representation of Dionysiac scenes of promiscuity. The following passage shows little discretion also:

> They set up full wine bowls in the middle of their assemblies and sneak off, one here, one there, to tryst in private with men. The pretext for all this is that they are maenads performing their rites, but they hold Aphrodite in higher regard than the bacchic god. [148]

Plato remembered

> hearing Sophocles the poet greeted by a fellow who asked, 'How about your service of Aphrodite, Sophocles – is your natural force still unabated?' And he replied, 'Hush, man, most gladly have I escaped this thing you talk of, as if I had run away from a raging and savage beast of a master.' [149]

We may assume, with little evidence, that this raging and savage beast attacked sometimes some women as well as men.

Jealousy

Jealousy (*phthonos*) was not a character trait restricted to women but seemed to have found in their lives more frequent occasions to flare up. It is a kind of fear that breeds in the swamps of insecurity and envy where competition is a threat. A woman can be another woman's best ally, but it can also be her worst enemy if the perception turns into resentment against a rival. A moderate feeling of competition can become a valuable incentive to progress, but a jealous one, rooted in envy, can be painfully divisive and destructive of every good social relations. [150]

Stepmothers were the frequent victims of this malady. When Alcestis was ready to die so that her husband

---

[148] *Bacchae*, 221-225: Loeb 495, 30.
[149] Plato, *Republic*, 1, 3B-C: Loeb237, 10.
[150] Euripides, *Fr., Antiope*, 209: Loeb 504, 108.

Admetus may live she made only one request: "Remember
to show your gratitude for this" and do not put a
stepmother over our children because "a stepmother comes
as a foe to the former children, no kinder to them than a
viper." [151] This kind of jealousy is of a mother rather than a
wife. It was indeed too much to ask but not too much to
wish for a generous wife and mother like Alcestis.

A "ménage à trois" created also an eruption of
jealousy between the two female partners in love for the
same man. After describing the marriage of Neoptolemus to
Hermione with Andromache as the concubine, Euripides
could not pass the opportunity to bemoan the jealousy such
a bedding arrangement can cause. Using the chorus of
Phthian women from Thessaly, he flatly admitted: "The mind
of a woman is a jealous thing and always ill-disposed
towards rivals in marriage." [152]

In the face of death, the same Andromache reflected
Euripides' misogynic bias concerning women's jealousy:

> It is strange that some god has given man remedies
> against snakes of the wild, yet where something
> worse than snake or fire is concerned, no one has yet
> found the specific [cure] against a woman [, a bad
> one: such a great bane we are to mankind]. [153]

A fifth-century Athenian man was not breaking any
rule when he took a concubine in addition to his wife or had
a one-night stand with a slave or a prostitute. It was
tolerated, yet resented perhaps in certain female circles.
Usually, however, the married man conducted his love
affairs outside the home, hoping that being kept out of the
women's sights would keep it also out of their minds. The
situation was hardly acceptable when he brought his
paramour home for a "ménage à trois". Clytemnestra killed
Agamemnon and Cassandra, his concubine brought home
after the war; Deianeira killed Heracles for bringing his
concubine Iole home; Hipparete attempted to divorce her
husband Alcibiades, also for bringing his concubine home.

---

[151] Euripides, *Alcestis*, 299-310: Loeb 12, 182-185.
[152] *Andromache*, 181-182: Loeb 484, 290.
[153] *Ibid.*, 269-273: Loeb 484, 300.

The presence of female servants in the house, either freeborn or slave, created for the master and his adult sons the temptation to abuse them sexually. Some men were very respectful and kept their distance, like Laërtes, Odysseus' father, who bought a young maid, Euryclea, and brought her home but "never lay with her in love, for he avoided the wrath of his wife", Anticleia. [154]   According to a court document of the fourth century, Apollodorus praised Lysias also for not bringing his alien mistress home for the fear of his wife's resentment. [155]

However, even without any hard evidence, we cannot give all Greek masters the same commendation for such a high standard of behavior. Men's passion can rise as quickly as a black cloud in spring. About the frequency of these affairs, a distinction ought to be made between one isolated encounter and a protracted relationship under the roof shared with a wife. The former may have happened often, perhaps as often as the occasions lent themselves; the latter rarely because of its intolerable consequences.

If one were to rely only on the playwrights of the fifth century, it would appear that certain female traits were related to age. When women were young or of middle age, they were sometimes generous and faithful like Alcestis and Andromache, but more often they were jealous, possessive, manipulative, even cruel at times toward their husband and children. Such was the towering Medea who killed her children out of jealousy in order to hurt her husband. But when women reached an older age and especially when they were with grandchildren and sometimes widowed, they were tender in their care, wise in their thoughts and courageous in their tolerance. They remained mothers of their grown-up sons and devoted grandmothers of their grandsons. Queen Atossa admonished her weak son, Xerxes, like Penelope did her brazen son, Telemachus. Queen Hecuba, the widowed and enslaved grandmother from Troy, cared for her adult daughters to the end and added her tears to the soil where she buried her grandson, Astyanax. Their jealousy vanished when the stimulation abated from their husbands' liberties now that they were either dead, away from home or very

---

[154] Homer, *Odyssey*, 1, 433: Loeb 104, 44.
[155] Demosthenes, *Against Neaera*, 59, 22: Loeb 351, 366.

old, except for Sophocles who died at the grand old age of ninety and still had a concubine at his side.

Gossip

Women had the gift of gab. [156] Sharing news with friends and relatives was, no doubt, a frequent occurrence among women. The birth of a child, the success of a husband, the ill-health of a mother, and all the little achievements and misfortunes in the household or the neighborhood were reported and repeated by mouth. The spoken words, delivered in person, were the normal medium of communication. In the Ancient World, true and positive news fulfilled an important function of social intercourse. But when it was either false or slanted to produce a negative response, it was gossip spread like a contagious virus. Women used it well after god Hermes "put speech in the first woman, Pandora." [157]

Men's reputations depended on their wives' good news rather than gossip. Aristotle acknowledged the baneful consequences of such reports by female spies like they had under Hiero of Syracuse. [158]

Women were also the victims of gossips spread by other women's tongues that conveyed shameless minds and a deceitful nature." [159] Their reputations could be tarnished and, as it was in the case of Alcestis described by Euripides, a maiden's chances to get married could be seriously jeopardized by them. With the comments made about her decision to waste her life for the salvation of her husband, Alcestis told her daughter that a stepmother may

> cast some disgraceful slur on your reputation and in the prime of your youth destroy your chances of marriage! [160]

The same Euripides made gossiping a trait of women's behavior when he wrote:

---

[156] Aristophanes, *Assemblywomen*, 120: Loeb 180, 258.
[157] Hesiod, *Works and Days*, 67-68: Loeb 57, 6.
[158] *Politics*, 5, 9, 1313b, 12-17: Loeb 264, 460.
[159] Hesiod, *Works and Days*, 80: Loeb 57, 8.
[160] Euripides, *Alcestis*, 315-316: Loeb 12, 184.

Women by nature love to criticize, and once they have found trifling reasons to find fault, they invent still more, such is the pleasure they take in speaking ill of one another. [161]

Odysseus' wife, Penelope, was weaving a pall in which her father-in-law, Laërtes, could be buried with respect, she explained,

For fear anyone of the Achaean women in the land should cast blame upon me, if he were to lie without a shroud, who had won great possessions. [162]

Reputation was the rudder to be held firmly by both men and women in order to steer their families in the right direction. Gossips could blow storms hindering their course.

<u>Inebriety</u>

Alcoholism was a widespread disease that debilitated some of the most prominent citizens, like Cleon and Alcibiades of Athens, Lysander of Sparta, and Alexander the Great of the glorious campaign through Asia. They drank in taverns and at symposia. It seems that women also enjoyed their wine, sometimes to excess, either in the privacy of a home, alone or with female friends, or on special occasions, especially at festivals.

About women's habits of eating and drinking to excess, Plato remarked that these were the last things they wanted the public to know. For this reason, they were forced to abstain from eating and drinking in public until mid-fourth century when he introduced the innovation of "public meals for the women." [163] We surmise that the practice did not become popular because Plato himself recognized the female penchant to secrecy in these matters:

The female sex would more readily endure anything rather than this: accustomed as they are to live a retired and private life, women will use every means

---

[161] *Phoenician Women*, 197-201: Loeb 11, 232.
[162] Homer, *Odyssey*, 19, 146-147: Loeb 105, 244.
[163] Aristotle, *Politics*, 2, 4, 1266a, 36-37: Loeb 264, 110.

to resist being led out into the light, and they will prove much too strong for the lawgiver. [164]

In the first lines of his play *Lysistrata*, Aristophanes implied that women were known to be immoderate. While waiting impatiently for her female friends to join her, she complained:

> Now if someone had invited them to a revel for Bacchus, or to Pan's shrine, or to Genetyllis at Colias, [all gods of wine and love], the streets would be impassible, what with their tambourines. [165]

The same Aristophanes, who was always in tune with his audience, used comedy to imply that the Athenian women had a serious problem controlling their wine drinking. In his *Women at the Thesmophoria* he showed them ready to burn Mnesilochus at the stake, not for the unseemly reason to save a baby girl, as they pretended, but for the real reason to quaff a leather flask of wine. [166] They ended up the losers in this squabble because he thwarted their strategy when he drank the wine to the last drop. [167]

Still in distress as a hostage, and probably a little tipsy, Mnesilochus sent a written summon for help to Euripides who must use disguises to reach him. First, he poses as Menelaus coming to claim his dear wife, [168] then as Perseus coming to save his Andromeda chained to a rock, [169] finally as an old woman who proposes a deal to the assembled women:

> If I can take him away with me, you'll never hear another insult. But if you refuse, whatever you've been doing behind your husbands' backs while they're away at the front, I'll denounce to them when they return. [170]

---

[164] Plato, *Laws*, 6, 781C: Loeb 187, 488.
[165] *Lysistrata*, 1-4: Loeb 179, 266.
[166] *Women at the Thesmophoria*, 730-738: Loeb 179, 546.
[167] *Ibid.*, 756: Loeb 179, 550.
[168] *Ibid.*, 871: Loeb 179, 564.
[169] *Ibid.*, 1011: Loeb 179, 582.
[170] *Ibid.*, 1166-1169: Loeb 179, 604.

The women accepted this threatening deal, because they preferred avoiding every revelation of their short-comings when their husbands were away, and let Mnesilochus go free.

Violence

In whatever state of mind they were, some women demonstrated that they could use more than words to destroy the cause of their misery. Clytemnestra killed her husband Agamemnon, Hecuba blinded her friend Polymestor, Jocasta and Creusa abandoned their babies to die, Agave was a monster of cruelty when she killed her son Pentheus, the mythical Procne killed her son Itys to punish her husband Tereus, and Medea also killed her sons for the same reason. She explained her action:

> A woman is full of fear, incapable of looking on battle or clod steel; but when she is injured in love, no mind is more murderous than hers. [171]

Women went sometimes beyond venting their ill feelings with complaints and resorted to acts of violence, always done with guile and deceit to compensate for their lack of strength. Worse still: some defended their wicked deeds "with fine words." [172]

A chorus of slave women in Aeschylus' play *The Libation-Bearers* reminisced about a woman's angst and "woeful deed" of violence when the Lemnian women killed their husbands: "No man holdeth in reverence that which merits Heaven's hate." [173]

The context of this chorus' lamentation was Clytemnestra's murder of her husband, Agamemnon, when he returned from the Trojan War.

> As he was stepping from the bath, on its very edge, she curtained the laver with a tented cloak,

---

[171] Euripides, *Medea*, 264-266: Loeb 12, 306.
[172] Id., *Fr, Meleager*, 528: Loeb 504, 626.
[173] *The Libation-Bearers*, 623-637: Loeb 146, 220.

enveloped her husbnd in a broidered robe's inextricable maze, and hewed him down. [174]

The cycle of violence continued when Electra made the plans to murder Clytemnestra and her lover Aegisthus, and encouraged her brother Orestes and his friend Pylades to do the deed while she kept "strict watch of what passes within the house, that so our plan may fit together well." [175] She stood at her brother's side when he first slew Aegisthus, then dragged their mother inside the palace and slew her. An unforgiving woman masterminded the two crimes. Orestes' words "Women are clever at inventing subterfuges" [176] were confirmed by those of Andromache to her maid: "You will find many ruses: you are a woman." [177]

When the body of Polydorus was recovered on the seashore and his mother Hecuba, queen of Troy, learned that the man she trusted, king Polymestor of Thrace, had killed him, she devised a way to carry out her vengeance. She sent out a servant to invite Polymestor to visit with her. When the king arrived with his two infant sons, she wrapped her plot in deceit (*dolos*):

> I want to say something privately to you and your sons. Please order your servants to stand at a distance from the house. ... First tell me whether my son Polydorus, whom you received into your house from my hand and his father's, is still alive. [178]

Polymestor responded to Hecuba's deceit with a lie of his own, assuring her that her son and all his gold were safe. She added cunningly that more gold was kept for him inside her tent. He followed her inside with the other Trojan women who slew his sons and stabbed his eyes with brooches. [179]

This crime took place between barbarians but Herodotus reported that Athenian women did the same to one of their own in a more lethal way. When the Athenian

---

[174] Aeschylus, *Eumenides*, 633-635: Loeb 146, 332.
[175] Id., *The Libation-Bearers*, 579-580: Loeb 146, 216.
[176] Euripides, *Iphigenia Among the Taurians*, 1032: Loeb 10, 260.
[177] Id., *Andromache*, 85: Loeb 484, 282.
[178] Id., *Hecuba*, 978-983: Loeb 484, 486.
[179] *Ibid.*, 1255: Loeb 484, 512.

troops were destroyed and only one soldier, perhaps a traitor, returned home to Athens alive and told of the calamity, the wives took it so "sorely to heart" that

> they gathered round the man and stabbed him with the brooch-pins of their garments ... thus was this man done to death. [180]

One of the tricks women used to affect the mood of their husbands was to serve them drugs extracted from herbs such as oleander, cyclamen or mandrake, usually mixed with wine. The quantity from moderate to excessive could determine the effect from relaxing anger, like Helen did in king Menelaus' court, [181] provoking lust and sleep, like Hera did to Zeus [182] or increasing affection and sexual desire, like the scribe of Nestor's cup stated: "Whoever drinks from this cup, desire for beautifully crowned Aphrodite will seize him instantly", [183] to causing utter madness and weird delusions, like Aristotle's pupil Theophratus explained in his *Enquiry into Plants* [184] or even killing the victim, like a mistress did unwittingly to her lover Philoneus in mid-fifth century [185] and Agave did to her son Pentheus, king of Thebes, when "her mouth dripped foam and her eyes rolled." [186]

This last scene in *Bacchae*, created by Euripides only for the theater of Tragedy, was blown out of realistic proportion in order to produce the effects of pity and fear through a reversal of fortune. No one could ever expect to see a mother in a bestial rage dismembering her son and carrying his head like a trophy. This scene of gruesome murder was unadulterated drama. The audience never sought in it a page of history but only the story of a ritualistic plunge into an abominable abyss of cruelty and murder, probably a cathartic form of lamenting their dire

---

[180] *Histories*, 5, 87-88: Loeb 119, 96.
[181] Homer, *Odyssey*, 4, 219 ff.: Loeb 104, 134.
[182] Id., *Iliad*, 14, 346 ff.: Loeb 171, 92.
[183] EWA 4, Pl. 73 and C.A. Faraone, *Ancient Greek Love Magic*, 12.
[184] *Enquiry into Plants*, 9, 11, 6: Loeb 79, 272.
[185] Antiphon, *Against the Stepmother*, 1, 19-20: Loeb, *Minor Attic Orators*, 308, 24.
[186] Euripides, *Bacchae*, 1122: Loeb 495, 120.

miseries in the year 405, preceding the surrender to the Spartan army at the end of the Peloponnesian War.

The story of Deianeira is more realistic, yet Sophocles' play *Women of Trachis* where it appeared is the most ambiguous of his seven plays preserved today. It requires careful attention. The character of Deianeira is unclear and the identification of her role in Heracles' death a challenge to the interpreters of this play. Was she the clever perpetrator of a murder or the silly victim of an accidental killing? The variance in the interpretations of this case is the result of Sophocles' own words that are at best difficult to reconcile and at worst contradictory. Our interpretation here is an attempt at penetrating the thoughts the audience had when they attended the first production of this play in about 435 BCE.

Deianeira was the daughter of Oeneus, king of the small state of Calydon in Aetolia. She became Heracles' wife after the death of his first wife Megara. She then came to Trachis in north Malis where he had his residence. She lived a solitary life in this city tucked in the desolate mountains of Northern Greece while Heracles was spending most of the years in foreign labors and campaigns, visiting his wife and children, "like a farmer", only "when he sows and when he reaps." [187] The oracle of Dodona in central Epirus had predicted for him "an untroubled life" but, if he did not return home this time, death after "a year and three months." [188] Deianeira said then that she dreaded the thought "to live on robbed of the noblest among men." [189] So, when the prophetic deadline came near, Heracles had already served his sentence and been kept in bondage in Lydia for over a year. Figuring out that he was on his way home, Deianeira entrusted her son Hyllus to go and search for his father, bring him home and prevent him to die. When On his way home, Heracles stopped at Oechalia, in north Euboea, where he killed king Eurytus and made his daughter, Iole, a concubine to share his household with his wife in Trachis.

When Deianeira heard about this arrangement she deeply resented it and despised a younger competitor in her

---

[187] Sophocles, *Women of Trachis*, 33: Loeb 21, 134.
[188] *Ibid.*, 76-85, 156-174 & 1164-1173: Loeb 21, 38-41, 144-147 & 226-229.
[189] *Ibid.*, 177: Loeb 21, 146.

marital bed. It appears that her wrenching jealousy motivated her action against Heracles. Posterity interpreted her name Deianeira to mean "man-murdering".

Three passages will serve us as anchors. The first passage deals with the origin of the poison that killed her husband. When Deianeira was still young, beautiful and recently married to Heracles and he was taking her to her new home in Trachis, he resorted to the services of the centaur Nessus to carry her across the treacherous waters of the river Evenus. Why did he, the strongest man on earth, not carry her himself? Mystery. The fact is that it was a mistake. As Nessus was carrying her in mid-stream," he laid lustful hands upon" her. [190] She shrieked and Heracles killed the centaur with his arrow. But before dying, Nessus collected from his wound and gave to Deianeira some of his blood poisoned by the multi-headed Hydra whom Heracles had previously slain. He gave it, as he said to her, as "a charm for the mind of Heracles, so that he shall never more see and love another woman instead of you". [191] Heracles could have heard the centaur's declaration since he could not have been far away. So, if he heard it, why did he dare bring a concubine home as a competitor to his wife's attention? If he did not hear it, he still acted irresponsibly, like a dunce and a fool he probably was, judging by the way he acted in king Admetus' palace, feasting with food and drink when his wife Alcestis had just died. [192]

As for the centaur's attempted rape, it was an act of lust which resulted in words of instruction to Deianeira and of warning to Heracles. Both should have been very suspicious of these words from the start. What kind of a rapist would give a charm to his victim so that she could keep her husband faithful, especially the one who was actually killing him? Was he so grateful? The real intent of his instruction to Deianeira could not have been any other than "to destroy the man who had shot him." [193] The underlying meaning of his instruction to Deianeira was to use the poison and kill Heracles if he indulged again in grievous extramarital amours. She understood it very well:

---

[190] *Women of Trachis*, 565: Loeb 21, 184.

[191] *Ibid.*, 572-577: Loeb 21, 184.

[192] Euripides, *Alcestis*, 747 ff.: Loeb 12, 230.

[193] *Women of "Trachis*, 710: Loeb 21, 196.

"For why, in return for what, could the monster have done a kindness to me, the cause of his death?" [194]

It seems quite clear that Deianeira understood from the start that Nessus' blood was a murder weapon and not, as he deceptively stated, a love-charm. She kept Nessus' blood as he instructed her, "hidden in a brazen pot", [195] so she kept "in a secret place the unguent, far from the fire and never warmed by the sun's ray." [196] She understood that, if she did not, something ominous would happen. On the other hand, she remembered his words, yet could not in her sane mind believe it was a drug (*pharmakon*) intended to intensify Heracles' love for her. At this time, she had no evidence either of the veracity of the centaur's words or of the effect his blood would have on her husband, but the circumstances already favored the understanding that Nessus' gift was anything but an aphrodisiac.

The second ambiguous passage in the story deals with what she did with the poisoned blood and how she obtained her evidence about what it really was. While Heracles was away from home, she weaved a robe for him as a dutiful wife would normally do. But when she received his concubine Iole in her house and learned of his imminent return, she burst into jealous indignation. She then remembered the robe and Nessus' warning to keep his blood away from fire or the sun's ray. Now, she needed to verify with evidence whether the centaur's gift was really a love-charm, as he had told her. She plucked a tuft of soft wool from a sheep, then privately, in the darkness of the house, so that the light would not reach and Iole and the servants would not see, she dipped it into the blood and tainted the robe with it, after which she folded the robe and laid it back into a casket. She then walked out of the house and negligently threw the tuft of sheep's wool on the ground, "into the sun's ray." The result, in her own words, became her unmistakable evidence:

> When it grew warm, it melted away into nothing and crumbled on the ground, looking most like the sawdust you see when somebody cuts wood. [197]

---

[194] *Women of "Trachis*, 707-708: Loeb 21, 194.
[195] *Ibid.*, 556: Loeb 21, 182.
[196] *Ibid.*, 685-686: Loeb 21, 194.
[197] *Ibid.*, 697-700: Loeb 21, 194.

Now she knew for sure that Nessus' words were all in deception and that the anointed robe would kill whoever would put it on near a fire or in the sunshine. So when she entrusted the casket containing this tainted robe to Lichas, instructing him to take it to Heracles as a gift from her, she was using him to deceive and kill. She knew that her gift was a death-weapon. She could have destroyed the poisoned robe or continued to keep it hidden. On the contrary, she kept her knowledge a secret and dispatched Lichas with the lethal robe.

Deianeira declared that she learned of the consuming power of the poisoned blood "too late" (*methusteron*) when it availed no more. [198] Perhaps, the sequence of events was as follows: she weaved a robe for Heracles, tainted it with Nessus' blood, thinking it was a love-charm to give him when he returned home, then dispatched Lichas with it to Heracles, before she threw the tuft of wool into the sunshine and discovered "too late" that it was not a love-charm but a weapon to kill Heracles. No doubt, she was bewildered by this new evidence, especially if she found it, as she said, "too late", to mean that she found it after she had dispatched Lichas. Then, why did she keep it a secret any longer, even at this late moment, when it was not "too late" to send promptly another messenger after Lichas and warn Heracles of the danger? She said she was in great fear of the dreadful outcome. So, if the meaning of her "too late" related only to her fear, she only wished to appear an innocent victim of the centaur when she actually knew that she was the deliberate murderer of her husband.

Other options about Deianeira's state of mind are still available. Perhaps she meant by "too late" that she would have used the deadly blood sooner, had she only known its power sooner, like as soon as the mistress invaded her household? This interpretation would only make her more culpable. Or was Deianeira no more than a risk-taker, a jealous and insecure wife whose mind was on the brink? "Too late" would then mean that she first ignored the evidence in the desperate and wishful hope of winning her husband back, then realized too late that the blood's lethal power was undeniably proven. No doubt, she was confused, laboring under the burden of extreme jealousy. Never-

---

[198] *Women of Trachis*, 710: Loeb 21, 196.

theless, her instructions to Lichas showed a clear and resolute mind. Therefore, the suggestion that she discovered the death-power of the tainted robe "too late" to prevent her action is nothing more than a piece in the pattern of deception she deliberately weaved. She would rather see her husband dead than share his love and lust with a younger woman in the same household. She would even kill herself rather than face forever the emptiness of her solitary life. Aphrodite and her son Eros were at work with her as they had been with Heracles.

Regardless of her frame of mind, Deianeira kept her pernicious knowledge a secret when she gave Lichas her benevolent instructions which reveal furthermore, under scrutiny, that certainly after giving her instructions she intended to kill Heracles, if not clearly at the time of the instructions, at least when the tainted robe was delivered to him. She may have been a risk-taker at the outset, being a person deranged by jealousy, but as the days went on she became a lucid and deliberate murderess.

Was Deianeira so deranged, however, that she perpetrated her crime intentionally and deliberately but not voluntarily? In other words, could she plead temporary insanity under the stress of an overwhelming fit of jealousy? The evidence shows that she remained in full control of the situation and of herself until the end. She had not crossed the line between being troubled and being insane. She used carefully crafted words to signify her will to kill Heracles, conveying her plan and yet hiding it at the same time:

> When you [Lichas] give it [the tainted robe], to him [Heracles], take care that no other person puts it on but he, and that neither the light of the sun, nor that the sacred precinct nor the blaze of the altar light upon it before he, standing there conspicuous in the sight of all, shall show it to the gods on the day when oxen shall be slaughtered. [199]

Deianeira tainted the robe before she knew it was making it lethal but instructed Lichas to deliver it to Heracles probably after she had discovered through the tuft of wool that it was actually lethal. Her instructions to Lichas

---

[199] *Women of Trachis*, 604-609: Loeb 21, 186.

are her indictment. Anyway, If she still lacked in a clear understanding of her action at this time, she could have acquired it completely during the five or six days that it took the messenger to travel from Trachis in Malis to Cape Cenaeum on the island of Euboea. Why did she not correct her instructions? Her omission makes her indictment definitive and irrefutable.

Bulls were symbols of strength and potency in Greek mythology. They were slain in sacrifice to the gods, especially Zeus and Dionysus, at an altar either near a domestic or public hearth or in front of a temple. At Cape Cenaeum, where this sacrifice of twelve bulls was to take place, it was more likely to take place at an altar near a hearth than in front of a temple because of the location next to "a sacred grove" in this "sea-swept cape in Euboea." [200] It was for sure in the blazing sunshine.

Deianeira's original vow was to give her husband the robe upon his return:

> For this was my vow, that if ever I saw or heard of his safe return home, I would duly clothe him in this tunic, and reveal to the gods a new sacrificer wearing a new robe. [201]

To give it to him tainted with poisoned blood was an afterthought, yet a clear and conscious one, and unfortunately another piece in the tapestry of her indictment. The monster Nessus had deceived her with his misrepresentation about the blood being a love-charm; now, after finding unexpectedly the evidence that it was a lethal weapon, she deceived everyone else and deliberately caused the torture and death of her husband.

Nevertheless, after the messenger Lichas left on his fateful journey, she had misgivings about her deed. She feared of having gone "too far" (ôs dedoika mê peraiterô). [202] In spite of it all, she let it all happen as she expected. Therefore, she was right to confess:

> For if I am not to prove mistaken in my judgment, I alone, miserable one, shall be his ruin; I know that

---

[200] *Women of Trachis*, 753-755: Loeb 21, 200.
[201] *Ibid.*, 610-613: Loeb 21, 186-189.
[202] *Ibid.*, 664: Loeb 21, 192.

the arrow that struck him tormented even Chiron [the centaur], who was immortal, and it destroys all the beasts whom it touches. How shall the black poison of the blood, coming from the fatal wound, not destroy my husband also? That is my belief. [203]

In keeping with tradition, the chorus introduced the divine into this tale of human tragedy: "And the Cyprian [Aphrodite], silent in attendance, is revealed as the doer of these things." [204]

Deianeira's son Hyllus described to her later the horrible scene of his father's torture:

As he [Heracles] was about to slaughter the many beasts for sacrifice, there came from home his own herald, Lichas, bringing your gift, the robe of death. He put it on, as you had instructed and slew twelve bulls. ... At first, poor man, he spoke the prayer cheerfully, rejoicing in the fine attire. But when the bloodshot flame from the sacred offerings and from the resinous pine blazed up, the sweat came up upon his body, and the thing clung closely to his sides, as a carpenter's tunic might, at every joint; and a biting pain came, tearing at his bones; then a bloody poison like that of a hateful serpent fed upon him. [205]

Agonizing Heracles was transported from Cape Cenaeum to nearby "mountain of Oeta, which belongs to highest Zeus." [206] The hero cried his torment with bitter words of anger against his jealous wife and died a cruel death.

Heracles' son Hyllus grieved bitterly for the loss of his father and reviled his mother for "killing the noblest man upon the earth, one such as you will never see again!" [207] He held his mother guilty of his father's death. [208]

Deianeira withdrew into the palace in Trachis, without a word to anyone, either to reveal her secret knowledge or

---

[203] *Women of Trachis*, 712-717: Loeb 21, 196.
[204] *Ibid.*, 860-861: Loeb 21, 208.
[205] *Ibid.*, 756-771: Loeb 21, 200.
[206] *Ibid.*, 1191: Loeb 21, 240.
[207] *Ibid.*, 811-812: Loeb 21, 204.
[208] *Ibid.*, 807-809: Loeb 21, 204.

to defend her action, and sitting on the bridal bed killed herself with a stroke of the sword. [209] Later, Hyllus felt guilty that he had charged is mother falsely and driven her to commit suicide. [210] So he tried to explain that she "did wrong by accident" [211] and did it only with the good intention of using the robe as a love-charm. In other words, he approved of his mother trying to win her husband back because her intent was good; she only missed her aim with the means she used. [212] Hyllus' naive belief in both Nessus' and his mother's deceptive gifts quieted his own sense of guilt and the rage of his father. In his distress, Hyllus took refuge also in a belief that the gods were responsible for this tragedy. It was indeed a subterfuge, full of tradition and superstition, which helped him heal the wounds in his soul and carry on with his life. In the end, crushed and unsure of his future, he cried about "the great unkindness of the gods displayed in these events ... and none of these things is not Zeus." [213]

Greek men and women knew that their destiny depended on their efforts. Women's major interest was naturally in their husbands' attention, especially in the bedroom. A story told by the orator Antiphon (480-411 BCE) duplicates Deianeira's story for the use of some magic device to lure a man. [214] In this instance, however, the women were innocent and their jealousy under control, although their skills fell short and the outcome turned out to be tragic. A wife and a slave concubine were sharing the love commitment of a certain Philoneus. He took them along with him when he visited Athens and stayed at the house of his married friend. The three women became cozy with each other and shared the knowledge they each had of their partners' sexual indifference. They thought of using a love potion on them. So they administered an aphrodisiac so powerful that it poisoned them.This story makes several points: first, the involuntary manslaughter of the husbands is our primary focus here, together with the sexual desire of

---

[209] *Women of Trachis*, 886-887: Loeb 21, 212.

[210] *Ibid.*, 940: Loeb 21, 216.

[211] *Ibid.*, 1123: Loeb 21, 232.

[212] *Ibid.*, 1136-1142: Loeb 21, 234..

[213] *Ibid.*, 1266-1278: Loeb 21, 248-251.

[214] See L. Foxhall, *The Politics of Affection*, in *Kosmos*, ed. by P. Cartledge et al., 63-64.

women and their secret ways of activating their complaints about it.

Against husbands who were rough, abusive or utterly misguided about an important issue, such as war and peace, the wives had no recourse other than inflicting pain in an indirect or symbolic fashion. In his *Lysistrata* of 411 BCE, Aristophanes referred to the "Herm-Docker clan" [215] meaning that, by opening their cloaks and exposing themselves, these women's husbands could suffer a mutilation similar to the one done to the Hermes statues by Alcibiades and his companions in 415 BCE. The reference was neither pointless nor insignificant when some of the perpetrators, still unidentified, were probably sitting in the audience.

As a general assessment, violence was never as frequently done by women as by men but, when violence was committed by women, it was done most often in reprisal for mental pain inflicted upon them.

Lamentations

Short of violence, lamentations were women's main release from sufferings and, at the same time, their main weapon in the face of danger. On the one hand, lamentations fed on their resentment, for example in jealousy, and their fear of imminent dangers and, on the other hand, provided the only weapon available when physical strength was lacking or not appropriate. Electra offered an example of such lamentations in the opening scene of Sophocles' play by her name. She lamented:

> But I shall not cease from my dirges and miserable lamentations. ... Revered children of the gods who look upon those wrongfully done to death [Agamemnon and Cassandra], who look upon those who dishonour the marriage bed in secret [Clytemnestra and Aegisthus] come, bring help, avenge the murder of our father, and send to me my brother [Orestes]! For I have no longer strength to

---

[215] *Lysistrata*, 1074: Loeb 179, 414.

bear alone the burden of grief that weighs me down. [216]

For Electra and most women of Ancient Greece lamentation was "a prop of suffering." [217] Men also, if their pride would tolerate it, could take in some lamentation, even with "floods of tears", a relief from the pain they sometimes endured in body or soul. [218] At the beginning of Euripides' play *Andromache* of about 427 BCE, Andromache, wife of the fallen Hector of Troy and now a slave-woman, was seated in front of a shrine. Before delivering her lamentation, she confessed that

> It is natural for women to get pleasure from their present misfortunes, by constantly having them on their lips. [219]

Of course, Andromache did not invent these lines: they were given to her by a male playwright, ever famous for his misogyny. The perception which men had of women as weaker, less courageous and, as a result, more prone to use lamentations as a defense, helped them toward considering themselves as superior by nature. From this point to a state of misogyny there was a very short distance and the Ancient Greeks crossed it very early in their history. The poet Hesiod of the eighth century and the lyric poets of the seventh and sixth centuries were avowed misogynists. Then, in the fifth century, Euripides acquired, justifiably or not, the reputation of being the enemy of women, as Aristophanes' play *Women at the Thesmophoria* amply demonstrated.

Such an attitude did not stop with Euripides. Plato of the fourth century had little trust in women. [220] His contemporary, the famous Cynic philosopher Diogenes disliked women as he despised the men who imitated them. [221] These were the thoughts of the male writers of Ancient

[216] Sophocles, *Electra*, 103-120: Loeb 20, 176.
[217] Aeschylus, *Fr.*, Uncertain Play, 213: Loeb 146, 498.
[218] Euripides, *Fr., Oenomaus*, 573: Loeb 506, 44.
[219] Id., *Andromache*, 93-95: Loeb 484, 282.
[220] *Republic*, 8, 549D-E: Loeb 276, 258.
[221] Diogenes Laërtius, *Lives of Eminent Philosophers*, Diogenes, 6, 46 & 65: Loeb 185, 48 & 66.

Athens until Aristotle came and summarized in his *Politics* his own philosophy of gender, as presented earlier.

Aristotle observed men and women in their sad moments and found a difference in the way they behaved witht their friends of the same gender. Both share their joys, he remarked but, when it comes to man, only

> He will not suffer others to lament with him, because he is not given to lamentation himself. But weak women and womanish men who like those who mourn with them and love them as true friends and sympathizers. [222]

Aristotle estimated that the reason for such a difference laid in the strength one has and the other has not. Men are strong enough not only to bear pain but also not to want to impose it on a friend. Women share their pain and gain strength in doing it, regardless of the pain they impose on their friends who do the same with them anyway. This is all of a man observing and talking!

The cause and manner of the lamentation made it morally and socially acceptable. In mythology, Alcyone's laments were perfectly justifiable when she lost her husband Ceyx with whom she lived a happy life, but her resulting suicide by drowning herself into the sea was not considered justifiable. Out of pity, however, a god changed her into a halcyon bird. [223]

Roles and Obligations

Religious Festivals

Women had an important role in the performance of religious rituals. In a fragment of the lost play *Melanippe Captive*, Euripides' heroine explained the importance of this role:

> Now as for dealings with the gods, which I consider prime importance, we have a very great role in them.

---

[222] *Nicomachean Ethics*, 9, 11, 1171b, 8-11: Loeb 73, 570.
[223] Euripides, *Iphigenia Among the Taurians*, 1089-1095: Loeb 10, 266 & *Fr.*, Unidentified Play, 856: Loeb 506, 480.

Women proclaim Loxias' mind in Phoebus' halls [at Delphi], and by Dodona's holy foundations, beside the sacred oak [in Epirus], womankind conveys the thoughts of Zeus to those Greeks who want to know it. Those rituals, too, which are performed for the Fates and the Nameless Goddesses are not open to men, but are promoted by women entirely. That is how the rights of women stand in dealings with the gods. [224]

Women of high standing could become priestesses, like the mythical Auge, the Egyptian Theonoe and the Greek Iphigenia. Their compensation was only prestige and a certain measure of authority in the cult of the god or goddess they served. Women of low standing could earn money selling chaplets and trinkets to worshippers of the gods. [225] All women had access to the shrines of gods and goddesses, for example Athena's Parthenon in Athens and the temple of Apollo at Delphi. The Athenian handmaidens of Creusa in Euripides' play *Ion* enjoyed their visit at Delphi, as they claimed:

Not only in holy Athens, then, are gods' fair-columned temples to be found or homage paid to Aguieus [Apollo, protector of roads]. Also at the shrine of Loxias [Apollo], Leto's son, the temple's twin facades gleam with fair-eyed loveliness. See, look here! [226]

The maidens reveled in the beauty of the site. "Friend, look over here!", says one. "But see here!," replied another. And another: "My eyes dart in all directions." Their artistic enjoyment could hardly be separated from their religious fulfillment at the sight of the shrine of their favorite gods Apollo, Artemis and Dionysus. Witnessing their excitement, Ion exclaimed: "Look at everything the law permits." [227]

---

[224] *Fr., Melanippe Captive*, 494, 12-22: Loeb 504, 596.
[225] Aristophanes, *Women at the Thesmophoria*, 443-457.: Loeb 179, 510-513.
[226] *Ion*, 184-190: Loeb 10, 336.
[227] *Ibid.*, 232: Loeb 10, 342.

Nubile girls made offerings of gifts at Brauron to Artemis and childless women did the same at Eleusis to goddesses Demeter and Persephone. [228] Between about 525 and 480 BCE, some wealthy women had four dedications to Athena inscribed on the Acropolis of Athens. [229]

The east frieze by Phidias on the Parthenon of Athens (440-432 BCE) depicts the procession of the *Great Panathenaea* quadrennial festival held in July/August, the month of Hekatombaion, the first month of the year. [230] Marshals guide the cortege, followed by the archon *basileus* and, behind him, the priestess of Athena *Polias* (guardian of the city) chosen by her peers from the Eupatrid family. They precede young girls (*arrêphorai*) who carry the robe (*peplos*) weaved in memory of Athena's victory over the Giants, and older maidens (*kanephorai*) who carry the sacred baskets of gifts, including the grain offered as symbol of fertility. Then older women and maidens come singing choral hymns. A man, perhaps the archon *basileus*, intervenes at the end to hold the robe presented to the city goddess Athena.

Every year on the last day of the month of Hekatombaion a minor Panathenaea was held in honor of Athena on the Acropolis where the young men and maidens were allowed to sing and dance all night. [231]

The wife of the archon *basileus*, called *Basilessa*, had by status a special role in the *Anthesteria*, the festival of the maturing wine on the 11th, 12th and 13th of the month of Anthesterion (Feb./March), in honor of god Dionysus. On the second day, the day of the wine jugs (*Choês*), she went to the god's sanctuary on the Agora. There she administered an oath of sexual abstinence to fourteen women called Venerable Ones (*Gerairai*) and then offered herself to the god as his wife.

At all the religious festivals but especially at the *Anthesteria* and the *Great Dionysia* in the month of Elaphebolion (March/April), women and even young girls

---

[228] *Inscriptiones Graecae*, 2, 2, 1388, 78-80 & 82-83 and 1400, 41-42 & 46-47: M.R. Lefkowitz & M.B. Fant, *Women's Life in Greece and Rome*, 119, p. 117.

[229] *Ibid.*, 1, 2, 756: *Ibid.*, 119, p. 117.

[230] EWA 11, Pl. 25. These were lunar months starting with the new moon and adjusted periodically to coincide with the course of the sun.

[231] Euripides, *Children of Heracles*, 779-783: Loeb 484, 86.

could drink wine, but never share in any contest with men. They were all singing, dancing and frolicking separately. [232]

We naturally think of Dionysus as the god of wine because generations of poets and artists have represented him with this attribute. He was originally the god of all life as it flows in the sap of trees and the blood of animals and humans. Therefore, life, not wine, was the core of the religious experience that took place at the *Great Dionysia*, in spring during the mild and rainy season so kind to the seeds of the earth. The celebration took some infectious forms of hysteria caused and also cured by rituals of mountain dancing as the votaries kept it under a controlled release. The culmination consisted of acting like wild animals, the bull or the lion that tear their prey to pieces and eat raw. Through this performance, the votaries experienced the mystical madness generated by the physical vitality and excitement symbolized by these powerful animals. As repulsive as it appears to outsiders, this ritual caused a transformation (*homophasia*) in the cultist's heart through communion with life's potency.

The "maids and matrons" were Bacchae (Bacchantes or Maenads), [233] dressed in white robes and their hair adorned with snakes and ivy. They danced, played musical instruments and carried the sacred thyrsus of Dionysus as they paraded in procession (*pompê*) to the countryside. The excitement caused by the presence of men became frantic and easily erotic, as shown in a painting inside an Attic *Kulix* (drinking cup) dated of 490 BCE. [234]

According to Euripides' story in *The Bacchae*, the devotees of Thebes paraded wildly to the idyllic Mount Cithaeron, a short distance to the southwest. There, they busied themselves preparing to celebrate their god Dionysus. All dressed in ritualistic fawn-skin attires and entwined hissing snakes, they played with gazelles and whelps of wolves, and faked miracles like making milk, red wine and honey surge from the ground. In their frenzy they slaughtered bulls and heifers and stripped their flesh in pieces. Some women were hurling their thyrsus against the chasing men and wounding them in blood. [235]

---

[232] Euripides, *Bacchae*, 114-119: Loeb 495, 20.
[233] Id., *Phoenician Women*, 656: Loeb 11, 280.
[234] EWA 12, Pl. 563.
[235] Euripides, *Bacchae*, 734 ff.: Loeb 495, 80.

The end of Euripides' play is a horrible scene of madness and cruelty, a creation of his wild and bizarre imagination. For dramatic reasons, he blew out of normal proportion the role of women in it. The wild Bacchae were not the Athenian wives we know from all other sources. He located the scene in Thebes, some thirty-six miles to the north, but produced his play for an Athenian audience in 405 BCE, when the two cities were at war with each other. No doubt, Athens, like Thebes, had its share of wild women because the wild men attending this Dionysiac festival counted on women to achieve ecstasy. Besides, the rites of Dionysus were celebrated in other locations, such as Mount Parnassus, near Delphi, where Ino went to join the Bacchae. [236]

When Xuthus of Athens adopted Ion, thinking the boy was his natural son but was unable to tell who his mother was, he admitted having indulged in an illicit affair in the folly of youth with a woman he assumed was one of Bacchus' maenads sharing in the revelry at Delphi. [237] In Thebes, some of these wild women were of the royal class. In Athens, all women were welcome, even wives and daughters of Athenian citizens.

Following the festival, a crowd of Athenian men and women rode or marched to Eleutherae, some twenty-seven miles away to the north, and brought the statue of Dionysus to Athens where it was placed at the theatre in preparation for the performance of Tragedies and Comedies during the following days of celebration.

The most sacred and revered of all the Athenian festivals was celebrated on the bay of Salamis, at Eleusis linked to Athens by a twelve-mile Sacred Way. In spite of all their secrecy, we know that these Eleusinian *Mysteries of Demeter* took place prominently in the early Fall of each year, in the month of Boedromion (Sept./Oct.) and are well certified by archaeology and literature. [238]

Every man and woman could be initiated by sacrificing a piglet symbolizing the death of Demeter's daughter, Persephone (*Korê*), and her abduction by Hades, the god of the Underworld. The priestesses brought gifts in a basket to the temple and offered them to the mother

---

[236] Euripides, *Fr., Ino*, test 3, 2: Loeb 504, 442.
[237] Id., *Ion*, 545-553: Loeb 10, 386-391.
[238] See W. Burkert, *Greek Religion*, trans. By J. Raffan, 285 ff.

goddess Demeter. The votaries bathed in the sea to purify themselves; they danced and sang hymns while holding some twigs from shrubs and trees. They fasted all day, until the night fell upon the earth. Then, the initiation rites took place outdoors, more obscure in their details than the surroundings where the light from torches could barely chase the darkness. The proceedings appeared to be high-spirited and inspiring. The descriptions are sketchy, yet suggest clearly that sinking into the dark Underworld in the fall and finding life again in the spring was a symbol of the earth vegetation and the inspiration for a spiritual and cathartic experience for all the participants. At the end, they shared in a feast whose main course was provided by the sacrifice of a great bull.

The Athenian women had another festival, one of their own, instituted long before the fifth century when they used it, according to Aristophanes, to attack Euripides who was then widely reputed to be a misogynist. They called this festival *Thesmophoria* in honor of goddess Demeter *Thesmophoros* whose major sanctuary was also at Eleusis. *Phoros* means "one who carries"; *Thesmos* conveys the dual meaning of "wealth" and "what is laid down". The latter meaning may refer to the law or to married women who had delivered a child and may have been the only participants in the festival, if they were also free. In Athens, the festival was held in the month of Pyanepsion (Oct./Nov.) at a site near the Pnyx where men assembled.

When Isaeus of the fourth century presented in court the proofs that his mother was the legitimate wife of his father Ciron, his second argument pertained to the time immediately following his parents' wedding celebration. He said:

> The wives of the demesmen afterwards chose our mother, together with the wife of Diocles of Pithus, to preside at the Themophoria and to carry out the ceremonies jointly with her. [239]

According to Herodotus, the Danaids brought these rites from Egypt and taught them to the native Pelasgic women of the Peloponnesus. But when the Dorian people

---

[239] *On the Estate of Ciron*, 8, 19: Loeb 202, 298-301.

migrated from the north and displaced the Pelasgians and the Ionians, the rites disappeared, except in the Peloponnesian central region called Arcadia. Since Herodotus could not have been unaware of the importance of the *Thesmophoria* in his times, he could have added that the rites migrated to Attica with the Ionians in about 1000 BCE.

For at least three and up to five days in Attica, in late October, the votaries abstained from sexual contact and fasted at least the entire second day. The ritual consisted of leading pigs into a cave where they were partly eaten overnight by snakes. Then the women brought the remains to an altar and mixed them with seeds. The symbolism of this ritual seems to suggest fertility because the Greek word for pig (*huos*) designated also the female organs.

We know enough about these rites to understand how strange and gory they were. Herodotus confessed that he knew much more about them than he cared to tell, although he never attended them in person. Not only did he remain silent about their annual celebration in Attica, but he stated explicitly:

> I could speak more exactly of these matters, for I know the truth, but I will hold my peace; nor will I say ought concerning that rite of Demeter which the Greeks called Thesmophoria, saving such part of it as I am not forbidden to mention. [240]

This reservation means no disrespect for goddess Demeter. The innuendo suggests only that he, like Aristophanes, did not have much respect for the women who performed them at the *Thesmophoria*. Nevertheless, in 411 BCE, Aristophanes produced his play *Women at the Thesmophoria*. He used Euripides' reputation as a misogynist, gravely damaged by his production of *Hippolytus* in 428, and sided with the women of this festival while disparaging him as a competitor.

Aristophanes' play involved women, played on stage by men who dressed like women in the context of a religious ritual reserved to women. The story line was simple: expecting the women to plot against him at the *Thesmophoria*, Euripides used a spy who dressed like a

---

[240] *Histories*, 2, 171: Loeb 117, 484.

woman, entered the precinct and pleaded his case. When the spy was discovered, he called on Euripides for help.

Aristophanes had never attended the *Thesmophoria*. So, he imagined what took place, perhaps with the assistance of some women informants. Worthy of note are the open discussion the women held as if they were in an assembly, the wine they appreciated dearly and the dances and songs they performed lustily on one tempo, then on another:

> Hey now, jump, swing around with a solid beat, Let all your songs peal out! Turn the step, and change the measure, raise a loftier music now. [241]

When the spy was freed at the end and a negotiated peace was settled between Euripides and the women, the ritual of dance and songs resumed as it had joyously started:

> Go light on your feet, form up a circle and all join hands; everyone mark the beat of the dance; step out with an agile foot! Our choreography should allow us to turn an eye in every direction. And all the while, everyone, for the race of Olympian gods lift your voice in reverend song as the dance turns crazily. [242]

About the *Thesmophoria*, Walter Burkert wrote:

> Once in the year at least, the women demonstrate their independence, their responsibility, and importance for the fertility of the community and the land. [243]

The presence of the gods and goddesses was pervasive in the life of the Greeks. It was an element of culture much more than a reason for religious fervor. They went from a sincere belief in the existence of the gods and their role in man's life to doubts and later disbelief, still with some measure of piety and a greater measure of superstition. They used the gods and goddesses as

---

[241] *Women at the Thesmophoria*, 985-986: Loeb 179, 578.
[242] *Ibid.*, 954-962: Loeb 179, 576.
[243] *Greek Religion*, trans. by J. Raffan, 245.

sponsors of their festivities. The sacrifices they made to them were only the beginning of what they enjoyed best, namely to get together and drink wine, sing, dance, and enjoy life in a country harboring much hardship.

At least once in a lifetime, all the Athenian women were involved in the democratic process of voting in a religious setting. According to an inscription found at the Acropolis on a marble stele of 450-445 BCE., they were all designated to vote for the lifetime appointment of a priestess of Athena *Nikê* (victory) for which whey were also all eligible. The appointee received "an annual salary of 50 dr., together with the legs and hides from public sacrifices." [244]

Another inscription of the early 4th century from Phalerum, west of Athens, revealed that Xenokrateia, probably a priestess, "founded the altar for the sake of instruction, for anyone who wishes to sacrifice over the good things achieved." [245]

Women could not have been active participants in these religious activities unless they enjoyed a fair degree of social freedom in order to organize, finance and celebrate them publicly. Athenian Women had a unique role in the religious life of the city.

Funerals

Wherever the Ionians settled, in Athens or in the colonies, the cremation of corpses did not take place during the fifth and fourth centuries as often as it did during the previous centuries. They preferred burying the bodies intact, if possible inside a coffin of pottery or wood, into a grave in the ground, sometimes with a plaster or tile facing. [246] Expediency was motivating their choice. If they resorted to cremation on an adjacent pyre, especially during the plague and war years between 430 and 400 BCE, they buried the ash urns in the ground. [247] Because of the technical difficulties, they opted only rarely to burn the

---

[244] R. Meiggs and D. Lewis, ed., *A Selection of Greek Historical Inscriptions*, 108.

[245] J.K. Davies, *Democracy and Classical Greece*, 180.

[246] D.C. Kurtz and J. Boardman, *Greek Burial Customs*, 96-97

[247] I. Morris, *Death-ritual and Social Structure in Classical Antiquity*, 140.

bodies inside the grave. The best known cemeteries in Athens were the Kerameikos and the Agora Dipylon. [248]

The role of women in funerals is well documented. Such funerals were of two types: one was public when it was conducted on behalf of the city (*polis*) either for a public figure or a warrior, all male; the other was privately conducted by the family (*oichos*) of the deceased, male or female, and involved only the family clan (*anchisteia*) and a few friends.

Only a few funerals were public and often political inasmuch as they were used to make a political or moral statement about someone who contributed his career to the good of society and the city. Two situations brought these funerals outside the confines of the family into the concern of the city: one was for the fallen soldiers, the other for the leaders of the city. Fewer in number, these funerals are better known as historical events.

In normal circumstances, when the death needed to be ascertained or the deceased was a prominent citizen, and perhaps a women such as a priestess like Praxithea, [249] the funeral was delayed, in most cases at least until the third day after death in order to allow more people to attend and present their respects. [250] The time between the death and the funeral, including the burial, was spent in wake and fasting. In some cases, especially in war times, the delay ended only at the most convenient time. On these more solemn occasions, unrelated women of at least sixty years of age could be retained to sing the dirges and utter the wailing cries. A funeral oration also was customarily delivered by a leader of the community, as Pericles did at the end of the first season of the Peloponnesian War, when the bodies of the fallen soldiers were returned to Athens. He then advised the women to be "of whom there is least talk among men whether in praise or in blame." [251]

Polynices was one of the seven captains who attacked the gates of Thebes. He was refused a burial, his body to be cast to the dogs and vultures. The other six captains and all the men who also died in the assault were to be cremated. According to customs that held together not only all Greece

---

[248] I. Morris, *Burial and Ancient Society*, 22 & 151.
[249] Euripides, *Fr., Erechtheus*, 370, 95-97: Loeb 504, 398.
[250] Plato, *Laws*, 12, 959A: Loeb 192, 530.
[251] Thucydides, *Peloponnesian War*, 2, 45, 2: Loeb 108, 340.

but also all human communities, [252] the Argive mothers came to assume all their funerary duties but Aethra, the mother of king Theseus of Athens, knew well that women must call on men's help to have things done, even in the funerary role largely reserved to women. Therefore, she advised the Argive mothers when they came to Thebes to bury their fallen sons: "It is proper for women, if they are wise, to do everything through their men." [253] The conditions on the battlefield were in this case different, yet the ritual was as close to normal as possible, except that the fallen soldiers were to be buried in a communal tomb. [254]

The compassionate king Theseus of Athens spared the women the overwhelming sorrow of touching their sons' mangled bodies. It was indeed a very unusual and unmistakable sign of great compassion to intervene as a man and a king, and to refuse to leave the care of the bodies of these fallen soldiers to the mothers and their slaves. He himself washed "the poor men's wounds", [255] wrapped the bodies in their shrouds and made the votive offerings at the temple he "dedicated to the dead." [256] Then he had them all cremated.

Theseus saw in his intervention no disgrace -- that feeling between "ashamed" and "disgusted" as Gilbert Murray explained [257] -- because he felt a loving care (*agapaô*) for the dead soldiers and believed in the democratic ways of kings. The mothers' hearts were torn with conflicting emotions: joy because of the king's compassion and sorrow because of the loss of their sons, "for when their children die, the grief in women's hearts is ever involved in the toil of lamentation." [258] Theseus' mother, Aethra, taught him to be compassionate and to honor the dead because their humanity makes them close to the gods.

The Athenians of the Classical Age knew their *Iliad* and how, some three hundred years earlier, Homer described the sight of the fair maiden Briseis grieving for the loss of Patroclus on the battlefield.

---

[252] Euripides, *Suppliant Women*, 311-313: Loeb 9, 46.
[253] *Ibid.*, 40-41: Loeb 9, 16.
[254] Euripides, *Fr., Erechtheus*, 360, 33: Loeb 504, 378.
[255] *Suppliant Women*, 765: Loeb 9, 88.
[256] *Ibid.*, 983: Loeb 9, 110.
[257] *Euripides and his Age*, 61.
[258] Euripides, *Suppliant Women*, 83-85: Loeb 9, 20.

Briseis, who was like golden Aphrodite, when she saw Patroclus mangled with the sharp sword, flung herself about him and shrieked aloud, and with her hands she tore her breast and tender neck and beautiful face. And in her wailing spoke the woman like the goddesses: 'Patroclus, most dear to my heart, wretch that I am, alive I left you when I went from the hut, and now I find you dead, ... So I wail for you in your death and know no ceasing, for you were ever kind.' So she spoke weeping, and to it the women added their laments; Patroclus indeed they mourned, but each one her own sorrows. [259]

Briseis was a foreign woman who shared with Patroclus the love of Achilles. She behaved like all women do in times of grief. This trait was not peculiar to Greek women, as the Greeks understood it.

In another scene, Homer described how King Priam of Troy brought back the body of Hector, his noble son, "on the bier in the wagon drawn by the mules" and Cassandra, Hector's daughter, announced its arrival at the city gates. All the men and women of the city assembled there "for on all came unbearable grief." Then king Priam led the cortege to Hector's house,

laid him on a corded bedstead, and by his side set singers, leaders of the dirge, who led the song of lamentation – they chanted the dirge, and to it the women added their laments. And among these the white-armed Andromache [Hector's wife] led the wailing, holding in her hands the head of man-slaying Hector.

She lamented about her fate and that of their son, "still but a babe", both conquered and to be made slaves of the Achaean victor. Then two women added their personal laments: Hecuba, Hector's mother, and the Greek Helen who eloped with Paris of Troy. The old king Priam closed the lamentations and directed the men of Troy to bring for nine days into the city abundant wood so that on the tenth day they could perform the final rites:

---

[259] Homer, *Iliad*, 19, 282-302: Loeb 171, 354-357.

They carried bold Hector out, shedding tears, and on the topmost pyre, they laid the dead man and cast fire on it.

The next morning, when they were all assembled again,

His brothers and his comrades gathered up the white bones, mourning, and large tears flowed over down their cheeks. The bones they took and placed in a golden urn, covering them over with soft purple robes, and quickly laid the urn in a hollow grave, and covered it over with great close-set stones. Then quickly they heaped the mound. ... When they had piled the mound, they went back again and gathering together duly feasted a glorious feast in the halls of Priam, the king nurtured by Zeus. In this way they held funeral for horse-taming Hector." [260]

Thus ended the *Iliad* of Homer. The ritual described here was for a barbarian prince and never followed literally in Greece at any time, but the roles of men and women were made as distinct as they were in Greece in later times.

After the Trojan defeat, Queen Hecuba was made a slave and one of the concubines claimed by the Achaeans. When she set up to prepare the body of her daughter, Polyxena, for burial, she requested the help of a servant:

You, old servant, take an urn, fill it with seawater and bring it here so that I may give my daughter her last bath ... and lay her out for burial. I cannot give her a funeral as she deserves but only as best I may (for what can I do?), gathering adornments from the captive women who share this tent with me. [261]

Hecuba prepared also the body of her grandson, Astyanax, for his burial. Again, Euripides told this story, this time in his play *The Trojan Women* of the fateful year 415 BCE. The Trojan women were still grieving for being shipped

---

[260] Homer, *Iliad*, 696-804: Loeb 171, 622-804.
[261] Euripides, *Hecuba*, 609-615: Loeb 484, 452.

as slaves to the strange lands of Argos, Salamis, Corinth or Athens, when the Greek messenger, Talthybius, entered carrying the dead child, Astyanax, who had been hurled from the tower at Troy. [262] So mutilated was the body that he had washed its wounds before bringing it for burial, not to his mother, Andromache, who was already gone with her new master, Neoptolemus, but to his grandmother, Hecuba.

The old queen took in her arms the child's mutilated body. Herself wounded with grief, she let her love claim the best of her motherly emotions as she looked at him: his curly hair, his hands so much like his father's, his sweet and proud lips with countless kisses for her. Then, she covered him with clothing, wreaths and garlands, and placed his body upon the shield "that preserved Hector's fair arm." [263] Now, all the women present performed the funeral rite, striking in rhythm upon their heads. [264] They lifted the shield on which the body rested and carried it to the burial place where they deposited it in a hollow grave prepared by Talthybius and his male attendants.

Whether Hecuba's behavior was a reflection of Trojan values and customs or a projection of Greek values and customs upon them, we do not know for sure. They were already so deeply ingrained in civilized behavior that they probably belonged equally to both. They were noble, tender, and respectful.

The argument has been cogently made, however, that the high rate of infant mortality -- perhaps up to 30/40 percent in the first year of life -- cheapened the value of infant life and diluted the intensity of the parents' grief for the loss of an infant child. The conditions were different when the child was of a promising lineage or had reached maturity and, therefore, demanded by tradition a more elaborate burial.

Worth mentioning is that the Athenian culture did not foster any form of ancestor worship, except for the national heroes like Achilles and Heracles.

The funerals heretofore considered were public and rare, although they carried with them a tradition that affected the private funerals as well. Most funerals were private and the name of the deceased remained unrecorded.

---

[262] Euripides, *Trojan Women*, 1121-1122: Loeb 10, 120.
[263] *Ibid.*, 1194: Loeb 10, 126.
[264] *Ibid.*, 1235-1236: Loeb 10, 130.

The silent monuments, however, are explicit about the duties of women and about their tender feelings, for example a vase of about 440 BCE in the white-ground technique. [265] Some fifteen terra cotta plaques executed by Exechias in about 540 BCE were placed around a women's tomb. They pictured like a frieze the phases of the funeral ceremony from lying in state and mourning privately to the burial at the gravesite. Women accompany the body transported on a chariot. The grief they convey is unmistakable. [266]

The literary sources such as the inscriptions, the laws, the histories and especially the dramas are explicit about the tender feelings expressed by mothers burying their children, and by children honoring each other and their parents with a proper burial. The role of women in the funeral rites is also well described in other written words.

The responsibility for planning and conducting the private funeral rites rested on the head of the family or, in his absence or incapacity, on the closest male relative. The orator Lysias reported that a son who was not worthy to fulfill his obligation toward his mother ought to be considered degenerate. [267]

The role of women was greater in the private funerals where tradition assigned certain tasks to women and allowed them to mourn loudly, with lamentations and cries at the death site and at the grave.

Except when death struck on the battlefield or in travel, or in an epidemic such as the plague of 430, [268] the body was laid out in the common quarters of the house where it received from the women the first funerary services. No special law except the law of tradition dictated their actions or restricted their expressions of mourning. The closest female relatives performed with the help of slaves the sacred task of preparing the deceased for burial (*prothesis*). They cleaned the body and dressed it with a simple tunic (*peplos*), but no more than three long outer garments (*himatia*) wrapped around the body and, for females, with some ornaments like earrings and necklace.

---

[265] Fantham, E. et al., *Women in the Classical World*, 97.
[266] *Ibid.*, 48-49.
[267] *Against Philon*, 31, 20-23: Loeb 244, 646-649.
[268] Thucydides, *Peloponnesian War*, 2, 50, 1-2 & 52, 1-4: Loeb 108, 346-353.

While the corpse laid in state on a bier some women cropped their hair and sang dirges, [269] others let their feelings of grief surge in cries of wailing, [270] holding the head of the deceased with one hand and raising the other in a sign of supplication. Some forms of self-mutilation, such as tearing hair and skin, and beating the head or the breasts, took place, sometimes to excess. [271] In the meanwhile, other women assembled the food and gifts, and placed them in baskets to be carried in procession to the burial site. The wake lasted all night.

Before sunrise of the third day after death, the men of the family clan (*anchisteia*) and a few close friends assembled at the house for the burial (*ekphora*). They carried the corpse in a wooden box if adult or in a jar if infant. They carried the jar in their arms, but usually placed the box on a cart. Walking in front, they pulled it or had it drawn by a horse or a mule through the narrow streets to the place of burial. In controlled noise-making, the women walked behind, except those of child-bearing age and children who did not participate in the procession. [272]

The uncertainty and void created by the loss of a guardian or husband produced the greatest of fear for the girls and women. They could do nothing without a man. Who would he be? Their options were limited and often frightening. So they shed tears and lamented as they tried to go on with their lives and the lives of those entrusted to their care. Plutarch reported that Solon, the lawmaker of the sixth century BCE, regulated the mourning that men and women could express at the burial site (*taphê*). He wrote:

> Laceration of the flesh by mourners, and the use of set lamentations, and the bewailing of any one at the funeral ceremonies of another, he borbade. ... Such offenders shall be punished by the board of [male] censors for women, because they indulge in unmanly

---

[269] Euripides, *Helen*, 1053-1054: Loeb11, 128.

[270] Id., *Heracles Mad*, 1025-1027: Loeb 9, 406 and *Trojan Women*, 105-121: Loeb 10, 24-27; see Id., *Fr., Archelaus*, 263: Loeb 504, 254.

[271] Id., *Suppliant Women*, 48-54: Loeb 9, 6 and Aeschylus, *Libation-Bearers*, 23-31: Loeb 146, 160.

[272] Plato, *Laws*, 12, 947D: Loeb 192, 494.

and effeminate extravagances of sorrow when they mourn. [273]

According to Demosthenes, Solon limited also the time women were allowed to stay at the burial site, because of their excessive wailing, and forbade the hiring of paid mourners. [274] The rationale for this law was implicitly given by Euripides in Dictys' words of consolation to Danae of Argos:

> Do you think that Hades is concerned at all for your laments, and will send your son back up [Perseus thought to have drowned] if you will go on grieving? Stop! You'd feel easier if you look at the troubles of those near at hand, if you'd be willing to consider how many of mankind have been exhausted by struggling with bonds, how many grow old bereft of children, and those who are nothing after ruling in the greatest prosperity: these are the things you should contemplate. [275]

And in Ino's words: "Understand mankind's condition and do not grieve beyond measure: you are not alone in being visited by evil fortune." [276]

After placing some wreaths of flowers on the tomb the women returned to the house to prepare for the funeral feast to follow and the men lowered the corpse into a shallow grave with a sufficient amount of rocky soil on top to protect it from scavengers and robbers. The grave could be shared with other members of the immediate families. [277]

This was the traditional procedure for a man's funeral and probably for an Athenian woman who had acquired a certain rank from her husband or from some special service she rendered, for example, as priestess or midwife. No doubt, many funeral services, especially in times of crisis like the plague of 430 BCE, were conducted with much less

---

[273] *Parallel Lives, Solon*, 21, 4-5: Loeb 46, 462-465; see Plato, *Republic*, 3, 395E: Loeb 237, 236.

[274] See N. Loraux, *Mothers in Mourning*, 20-28.

[275] Euripides, *Fr., Dictys*, 332: Loeb 504, 350-353.

[276] Id., *Fr., Ino*, 418: Loeb 504, 456.

[277] Id., *Fr., Erechtheus*, 370, 68: Loeb 504, 394.

care. [278] The baskets of offerings were then the first ritual to be neglected.

The orators of the fourth century brought a touch of dark reality to the picture of grief exhibited at funerals. These were some of the rare occasions in which men and women, perhaps total strangers to each other, were assembled in one cortege from the house to the gravesite. First, the choice of the route could be a matter of dispute. [279] Also, some evil encounters could not always be prevented by the solemnity of the circumstances. Lysias reported in the first quarter of the fourth century that a male seducer caught sight of a young wife when she was attending the funeral of her mother-in-law. The wife's husband was Euphiletus and the lover Eratosthenes, the two we met already when dealing with adultery and its punishment. [280]

To bury the deceased men and women of Athens, except the convicted criminals, was a sacred obligation. [281] The story of the activist Antigone will be told later because it transcends the obligation of providing a decent burial. Several other incidents demonstrated this obligation.

One incident involved Nicias, the Athenian general who negotiated the famous peace of 421 BCE that is known by his name. Once he "chose rather to renounce his victory and his glory than to let two citizens die unburied." [282]

After the victory of the Athenian fleet against the Spartans in 406 BCE at the Arginusae islands, south of Lesbos, a storm broke out and prevented the generals from rescuing the crews of twenty-five sunken ships. When the news reached Athens that these sailors had not been given a proper burial, some extremists in the Council proposed to put the six generals to death for neglecting their duty. Socrates was the only one who objected for the sake of moderation and a fair trial. But the motion passed and the generals were executed. A few days later, however, the Council members recognized their ill-advised decision and condemned to death the extremists who misled them.

---

[278] Thucydides, *Peloponnesian War*, 2, 52, 2: Loeb 108, 350.
[279] Isaeus, *On the Estate of Ciron*, 8, 22: Loeb 244, 302.
[280] *On the Murder of Eratosthenes*, 8 & 20: Loeb 244, 6 & 20; see above, p. 104.
[281] Xenophon, *Hellenica*, 1, 7, 20: Loeb 88, 77.
[282] Plutarch, *Parallel Lives, Nicias*, 6, 6: Loeb 65, 228-231.

This incident tells more than the confusion that plagued the Athenians a short time before their surrender to Sparta. It tells also of the importance of a proper burial, lest the soul kept wandering restlessly. It could be done with a sense of moderation, such as resorting to a symbolic ritual, like Antigone did, when the circumstances did not allow the actual burial in the ground, but it ought always to be done. King Theseus called it "the custom of all the Greeks" and explained why: "We do not possess our bodies as our own; we live our lives in them, and thereafter the earth, our nourisher, must take them back." [283]

Tradition supported some rituals performed at the grave on the third and ninth days after the burial [284] and only one annual celebration in honor of the dead, namely during the three-day spring festival called *Anthesteria*. There seemed to be little formality in the rituals prescribed for these occasions, except that the participants offered sacrifices to god Hermes and incantations to ward off the baleful return of the ghosts of the dead. The festival was not held with only sad events since, before it ended, the same Athenians offered special thanks to god Dionysus for giving them the new wine. The guardian of each household had brought his own wine to the celebration and the result was nothing less than the general inebriation of both men and women, as it appeared to be a convenient way to drown their grief. [285]

The respect paid to the dead was extended only to close relatives, except for the war casualties who were entitled to special honors. Custom prescribed the respectful burial of parents by their children [286] and frequent visits to their tombs, as Orestes, Electra and the Libation-Bearers did for Agamemnon [287] and Hermione for her aunt and foster-mother, Clytemnestra. Her mother, Helen, had hesitated at first to send her with the offerings, but "it wouldn't be proper for servants to bring these offerings." [288] Out of

[283] Euripides, *Suppliant Women*, 526 & 534-536: Loeb 9, 64.
[284] Isaeus, *On the Estate of Menecles*, 36: Loeb 202, 60.
[285] See J. Bremmer, *The Early Greek Concept of the Soul*, 102-122 and S.C. Humphries, *The Family, Women and Death*, 13 ff.
[286] Euripides, *Medea*, 1034: Loeb 12, 378.
[287] Id., *Electra*, 90-92: Loeb 9, 160 & Aeschylus, *The Libation-Bearers*, 167 ff.: Loeb 146, 174.
[288] Euripides, *Orestes*, 106: Loeb 11, 422.

respect, she changed her mind and gave her daughter to bring to her sister's grave some of her own hair and an offering of "milk and honey mixture and the foaming wine" as libations. [289]

We know also that Orestes, expecting to die, wished that his sister, Electra, will give to his tomb "the gift of her tears and cut hair" [290] and Iphigenia, believing he was dead, talked of offering "to him these libations, this mixing bowl for the dead", containing milk, wine and honey. [291]

According to R. Garland, a series of flasks, called lêkuthoi -- white-ground, narrow-necked with one handle and containing oil or ointment -- show that they were popular grave-gifts from the 460's to 410's BCE. They displayed some iconography representing visits to a tomb, in most cases by women carrying gifts in shallow baskets or extending their arms in greeting. [292]

Now is the time, at the end of reviewing funeral practices and rituals in Ancient Greece, to expose the strange behavior of Admetus as expression of grief for the loss of his wife, Alcestis. He promised to mourn her all his life since she volunteered to die so he could live. [293] This was well and good, but he dared commission "skilled craftsmen" to fashion in her image a mannequin which he will lay in bed with him and hold as if it were his dear wife. [294] Although strange, his intentions were more noble and sincere than those of some Egyptian embalmers whom Herodotus accused of necrophilia. [295] Admetus was a weak character and Alcestis the only source of his strength. How fortunate he was not only as a king but especially as a husband when Heracles returned her "from below to the light of day." [296]

---

[289] Orestes, 115: Loeb 11, 424.
[290] Euripides, Iphigenia Among the Taurians, 703: Loeb 10, 220.
[291] Ibid., 158-169: Loeb 10, 166.
[292] The Greek Way of Death, 107-108.
[293] Euripides, Alcestis, 336-337; Loeb 12, 186.
[294] Ibid., 348-356: Loeb 12, 186-189.
[295] Histories, 2, 89: Loeb 117, 372.
[296] Euripides, Alcestis, 1139: Loeb 12, 270.

The Theater

Another question that may never be answered satisfactorily concerns women's attendance at the theater productions of Classical Tragedy and Comedy. [297] The evidence is fragmentary and elusive. The consensus among scholars applies to the following assertions: First, women did not perform on stage although they were often featured on stage either as actors or chorus members. Male citizens filled all the roles. Second, women were allowed in the audience but under certain conditions. They were not allowed at the *Great Dionysia* productions in late-march, which were open to male citizens only, either from Attica or the colonies. They were present at the Festival of Dionysus but only on the days preceding the theatrical performances and participated in the procession where they danced and sang, and one or more among them carried baskets of offerings. Women were allowed at the *Lenaea* in the month of Gamelion (Jan./Feb.) of each year and at other local productions. They were then seated, not with men but in a special section at the rear of the tiered seating space, called *kavêa*.

Two passages are often quoted on this subject. They are not conclusive, yet they seem to delineate some perimeters. The first passage appears in the play *Peace* of Aristophanes. In preparation for his wedding to Cornucopia, Trygaeus offered a sacrifice to Peace. He enjoined his servant to "throw the spectators some of the barley pips" [298] After the servant had complied, he certified that every spectator "got a pip". Then Trygaeus asked the question crucial to the present inquiry: What about the women? The servant replied with a double entendre, based on *kritha* (barley pip) and *krithê* (penis): "Their husbands will give it to them tonight!", which may imply two different situations: first, that they were not present in the audience and will get their corn at home when their husbands return from the theatre or, second, that they were seated far in the back of the cavea where the pips could not be thrown far enough to reach them. The second option of this alternative is probably the correct one because Aristophanes implied in

---

[297] See J.R. Laurin, *Poets of Tragedy in Classical Athens*, 164-168.
[298] *Peace*, 962: Loeb 488, 548.

Frogs that women were present at one of Euripides' plays, *Bellerophon*, over which respectable women could have felt shame, therefore they could have been present at other plays less disturbing, including some of his own, like *Peace*. [299] If they were present, sitting in the back, why did the husbands who were sitting in front did not make the effort to give ther wives some of the barley pips they caught? Too much trouble is probably the answer. Therefore this passage is not conclusive either way it is interpreted.

The second passage is from Plato's *Laws*. The dialogue takes place between an Athenian Stranger and the Cretan Clinias. The Athenian objects to bringing to Athens the type of Cretan Tragedy which serves to "harangue women and children, and the whole populace" against the institutions of the state. [300] Plato seems to imply that the Cretan custom of allowing women, children and slaves to the theater performances was allowed in Athens only after the magistrates had determined whether the production was suitable to "women who are to make the best of themselves, let alone to men." [301] So, the most we may conclude from this passage is that women may have attended certain performances deemed acceptable by the magistrates. Comedy was probably excluded as too gross for women's ears and eyes, and some Tragedy, like Euripides' *Bacchae*, too violent for women's emotions. We may never know for sure which plays were selected for general audiences. Therefore, at best, the door is ajar, not wide open, to have women present at some theater productions.

Other minor pieces of evidence can confirm the position that women attended at least some of the plays at the theatre, If it is true that some women took hemlock after seeing one of Euripides' plays, as stated earlier, and boys died of fright and women had miscarriages for seeing the chorus of Furies on stage at one of Aeschylus' plays, *The Eumenides*. [302] The exaggeration is obvious but the presence of women at the theatre is well taken. Plato explained later that the poets in the theatre "found a kind of rhetoric which is addressed to such a public as is compounded of children and women and men, and slaves as

---

[299] *Frogs*, 1050-1051: Loeb 180, 168.
[300] Plato, *Laws*, 7, 817C: Loeb 192, 98.
[301] Id., *Republic*, 3, 398E: Loeb 237, 246.
[302] *Life of Aeschylus*: see H.D.F. Kitto, *The Greeks*, 233.

well as free." [303] It appears, therefore, that the staging and attendance of women at the theatre contributed to making the plays a "democratic act" open to all people. [304]

All in all, women were limited in Athens to appearing in public as a group at weddings and funerals, Festivals and certain athletic events, and probably certain theatrical productions, such as Euripides' *Alcestis*, which the magistrates approved for their moralizing contribution. Otherwise, they socialized only with members of their extended family and with female friends, mostly in their neighborhood.

Fashion

Fashion is a part of women's social life, because it is selected and worn to be seen by others and to make a statement about one's self to others, in Ancient Athens to women rather than men, except their husbands.

The garments that covered most female figures in art were designed to adorn them and to protect their modesty in front of the viewers. According to Euripides, "modesty is born in the eyes" [305] but the fact is that it lives in the garments that will now guide us through the fashion of their time. In general, they were simple in the Archaic period; [306] then became gradually more sophisticated and elegant during the Classical period [307] and more extravagant and luxurious in the Hellenistic period. [308]

No sample of garments has been preserved because linen from the plant flax and wool from the fleece of sheep disintegrated with time. Silk was sparingly used until the Seleucids established the Silk Route to China in the third century BCE. Then silk became a material of choice, and also cotton fiber, probably imported from Egypt. Our sources of information, either from literature or iconography, are often obscure and inconsistent in the details but fairly reliable in the general view.

---

[303] Plato, *Gorgias*, 502D: Loeb 166, 450-453.
[304] Aristophanes, *Frogs*, 951: Loeb 180, 154.
[305] *Fr., Cresphontes*, 457: Loeb 504, 512.
[306] EWA 1, Pl. 337 & 356 and 7, Pl. 12.
[307] EWA 3, Pl. 368; 4, Pl. 218 & 7, Pl. 63.
[308] EWA 2, Pl. 55; 3, Pl. 80 & 12, Pl. 512.

The mythical Amazon women of Scythia and Lapith women of Thessaly were for their beauty the frequent subjects of Greek art works but were not at all the models of the Athenian women since they probably wore in life the same attire as men, being involved in similar activities of war.

The Athenian women always dressed modestly, yet enticingly. In public, their dresses were all long and leaving only the head, the arms and the feet exposed to view. For private chores inside the house, their robe was shorter and adapted to their work.

Homer described in the *Iliad* how goddess Hera adorned herself to entice her husband Zeus.

> With ambrosia first did she cleanse every stain from her lovely body, and anointed herself richly with oil, ambrosial, soft, and of rich fragrance. ... She combed her hair and with her hands plaited the bright tresses, fair and ambrosial, that streamed from her immortal head. Then she clothed herself in an ambrosial robe ... [with] many embroideries; and she pinned it at the breast with brooches of gold, and she girt about her a belt set with one hundred tassels, and in her pierced ears she put earrings with three clustering drops; and abundant grace shone from them. And with a veil over all did the fair goddess veil herself, a veil fair and bright, all glistening, and it was white as the sun, and beneath her shining feet she bound her fair sandals. [309]

Then Hera called on Aphrodite to direct the final touch of her adornment. Thus it went:

> Take now and place in your bosom this strap [brassiere], inlaid, in which all things [breasts] are fashioned. [310]

In the *Odyssey* also, Homer described briefly how the nymph Calypso adorned herself for the pleasure of Odysseus:

---

[309] Homer, *Iliad*, 14, 170-186: Loeb 171, 78-81.
[310] *Ibid.*, 14, 219-220: Loeb 171, 82.

The nymph clothed herself in a long white robe, finely woven and beautiful, and about her waist she threw a beautiful girdle of gold, and on her head she placed a veil. [311]

When Euripides of the fifth century was pursued by the Athenian women who wanted revenge for his incessant lampooning, he sought a spy to infiltrate their meeting and plead his case. A kinsman, his father-in-law Mnesilochus, accepted the assignment for which he had to be fixed like a real lady in dress and appearance. He was first shaved with a razor, then covered with a dress and a brassiere, a wig and a hat, a wrap also and pumps on his feet. [312]

In his play Bacchae (405 BCE), Euripides described how king Pentheus disguised himself as a woman in order to spy on the maenads' behavior at the Dionysiac festival: long hair crowned with a headdress, girdle tight under the evenly hanging long dress, reaching to his feet, a thyrsus in his hand and a dappled fawnskin. [313] We can assume that women dressed in this fashion only for the festival of Dionysus.

The Greek women dressed in a simple and elegant fashion. They had learned as young girls to weave large pieces of material, either linen or wool. Cutting and sewing was used very sparingly. The tunic called peplos was a large rectangular drape wrapped loose around the body. [314] It was much longer in width than in height from feet to shoulders over which it was folded, with two holes at the fold for the arms. The folded portion could be raised over the head and used as a veil. Nevertheless, the peplos was not always plain and rectangular if we judge by the records of dedications to goddesses. We know of one peplos scalloped, embroidered, and with letters woven in and of another dotted and with a broad purple border with a wave design. [315]

The Dorian style of dress included a brooch or clasp (peronê) to hold the folded dress on the right or the left

---

[311] Homer, Odyssey, 5, 230-232: Loeb 104, 198.
[312] Aristophanes, Women at the Thesmophoria, 213 ff.: Loeb 179, 484 ff.
[313] Bacchae, 828 ff.: Loeb 495, 92.
[314] EWA 1, Pl. 351 & 11, Pl. 125.
[315] Inscriptiones Graecae, 2, 2, 1514: M.R.Lefkowtz and M.B. Fant, Women's life in Greece and Rome, 123, p. 120.

shoulder, either for the convenience of freeing the arm for work or for a fashionable display of an ornament while breaking the vertical fall of the garment. [316] It added a touch of elegance, probably imported from Troy. [317] It could also become a dangerous weapon. Oedipus used Jocasta's brooch to blind himself; [318] Hecuba and her fellow Trojan women used their brooches to blind king Polymestor of Thrace. [319]

Herodotus wrote in mid-fifth century that the brooch women wore was so lethal as a weapon and probably used so often that it became forbidden by law. The occasion had been created by the hostilities between, on one side, the Epidaurans, the Aeginetans and the Argives and, on the other side, the Athenians who sent a few triremes to retrieve from Egina the image of two minor goddesses, Damia and Auxesia. A battle ensued. Suddenly, a thunderclap and an earthquake stopped the engagement and, although the accounts of the detail of the events varied, all the Athenians were killed except one man who returned to Athens. Herodotus continued:

> Albeit even this one (say the Athenians) was not saved alive but perished as here related. It would seem that he made his way to Athens and told of the mishap; and when this was known (it is said) to the wives of the men who had gone to attack Aegina, they were very wroth that he alone should be safe out of all, and they gathered round him and stabbed him with the brooch-pins of their garments. ... Thus was this man done to death. [320]

Such a horrible crime frightened the Athenians. As a result, they decreed that the Athenian women should "change their dress to the Ionian fashion" from the Dorian fashion they currently followed. Herodotus added: "Henceforth they were made to wear the linen tunic, "that so they might have no brooch-pins to use." This decree applied only to Athens and Attica. In retaliation, the Argives and

---

[316] EWA 3, Pl. 373; 2, Pl. 48 & 7, Pl. 47.
[317] Euripides, *Electra*, 317: Loeb 9, 186.
[318] Sophocles, *Oedipus King*, 1268-1272: Loeb 20, 458.
[319] Euripides, *Hecuba*, 1255: Loeb 484, 512.
[320] Herodotus, *Histories*, 5, 87-88: Loeb 119, 96.

Aeginetans made a law for their women "that their brooch-pins should be made half as long again as the measure then curtomary." [321]

Even if Herodotus embellished his story and made sure the Athenians would not be offended by it, he confirmed the use of brooches by Greek women, as represented in iconography, for example on a relief of about 480 BCE from Pharsalos in Thessaly [322] and a statue of Eirine of about 370 BCE. [323]

At the waist, the long garment was often gathered in with a girdle or belt [324] where it could be folded again over the belt to make a pouch. [325] During the late Classical period the *peplos* was folded only slightly over the belt instead of folded over at the top. Another mode of fashion in the late period was to set the belt not at the waist but higher under the breasts, in a fashion resembling the Empire Style of the Napoleonic Era.

The *peplos* of young girls was longer than needed so that it could be let down at the waist as they grew up. On the other hand, for the convenience of play, all young girls wore also a shorter *peplos* with a belt and a slit on one side to free the leg. Athletic girls, artisans, slaves and warriors like the Amazons, wore also a short *peplos*, called *exômis*, sleeveless, with one bare shoulder for the ease of their movements. [326]

Under the *peplos*, women wore a chemise or slip called *chitôn*, similar to the one men wore, short and sleeveless. It was made of two panels of cloth sewed up on the sides and at the top, like a bag pierced with three holes for the head and the arms. During the fifth century, the *chitôn* was made more tightly wrapped around the body than the *peplos*. Other brief undergarments may have been worn under the *chitôn*, like panties, surely simple and functional.

The third piece of garment, worn especially outdoor in wintertime, was the *Himation*, which was a cloak made of a large oblong piece of cloth draped usually over the left

---

[321] Herodotus, *Histories*, 5, 88: Loeb 119, 96.
[322] EWA 7, Pl. 47.
[323] EWA 3, Pl. 373.
[324] EWA 2, Pl. 49 & 3, Pl. 385.
[325] EWA 12, Pl. 120.
[326] EWA 3, Pl. 377; 11, Pl. 123; 12, Pl. 138 & 13, Pl. 41.

shoulder and folded over the head. The short *himation* worn by men was called *klamus* (rich) or *tribôn* (poor).

The common shoes were sandals tied to the feet and ankles with leather thongs or pumps without any ties at all, also known as "pleasure-boat slippers." [327] In better circumstances, women wore closed leather shoes and socks. [328] It appears that they had many pairs of shoes because, as Ischomachus told Socrates, each set had to be put in its proper place. [329] The same Ischomachus sounded modern when he revealed that his wife "was wearing boots with thick soles to increase her height." [330]

The hair was styled sometimes hanging down, other times short and parted in the middle, with a band around at the forehead, or gathered in a chignon with a snood or a net. Helen was known to have beautiful red hair. [331] Once, in one of Euripides' plays, as soon as she exited the stage, Electra snapped: "See how she cut off just the ends of her hair, trying to keep her beauty unchanged!" Such a remark would have been catty if Helen's beauty had not been the cause of the miseries, not only of the Atreid family but of all of Hellas. [332] Distraught and humiliated, Electra cut off her hair very short and, as she admitted, kept it filthy at times. [333]

Unless it is shown or given a measure, "very short" is an imprecise term. How short did Electra cut her hair? In Euripides' *Electra*, line 107, the comment about her shorn head is made contextually with the painful practice of carrying on it a heavy water jug. This comment must be related to *Electra*, line 241, where the shortness of her hair is related to the Scythian practice of either shaving with a razor at the surface of the skin or cut close to the skin with a knife. Such a short hair seems to fit ill with the statement at *Electra*, line 184: "Look at my filthy hair". If her hair was long enough to be groomed or combed, it had not been cut off close to the skin but was kept at least long enough to reach down to her earlobes. In other words, it was long

---

[327] Aristophanes, *Lysistrata*, 45-47: Loeb 179, 272.

[328] Aeschylus, *Fr., Phineus*, 144: Loeb 146, 469.

[329] Xenophon, *Oeconomicus*, 8, 21: Loeb 168, 436.

[330] *Oeconomicus*, 10, 2: Loeb 168, 446.

[331] Hesiod, *Catalogue of Women*, 67, 41: Loeb 503, 194.

[332] Euripides, *Orestes*, 128-131: Loeb 11, 424.

[333] Id., *Electra*, 107, 184 & 241: Loeb 9, 160, 168 & 174.

enough to be combed, yet short enough to signify her distress and humiliation. The context confirms this interpretation. Electra was a banished princess, married to a peasant with whom she had no sexual relations. Furthermore, she was distraught by the belief that her brother Orestes was either lost or dead. It is no surprise that, when he came to her humble residence in the hills, he saw her but did not recognize her, taking her for a servant. Iconography also confirms that women often wore their hair in this fashion. The exception was in letting it be seen unkempt in public.

Electra said it well, not without some venom, that a woman "has no need to show a lovely face to those outside the house, unless she is looking for mischief." She was then addressing her mother Clytemnestra: As soon as your husband Agamemnon left for the war, "you began to primp your golden tresses before a mirror." [334] For sure, the mirror, made of polished earthenware or bronze, was a woman's best friend.

Cosmetics, such as face powder and rouge, and other ornaments, such as earrings, necklaces and bracelets, were well known and used with good taste. The coloring came from plants, herbs, and lead carbonate. The jewelry represented a variety of motifs, mostly female figures and primarily Aphrodite. Perfume was also popular. The better kind had to be imported, probably from Arabia. The whiter was a woman's face the more dignified and beautiful she felt, sometimes for illicit adventures. So, women used a strigil to clean their face and lead white powder to make it look whiter, like Japanese geishas do. [335] Xenophon revealed the same practice by Ischomachus' wife. He told her, however, that she was not pleasing him more "by the colour of white powder and rouge" than by "her own pure body." [336] In spite of these and similar words of displeasure, most women continued to use cosmetics and perfume. [337]

We do not know of any example of nightgowns, either because they were never modeled or were lost. We

---

[334] Euripides, *Electra*, 1073-1075: Loeb 9, 268.
[335] See Aristophanes, *Assemblywomen*, 878 & 929: Loeb 180, 370-375; also, Lysias, *On the Murder of Eratosthenes*, 1, 17: Loeb 244, 10 and Xenophon, *Oeconomicus*, 10, 2: Loeb 168, 446.
[336] Xenophon, *Oeconomicus*, 10, 2-7: Loeb 168, 446-449.
[337] Aristophanes, *Lysistrata*, 42-48: Loeb 179, 272.

can infer, however, from Aristophanes' *Lysistrata* that women wore "see-through underwear", hidden under a dress during the waking hours but convenient at night for comfort and pleasure.

Artistic Evolution

Paintings and sculptures of women, most of them in formal dress, confirm the description of women's fashion in the Archaic and Classical Ages of Athens. The development of artistic productions became a sign of the changing times at the turn of the century, in the last years of the fifth century BCE, when the Peloponnesian War was crawling in blood toward its miserable end. Until this time, the male figure was often represented nude and the female figure of goddesses and mortal women was always represented dressed in a garment. The so-called "Lady of Auxerre", dated of the second half of the seventh century, emphasized and even pointed at the breasts, but this was a symbol of motherhood rather than sensuality. [338] Besides, such an emphasis had become a tradition since Minoan times. The "Snake Goddess" of Knossos, Crete, was a clear symbol of fertility as two statuettes in faience, as early as 1700-1600 BCE, represented her as bare-breasted. [339]

A change took place during the latter years of the Peloponnesian War that ended in 404 BCE. For the first time, women posed in the nude as models and were shown standing in the nude. The scanty data at our disposal reveal with sufficient certainty that an artist by the name of Zeuxis (short for Zeuxippus) was the innovator of this new trend. We are not sure where he was born and exactly when, but we read in Plato's *Protagoras* that he lived in Heraclea, southeast Italy, [340] a colony founded in 432 BCE, and we know that he was a famous painter during the last twenty-five years of the fifth century. We find him in Athens before 424 when he became a pupil of the painter Apollodorus and was still there in 422 when he participated in a symposium with Socrates. [341]

---

[338] EWA 1, Pl. 342.
[339] EWA,4, Pl. 55.
[340] *Protagoras*, 318B: Loeb 165, 122.
[341] Xenophon, *Banquet*, 4, 63: Loeb 168, 443.

In sculpture and painting, the nudes were more frequently male than female, yet a few female subjects were favored by the artists. Of all the goddesses, Aphrodite was the most frequently represented in the nude. Among women, Helen of Sparta and Troy was regarded as the most beautiful in the world. Zeuxis of the late fifth century sculpted a statue of her in the nude and made a painting of her also, at the request of the Italian city of Crotona, for which, according to Valerius Maximus (fl. c. 20 CE), he had some of the most beautiful women of the city pose as models. [342] He chose from each the part of the body he evaluated as the most beautiful and painted it in one figure of Helen on a panel which was later displayed in Rome. This painting is now lost, as well as a copy he made for Athens where he lived for some years and may have promoted this new interest among the male artists. [343]

Other women, more real than Helen, served also as models to sculptors and painters. Theodotê, Alcibiades' female companion (hetaira), posed for painters in late fifth century [344] and Phryne, Praxiteles' paramour, posed in mid-fourth century as model for his delicate and sensuous Aphrodite of Knidos. [345]

Theodotê, mentioned above, seemed to have been entangled in the web of the past while trying to free herself for a more liberal future. Xenophon told that she was very beautiful and that "the artists visited her to paint her portrait, and she showed them as much as decency allowed." [346]

On this recommendation, Socrates could hardly wait to go and see such a beauty beyond expression. When he arrived at her house she was posing for a painter and surely showing more of her body, but not more than what would make her suggestive and enticing, since she hoped to persuade the best of the male viewers to take her as a paid escort. When the session ended, she dressed herself fully and elegantly and appeared with her mother before Socrates who, indeed, was delighted like every Athenian man in his sixties would be at the sight of a gorgeous young lady. At

---

[342] *Memorable Doings and Sayings*, 3, 7, Ext. 3: Loeb 492, 312.
[343] Xenophon, *Oeconomicus*, 10, 1: Loeb 168, 446.
[344] Id., *Memorabilia*, 3, 11, 1: Loeb 168, 238-241
[345] EWA 3, Pl. 374 & 11, Pl. 238.
[346] Xenophon, *Memorabilia*, 3, 11, 1: Loeb 168, 240.

the turn of the century, a change was taking place about the public appreciation of the female body.

For the first time, starting in mid-fourth century, the nude female figure appeared in a standing position and for general viewing. Prior to this time, the rare portrayals of female nudity, such as the Flute-girl [347] and the Dying Niobid [348] of mid-fifth century, were sitting or leaning and, furthermore, intended for male viewing only, like the image of *hetairai* and prostitutes on vases used at symposia.

If the sculptor Praxiteles was not first to show nude female bodies in art, he was first to make it acceptable. His *hetaira*, Phryne, posed for him as a model, then his Aphrodite of Knidos sculpted in marble in about 350 BCE became a model for other artists to imitate. From this time on, and during the entire Hellenistic period, Aphrodite was painted and sculpted in the nude, standing like the "Medici Aphrodite" of early third century or crouching like the "Crouching Aphrodite" of mid third century [349] or disrobing like the Aphrodite from Melos, known as the Venus de Milo of about 150 BCE. [350] The poses became more erotic and variable with the years, as the freedom women received from men grew out of the political instability and social uncertainty of the time.

This change in the artistic representation of women was symptomatic of the more profound changes which helped women making progress toward greater independence: not a huge leap but only a small step, because their legal, political and social standing did not change. Only their life style became more free and assertive in the society of Athens.

In spite of women's apparent gains, it is worth remembering again that Athens was a man's world and that the statues and paintings of goddesses and mortal women were addressed to men, not to women. These painted and sculpted women expressed men's views about feminine beauty, namely that it was there for men to use for their enjoyment, whether it was in a simple or lavish garment or in the nude.

---

[347] EWA 3, Pl. 350.
[348] EWA 3, Pl. 360.
[349] EWA 7, Pl. 157.
[350] EWA 7, Pl. 176.

About the real life of women in the society of Ancient Athens, it is worth remembering also that there lies the major difference between their life and the life of women in our modern world. The life of women engaged in homemaking, such as cooking, cleaning, caring for husband and children has not changed fundamentally. Instead of slaves, modern women have sophisticated tools and appliances. The motions have remained the same, except for clothing which has now been assumed by the industrial production and the department stores. The major changes between then and now are in the social life of women, outside the home, and the difference has not yet penetrated completely the entire world of today.

*   *   *

CHAPTER TEN

ACTIVIST WOMEN

<u>Mythology</u>

Of all the goddesses inspiring the devotion of the Athenian women, none was more popular than Athena, under various titles such as *Nikê* (victory), *Polias* (city), *Parthenos* (virgin) and *Promachos* (warrior). As a result, no myth was better known and celebrated with more pomp in Athens than the myth of Athena, protectress (*phulax*) of the city-state. The Greeks honored her at public festivals and privately, Like Melinna did when she set up a memorial and donated some of her possessions acquired through handi-work and bartering with other women.[1]

Athena was a female deity, yet in the minds of male writers and artists she was not entirely feminine. They represented her not only as motherless but as a virgin who had rejected the major role of motherhood. They depicted her wearing the warrior's helmet and aegis, and holding a spear in her hand. Homer cared to place her in the thick of battle at Troy [2] and Aristophanes of conflict inside the walls in Athens. [3] She was not only the guardian of Athens against all enemies but also the creator of the highest court of law, the *Areiopagos*, [4] for the city-state and the benefactress who planted on the Acropolis the olive tree that never dies. Athena changed the wandering punitive Erinyes into peaceful Eumenides with a dwelling beneath the earth. [5]

Augustine of Hippo in the early fifth century CE wrote that, when king Cecrops of Athens, inquired with the oracle

---

[1] See M.R. Lefkowitz and M.B. Fant, *Women's Life in Greece and Rome*, 55, p. 28.
[2] *Iliad*, 5, 121-132: Loeb 170, 214-217,
[3] *Lysistrata*, 344-347: Loeb 179, 312.
[4] Aeschylus, *Eumenides*, 614: Loeb 146, 330.
[5] *Ibid.*, 1021-1023: Loeb 146, 368.

at Delphi about the name of his city, an olive tree and a water spring appeared unexpectedly on the Acropolis. He then heard that the olive tree signified Athena and the water spring Poseidon, and that all the residents of Athens, men and women, should be called upon to name their city after either one of these deities.

> When Cecrops received this oracle, he called together all the citizens of both sexes – for at that time it was customary in that area that the women also should have a part in public deliberations – to take a vote. When therefore the multitude was consulted, the men voted for Neptune [Poseidon] and the women for Minerva [Athena]; and because the women were found to be one more, Minerva was victorious. Then Neptune in his wrath devastated the lands of the Athenians by great floods of sea-water. [6]

The women of Athens were punished for this calamity: first, "they should no longer have any vote"; second, "none of their children should be named after their mothers" and, third, "no one should call them Athenians". So it happened that, when Athens received its name after a female deity, Athena, [7] all the women of Athens were deprived of the civic involvement they had heretofore enjoyed.

This myth, surely invented by men, was a way of justifying not only the choice of a city's name but also the exclusion of women from public affairs. It refers to prior times when women deliberated and voted with men on public issues and to new times inaugurated by Cecrops when women were relegated to the home as wives and mothers. So, at the same time, Athena became the housewife's (erganê) model and invented needlework and weaving for which she was honored with a new robe (peplos) presented to her every four years at the Great Panathenea.[8]

Aristophanes had a fantasy of his own about Athena. When the birds gathered to build their utopian city in the

---

[6] *The City of God*, 18, 9: Loeb 415, 390-393.
[7] Euripides, *Ion*, 8-9 & 1555-1556: Loeb 10, 322 & 504.
[8] EWA 11, Pl 125: East frieze of the Parthenon. Also, Hesiod, *Works and* Days, 63-64: Loeb 57, 6 and Homer, *Iliad*, 14, 178-179: Loeb 171, 78 & *Odyssey*, 7, 110: Loeb 104, 254.

sky, they invited Peisetaerus and Euelpides to join them. The Athenian pair flew up by using their own wings. Then, Peisetaerus retained Athena *Polias* as "Citadel Guardian", as she was of Athens, although she would appear somewhat estranged up there, as she, "a god born a woman stands there wearing full armor, while Cleithenes plies a spindle." [9] This role reversal did not sit well with Euelpides who went off to supervise the construction of the city walls in the sky, then left, probably in a huff, and never returned.

It seems obvious that Athena stood to represent both sexes, displaying the attributes and features of a woman, yet being born of father Zeus without a mate and unwedded herself, [10] also wearing a helmet and holding a lance like an Athenian warrior. [11]

Athena was female in body and skill, but male in mind and courage. She symbolized that neither gender was perfect and complete but also that the two genders, male and female, were unequal. Like the body submits to the soul, the female must submit to the male and be ruled by him. Her image in Classical Athens was the legacy of a long tradition of male chauvinism.

Nevertheless, the model chosen by Athenian men for their beloved city-sate was not a man but a woman who had the qualities they understood to be masculine. Therefore, when they made her the first activist goddess in myth, they raised the possibility of finding activist women in real life.

As the goddess of love, Aphrodite had no favorites between men and women when she stood between them dispatching to both her son Eros as matchmaker in their erotic love. Her role was ambivalent not only by gender but also by outcome, as it provided both the pleasures of sexual love and the miseries of its enslavement.

The men of Ancient Greece created not only gods to their resemblance but also goddesses for their pleasure and according to their world's views. So their image was

---

[9] Aristophanes, *Birds*, 826-831: Loeb 179, 132.
[10] Aeschylus, *Eumenides*, 664-666: Loeb 146, 334-336 and Euripides, *Ion*, 452-455: Loeb 10, 372-374.
[11] See Athena *Promachos* (Defender) was painted in Athens on a panathenaic prize amphora in terracotta and attributed to the Marsyas Painter, 340-339 BCE: The J. Paul Getty Museum at Malibu, CA, 79.AE.147. See above, p. 8.

feminine and their functions in accord with men's values, for example, of justice (*dikê*), victory (*nikê*), peace (*eirênê*). [12]

A group of mythical women also bridged the gap between men and women. They were the Amazons, women by biology but, as they excelled in courage, behaving like "peers of men". [13] Their name came from *a-mazos* (without breast) because their right breast was removed at birth so they could later in life use weapons more freely. They were warrior women who did not marry before they had "killed an enemy in battle" and many never succeeded doing it. Those who were married

> Followed their ancient usage; they ride a-hunting with their men or without them; they go to war, and wear the same dress as the men. [14]

The unmarried Amazons were fierce warriors and promiscuous females. They were beautiful and wild, outside the boundaries of civilization, as the Greeks understood them, not only geographically in some northeastern barbarian region called Scythia, but socially and morally as they broke the norms of a civilized life style. Theirs was a cross between the life style represented by goddesses, namely the unwed and nature-wild Artemis and the erotic and sex-wild Aphrodite. But unlike Demeter who also stood between Artemis and Aphrodite, yet was a civilized wedded mother, the Amazons were barbarian and promiscuous beauties living the wild dreams of free sex in a female-dominated society.

According to legend, when king Theseus of Athens abducted the Amazon princess Antiope, he provoked the Amazon women to invade Attica and besiege Athens. Antiope was then compelled to fight on his side against her own kind who were repelled and defeated. [15]

In the context of the Athenian Classical Age, after the real victory over the Persians in 480 BCE, this mythical victory was significant as a symbol: it meant that King Theseus' victory inaugurated a style of society in which men

[12] Aristophanes, *Peace*, 520 ff.: Loeb 488, 494.
[13] Homer, *Iliad*, 3, 189 & 6, 186: Loeb 170, 142 & 288.
[14] Herodotus, *Histories*, 4, 116-119: Loeb 118, 316.
[15] See Lysias, *Funeral Oration*, 2, 4-6: Loeb 244, 32-35.

dominated women and women contributed generously to family life.

These female models were chosen by men as dominant among the deities and the mythological figures of Athens. Men were involved in civic affairs where the virgin Athena, like a male leader, inspired them to be dedicated and loyal to their city. Men were also warriors and the Amazons, although their mythical enemies, inspired them to be brave and beautiful in combat. Women had a different mission, in the background behind men, as providers of citizens for the city and of soldiers for her defense.

Politics

The fact is well established that the Athenian woman had no role in the government and the courts of her city-state. She was a free member of the society of Athenians but exercised this freedom only under the rule of her guardian, be he father or husband. As a wife, she was given some responsibilities in raising the children and managing the household and was accountable to her husband. In the public government of the city she had no role or responsibilities, in spite of Plato's late theorizing about some degree of involvement. In the society of Athens, her freedom meant a status and some privileges allowed by her husband, not a role adjacent to his.

Nevertheless, certain women with a stronger or more radical character exerted some influence on the formation or implementation of policies devised by their husbands. The historian Herodotus reported an incident of women's intervention that, if true, must have been very rare. In 481/80 BCE, Greece was threatened by a supreme assault from the Persians' overwhelming forces. Lycidas, a member of the Athenian Council, advocated the policy of submitting to the Persians. His proposal caused such an outrage that the Council members supported by a few henchmen stoned him to death. The Athenian women who heard about it "went of their own motion to the house of Lycidas, and stoned to death his wife and his children." [16]

This story is suspicious because it is so much out of character. Written only forty years after the incident,

---

[16] *Histories*, 9, 5: Loeb 120, 162.

Herodotus may have heard this story as a sanitized hearsay, the true story being that the men did it all but placed the opprobrium for killing women and children on their women rather than suffer the pollution themselves. Also, the telling of this story at the time the Athenians were on the brink of a war with Sparta may be more significant than the story itself. It suggested how far women could go in times of crisis.

The following stories of four activist women, all unmarried, will illustrate how far they were willing to go for the defense of a value such as the love of family and the loyalty to city.

Antigone

At about the time Herodotus was publishing his *Histories*, Sophocles was producing his masterpiece of Tragedy, the play *Antigone* of 443/441 BCE, in which he used the story of Antigone to illustrate the unusual power of a woman with the mind of a man. Antigone's sister, Ismene, acted more like a traditional woman, subservient in every way to a man, Creon, her king and, as her uncle, her guardian (*kurios*). But Antigone, more like a man, understood better the values not only of kinship in the family but also of freedom in the Athenian society. She held that her two brothers, Polynices as well as Eteocles, were free citizens with civic rights of burial. [17] But King Creon issued a decree against Polynices' right of burial because he attacked his city. Antigone declared her intention to resist the king's order and bury her brother. Creon countered: "While I live a woman shall not rule." [18]

The male writers of Ancient Greece attributed some depreciation of mental capacity to the female, in comparison with the male, for the physical strength that they perceived as diminished in the female. By strength, they meant the ability to accomplish physical tasks equal to males' running, lifting and fighting. But they shortchanged the meaning of strength by not including in it the ability to endure under mental pressure or physical pain.

---

[17] Sophocles, *Antigone*, 450 ff.: Loeb 21, 44.
[18] *Ibid.*, 525: Loeb 21, 50.

Strength is like a tree with two major branches: one being might and the other fortitude. In order to excel at physical tasks, one like Heracles or Achilles had to be mighty, but, in order to endure, one like Antigone had to have fortitude. She was unable to compete with a strong man who could dig a grave. On the other hand, she had the mental fortitude to resist a king's decree and perform her brother Polynices' symbolic burial when she heaped up a tomb for him. [19] She displayed extraordinary determination and endurance that made her equal to men in heroism. She even surpassed them, not in any physical exploit, but in relentless fortitude.

The conflict between the edict of a king and the Greek tradition, sanctioned by the gods, about all Greek citizens and their families having a human right to a proper burial, created a crisis that forced Antigone to step out of character as a woman and take a man's stand in the public affairs of the state. She proved that women, on occasions, had the insight and the fortitude to adopt a role in the political arena, even if it implied breaking the anonymity in which men wanted them confined and confronting men as equal to them. Antigone may have demonstrated on stage actions other unknown women may have attempted to do in real life. The fact was that, far from offending the audience, the play was an enormous success that resulted in the honorary selection of Sophocles as one of the ten generals in the expedition against the Samians in 440 BCE. [20] Antigone stood up for values respected in Ancient Athens and until today in favor of women's rights, for example to argue for their freedom in the political debates about contraception.

After the Peloponnesian War began in 431 BCE, the dramatists testified to the tensions in the Athenian society between the peacemakers and the warmongers. If the stage cannot be too far from real life, lest the audience be totally frustrated, some women probably attempted to acquire at this time some influence over the political decisions concerning war and peace.

Antigone's sacrifice of her life was an act of protest against a decree made according to the common belief in

[19] Sophocles, *Antigone*, 80-81: Loeb 21, 10.
[20] Thucydides, *Peloponnesian War*, 1, 115, 2-5: Loeb 108, 190.

the absolute power of a king. She refused to submit and consent, like her sister did, and died for her cause, like Macaria, by her own hand. She was a virgin not yet claimed by a husband when she stood up and defied king Creon's decree prohibiting the rites of burial for her brother Polynices.

The two brothers, Polynices and Eteocles, killed each other in single combat for the right of succession to king Oedipus on the throne of Thebes. The recognized successor, King Creon, their uncle, decreed that Eteocles would be given a burial but Polynices would be left unburied and to be devoured by vultures and dogs because he attacked his native city. Then, their sister Antigone declared her intention:

> Yea, and I declare unto your Cadmean rulers – If none other be willing to take part with me in burying him, I will bury him, and I will risk the peril of burying mine own brother; nor do I feel shame thus to be an unsubmisssive rebel to the State. Strange power – the bond of common blood whence we are sprung from wretched mother [Jocasta] and unhappy sire [Oedipus]. ... His flesh no gaunt-bellied wolves shall rend – let no one 'decree' me that! Woman that I am I will contrive for him a burying and a grave, bearing the earth in the fold of my linen raiment. With my own hands I will cover him. Let no man 'decree' (*doxa*) it otherwise. Courage! I shall find the means to act. [21]

Such a defiance of the law for the sake of family loyalty (*philia*) would have been brave and poignant even from a man, but it was much more so from a woman who did not have any rights of citizenship. Her defiance stood against not only the decree of Creon but also against the traditional rule of female subservience to him as her guardian and her king, yet it defined the role and responsibility of women in the funerary practices of Athens. In Creon's estimation, the prescribed law of a king superseded the traditional rule of burial. In the estimation

---

[21] Aeschylus, *Seven Against Thebes*, 1032-1047: Loeb 145, 412-415.

of a woman, the traditional rule of burial superseded not only the king's prescribed law but also the traditional rule of subservience of women to men. The first was divine, the other two were human:

The rule of female subservience, she implied, was a tradition and a law (*nomos*) also, but one imposed by men without the sanction of the gods. This argument was revolutionary in democratic Athens as much as it was in autocratic Thebes. But her inner persuasion was so firm that she was willing to die for it. [22] She will, therefore, remain subservient to men as long as their command does not oppose the laws of nature sanctioned by the gods.

The implications of her stand were far-reaching. As her guardian (*kurios*), Creon, had no right to command her to submit to the unnatural act of refusing a proper burial to a brother who was not a deviant criminal but a son who was defending his right of succession. In civil wars, both sides can claim to be right. As king, Creon believed that the gods had sanctioned his prohibition. He was warranted to believe that his power (*kratos*) as a whole was of divine origin, but not that each of his decrees received divine approval. Therefore, the conflict of decree (*doxa*) versus Justice (*dikê*) in the family and the state favored Antigone because the gods sanctioned her decision for the sake of justice.

Sophocles recognized tradition as a norm of conduct (*nomos*), equal and sometimes superseding the law by decree, also called *nomos*, enacted by men. He made this point through a woman's voice.

After Antigone was caught performing the rites of burial for her brother, Polynices, she argued that the unwritten laws of God superseded all laws of men:

> Yes, for it was not Zeus who made this proclamation, nor was it Justice who lives with the gods below that established such laws among men, nor did I think your proclamations strong enough to have power to overrule, mortal as they were, the unwritten and unfailing ordinances of the gods. For these have life, not simply today and yesterday, but forever and no one knows how long ago they were revealed. [23]

---

[22] Sophocles, *Antigone*, 459: Loeb 21, 44.
[23] *Ibid.*, 450-457; Loeb 21, 44.

Antigone's courage was undeniable because it was unheard of for a woman to pursue such a task against a man's will, outside the home, in the public arena of politics reserved to men. Like a woman, however, she was fighting for the value of kinship in the family, expressed in the right to a ritualistic burial for all family members. She was a true woman with a man's will.

Antigone executed her vow to bury her brother Polynices. When she did it, the guards caught her and then deputized one of their own to bring her to king Creon and the elders of Thebes. He shouted the charge:

> She herself was burying the man! ... Yes, I saw her burying the corpse ... We saw the girl, she cried out bitterly ... when she saw the corpse laid bare ... At once she brought in her hands thirsty dust, and from the well-wrought brazen urn that she was carrying she poured over the corpse a threefold libation. [24]

Too weak and without the tools to dig a hole, Antigone simply let the body lay down on the ground and sprinkled a thin layer of dust to cover it and protect it from the ravenous animals. She argued against Creon that the unwritten laws of God superseded all laws of men. In the face of her guardian and king, who had publicly forbidden the burial, she defended her obligation to perform the rites for one who was not only her brother but a citizen of Thebes.

Thus, Antigone not only fulfilled the task of burying her brother, but also assumed the role of defending the right of all citizens to receive a proper burial. Her actions and words were making a political statement, besides being an expression of love for a brother and of respect for his humanity. His status as a human being, a citizen, a prince and a contender for the throne of Thebes seemed to have had less to do with her motivation than the fact that he was her brother. She would have done the same, had he been a commoner and she a peasant girl. He was a brother and, as she awkwardly explained, he could not be replaced. [25]

---

[24] Sophocles, *Antigone* 403-431: Loeb 21, 38-43.
[25] *Ibid.*, 904 ff.: Loeb 21, 86-89.

Also, although her brave action was not motivated as a challenge to the authority of King Creon, it became his greatest challenge, one he handled to his own detriment when he lost not only Antigone but also his own son Haemon with her. She linked the issue of her brother's burial to civilization devised by men and sanctioned by the gods. A decent burial of the dead was indeed a part of civilization like the use of language, the cultivation of the land, the mastery of the sea and the social organization of the community.

The guard's charge against Antigone was proven by her own admission: "I say that I did it and I do not deny it." [26] Her sister Ismene was now ready to take a stand before Creon and die with her – "How can I live alone without her?" she cried. [27] Without the support of her immediate family and of a husband and children of her own, what was left in life for her but the miseries of servitude, as it would be for most women of Ancient Greece? Fear was now her motive and deception her means for wanting to join her sister.

Creon's sentence for Antigone's transgression was to "die at once close at hand, in the sight of her bridegroom" [28] Haemon, Creon's son who defended her and will die with her in a rocky cavern. She will die "unwept, friendless, unwedded," [29] not of stoning as she first expected but of starvation in a cave.

In the meanwhile, the seer Tiresias intervened and Creon commuted Antigone's sentence. He even rushed to rescue her from death. Alas, he was too late. When he arrived with his attendants, he saw her "hanging by the neck" and his son "lying near, his arms around her waist, lamenting for the ruin of his bride in the world below." [30] Then, in defiance of his father confronting him, Haemon killed himself with the sword. After hearing of these calamities, Eurydice, wife of Creon and mother of Haemon, committed suicide: she "pierced by the sharp sword." [31]

Antigone accepted to be sacrificed for a cause she could not have defended with impunity in real life as she did

---

[26] Sophocles, *Antigone*, 443: Loeb 21, 42.
[27] *Ibid.*, 566: Loeb 21, 56.
[28] *Ibid.*, 760-761: Loeb 21, 74.
[29] *Ibid.*, 876: Loeb 21, 84.
[30] *Ibid.*, 1221-1223: Loeb 21, 114.
[31] *Ibid.*, 1301: Loeb 21, 122.

on the Sophoclean stage. Her belief that every citizen
deserved a decent burial was traditional but the
circumstances in which she defended it were exceptional,
especially for a woman. By opposing the will of her ruler
Creon she showed the audacity, determination and self-
confidence expected of a man of great character (*anêr*), a
leader and a hero.

Lysistrata

Women placed the blame on men for the disastrous
conduct of the war between Athens and Sparta. Their
mouthpiece and exploiter, Aristophanes, made this
indictment in a comedy of 411 BCE, the most disastrous
year of the war. His play *Lysistrata* was not only a plea for
peace but also a brilliant and funny illustration of women's
reaction to public events that affected their lives profoundly.
We can hear them discussing privately, in the neighborhood
and at the water fountain, the disastrous strategy of foreign
affairs. They needed peace at all cost. Not only their own
lives but those of their husbands and children depended on
it. Now their leader, Lysistrata, had a plan and all the self-
confidence to make it work:

> It's true I'm a woman, but still I've got a mind: I'm
> pretty intelligent in my own right, and because I've
> listened many a time to the conversation of my father
> and other elders, I'm pretty well educated too. [32]

Lysistrata's stratagem conveyed to the Athenian
women of her party was ingenious, yet not totally original:
while the husbands were still asleep, she gathered the wives
at dawn near the Gate of the Acropolis (*Propulaion*) and
persuaded them to withhold all sex with their husbands
until they make peace. Their prayer to Athena reflected their
purpose: "Rescue from war and madness Greece and their
fellow countrymen." [33] The stakes were very high, as
Lysistrata pointed out: "The salvation of all Greece lies in
the women's hands!" [34]

---

[32] Aristophanes, *Lysistrata*, 1124-1127: Loeb 179, 418.
[33] *Ibid.*, 342-343: Loeb 179, 312.
[34] *Ibid.*, 29-30: Loeb 179, 270.

Persuaded that peace is the reward, the women accepted to follow Lysistrata, withholding sex from their husbands and taking over the Acropolis in order to control the treasury. The plan was hilarious because it was far-fetched. The wives' chances to win were indeed greater on the domestic front than on the Acropolis. Nevertheless, they vigorously repelled an attack and resisted the urge to satisfy their husbands.

The leader of the chorus of women made the indictment clear:

> Even if I was born a woman, don't hold it against me if I manage to suggest something better than what we've got now. I have a stake in our community: my contribution is men. You miserable geezers have no stake, since you've squandered your inheritance, won in the Persian Wars, and now pay no taxes in return. On the contrary, we're all headed for bankruptcy on account of you! [35]

War had always been the affair of men, although women had on occasions lent them a helping hand, guarding the wall [36] or, in the early fifth century, organizing the defense, like Telesilla of Argos did against the Spartan invaders. [37] Now women were taking command: "war shall be the business of women-folk!" [38] They will stop the war and run the affairs of the State the way they run their own household. How is it done? Lysistrata did not say in any descriptive words except by unsnarling the war with ambassadorial negotiations compared to a great ball of yarn all tangled up and pulled "now this way, now that way." [39]

After much fighting and prodding, the men finally surrendered to their wives. Their leader confessed:

> The ancient adage is right on the mark and no mistake: "Can't live with the pests or without the pests either." [40]

---

[35] *Lysistrata*, 649-655: Loeb 179, 356-359.
[36] Homer, *Iliad*, 18, 514: Loeb 171, 324.
[37] Plutarch, *Moralia*, 245C-F: Loeb 245, 488.
[38] Aristophanes, *Lysistrata*, 538: Loeb 179, 340.
[39] *Ibid.*, 567-570: Loeb 179, 346.
[40] *Ibid.*, 1038-1039: Loeb 179, 410.

At the end, both sides, the activist women and the warmongering men, agreed to sign a treaty of peace and respond to Lysistrata's invitation to a feast. The Spartan men reclaimed their wives and the Athenian men theirs, pledging to "be sure never again to make the same mistakes." Then, all together, they had "a dance for the gods." [41]

The husbands and wives of *Lysistrata* were burning with lust only for each other. They broke no rule of propriety or decency. In some fashion, the men showed a greater measure of morality because they avoided the options provided to them either from female prostitutes or boy friends. Wives did not have these options and were only eager to go back home to their husbands.

The story was a farce, the picture a caricature, but the message of peace was for ever the most important contribution of this play which, unfortunately at the time of its production in the thick of the Peloponnesian War, had little impact on the Athenian conduct of foreign affairs. Peace came to Athens in 404 only by way of surrender to Sparta, accompanied by the plundering of the city and the dire sufferings and despair of the citizens who survived.

Praxagora

In another play, *Assemblywomen* of about 392 BCE, when Athens was trying to rebuild her prestige and restore her prosperity after the Peloponnesian War, Aristophanes made again the claim for women's involvement in public affairs. Knowing how pointed his verbal attacks had been during the war on real warmongering politicians like Cleon and Hyperbolus, we have a sense of some realism in the following storyline.

The action began in the pre-dawn. Praxagora, whose name meant "Woman Effective in Public", got up quietly, lighted a lamp to chase the darkness and exited her house. While waiting for other women to arrive and join her, she addressed the lamp as if it were a secret deity, privy to her most intimate actions. Then, one by one, the women gathered around her according to a plan discussed and

---

[41] *Lysistrata*, 1273-1278: Loeb 179, 436.

"agreed on at the Scira", the "Mothers' March". [42] Such a gathering of women was unacceptable, unless the reason was of major importance. In 415 BCE, during the war, Euripides had lent these words to Andromache in his play *The Trojan Women*:

> Whether or not there is anything blameworthy in a woman's conduct, the very fact that she goes out of the house draws criticism. [43]

So these women must have had good reasons to meet Praxagora clandestinely outside her house, and all, more than eleven of them, to be dressed in their husbands' tunics, mantles and Laconian shoes, holding walking sticks, wearing faked beards and showing hair in their armpits and a suntan over their skins. They wanted to be taken as men when, according to plan, they will walk to the Pnyx and appear at the Assembly (*Ekklêsia*). There they will adapt their language and mannerism to those of men, as they had diligently practiced. [44] These frustrated women intended to "take over the government and do something good for the city. As it is, our city is oarless and becalmed." [45]

Like *Lysistrata*, this play *Assemblywomen* had little impact on the public policies set up by men. Athens continued her involvement in the so-called Corinthian War that looked like a new Peloponnesian War. Now Athens was on the side of Corinth, Argos and the Boeotian League against Sparta. The Athenian general Iphicrates won an important battle at the seaport of Lechaeum on the Corinthian Gulf in 390. The war would have continued if the Persians had not imposed the King's Peace on those pugnacious cities in 387/386 BCE.

Public demonstrations of the kind Lysistrata and Praxagora organized in Athens were unheard of except on stage. The women selected a battlefield and declared war on men, one with water poured on them when they attempted to climb the Acropolis, the other with words when they assembled at the Pnyx.

---

[42] Aristophanes, *Assemblywomen*, 59: Loeb 180, 252.

[43] *The Trojan Women*, 647-649: Loeb 10, 80.

[44] Aristophanes, *Assemblywomen*, 116-119: Loeb 180, 258.

[45] *Ibid.*, 107-109: Loeb 180, 258.

Like the myths of ancient lore, these plays were fantasies with a message. In Aristophanes' plays, the primary message was that women can do a better job of government than men. The secondary message was perhaps that they will take over the job if men continue to behave irresponsibly. These plays were a subtle and funny way of putting the men on notice by none other than another man, Aristophanes.

Agave

In Euripides' Tragedy *Bacchae* of 405 BCE, the message was shrouded in violence beyond nature and conventions, sometimes without understanding. The women votaries of god Dionysus won their battle against king Pentheus, not only when he divested himself of his own male identity and dressed like a woman, but especially when he was captured, dismembered and devoured by these mad maenads. The message of a female revolt against the male domination was hidden under the scenes of carnage. The women tore down on stage the walls that protected the civility of the man-dominated Thebes. A mother destroying the fruit of her own womb was the symbol of the new order that women, guided by Dionysus, were bent on creating. Agave, mother of Pentheus, boasted to her father, Cadmus:

> Father, you have the right to boast loudly that you begot the world's bravest daughters: I said all of them, but especially me, since I left my loom and shuttle and taken on greater things, hunting beasts with bare hands. I grasp, as you see, a prize of victory here so that it can be nailed up on your house's walls. [46]

Euripides' story can be interpreted as a stage of war introducing a new order of female domination. God Dionysus, like the commander of the Maenads, declared his plan in the opening prologue:

> But if the city of Thebes gets angry and tries to bring the bacchants from the mountain by force of arms, I

---

[46] Euripides, *Bacchae*, 1233-1240: Loeb 495, 134.

will meet them in battle at the head of an army of maenads. [47]

The scenes were a gruesome fantasy with a message from women and a savage cry for freedom and equality. The message was lost on the Athenian audiences because of the madness of its delivery. Agave was restored to sanity at the end and led into exile with no place she could call her home. She had lost it all as her punishment by men. The audiences understood the futility of women's demonstrations and enjoyed them, either in comedy or tragedy, as entertainment without any consequence. In reality, however, the Athenian men were not ready to listen and look into their life style, much less to change it. Women continued to live with their inner tensions, leaving their personal conflicts completely unresolved. All in all, most women never had any conflicts and those who did found their best lot in quiet resignation.

Sacrificial Deaths

The sacrificial deaths of Iphigenia, Macaria and Polyxena may be deemed acts of activism for they were sought or accepted freely for a public cause in the context of belief in the gods. Their tragic deaths demonstrated also how generous and courageous these young girls were at their live's final moment.

Iphigenia

In a brilliant tragedy, Euripides told the story of Iphigenia, Agamemnon's daughter, who was sacrificed to goddess Artemis for the good of her country. Her father was commander-in-chief of the Achaean troops held at Aulis, unable to sail because of unfavorable winds. The seer Calchas announced that Iphigenia's life was the ransom demanded by the goddess for the gift of sailing to Troy.
Iphigenia's father used the deception of her marriage to the hero Achilles to bring her and the family from Argos to Aulis. For a while, Iphigenia prepared for her wedding. Only later, did she understand that her preparation was for

---

[47] *Bacchae*, 50-52: Loeb 495, 16.

the sacrifice of her life. The two preparations followed their
respective rituals that included several similarities. For this
reason, some scholars have associated very closely the
rituals of sacrifice and wedding. [48] The similarities between
rituals are inevitable but, in Iphigenia's case, one is rejected
in favor of the other. The wedding invitation and
preparation were only a deception that served
Agamemnon's purpose for a while but was later revealed.
Confronted with her sacrifice, Iphigenia did not think of it as
a wedding. She did not fantasize a marriage to Achilles in
Aulis or Hades. If she happened to think about marriage, it
was only about the violation of its sanctity by the elopement
of her aunt Helen with Paris of Troy. This, after all, was the
cause of her ultimate sacrifice. Her dominant thought was
about her own sacrifice, how divine it was in its inspiration
and patriotic in its outcome. Indeed, a sacrifice made to the
virgin goddess Artemis fell short of being a wedding under
the aegis of Aphrodite, the goddess of love.

Whether the expedition to Troy was justified by the
motive of retrieving Helen is irrelevant to Euripides's tragedy
and Iphigenia's sacrifice. Her action can be explained only
by the divine condition set by Artemis for the departure of
the Achaean fleet from Aulis. However, if Artemis' demand
was the condition that prompted Iphigenia's ultimate
sacrifice, its purpose was not to satisfy her demand blindly.
Without the good of Hellas as its patriotic purpose, her
sacrifice would have been meaningless and, consequently,
not accepted, especially by her father.

At first, Iphigenia begged for her life, but when she
came to understand that her fate was to die for her country
she realized that

> Truly it is not right that I should be too in love with
> my life. ... [Heroes will] fight bravely against the
> enemy and die on behalf of Hellas: shall my single
> life stand in the way of all this? What just plea can we
> make to counter this argument? [49]

Then the deep feeling of inferiority appeared again,
as it did at every turn of a woman's life:

---

[48] For example, H.P. Foley, *Ritual Irony*, 65-105.
[49] Euripides, *Iphigenia at Aulis*, 1385-1391: Loeb 495, 316.

And there's another thing to be said. This man
should not do battle with all the Greeks and be killed
for a woman's sake. Better to save the life of a single
man than ten thousand women! [50]

Iphigenia's mother, Clytemnestra, was crushed with
grief and anger when her daughter saw no choice but to
surrender to her fate: "I shall give myself to Greece" -- "Allow
me to save Hellas if I can." [51] Clytemnestra was the only
witness who never accepted her daughter's sacrifice
because her heart harbored such anger against her husband
that no other feeling ever dislodged it. She carried this
anger to paroxysm more than ten years later, when she
exacted from him as reparation the loss of his own life in a
brutal murder.

In the end, Achilles praised Iphigenia's "noble heart".
[52] She proceeded to the temple where the sacrifice must be
performed and turned herself in to her father:

Father, I have come to you. I willingly grant that your
men may bring me to the goddess' altar and sacrifice
me, if it is what the oracle requires. [53]

The story of Iphigenia's sacrifice fascinated the minds
of young girls. She was a virgin, a loving daughter and an
aspiring wife. She made the ultimate sacrifice for a cause
higher than motherhood. She was the perfect model of
patriotism for girls in their nubile years, prior to their
wedding. By her demand, goddess Artemis had caused her
to accept immolation. Thus, she became also the model of
the devotees of Artemis, especially at Brauron, east of
Athens, where the goddess had her major shrine.

Iphigenia' sacrifice had been sanctioned in advance
by the gods. Therefore, it was acceptable by Greek
standards because it met both requirements of contributing
to the benefit of Hellas and being also approved by the
gods. In times past, king Erechtheus used an Athenian
victory against Eumolpus, the religious leader of Eleusis, to
justify the slaying of all his daughters, except Creusa, Ion's

---

[50] Euripides, *Iphigenia at Aulis*, 1392-1394: Loeb 495, 316-319.
[51] *Ibid.*, 1397 & 1420: Loeb 495, 318-321.
[52] *Ibid.*, 1421: Loeb 495, 320.
[53] *Ibid.*, 1552-1556: Loeb 495, 334-337.

mother. He was punished for it when "the blow of the sea-god's [Poseidon's] trident killed him, [54] because his sacrificial action had not been sanctioned in advance by the gods.

Furthermore, to be chosen for such a noble sacrifice was not the prerogative of maidens, although it was more frequently demanded of them than of young men. Menoeceus was one who was chosen to be sacrificed for the sake of Thebes threatened by the dispute between Oedypus' two sons, Eteocles and Polynices, about the dynastic succession. The prophet Tiresias came to their uncle Creon who was holding the power temporarily and declared to him the will of Ares, the god of war: "You must slaughter your son Menoeceus here, for the country's sake." [55] Unlike Agamemnon, Creon refused to accede to the divine will: "Never shall I go so far in wretchedness as to offer my child to the city for slaughter!" [56]

In this case, Creon was right. His son chose to sacrifice himself, when he "plunged the dark sword into his throat, achieving survival for this land", [57] but he did not prevent the two brothers from killing each other, thus failing to break the curse upon Oedipus' family, because the god's sanction was, in this case, misunderstood by the young Menoeceus. The god's will was for a man to sacrifice himself in combat, not in immolation.

Macaria

A second instance of a noble sacrifice by a maiden involved the children of Heracles, known as Heracleidae. After the hero's death, his archenemy Eurystheus of Argos was threatening their lives when they were hiding at the altar of Zeus at Marathon. The danger grew so grave that it required, beyond supplications, some great and courageous offering to the gods. Only the sacrifice of a maiden would ensure the safety of the entire city, like Iphigenia's sacrifice at Aulis had achieved the good of Hellas. However, unlike Iphigenia who was drafted, Heracles' only daughter, Macaria ("The Blessed Girl"), addressing her father's kinsman Iolaus,

---

[54] Euripides, *Ion*, 282: Loeb 10, 350.
[55] Id., *Phoenician Women*, 913-914: Loeb 11, 310.
[56] *Ibid.*, 963-964: Loeb 11, 316.
[57] *Ibid.*, 1092-1093: Loeb 11, 328.

volunteered for this supreme sacrifice: "I am ready, old man, of my own accord and unbidden, to appear for sacrifice and be killed." [58]

Macaria argued that she could as easily be killed anyway if Marathon was attacked and, if she fled into exile, every people would reject her as a shameful coward. She therefore concluded: "For, mark it well, by not clinging to my life I have made a most splendid discovery, how to die with glory." [59]

Her guardian, Iolaus, felt proud of her for such a noble and brave offer, worthy of her valiant father, Heracles. Her courage, marred with grief, remained unshaken when she bade farewell to her family and committed herself to a fateful suicide. Her sacrifice ensured, as she believed, the victory of her father's family over king Eurystheus' Argive troops.

Polyxena

A third instance of sacrifice by a maiden displayed the same courage but from a Trojan girl, Polyxena, daughter of king Priam and queen Hecuba. In Euripides' play, an old man, the Greek Talthybius, described in detail the sacrifice of this brave virgin. When the Achaean troops were gathered all around, Achilles' son, Neoptolemus, led Polyxena by the hand to the top of a mound. Then he made an offering to his dead sire, Achilles, and, after silence had spread over the troops, he uttered a prayer:

> Son of Peleus, my father, receive these libations, ...
> Come and drink the blood of a maiden, dark and undiluted, which is the army's gift and mine! Be propitious to us; grant us your leave to cast off the mooring cables from our sterns, and allow us all, journeying home in peace, to reach our native land! [60]

Neoptolemus took his golden sword from the scabbard, while young warriors came to hold this beautiful

---

[58] Euripides, *Children of Heracles*, 501-502: Loeb 484, 56.

[59] *Ibid.*, 533-534: Loeb 484, 58; see Id., *Fr.*, Unidentified Play, 854: Loeb 506, 480.

[60] Euripides, *Hecuba*, 534-541: Loeb 484, 446.

and valiant girl, but with a gesture she stopped them and declared:

> I die of my own accord! Let no one touch my person, for I shall offer you my neck bravely! In the gods' name, leave me free when you kill me, so that I may die a free woman! [61]

Then the proud princess pulled her robe down to her waist "and showed her breasts, lovely as a goddess' statue." [62] After she kneeled, Neoptolemus who felt pity for her struck her neck with the sword. Polyxena fell and died with grace and modesty, and as freely as Iphigenia and Macaria. Iphigenia, however, was spared at the end, thanks to Achilles' intervention, when goddess Artemis substituted a hind in her stead on the altar of sacrifice. [63] Each one was, as Hecuba said, "bride that is no bride, virgin that is virgin no more", [64] like a bride whose wedding could take place only in Hades.

Erechtheus' Daughter

This story is not as well known as the preceding ones. Nevertheless, what is known mostly through another Euripidean play kept only in fragments is clear about the sacrifice of a maiden to save the city, as required by a divine oracle.

Erechtheus was a leader of Athens in the early times of her rise as a city. Another leader, Eumolpus, who probably came from Thrace, in northeast Greece and settled in Eleusis, a short distance north of Athens, acquired the desire of conquering Athens by force of arms. Erechtheus and probably the citizens under him became frantic with fear and apprehension. So, as leader, he did what all good leaders in Ancient Greece would do: he consulted with the oracle at Delphi.

The oracle added to Erechtheus' anxiety, declaring that, If he wanted to defeat his enemy and save his city, he had to sacrifice one of his three daughters. When he came

---

[61] Euripides, *Hecuba*, 548-551: Loeb 484, 448.
[62] *Ibid.*, 560: Loeb 484, 448.
[63] Id., *Iphigenia at Aulis*, 1421-1432: Loeb 495, 320.
[64] Id., *Hecuba*, 611-612: Loeb 484, 452.

home and shared the news with his wife, Praxithea, he
heard from her only words of encouragement:

> I for my part shall offer my daughter to be killed. My
> reasons are many, and the first of them is that I could
> get no other city better than this. ... Next, we bear
> our children for this reason, to protect the gods'
> altars and our homeland. The city as a whole has a
> single name, but many inhabit it; why should I
> destroy them when I can give one child to die for all?
> ... This girl – not mine (in fact) except in birth – I shall
> offer for sacrifice to defend our land. [65]

Then, Praxithea concluded with words that sounded
more like a command than an advice:

> Citizens, use the offspring of my womb, be saved, be
> victorious! At the cost of just one life I surely shall
> not fail to save our city. My homeland, would that all
> your inhabitants loved you as I do; then we could
> dwell in you easily, and you would suffer no harm. I
> love my children, but I love my homeland more. [66]

The rest of the story was a mixture of joy and pain
for the generous mother, Praxithea: the joy of victory over
the enemy and freedom of the Athenians, and the pain of
losing her husband in the battle [67] and her three daughters,
since the other two committed suicide in solidarity with
their sister who was sacrificed to the gods for the sake of
the city, without being ever consulted in the matter.

The three daughters were buried "in (the same) earth
tomb, in recognition of their nobility" and became renowned
throughout Greece as the Hyacinthid goddesses with a ritual
and a sanctuary. [68]

---

[65] Euripides, *Fr., Erechtheus*, 360, 4-39: Loeb 504, 374-379.
[66] *Ibid.*, 360, 50-55 & 360a: Loeb 504, 378-381.
[67] *Ibid.*, 369, 36-44: Loeb 504, 392.
[68] *Ibid.*, 370, 73-89: Loeb 504, 396.

CHAPTER ELEVEN

ALIENS AND SLAVES

Attica belonged to the Athenian citizens. In 451 BCE, Pericles persuaded the Assembly to adopt a decree requiring a citizen to be the legitimate son of two Athenian parents and not only of an Athenian father as traditionally accepted. By so doing he reduced by half, from about 60,000 to 30,000, the pool of Athenian citizens and adroitly eliminated his rival Cimon the Younger whose father was the famous Greek general Miltiades and his mother the Thracian princess Hegesipyle, a non-Athenian.

Following Athens' capitulation to Sparta in 404 and the brief rule of the Thirty Tyrants, the democratic archon Euklides reinstated the neglected law of dual parentage. The law even authorized Athenian men to marry more than one Athenian woman. Socrates may have used this extension of the law. Later in the fourth century, when the Athenian men were in short supply, it even became illegal for an Athenian man to marry a non-Athenian woman.

As a result of these laws, enacted not as much for the protection of women as for the restoration of the Athenian citizenry, a roster was kept of Athenian citizens and their parentage was scrutinize carefully before they took any public office.

A decree of 346 BCE that mandated a review of the deme lists resulted in a court case. According to Demosthenes, Eubulides charged that a certain Euxitheus ought to be disfranchised because of his lack of full Athenian parentage. [1] The outcome of his exclusion was serious: he was losing not only his citizenship with all the rights, such as the right to bury his alien mother according to religious rituals, but also the ownership of his land. The loss of ownership must have been a punishment because,

---

[1] *Against Eubulides*, 57, 2 ff.: Loeb 351, 232 ff.

although a non-citizen, he was an alien resident with the legal right to own land.

Two categories of non-citizens, men and women, resided in Attica for all or part of their lives: the first category was the free aliens who could be permanent or temporary residents as they chose and have certain rights under the law – a man was called metic (*metoikos*) and a woman, according to her occupation, either companion (*hetaira*), concubine (*pallakê*) or prostitute (*pornê*) -- and the second category was the slaves who enjoyed no freedom and therefore were at the mercy of their masters for everything in their lives.

Free Aliens

The free alien tourists or residents came either from other regions of Greece – the Peloponnesus or Mainland Greece -- or from the colonies -- especially Asia Minor (present-day Turkey), the Aegean islands, Sicily or Southern Italy. They came for a few days any time in the year, in a normal flow during the good season from spring to fall and in large numbers at festival times, especially the *Anthesteria* honoring god Dionysus in February/March (month of Anthesterion) and the *Panathenaea* for a variety of contests and games every four years in July/August (month of Hecatombaion). All free women were allowed to attend at least part of these festivals.

Our interest is primarily in the free aliens who resided for some time or for a life time in Attica. Standing on three dates for the fifth century BCE, the numbers of the non-citizen, yet free, population in Attica could be estimated as follows: in 451 (decree of dual parentage) 25,000 permanent free aliens, in 431 (beginning of the Peloponnesian War) 30,000 permanent free aliens and in 404 (end of the Peloponnesian War) 13,500 permanent free aliens. During the fourth century BCE, the population of permanent free aliens probably dropped a little to about 10,000 men and women.

The free alien residents were either born in Athens or came from any other regions held by the Greeks or, more rarely, from other so-called barbarian regions, like Scythia or Phrygia. If they were married women, their rights were limited to those given to non-citizens after the law of dual parentage.

A companion (*hetaira*) was not legally married to an Athenian citizen but was living with him as if she was his wife, providing for him all the assistance and attention he expected from a wife. She occupied the highest position among the alien women living in Attica. She was a permanent companion who tried to emulate and often outpace the wife in the performance of all the services required to keep a man happy and prosperous. She fixed meals, weaved clothes and blankets, managed the household, entertained the guests and responded to the sexual desires of her man.

The *hetaira* had to overcome a feeling of inferiority in the competition with the wife and her children by developing some intellectual advantage. Several of them, like Diotima, [2] Thargelia, [3] and especially Aspasia, [4] could entertain men with a witty and erudite conversation.

The brilliant and unscrupulous Aspasia of Miletus compensated well for any feelings of inferiority, if she had them at all, when she became Pericles' *hetaira*, replacing his Athenian wife after he divorced her amicably in 445 BCE. He was then about fifty years of old and she was only half his age. She became admired by many for her charm and intellect, and disliked by others who later went as far as taking her to court for impiety and embezzlement. [5]

Pericles, the leader during the most prosperous years of the fifth century, was first married to an Athenian woman who had already been married and had a son, known as Callias the Rich. Her first husband, Hipponicus, either died or divorced her, placing her perhaps in the position of an heiress obligated to marry a kinsman. She gave Pericles two sons, Xantippus and Paralus, who later died of the plague like their father. When Pericles divorced her, he immediately fell under the spell or was already under the spell of this Aspasia of Miletus who was now living in Athens and became his *hetaira* for the rest of his life. According to Plutarch, Pericles

---

[2] Plato, *Symposium*, 204 ff.: Loeb 166, 182 ff.
[3] Plutarch, *Parallel Lives, Pericles*, 24, 2: Loeb 65, 68.
[4] *Ibid.*, 24, 1-3: Loeb 65, 68.
[5] *Ibid.*, 32, 1-3: Loeb 65, 92.

himself took Aspasia, and loved her exceedingly. Twice a day, as they say, as going out and coming in from the market-place, he would salute her with a loving kiss. [6]

Aspasia gave him a son, Eupolis, who later became a citizen by decree, because he did not meet the requirement of dual Athenian parentage. Plutarch described their relationship further:

And so Aspasia, as some say, was held in high favour by Pericles because of her rare political wisdom. Socrates sometimes came to see her with his disciples, and his intimate friends brought their wives to her to hear her discourse, although she presided over a business that was anything but honest or even reputable, since she kept a house of young courtisans. ... However, the affection Pericles had for Aspasia seems to have been rather to an amatory sort. [7]

It is hard to conceive any society more liberal and morally relaxed than Athens was in the Periclean Age. Aspasia's reputation, even before she arrived in Athens, was probably tarnished by her activities as a madam in Megara. If Pericles knew it, and probably did, he certainly did not mind, because she was known later for providing him and his friends with good times with prostitutes. So, her conduct did not avoid bringing out some detractors, especially a certain Hermippus who accused her of receiving into her house freeborn women for the uses of Pericles. [8] Hermippus took her to court and made impiety his general indictment. Pericles defended her passionately and had the case dismissed. But his image was tarnished by it. Plutarch who reported the incident implied that he encouraged the hostilities with Sparta in order to divert attention from his personal troubles. [9] Nothing new under the sun!

Aspasia's influence was clearly recognized by the historian Plutarch of the late first century CE, who used

---

[6] *Parallel Lives, Pericles,* 24, 5-6: Loeb 65, 70.

[7] *Ibid.,* 24, 3 & 5: Loeb 65, 68-71.

[8] *Ibid.,*32, 1: Loeb 65, 92.

[9] *Ibid.,*33, 6: Loeb 65, 96.

previous accounts as sources of his biographies. He stated that Pericles proposed to the Assembly to declare war against the Samians "to gratify Aspasia," [10] in 439, prior to the Peloponnesian War.

Pericles was a great politician, with extraordinary leadership ability, but he was not as pious as Solon or as wise as Cleisthenes and certainly more lax than both in his morals. Another anecdote reported by Plutarch involved the sculptor Phidias to whom Pericles entrusted the Parthenon project. They were close friends who allegedly took advantage of the beauty of the site to do certain things less than honorable. Some slanderers or malcontents accused Phidias of using this site under his control to procure freeborn women for Pericles' sexual enjoyment. [11] The presence of prostitutes in this area of intense foot traffic by men of all types is a fair assumption. That the gossips included these two men who were the most prominent citizens of Athens is a fair assumption also. Plutarch's moralizing bend may have influenced his selection of anecdotes and, on occasions, his uncritical reporting.

On the other hand, a contemporary playwright, Aristophanes, who reflected the general perception of his time, made the same observation when he attributed a prelude to the Peloponnesian War to Aspasia when Pericles issued a decree of 432 BCE that imposed a blockade on Megara and ignited a war, in retaliation for allegedly stealing "a couple of Aspasia's whores". This silly reason, given in the comedy Acharnians of the year 425, after Pericles' death in 429 but while Aspasia was still alive and a prominent figure in Athens, not only served the purpose of discrediting the war but also revealed the perception the citizens of Athens had of Aspasia's influence on public affairs. [12]

In another play, Peace of 421 BCE, the same Aristophanes attributed the origin of the war to a distraction from Phidias' embezzlement of funds rather than Aspasia's retaliation. [13] But a historian is more credible than a playwright in these matters. The real reason for this decree

---

[10] Parallel Lives, Pericles, 24, 1: Loeb 65, 68.
[11] Ibid., 13, 9: Loeb 65, 44.
[12] Acharnians, 525 ff.: Loeb 178, 120.
[13] Peace, 603-615: Loeb 488, 502-505.

of war was given by Thucydides in his history of the war: the Athenians charged

> the Megarians with encroachement upon the sacred land and the border-land not marked by boundaries, and also with harbouring runaway slaves. [14]

As a whole, it seems that Aspasia used her political influence exceptionally well, not only in the privacy of Pericles' household where love was their bond, but also in his public life where power was their common goal. Thanks to Pericles and her own remarkable qualities, she became the most prominent woman of this time. Her legal status as non-Athenian and her political role almost equal to men's role made her resented by the common Athenians of both sexes. If the rumor carried any truth that the Peloponnesian War was started for her sake in 431 BCE, it was reminiscent of the Trojan War that, according to legend, had been fought for a woman, Helen of Sparta.

After the death of Pericles in 429, Aspasia continued living in character, meddling in politics and sex. In summary, she became the *hetaira* of Lysicles, a sheep dealer whom she made the chief man in Athens, in spite of his low birth and character. It seems to be true that she then taught the art of speaking not only to him but to many other men, and probably not only rhetoric since many considered her a professional harlot. Her influence on public affairs, so it seems, continued to be prominent even after Lysicles died prematurely in winter 428-427 BCE. She may have died much later, in 410 BCE, in obscurity and at the age of about sixty, old by measure of Greek longevity.

Another alien woman who seemed to have had some political influence in Athens of the fifth century was Elpinice, the sister of General Cimon, rival of Pericles. As a close friend of his, [15] she pleaded with him and probably offered him some sexual favors in order to calm his enmity against her brother for whom she was seeking a return from exile. She won her case shortly before her brother died in 451 or shortly thereafter, during a naval expedition against the Persians. Plutarch told us also that Elpinice had intimate

---

[14] *Peloponnesian War*, 1, 139, 2: Loeb 108, 238.
[15] Plutarch, *Parallel Lives, Pericles*, 10, 4 & 28, 4: Loeb 65, 30 & 80.

relations with a famous painter, Polygnotus of Thasos, who once painted her portrait on the porch (*stoa*), called Poecile, with a group of Trojan women. Her reputation had already been tarnished more seriously when she lived with her brother Cimon, not secretly, but as his married wife. She later married Callias, one of the richest men in Athens and the son of Pericles' divorced wife. She had been left an orphan with her brother Cimon and neither had ever learned to control their amorous tendencies. [16]

Concerning the status of *hetairai* in the Athenian society, a court case reported by Demosthenes is of particular interest. An Athenian citizen, named Stephanus, and his *hetaira*, Neaera, were living together in Athens. She was posing as his wife, although she was of Megaran origin and had previously been engaged by Nicarete, a high-society madam, to be a prostitute in Corinth. Neaera of the early fourth century faked her status so well that she almost succeeded in having her daughter recognized as a legitimate Athenian girl, although she was incapable by law to give her husband children who qualified to be citizens. Stephanus hid his predicament and pretended that she was his legitimate wife. Their hidden situation became critical when he gave their daughter in marriage to an Athenian citizen. An informant divulged his marital arrangement to two prosecutors, Theomnestos and Apollodorus, who took him to court. There they represented Neaera as an alien adulteress and, as a result, dishonored Stephanus as a citizen and succeeded in depriving him of his civic rights. They did not blame him for having her for pleasure or daily service, but for having her as a wife, because only wives were "to bear us legitimate children and to be faithful guardians of our households." [17]

Female companions, concubines and prostitutes, categorized by their place of work -- home, temple, symposium, brothel or street -- were all recruited among the non-Athenians. They were all practicing their skills openly, the best of them through pimps or madams, who set the fees and never failed to collect them. [18] No laws restricted men's sexual activities, except in adultery, and no police

---

[16] Plutarch, *Parallel Lives, Cimon*, 4, 5-7: Loeb 47, 414.
[17] Demosthenes, *Against Neaera*, 59, 122: Loeb 351, 446.
[18] Euripides, *Fr., Sciron*, 675: Loeb 506, 154.

force supervised any kind of conduct beyond the prescriptions of moderation and mutual respect based on customs and common sense. Athenian men accepted pleasure as a boon but realized its risks. Without any Sacred Books of instructions to follow, they behaved respectably. Some failed, like Callias who lost a fortune on girls and parties. As for the Athenian women, their sheltered life forced most of them to be chaste.

The occasion most often depicted on vases of the late sixth and fifth centuries was the men's symposium which included female entertainers. They served wine, played music, especially with the flute, competed at the game of *kottabos* by flicking the dregs of the wine at a target, and offered sexual satisfaction on demand, either during or after the gathering. [19]

One of the duties of the ten city controllers (*astunomoi*) was

> To supervise the flute-girls and harp-girls and lyre-girls to prevent their receiving fees of more than two drachmas, and if several persons want to take the same girl, these officials cast lots between them and hire her out to the winner. [20]

Aristophanes used many vulgar and libidinous women in his comedies, especially at the end in the simulation of a wedding (*gamos*). Only free foreign women residing in Athens could reach in public the sexual intensity of these feasts. They provided a service to men in real life and gave the dramatist some material for wild scenes of comedy. Athenian wives of citizens would have recognized this reality without participating in it.

The divide between the Athenian citizens, men and women, and all the other residents of foreign extraction should not minimize the important role some of these aliens played in the community of Athens, especially after the law of dual parentage was passed in 451 BCE. Their number increased but the power they held heretofore weakened greatly because they were excluded from every

---

[19] See Plato, *Symposium*: Loeb 166, 80-245 and Xenophon, *Banquet*, 1-9: Loeb 168, 534-635; see Euripides, *Fr., Oeneus*, 562: Loeb 506, 36.
[20] Aristotle, *Athenian Constitution*, 50, 2: Loeb 285, 138.

direct involvement. As non-citizens, they needed citizens to sponsor them. They paid several taxes, single women half as much as individual men, to support the government in which they had no voice. They were prohibited by law to marry in the Athenian citizen class and required to seek permission to own land or dwelling. They were allowed, however, to use the court system for redress of their grievances. They could even obtain citizen status by order of the Assembly. As a result of these political and economic restrictions they turned to occupations requiring no land ownership, like manufacturing, shopkeeping, trading and banking, like the Jews of the dispersion (*diaspora*) were forced to do in later centuries.

The free alien wives in these marriages imitated the Athenian wives and blended well with their life style, always secluded from political involvement. They had children, managed their household, visited with friends, lived a virtuous life, honored their dead and made religious dedications. They were free and respectable. Some, like Cimon's wife, were married to Athenian men. The majority, however, were married to alien husbands who found in Athens the best location to practice their trade or craft.

Non-Greek Women who were not slaves by birth were called barbarian and given due consideration to their status and behavior. Aeschylus created in his play about the Persians a queen mother Atossa of great wisdom and piety. Euripides depicted Medea as a bright and passionate woman, in spite of all her madness. He compared her to a lioness whose nature was fiercer than "Tyrrhenian Scylla", the female monster who personified the treacherous rock at the narrow straits of Messina between Italy and Sicily where, with the whirlpool of Charybdis, it created one of the most dangerous passages for sea voyagers. Euripides' comment sounded like an excuse when he explained that Medea, a barbarian, committed a crime no Greek woman would have dared to commit. She killed her children in revenge for her abandonment by Jason, her Greek husband. [21]

In spite of being welcome for the contribution they could make to the welfare of the Athenian-born citizens and their native wives, all foreigners generated feelings of fear on both sides: the Athenians feared to be betrayed or

[21] Euripides, *Medea*, 1336 ff.: Loeb 12, 404.

outsmarted and the foreigners to be rejected, like Ion did when he decided to move from Delphi to Athens. History often repeats itself. [22] Euripides must have had a bad experience with certain foreign residents, probably Athenian male with female consort, for lending Praxithea this complaint about them: "Someone who settles in one city from another is like a bad peg fixed in a piece of wood: he's a citizen in name, but not in reality." [23] So also was the woman who walked through life behind her man.

Slaves

The woman who was a citizen only by the proxy of her Athenian guardian and was not free resident was a slave (*doulos*) either by birth or acquisition, usually conquest. [24] The conquered female slave was either barbarian like the Trojan women or Greek like those from the Aegean islands who fought Athens in the Peloponnesian War. [25]

"God has marked out slaves as a class for the inferior estate", wrote Euripides. [26] Among the slave women, the concubine (*pallakê*) was at the top of this inferior class. In the time of the Argonauts, Hypsipyle, the daughter of king Thoas of the island of Lemnos, was sold into slavery and became the nursemaid of Opheltes, son of king Lycurgus of Nemea in Greece. [27] The soldiers away from home felt they had a right to a concubine. Achilles had his war-prize, Briseis, who became as close to him as a wife and Agamemnon his Chryseis whom he loved more than his wife, as he said:

> I would far rather keep her at home. For in fact I prefer her to Clytemnestra, my wedded wife, since she is in no way inferior to her, either in form or in stature, or in mind, or in handiwork. [28]

---

[22] Euripides, *Ion*, 607-608: Loeb 10, 398.
[23] Id., *Fr., Erechtheus*, 11-13: Loeb 504, 376.
[24] Aristotle, *Politics*, 1, 1255a, 2, 13-2, 1255b, 2, 19: Loeb 264, 22-29.
[25] Thucydides, *Peloponnesian War*, 3, 68, 3 & and 4, 48, 4: Loeb 109, 122 & 296.
[26] *Fr., Antiope*, 218: Loeb 504, 200.
[27] See Euripides, *Fr., Hypsipyle*, 752-765b: Loeb 506, 260-295.
[28] Homer, *Iliad*, 1, 112- 115: Loeb 170, 20.

At the end of the war, Agamemnon acquired Cassandra, princess of Troy -- "the choicest flower of rich treasure ... my army's gift" [29] -- and took her home with him. She held the highest status of all the slaves.

Standing on the same three dates previously used for the fifth century BCE, the number of slaves living in Attica during the fifth century BCE could be estimated as follows: in 451 (decree of dual parentage) 146,000 slaves, in 431 (beginning of the Peloponnesian War) 162,000 slaves and in 404 (end of the Peloponnesian War) 86,500 slaves. During the fourth century BCE, the population of slaves dropped considerably from 86,500 to between 20,000 and 30,000 because the military campaigns which were the main source of acquisitions were greatly reduced.

It is difficult to estimate the number of slaves per household but it seems well founded to believe that the numbers were in correlation with prosperity, larger in the wealthier households but not as large, at all levels of wealth, as they were in the Persian households. At the peak of her prosperity in 431 BCE, Athens had an average of slightly more than three slaves per household, a reality which makes Euripides' statement quite true: "For we who are free live by slaves" who make us free from toils. [30]

When the Spartan troops established their encampment at Deceleia, north of Athens, in 413 and led forays throughout Attica for their subsistence, as Thucydides informed us,

> more than twenty thousand slaves had deserted, a great part of them artisans, and all their sheep and beasts of burden were lost. [31]

Most male artisans took their family with them, so the number of slave women dwindled also and forced the Greek families to face their horrible ordeal without help either in the household or on the farm.

A good slave was "one with a free-man's heart even if he lacks a free-man's name." [32] - "Only one thing brings shame to slaves, the name. In all else a slave who is valiant

---

[29] Aeschylus, *Agamemnon*, 954-955: Loeb 146, 80.
[30] *Fr.*, Unidentified Play, 1019: Loeb 506, 576.
[31] Thucydides, *Peloponnesian War*, 7, 27, 5: Loeb 169, 48.
[32] Euripides, *Helen*, 728-730: Loeb 11, 94.

is not at all inferior to free men." [33] -- "The name of slave will not corrupt one who is good; many slaves are better men than those who are free." [34] -- "For many slaves their name is a thing of shame, but their mind is freer than those who are not slaves." [35] And again from Euripides:

> For my part I do not know how we should assess nobility. For I declare that those who are brave and just by nature, though they be born from slaves, are nobler than those who are mere empty appearances. [36]

The context of these quotations was about male slaves, but the content applied as well to female slaves who were assisting their mistress in nurturing her children and managing her household. The maidservants in Euripides' play *Ion* testified with poetic grace and beauty to the major role of slave women:

> The prime of youthfulness that bears fruit, for these will have from their fathers wealth hereditary to give to children in turn. ... May I have in preference to wealth and kingly halls the careful nurture of dear children. [37]

Some slaves of both genders worked outside the homes in ways pleasing to men. The majority of them, however, and almost all the female slaves were attached to a household, under the immediate authority of the wife. None of them had any rights but had all the obligations pertaining to the loyal service of their master, always the husband ultimately, even if the wife was their manager. He had the final word about their assignments but the wife directed the activities of their daily routine inside and outside the house. Inasmuch as they did not deserve any form of protection, the female slaves could walk alone to the fountain or the marketplace, and do errands as demanded.

---

[33] Euripides, *Ion*, 854-856: Loeb 10, 420.
[34] Id., *Fr., Melanippe Wise*, 511: Loeb 504, 610.
[35] Id., *Fr., Phrixus*, 831: Loeb 506, 454.
[36] Id., *Fr., Melanippe Captive*, 495, 40-43: Loeb 504, 602.
[37] Id., *Ion.*, 475-491: Loeb 10, 376.

Athens had in this subservient class a solid block of faithful and virtuous women who made it possible for the Athenian class to live a life of greater leisure and enjoyment. To be virtuous for a slave woman meant to be faithful to her mistress and keep her business secret. [38] If the mistress was wicked, for example conducting a clandestine sexual affair with a man or perhaps a woman, or wanting her child to be destroyed, the slave servant carried the mistress' orders. In her infatuation for her stepson Hippolytus, Phaedra used her servant to deliver secret messages to him. [39] Also, as Euripides further stated, "it is not possible for a slave to speak the truth if it happens not to suit his master" [40] and this applied to the female as well as the male servants.

If a slave, man or woman, was called upon to testify about the master in a case involving the courts, either one was not expected to tell the truth if it was to be in any way damaging to the master becaue the slave was always considered secretive and loyal. For this reason, every word of evidence they provided spontaneously was disbelieved. In order to get to the bottom of a case and dredge the mud against a master, the interrogators resorted to torture, probably only beating, and only then believed and used the testimony of a slave. [41]

For good or for bad assignments, servants always needed to be supervised because they never could be completely trusted even in their daily lives. [42] To this extent, nobody, slave or not slave, could ever be trusted completely. Caution, therefore, was ever a fair guide in all engagements with other people.

In the social order of Classical Athens, the female slaves were an extension of the Athenian women. Inasmuch as the male head of the household owned them, they did all his bidding in total subservience and responded to all of their mistress' demands and assisted her in every domestic chore, for she was holding an extension of the power of

---

[38] Euripides, *Fr., Eurystheus*, 375: Loeb 405, 408.
[39] Id., *Hippolytus*, 645-650: Loeb 484, 186; see Id., *Fr., Danae*, Appendix, 41-42: Loeb 504, 342.
[40] Id., *Fr., Busiris*, 313: Loeb 504, 320.
[41] Isaeus, *On the Estate of Ciron*, 10: Loeb 202, 292.
[42] Euripides, *Fr., Alcmeon in Psophis*, 86: Loeb 504, 98 and *Fr., Alcmene*, 93: Loeb 504, 108.

their owner, lord and master. The slaves shared in their master's affliction as well as success. [43] Aristotle debated these concepts at some length in his *Politics*. [44]

The playwrights of Tragedy attributed to slave women some of their most noble and endearing characters. Euripides exploited the courage and tenderness of the Trojan Hecuba and Andromache in two plays by their names. Their defeat in war had caused them to be made slaves of their conquerors.

Female slaves had no opportunity of their own to improve their social status except through their husbands' promotion, and their husbands could rise only when their outstanding service to the State justified their masters' goodwill. For example, Pasio of Demosthenes' oration was once a slave of the bankers Antisthenes and Archistratrus. They prevailed upon the Assembly to make him a citizen with his two sons, so he could handle their real estate loans. He became a very wealthy man. While he was managing their banking operation, he acquired a capable slave employee, called Phormio, whom he manumitted, then selected to become the husband of his wife, Archippe, after his death which occurred in 370/69 BCE. Phormio married her without delay in 368 and the Assembly declared him an Athenian citizen in 361/60 BCE. Archippe was probably born a slave but was promoted with her husbands. As a result, she lived a life of luxury as a high-society freedwoman. [45] In his will, Pasio bequeathed to her as dowry two talents, an apartment house and all that she used in their house, including her slaves, which she took to Phormio's house when they married according to the instructions. [46] It is not clear whether she was granted automatically all the privileges of the Athenian women, like owning property, which she did at least as dowry managed by her husband. In any case, with all her good fortune, she could not have had a better life. By Phormio she also had two children who had legal problems of their own after their father's death. Considering how well these slaves and

---

[43] Euripides, *Fr., Alcmeon in Psophis*, 85: Loeb 504, 96.

[44] *Politics*, 1, 2, 1254, 19-1255b, 40: Loeb 264, 22-31.

[45] Demosthenes, *For Phormio*, 36, 47: Loeb 318, 354; *Against Stephanus I*, 45, 25: Loeb 155, 194 and *Against Stephanus II*, 46, 13: Loeb 155, 252.

[46] Id., *Against Stephanus I*, 45, 27: Loeb 155, 196.

masters helped each other, a saying of Euripides seems befitting: "How pleasing it is for slaves to have good masters, and for masters a slave who is friendly to their family." [47]

Aristotle was liberal toward his slaves when he wrote his will and granted them that, if they are sold, they shall continue to be employed but, if they deserve it, they shall be given their freedom. [48]

In general, dramatists did not delve so deeply into our human condition. They usually gleaned on the surface like Ruth in Boaz's field. Euripides was different: he often thought like a psychologist and a counselor while writing a drama involving slaves, for example when he made the nurse in his *Hippolytus* say with some humility: "I have much less praise for excess than for moderation. The wise will bear me out." [49] And again:

> This is one of the wise principles mortals follow – dishonorable deeds should remain hidden from view. Mortals, you know, should not try to bring to their lives too high a perfection: no more would you make fine and exact the roof over a house. ... No, if the good you have done outweighs the bad, then on the human scale you would be fortunate indeed. [50]

After this old nurse failed to persuade Phaedra to accept her own feelings, no matter how shameful they were, she finally mused, it seems, from experience:

> If I had had success, I would have been numbered among the very wise. For our wisdom varies with the outcome. [51]

Phaedra was blessed to have a servant slave as caring as this nurse, even if she was not successful in preventing

[47] *Fr., Meleager*, 529: Loeb 504, 626.
[48] Diogenes Laërtius, *Lives of Eminent Philosophers*, Aristotle, 5, 15: Loeb 184, 458; see Demosthenes, *Against Evergus and Mnesibulus*, 47, 55: Loeb 155, 310.
[49] Euripides, *Hippolytus*, 264-266: Loeb 484, 148.
[50] *Ibid.*, 465-472: Loeb 484, 168.
[51] *Ibid.*, 699-701: Loeb 484, 192.

the premature deaths of Phaedra and Hippolytus. In another play, the same Euripides said:

> A wife should always be served by such a woman as will not be silent over what is right, but who hates what is shameful and keep it before the eyes. [52]

When the slave women of Argos were in Tauri land with Iphigenia and saw that the end of their captivity was at hand, they displayed their wisdom by chanting a choral song inspired by a heartfelt longing for the land where they were born and grew up happy and prosperous. They sang about a man, and a woman as well:

> How fortunate I hold the man who is luckless throughout his life! In hard necessity he feels no pain, whose constant companion has been shifting misery. But to come to grief after blessedness is a heavy fate for mortals. [53]

After the Theban maidservants of the chorus, in Euripides' play *Ion*, witnessed the clever, yet immoral, scam Xuthus perpetrated on his wife Creusa by adopting Ion as his son, they exclaimed through the voice of their leader:

> Oh, oh! How I hate villainous men, who plot injustice and then make the handiwork look fair with clever ruses! I would prefer to have someone ordinary but honest for a friend rather than a clever knave. [54]

Such a comment was one of caution in relationships but also a sign of the appreciation held by the Ancient Athenians not only for the physical but also the mental quality of their slaves. Combined with humility and loyalty, they could be the best friends of their masters and mistresses, otherwise

---

[52] Euripides, *Fr., Ino*, 410: Loeb 504, 450.
[53] Id., *Iphigenia Among the Taurians*, 1118-1122: Loeb 10. 268.
[54] Id., *Ion*, 832-835: Loeb 10, 418.

There is no greater burden than a slave who has greater ideas than he should, nor a possession more vile nor more worthless in a household. [55]

*

*

*

[55] Euripides, *Fr.*, *Alexander*, 48: Loeb 504, 50 and *Fr.*, *Antiope*, 216, Loeb 504, 224.

CHAPTER TWELVE

DEATH

Natural Death

The end of human life took place in two phases: one was ugly and mournful, the other beautiful and hopeful. The former was personified by two goddesses: Gorgon (*Gorgos*) with the monstrous face and Doom (*Kêr*) who thirsted on human blood. [1] Their role was to end life and inflict corruption on the body. The other phase was personified by the god Death (*Thanatos*) whose role was to take the deceased to the Underworld. [2] In the Greek pantheon, the ugly and painful phase of dying was given to goddesses, the phase of beauty to a god. Still, the passage he guided from this world to the next could be made more soothing and memorable when women performed their sacred functions of funerary rituals and grave visitations. In death as in life the image of women suggested phantoms of darkness and fear mixed with images of comfort and care.

The women's way of dying was not different from the men's way. Women had no control over their own demise and no peculiar way of departing which were unknown to men, except in childbirth which was probably frequent. Their life expectancy is estimated to have been about 36-37 years of age. [3] Men, like Oedipus and Socrates, preferred to die humbly, without any ostentation. Unless they were murdered or committed suicide, usually as a result of some men's actions, women were not given even this much of attention in death because they did not receive it in life.

---

[1] Homer, *Iliad*, 5, 741: Loeb 170, 260 and 18, 535: Loeb 171, 326.
[2] *Ibid.*, 16, 693: Loeb 171, 212.
[3] See J. Lawrence Angel, *Paleoecology, Paleodemography and Health*, in *Population, Ecology, and Social Evolution*, ed. by S. Polgar, p. 178 and Table. Men's life expectancy is estimated at about 45 years of age, variable according to war and peace.

Alcestis, however, was the exception, again because of a husband for whom she sacrificed her life.

> When she learned that the fated day had come, she bathed her fair skin in fresh water, and taking her finery from her chambers of cedar, she dressed herself becomingly. [4]

Alcestis was conscious and in good health. She extolled her sacrifice rather than her death. Unlike her, most women on their deathbed were fatally ill or injured, and could not display the same concern for their appearance. The biology of death was never examined with any careful attention. The Greek fascination was for life to benefit the world; therefore, if certain individuals "do the earth no good, they should vanish and die and get out of the way of the young!" [5]

At the moment of death, the person's soul (*psychê*) left the body and began a new life as its shadow (*eidôlon*) in the Underworld. The soul remained related to the person to whom it belonged in life and did not assume any other form of life, either animal or divine. For example, Clytemnestra's soul, appearing as a ghost, could show the wounds that caused her death. [6] Plato explained in a dialogue between Callicles and Socrates who was the teacher:

> Death, as it seems to me, is actually nothing but the disconnexion of two things, the soul and the body, from each other. And so when they are disconnected from one another, each of them keeps its own condition very much as it was when the man was alive, the body having its own nature, with its treatments and experiences all manifest upon it. ... And so it seems to me that the same is the case with the soul too, Callicles; when a man's soul is stripped bare of the body, all its natural gifts, and the experiences added to that soul as the result of his various pursuits, are manifest in it [to the judge in the Underworld]. [7]

---

[4] Euripides, *Alcestis*, 158-160: Loeb 12, 170.
[5] Id., *Suppliant Women*, 1112-1113: Loeb 9, 124.
[6] Aeschylus, *Eumenides*, 103: Loeb 146, 280.
[7] *Gorgias*, 524B-D: Loeb 166, 520-523.

Plato continued explaining that, in the Underworld, the souls of the incurable sinners, especially those of tyrants, were submitted to punishments which served as deterrents against evil habits and actions that the living were tempted to accept. On the other hand, the souls of those who committed curable sins, like mild insolence or licentiousness, could learn from pain and suffering and be cured in Hades as they could have learned and be cured in life. It was not too late for them to be liberated through their submission to suffering in Hades and to become happy in their new life. [8]

The Ancient Greeks believed that, since the soul (*psychê*) did not die with the body but survived in Hades, it could be reached by the survivors on earth. Before offering her life in sacrifice, Polyxena asked her mother Hecuba what message she could take to her deceased brother Hector and father Priam. [9] If she expected to deliver a cry for help from the most miserable of all women, she did not seem to expect much help to come from the dead.

In their minds, however, the Ancient Greeks had for the dead of either gender a reverence so great that they thought of them as being somehow alive, although weak and defenseless. Because the obscurity of the Underworld fostered their feelings of apprehension and insecurity, they resorted to the use of superstitious formulas in order to ward off any malevolence from the dead. On the third day of the festival of *Anthesteria*, previously noted, they offered sacrifices to god Hermes of the Underworld for the sake of the dead whose spirits were wandering. In order to parry their baleful actions they chewed tender leaves and smeared the doors of their houses with dark brown pitch.

Some of the prolonged expressions of grief were foreboding acts of revenge, not from the dead but from the living, for the untimely loss of a dear one by murder. The case of Electra and Orestes is the most pathetic and destructive that we know. They hated their mother, Clytemnestra, for murdering their father, Agamemnon, and sought to avenge him. Electra's lamentations, if they were a part of a woman's role in grieving for the dead, were corrupted by her motivation of revenge. Such is the irony of

---

[8] *Gorgias*, 525B-E: Loeb 166, 524-527.
[9] Euripides, *Hecuba*, 422: Loeb 484, 436.

life that the best of customs can sometimes be misguided toward evil ends.

Suicide

Like murder, suicide was a form of complaint directed against someone, including oneself. It was more secret than murder because it left no trace in the courts and invited less scrutiny in social circles. It could be hidden easily except in the cases large enough to warrant reporting in literature. Therefore, the sources of information reveal only a part of reality. Suicide was probably very rare among married women, more frequent among unmarried, divorced or widowed women who felt their lives were worthless without a husband, especially if they had no other close relative. Motherhood and the family were the keys to the survival of women.

Women were not considered heroic when they committed suicide because they felt unable to bear the burden of life. Men also who did it only from "sloth and unmanly cowardice" were not considered heroic and, for this reason, were given a modest burial, away from the burial grounds of the respectable citizens. [10] If a woman committed suicide out of shame or guilt for a certain deed, like Jocasta for marrying her own son, Deianeira for killing her husband Heracles or Phaedra for loving her stepson Hippolytus, she was excused, if not forgiven, for her action. A woman was expected to be weak and sometimes to harbor the madness of despair that leads to suicide.

The playwrights of Tragedy included the suicide of some of their leading female characters. They always had it taking place off stage and reported to the audience by some messenger. The predominant motive they attributed to these women was shame and the preferred form was by hanging rather than the sword. Deianeira was an exception as she killed herself "by the stroke of the cruel iron," striking herself "with a two-edged sword in the side below the liver and the seat of life." [11] She did it in shame for

---

[10] Plato, *Laws*, 9, 873C-D: Loeb 192, 266.
[11] Sophocles, *Women of Trachis*, 886-887 & 930-931: Loeb 21, 212 & 216.

killing her husband, Heracles, and for causing the anger of her son, Hyllus. [12]

Queen Jocasta hanged herself because she could not bear the recognition of being married to her son, Oedipus. [13] Antigone, Oedipus' daughter, and Eurydice, king Creon's wife, hanged themselves in anger against him: Antigone for his refusal to allow the burial of her brother Polynices and Eurydice for his death sentence on Antigone, previously promised in marriage to her son, Haemon, who also committed suicide for losing her. [14]

Phaedra, the wife of king Theseus of Athens, bestowed her love not on him alone but also on his son, Hippolytus. She had no right to make a lover of him, her stepson. So, in shame and fear, "she tied aloft a noose to hang herself." [15]

Imitating the action of hanging herself, Evadne threw herself onto the pyre where her husband's body was being cremated. [16]

The playwrights of Tragedy lent the thought of suicide, but not the deed, to other female characters of their plays. The thought was always related to the loss of a husband, as if these male writers were saying that a wife had no life of her own. When the rumors of Agamemnon's death in battle at Troy reached his wife Clytemnestra, she said that the thought of suicide by hanging came to her mind. She said it in guile and deceit, because she did not mean it, but it was understood as being the normal reaction of a wife deprived of her husband. [17] Like her sister, Helen had the thought also of committing suicide by stabbing herself, a nobler way to die, when Teucer, one of the Achaean warriors at Troy, found her in Egypt and informed her that her husband, Menelaus, was lost at sea and her mother, Leda, had herself committed suicide by hanging in shame of her daughter's disastrous behavior. [18]

---

[12] Sophocles, *Women of Trachis*, 940: Loeb 21, 216.
[13] Id., *Oedipus King*, 1263: Loeb 20, 458.
[14] Id., *Antigone*, 1220, 1236 & 1301: Loeb 21, 114, 116 & 122.
[15] Euripides, *Hippolytus*, 802: Loeb 484, 202.
[16] Id., *Suppliant Women*, 1070-1071: Loeb 9, 120.
[17] Aeschylus, *Agamemnon*, 877: Loeb 146, 72.
[18] Euripides, *Helen*, 134-138, 200-201, 293 & 350-356: Loeb 11, 28, 34, 42 & 48.

Even when suicide was used for its dramatic value, it was never exploited by the survivors as the expression of a wish of good riddance. The dramatists told about it, sometimes with some details, but never with a judgment of right or wrong or with glee. It was always a response to unbearabke pain which met the standard of Tragedy in pity and fear.

Ritual Sacrifice

The sacrifice of one's life for a cause greater than life was reviewed in previous chapter ten, in the context of women's activism. It is a form of suicide, not reprehensible but noble and commendable. Some soldiers did it with courage in the losing battles of the Peloponnesian War and some maidens did it also to placate the gods and ensure a victory against enemies of their family or state.

Times have not completely changed. When the young man Mohamed Bouazizi burned himself to death in protest in December 2010 in Tunisia he ignited the light of democracy, like a lighthouse in the dark night, and caused the Arab Spring to spread throughout the Near East.

These stories about maidens of Ancient Greece may have been fictions of the poets' imagination and perhaps some may have been true. The point they made, however, was not for veracity but for inspiration of patriotism favoring the state as the greatest of all values, above self, family and clan.

Memories

The site of the burial was marked, probably with only a small mound of stones until the last third of the fifth century BCE when a few sites began to be marked with a gravestone and occasionally a monument with a statue of the deceased, a bas-relief and an inscription, depending on the wealth of the family. The very rich families displayed their wealth by having in addition an enclosure around their family burial plot.

The erection of funerary monuments, however, was not the common practice in Attica. The rare ones represented in statue or on bas-relief the great men and perhaps a few great women whose death, according to the

Troezenian women of Euripides' *Hippolytus*, "have greater power to move." [19] Some Athenian women and most non-Athenian women were buried without a marker, away from their family. The preceding Heroic Age was kinder, as it favored a stele to mark every tomb. [20]

The ordinary wife or mother was often buried without a marker, away from her husband and sons. Her anonymity in death reflected her anonymity in life. Sarah B. Pomeroy can be trusted when she estimates that ten percent of the Athenian women did not have a marker to indicate their place of burial, which she explains with two reasons, one for lack of funds and the other for lack of respect. [21]

The name given to women and to men on the funerary monuments at the Athenian Agora indicated how the status of the deceased's life was perceived. The majority of women were referred to as wife (*gunê*) or daughter (*thugatis*), very rarely as mother. Also, men were never called husband or father, and very rarely son. They had a name of their own and it was the only name used to identify them in the inscription. The stele reproduced on the cover of this book shows husband and wife with their name, Philoxenos and Philoumene, inscribed above their heads.

Women and children showed their subservience to men even in death and this should be no surprise at least for one reason: the monuments were designed and paid for by men. The women's name as wives and daughters, however, showed more than their dependence as subservient partners of men; they showed also the men's appreciation, respect and love they harbored for them. Furthermore, such a public display indicated that the family (*oikos*) was not purely a private institution but part of the city (*polis*) where it flourished by producing her citizens.

The affectionate poses captured on gravestones and reliefs revealed the warm memories the husbands kept of their wife and daughters after their demise, as seen in the following scenes presented here as examples of many more:

1.   A husband bidding farewell to his wife: they clasp hands while he is staring at her whose head is bowed in

---

[19] *Hippolytus*, 1465-1466: Loeb 484, 262.
[20] Homer, *Iliad*, 17, 434: Loeb 171, 260.
[21] See S.B. Pomeroy, *Families in Classical and Hellenistic Greece*, 121.

expression of grief. This relief appears on an Attic funerary vessel for oil or perfume, called *Lêkuthos*, of c. 375 BCE from Salamis. [22]

2.   A young mature woman, called Mnesarete is seated, head bowed in a pensive pose and facing another young woman, perhaps a younger sister, offering a gift. This Attic relief is on an upright rectangular marble slab, called *stêlê*, of the first half of the fourth century BCE from Piraeus. [23]

3.   A mature woman standing and, in a gesture of endearment, extending one hand to touch the face and the other to clasp the arm of another woman, seated and looking at her, while a girl is observing from behind in bewilderment. This Attic relief is on a marble gravestone of the second half of the fourth century BCE. [24]

4.   Facing each other, with loving intensity, the soldier Philoxenos, in battle gear, and his wife Philoumene, in classical dress, are clasping hands in farewell. This Attic grave stele is in pentilic marble and dated about 400 BCE. [25]

5.   One other funerary monument, erected shortly after the Peloponnesian War which ended in 404 BCE, is different from the common ones for women. They were usually referred to, never as mothers but as wives or daughters of the men who designed and paid for the monuments. When a son neglected to build one for his departed mother, his father being already dead or incapacitated, his sister assumed the responsibility with the approval of her husband. In this case, the monument was a relief showing a mother, Amphirete by name, seated and holding a baby girl on her lap. She is also holding a bird in her right hand, probably to signify the departed soul of the child who must have died at about the same time as she did, perhaps from a complication originating in childbirth. The inscription is explicit about the loving relationship of mother and child.

I hold this dear child of my daughter, whom I held on my knees when we were alive and looked with our

---

[22] EWA 2, Pl. 59; see J. Oakley, *Picturing Death in Classical Athens: The Evidence of the White Lekythoi.*

[23] EWA 3, Pl. 369.

[24] EWA 2, Pl. 58.

[25] The J. Paul Getty Museum at Malibu, CA, 83,AA,378, reproduced on the cover of this book. See also H.D.F. Kitto, *The Greeks*, 228, about Damasistrate.

eyes upon the light of the sun, whom now dead, I dead hold. [26]

Such a design emphasizing motherhood and the female lineage is unique in the history of Classical Athens. The timing at the turn of the century is also significant as an indication of the liberties women could take during these changing times.

*

*

*

[26] *Inscriptiones Graecae II*, 2, 10650: C. W. Clairmont, *Classical Attic Tombstones*, 1, 660.

EPILOGUE

The picture of the life of women in Classical Athens of the fifth and fourth centuries BCE has appeared to be in chiaroscuro, with more shade than light because the men's towering figure dominated the scene. The writings about women, all by men, especially Euripides, were so often misogynous that the dark lines obscured the bright ones in the eyes of modern readers. At the end of our long survey, both author and readers feel a need to summarize, not the list of facts larded with more than thirteen hundred references, but the general perspective in which these facts were interpreted.

Our closing words about perspective are an attempt at restoring some measure of balance on one final page without denying the accuracy of the data painfully collected in the previous four hundred and twenty-five pages. [1] Although the accuracy of our interpretation of any one statement, including the translations from Ancient Greek into modern English, may be questioned and probably found to be sometimes wanting, the conglomerate of statements certainly leads to a few undisputed tenets.

First, women were considered by men and considered themselves inferior to men in status and life style. As a result, they were restricted in their activities to certain roles, all in some way related to motherhood as a contribution not only to the family but also to the state. Also, unlike the Spartan women, the Athenian women were feminine in deeds and character, although they were not generally as physically strong as men. Therefore, although they could not compete with men in certain activities, they knew how to make themselves desirable by men who loved them even when, according to our standards, they cheated on them. Besides, nobody could deny that the Athenian men loved their family, therefore loved also the person that made it possible in the first place and nurtured it with skill and love later.

---

[1] H.D.F. Kitto made the same attempt in *The Greeks*, esp. p. 222-236.

Furthermore, the men's activities in literature, art, government and social life proved that they were, as a group, intelligent, law-abiding and highly civilized for their time in history and in comparison with all other known peoples of their time. So they generally respected women, appreciated their good work and virtues, and carefully guarded them out of love more than jealousy.

Some facts, particularly the negative ones, related by the dramatists, especially Euripides, and the historians, especially Herodotus, tended to be reported for effect rather than accuracy. Furthermore, many facts remained unknown about the life of women in Ancient Athens because the documentation was lost or simply nonexisting, for example about the conversations husbands and wives had besides those reported by Xenophon about the management of the household. Therefore, to admit some measure of our ignorance is the right attitude at all times. Such ignorance on our part is enlarged by the distance between the culture of our modern world and that of the Ancient Greek world. As a result, our interpretations must always be guarded, because what appears now negative at first sight may be positive after all, for example Pericles' statement about women keeping silent.

In conclusion, the women of our modern industrialized and digitallized countries would not want to live the life of the women of Ancient Athens, but many women of modern less-developed countries of Africa or Asia would not only want it, if it were possible, but would gain from it. Every change along the centuries between then and now has not been for the benefit of women everywhere in the world. The struggle is still ongoing toward making their lives a better lot through progress in equality of treatment and opportunity as well as respect for their special contributions and needs.

The stellar victories of women at the London Olympic of 2012 have shaken the argument, expounded especially by Aristotle, that women's physical and emotional weakness, in comparison with men's strength and reasoning ability, was the cause of her natural inferiority to men in all things. These games have proved the vitality of women, in mind and body, and revealed their rising competitive spirit, skills and physical power, enhanced by the improved quality of their facilities, nutrition, education and medical care. All girls and women need access to such enhancements if ever the male prejudice and, in some places, the violent resistance levied against their equality with boys and men can be suppressed for the benefit of mutual respect everywhere in the world.

*

*

*

SELECT BIBLIOGRAPHY

ABBREVIATIONS

ed. = edited; **et al.** = and others; Id. = same author; **Intro.** = introduction; **P.** = press; **Pub.** = publisher or publication; **rev.** = revised; **trans.** = translated; **U.** = university.

Sources (Quoted in this book)

Adams, Charles Darwin, ed. & trans. *Aeschines, Speeches*. Loeb 106.
Armstrong, G. Cyril, ed. & trans. *Aristotle, Metaphysics*. Loeb 287.
Babbitt, Frank Cole, ed. & trans. *Plutarch, Moralia*. Loeb 222 & 245.
Balme, D. M., ed. & trans. *Aristotle, History of Animals*. Loeb 439.
Bowersock, G. W., ed. & trans. *Xenophon, Hiero* et al. Loeb 183.
Brownson, Carleton L., ed. & trans. *Xenophon, Hellenica*. Loeb 88.
Burtt, J. O., ed. & trans. *Minor Attic Orators, Lycurgus* et al. Loeb 395.
Bury, R. G., ed. & trans. *Plato, Laws*. Loeb 187 & 192.
Id., *Plato, Critias* et al. Loeb 234.
Campbell, David A., ed. & trans. *Greek Lyric, Sappho* et al. Loeb 142.
Id., ed. & trans. *Greek Lyric, Stesichorus* et al. Loeb 476.
Collard, Christopher, ed. & trans. *Euripides, Fragments*. Loeb 504 & 506.
Cropp, Martin, ed. & trans. *Euripides, Fragments*. Loeb 504 & 506.
Cunningham, I. C., ed. & trans. *Theophrastus, Characters* et al. Loeb 225.
Dimock, George E., rev. ed. & trans. *Homer, Odyssey*. Loeb 104 & 105.
Emlyn-Jones, Chris, ed. & trans. *Plato, Republic*. Loeb 276.
Encyclopedia of World Art. McGraw-Hill Book Co., 15 vols, 1968. Many articles and plates.
Evelyn-White, Hugh G., ed. & trans. *Hesiod, Theogony* et al. Loeb 57.
Id., *Hesiod, Catalogue of Women* et al. Loeb 503.
Id. Homer. *The Odyssey*. Trans. with intro and notes by Bernard Knox. Viking, 1996.
Fantham, Elaine et al. *Women in the Classical World: Image and Text*. Oxford U.P., 1994.
Forster, Edward Seymour, ed. & trans. *Isaeus*. Loeb 202.
Fowler, Harold North., ed. & trans. *Plato, Euthyphro* et al. Loeb 36.
Id., *Plato, Theaetetus* et al. Loeb 123.
Id., *Plato, Cratylus* et al. Loeb 167.
Freese, John Henry, ed. & trans. *Aristotle, Art of Rhetoric*. Loeb 193.
Godley, A. D., ed. & trans. *Herodotus, Histories*. Loeb 117 & 119.
Green, William M., ed. & trans. *Augustine, City of God*. Loeb 415.

Halliwell, Stephen, ed. & trans. *Aristotle, Poetics* et al. Loeb 199.

Henderson, Jeffrey, ed. & trans. *Aristophanes, Plays*. Loeb 178, 179, 180,
488 & 502.

Hett, W. S., ed. & trans. *Aristotle, On the Soul* et al. Loeb 288.

Hicks, R. D., ed. & trans. *Diogenes Laërtius, Lives of Eminent
Philosophers*. Loeb 184 & 185.

Hormerod, H. A., ed. & trans. *Pausanias, Description of Greece*. Loeb 188.

Hort, Arthur F., ed. & trans. *Theophrastus, Enquiry into Plants* et al. Loeb
79.

Jones, W. H. S., ed. & trans. *Pausanias, Dscription of Greece*. Loeb 93 &
188.

Id., *Hippocrates, Epidemics* et al. Loeb 147.

Kovacs, David, ed. & trans. *Euripides, Plays*. Loeb 9, 10, 11, 12, 484 &
495.

Lamb, W. R. M., ed. & trans. *Plato, Protagoras* et al. Loeb 165.

Id., *Plato, Symposium* et al. Loeb 166.

Id., *Lysias*. Loeb 244.

Lefkowitz, Mary R. and Maureen B. Fant. *Women's Life in Greece and
Rome: a Source Book in Translation*. Johns Hopkins U.P., 2n ed., 1992.

Lloyd-Jones, Hugh, ed. & trans. *Sophocles, Plays*. Loeb 20, 21 & 483.

Loeb Classical Library. Harvard U. P. and William Heinemann Ltd. 1911 ff.
Greek text with English translation.

Longrigg, James. *Greek Medicine from the Heroic to the Hellenistic Age. A
Source Book*. Routledge, 1998.

Maidment, K. J., ed. & trans. *Minor Attic Orators, Antiphon* et al. Loeb
308.

Marchant, E. C., ed. & trans. *Xenophon, Memorabilia* et al. Loeb 168.

Id., *Xenophon, Hiero* et al. Loeb 183.

Meiggs, Russell and David M. Lewis. *A Selection of Greek Historical
Inscriptions to the End of the Fifth Century B.C.* Clarendon P., 1969.

Murray, A. T., ed. & trans. *Homer, Odyssey*. Loeb 104 & 105.

Id., *Homer, Iliad*. Loeb 170 & 171.

Id., *Demosthenes, Against Aphobus* et al. Loeb 318.

Id., *Demosthenes, Against Eubulides* et al. Loeb 351.

Peck, A. L., ed. & trans. *Aristotle, History of Animals*. Loeb 437 & 438.

Id., *Aristotle, Generation of Animals*. Loeb 366.

Perrin, Bernadotte, ed. & trans. *Plutarch, Parallel Lives*. Loeb 46, 47, 65,
80 & 99.

Pomeroy, Sarah B. *Xenophon, Oeconomicus: A Social and Historical
Commentary with a New English Translation*. Clarendon P., 1991.

Preddy, William, ed. & trans. *Plato, Republic*. Loeb 276.

Rackham, H., ed. & trans. *Aristotle, Nichomachean Ethics*. Loeb 73.

Id., *Aristotle, Politics*. Loeb 264.

Id., *Aristotle, Athenian Constitution*. Loeb 285.

Rusten, Jeffrey, ed. & trans. *Theophrastus, Characters* et al. Loeb 225.

Sanford, Eva M., ed. & trans. *Augustine, City of God*. Loeb 415.

Selincourt, Aubrey de, trans. *Herodotus, The Histories*, rev. and intro. by John Marincopa. Penguin Books, 1972.

Shackleton, D. R., ed. & trans. *Valerius Maximus, Memorable Doings and Sayings*. Loeb 492.

Shorey, Paul, ed. & trans. *Plato, Republic*. Loeb 237.

Smith, C.F., ed. & trans. *Thucydides, Peloponnesian War*. Loeb 108, 110 & 169.

Smyth, Herbert Weir, ed. & trans. *Aeschylus, Plays*. Loeb 145 & 146.

Tobi, Levenberg Kaplan et al, ed. The J. Paul Getty Museum; Handbook of the Antiquities Collection, Los Angles and Malibu, California, 2001.

Todd, O. J., ed. & trans. *Xenophon, Memorabilia* et al. Loeb 168.

Van Hook, La Rue, ed. & trans. *Isocrates, Helen* et al. Loeb 373.

Vince, C. A., ed. & trans. *Demosthenes, Orations*. Loeb 155.

Vince, J. H., *Demosthenes, Orations*. Loeb 155, 202, 238 & 299.

Wright, Frederick A. *Feminism in Greek Literature from Homer to Aristotle*. Kennikat Press, 1969.

Wyatt, William F., rev. ed. & trans. *Homer, Iliad*. Loeb 170 & 171.

Wycherley, R. E., ed. & trans. *Pausanias, Description of Greece*. Loeb 298.

Literature (Quoted or recent)

Angel, J. Lawrence. *Paleoecology, Paleodemography, and Health*, in *Population, Ecology, and Social Evolution*, ed. by Steven Polgar, 1975, p. 167-190.

Blok, Josine H. *Virtual Voices: Toward a Choreography of Women's Speech in Classical Athens*, in Lardinois, A. et al., *Making Silence Speak: Women's Voices in Greek Literature and Society*, p. 95-116. Princeton U.P., 2001.

Id., *Becoming Citizens: Some Notes on the Semantics of 'Citizen'*, in Archaic Greece and Classical Athens, Klio 87 (2005) 7-40.

Boardman, John: see Kurtz, Donna C.

Bremmer, Jan. *The Early Greek Concept of the Soul*. Princeton U.P., 1983.

Id., ed. *From Sappho to de Sade: Moments in the History of Sexuality*. Routledge P., 1989.

Brisson, Luc. *Sexual Ambivalence. Androgyny and Hermaphroditism in Greco-Roman Antiquity*. Trans. by Janet Lloyd. U. of California P., 2002.

Brulé, Pierre. *Women of Ancient Greece*. Edinburgh, 2003.

Burkert, Walter. *Greek Religion*. Trans. by John Raffan. Harvard U.P., 1985.

Cartledge, Paul. *The Greeks: A Portrait of Self and Others*. Oxford U.P., 1993.

Cartledge, Paul, Paul Millett and Sitta von Reden, eds. *Kosmos: Essays in Order, Conflict, and Community in Classical Athens*. Cambridge U.P., 1998.

Clairmont, Christoph W. *Classical Attic Tombstones*. 6 vols & supplement, Akantus, 1993-1995.

Clough, James, trans: see Flaceliere, Robert.

Cohen, Edward E. *Athenian Economy and Society:A Banking Perspective.*
Princeton U.P., 1992.

Cole, S.G. *Landscape, Gender, and Ritual Space: The Ancient Greek
Experience,* U. of California P., 2004.

Connelly, Joan Breton. *Portrait of a Priestess: Women and Ritual in
Ancient Greece.* Princeton U.P., 2007.

Dalby, Andrew. *Food in the Ancient World from A to Z.* Routledge, 2003.

Davidson, Alan: see Wilkins, John.

Davidson, James. *Private Life,* in *Classical Greece, 500-323 BC,* ed. by
Robin Osborne, Oxford U.P., 2000, p. 139-169.

Davies, John Kenyon. *Democracy and Classical Greece.* Harvester P. Ltd.,
2nd ed., 1993.

Dillon, Matthew. *Girls and Women in Classical Greek Religion.* Routledge,
2002.

Dobson, Mike: see Wilkins, John.

Dover, Kenneth J. *Greek Homosexuality.* Harvard U.P., 1978.

Easterling, P.E., ed. *The Cambridge Companion to Greek Tragedy.*
Cambridge U.P., 1997.

Evans, Nancy A. *Sanctuaries, Sacrifices and the Eleusinian Mysteries,* in
Numen 49.3 (2002) 227-264.

Id., *Feasts, Citizens, and Cultic Democracy in Classical Athens,* in Ancient
Society 34 (2004) 1-26.

Fant, Maureen B.: see Lefkowitz, Mary R.

Fantham, Elaine et al. *Women in the Classical World: Image and Text.*
Oxford U.P., 1994.

Faraone, Christopher. *Ancient Greek Love Magic.* Harvard U.P., 1999.

Flaceliere, Robert. *Love in Ancient Greece.* Trans. by James Clough. Crown
Pub. Inc., 1962.

Fletcher, Judith: see Sommerstein, A.H.

Foley, Helene P . *Ritual Irony: Poetry and Sacrifice in Euripides.* Cornell
U.P., 1985.

Id., *Female Acts in Greek Tragedy.* Princeton U.P., 2001.

Id., *Mothers and Daughters,* in *Coming of Age in Ancient Greece,* ed. By J.
Niels and J.H. Oakley, 2003, p. 113-137.

Forskyke, Sara. *Slaves Tell Tales.* Princeton U.P., 2012.

Foxhall, L. *The Politics of Affection,* in *Kosmos,* ed. *by P. Cartledge et al.,
63-64.*

Gallant, Thomas W. *Risk and Survival in Ancient Greece. Reconstructing
the Rural Domestic Economy.* Stanford U.P., 1991.

Garland, Robert. *The Greek Way of Death.* Cornell U.P., 2nd ed., 2001.

Geoffroy-Schneider, Berenice. *Greek Beauty.* Assouline, 2003.

Goff, Barbara, ed. *History, Tragedy, Theory: Dialogues on Athenian
Drama.* U. of Texas P., 1995.

Golden, Mark. *The Exposure of Girls in Athens,* in Phoenix 35 (1981)
316-331.

Goldhammer, Arthur, trans.: see Schmitt-Pantel, Pauline.

Gomme, Arnold W. *The Population of Athens in the Fifth and Fourth Centuries B.C.* Argonaut Inc. Pub., 1967.

Green, Peter, *Classical Bearings. Interpreting Ancient History and Culture.* Thames & Hudson, 1989.

Greenberg, Mark, ed. in Chief. *The J. Paul Getty Museum: Handbook of the Antiquities Collection.* Los Angeles, 2002.

Hall, Edith. *The Sociology of Athenian Tragedy*, in *The Cambridge Companion to Greek Tragedy*, ed. by P.E. Easterling, 1997, p. 93-126.

Harvey, David: see Wilkins, John.

Henry, Madeleine M. *Prisoner of History: Aspasia of Miletus and her Biographical Tradition.* Oxford U.P., 1995.

Honeyman, Don: see Lloyd-Joes, Hugh.

Hornblower, Simon & Antony Spawforth, eds. *The Oxford Companion to Classical Civilization.* Oxford U. P., 1998.

Humphreys, Sarah C. *The Family, Women and Death: Comparative Studies.* U. of Michigan P., 2nd ed., 1993.

Johnston, Sarah Iles. *Restless Dead: Encounters between the Living and the Dead in Ancient Greece.* U. of California P., 1999.

Jones, W. H. S. *Philosophy and Medicine in Ancient Greece with an Edition of Peri Archaies Intrikes.* Johns Hopkins U.P., 1946 & 1978.

J. Paul Getty Muiseum: see Greenberg, Mark, ed. in Chief.

Kitto, H. D. F. *The Greeks*, Illustrated Edition with a New Preface by the Author. Aldine Pub. Co., 1964.

Kosmopoulou, A. *'Working Women': Female Professionals on Classical Attic Gravestons*, in Annual of the British School at Athens, 96 (2001) 281-319.

Kurtz, Donna C. and John Boardman. *Greek Burial Customs.* Cornell U.P., 1971.

Lardinois, André and Laura McClure, eds. *Makinng Silence Speak: Women's Voices in Greek Literature and Society.* Princeton U.P., 2001.

Laurin, Joseph R. *Homosexuality in Ancient Athens.* Trafford Pub., 2005.

Id., *Poets of Tragedy in Classical Athens.* Trafford Pub., 2008.

Id., *Heracles and Oedipus in Greek Classical Drama.* Trafford Pub., 2008.

Lefkowitz, Mary R. and Maureen B. Fant. *Women's Life in Greece and Rome: A Source Book in Translation.* The Johns Hopkins U.P., 3rd ed. 2005.

Lewis, D.: see Meiggs, R.

Lloyd, Geoffrey. *Science, Folklore and Ideology: Studies in the Life Sciences in Ancient Greece.* Cambridge U.P., 1983.

Lloyd-Jones, Hugh. *Females of the Species. Semonides on Women.* Photographs by Don Honeyman of Sculptures by Marcelle Quinston. Noyes P., 1975.

Longrigg, James. *Greek Medicine from the Heroic to the Hellenistic Age. A Source Book.* Routledge, 1998.

Lonsdale, Steven H. *Dance and Ritual Play in Greek Religion.* Johns Hopkins U.P., 1993.

Loraux, Nicole. *The Experiences of Tiresias: the Feminine and the Greek Man*. Trans. by Paula Wissing. Princeton U.P., 1995.

Id., *Mothers in Mourning; with the Essay, Of Amnesty and its Opposite*. Trans. by Corinne Pache, Cornell U.P., 1998.

Id., *Born of the Earth: Myth and Politics in Athens*. Trans. by Selina Stewart. Cornell U.P., 2000.

Martinez, David. *Love Magic and Vows of Abstinence, in Ancient Magic and Ritual Power*, ed. by M. Meyer and P. Mirecki, 2001, p. 335-359.

McLure, Laura.: see Lardinois, A.

Meiggs, Russell and David Lewis. *A Selection of Greek Historical Inscriptions to the End of the Fifth Century BC*. Oxford U.P. 1988.

Meyer, Marvin and Paul Mirecki, eds. *Ancient Magic and Ritual Power*. Brill Academic Pub., 2001.

Millett, Paul: see Cartledge, Paul, *Kosmos*.

Morris, Ian. *Burial and Ancient Society. The Rise of the Greek City-state*. Cambridge U.P., 1987.

Id., *Death-ritual and Social Structure in Classical Antiquity*. Cambridge U.P., 1992.

Morwood, James and John Taylor. *Pocket Oxford Classical Greek Dictionary*. Oxford U.P., 2002.

Munn, Mark. *The School of History. Athens in the Age of Socrates*. U. of California P., 2000.

Murray, Gilbert. *Euripides and his Age*. Oxford U.P., 2nd ed., 1946.

Neils, Jenifer and John H. Oakley. *Coming of Age in Ancient Greece: Images of Childhood from the Classical Past*. Yale U.P., 2003.

North, Helen. *Sophrosyne: Self-knowledge and Self-restraint in Greek Literature*. Cornell U.P., 1966.

Nussbaum, Martha C. and Julia Sihvola, eds. *The Sleep of Reason: Erotic Experience and Sexual Ethics in Ancient Greece and Rome*. U. of Chicago P., 2002.

Oakley, John H. *Picturing Death in Classical Athens:The Evidence of the White Lekythoi*. Cambridge U.P., 2003.

Id., see Neils, Jenifer.

Oakley, John H. and Rebecca H. Sinos. *The Wedding in Ancient Athens*. U. of Wisconsin P. 1993.

Osborne, Robin. ed. *Classical Greece: 500-323 BC*. Oxford U.P., 2000.

Id., see Rhodes, P.J.

Pache, Corinne: see Loraux, Nicole, *Mothers in Mourning*.

Polgar, Steven. *Population, Ecology, and Social Evolution*. Mouton Pub., 1975.

Pomeroy, Sarah B. *Families in Classical and Hellenistic Greece: Representations and Realities*. Clarendon P. 1997.

Purvis, Andrea. *Singular Dedications: Founders and Innovators of Private Cults in Classical Greece*. Routledge, 2003.

Quinston, Marcelle: see Lloyd-Jones, Hugh.

Raffan, J., trans.: see Burkert, W.

Reden, Sitta von: see Cartledge, Paul, *Kosmos*.

Rhodes, Peter John and Robin Osborne. *Greek Historical Inscriptions 404-323 B.C.* Oxford U.P., 2007.

Richlin, Amy, ed. *Pornography and Representation in Greece and Rome.* Oxford U.P., 1992.

Robb, Kevin. *Literacy and Paideia in Ancient Greece.* Oxford U.P., 1994.

Rutter, N. Keith and Brian A. Sparkes, eds. *Word and Image in Ancient Greece.* Edinburgh U.P., 2000.

Schaps, David M. *Economic Rights of Women in Ancient Greece* [to 146 BCE]. Edinburgh U.P., 1979.

Schmitt-Pantel, Pauline, ed. *A History of Women in the West.* Trans. by Arthur Goldhammer. Harvard U.P. vol. 1: 1992.

Sealy, Raphael. *Women and Law in Classical Greece.* U. of North Caroline P., 1990.

Seidensticker, Bernd. *Women on the Tragic Stage,* in *History, Tragedy, Theory: Dialogues on Athenian Drama,* ed. by B. Goff, 1995, p. 151-173.

Sigerist, Henry E. *A History of Medicine.* vol. 2: *The Golden Age of Greek Medicine,* p. 213-335. Oxford U.P., 1961.

Sinos, R. H.: see Oakley, J.H., *The Wedding.*

Sissa, Giulia. *The Sexual Philosophies of Plato and Aristotle,* in *A History of Women in the West,* ed. by P. Schmitt-Pantel, 1992, Vol. 1, p. 46-82.

Snodgrass, Anthony. *The Uses of Writing on Early Greek Painted Pottery,* in *Word and Image, in Ancient Greece,* ed. by N.K. Rutter and B.A. Sparkes, 2000, p. 22-34.

Sommerstein, Alan H. and Judith Fletcher, eds. *Horkos: The Oath in Greek Society.* Phoenix P., 2007.

Sparkes, Brian A. ed.: see Rutter, N. Keith.

Spawforth, Antony, ed.: see Hornblower, Simon.

Stewart, Selina: see Loraux, Nicole, *Born of the Earth.*

Symonds, John A. *Studies of the Greek Poets.* U. P. of the Pacific, vol. 1, 2002.

Taylor, John, ed.: see Morwood, James.

Usher, Stephen. *Greek Oratory. Tradition and Originality.* Oxford U.P., 1999.

Webster, T.B.L. *Tragedies of Euripides.* Methuen Pub., 2nd ed., 1970.

Wiles, David. ed. *Greek Theatre Performance: An Introduction.* Cambridge U.P., 2000.

Id., *Women, Politics and Myth,* in *Greek Theatre Performance: An Introduction,* ed. by D. Wiles, p. 66-88.

Wilkins, John, David Harvey and Mike Dobson, eds. *Food in Antiquity.* Foreword by Alan Davidson. U. of Exeter P., 1995.

Winkler, John J. *The Constraints of Desire: the Anthropology of Sex and Gender in Ancient Greece.* Routledge P., 1990.

Wissing, Paula, trans.: see Loraux, Nicole, *The Experiences of Tiresias.*

Woodhouse, S. C. *English-Greek Dictionary. A Vocabulary of the Attic Language.* Routledge and Kegan Paul, 1964.

Wright, Frederick Adam. *Feminism in Greek Literature from Homer to Aristotle.* Routledge, 1923.

Wycherley, R. E. *How the Greeks Built Cities. The Relationship of Architecture and Town Planning to Everyday Life in Ancient Greece.* W.W. Norton & Co., 2nd ed., 1976.

*

*

*

GLOSSARY

A: 380.
Agapaô: 354.
Akoitis: 22.
Akropolis: 24.
Alabastron: 212.
Aletês: 41.
Amphidromia:
125, 146, 150,
190.
Amphora: 8, 59.
Anchisteia: 33,
115, 146, 154,
158, 169, 202,
203, 266, 353,
359.
Andreia: 283.
Androgunos: 26.
Andrôn: 157.
Anêr: 21, 22, 156,
283, 286, 388.
Anthesteria: 41,
210, 346, 362,
401,419.
Anthrôpos: 21, 22,
138, 300.
Aoros: 122.
Archê: 30.
Archôn: 33, 237,
272, 277.
Areiopagos: 377.
Aretê: 136, 226,
244.
Arista: 175.
Arktos: 41, 210.
Arrên: 29.
Arrêphoros: 41,
181, 346.
Asebeia: 169.
Astunomos: 407.
Athenaios: 10, 25,
121.
Aulos: 208.

Basilessa: 346.
Basileus: 346.

Basilikôs: 87.
Bouleutêrion: 124.

Charis: 140.
Chitôn: 370.
Choês: 346.

Deipna: 175.
Dekatê: 125, 190.
Demos: 203.
Dêmotas: 120.
Diaphora: 31.
Diaspora: 408.
Dikê: 57, 110,
380, 385.
Dinos: 59, 62
Dionysia: 41, 324,
346, 364, 368.
Dolos: 332.
Dorpa: 175.
Doulos: 409.
Doxa: 384, 385.
Dustuchestaton:
92.

Eidôlon: 418.
Eidos: 29-31, 88.
Eirênê: 380.
Ekklêsia: 391.
Ekphora: 359.
Eleutherius: 162.
Embruon: 142.
Enguê: 271, 282.
Ennea: 170.
Enneakrounos:
170.
Epaulia: 72.
Epiklêros: 267.
Eponumos: 277.
Erastês: 321.
Erganê: 378.
Erômenos: 99,
320.

Erôs: 52, 70, 79,
80, 224, 253,
288, 316, 318.
Êttôn: 109.
Euhan: 69.
Exômis: cover,
370.

Gamelia: 72, 271.
Gameô: 59.
Gamikos: 59.
Gamos: 59, 64,
139, 318, 407.
Genos: 29-31, 33,
44, 268.
Gerairai: 346.
Gnomê: 89.
Gorgos: 417.
Graphê: 56, 110.
Gunaikonitis: 116,
157.
Gunaikos: 21, 22.
Gunê: 22, 71, 138,
423.

Hedna: 50.
Hetaira: 46, 56,
99, 112, 185,
276, 307, 374,
375, 401, 402,
405, 406.
Hetairistria: 322.
Himation: 359,
370, 371.
Homophasia: 347.
Horkos: 33, 57.
Hubris:224.
Hudria: 59, 170,
212, 213.
Huos: 350

Iatros: 135.
Ischus: 89.

Kanephoros: 346.

INDEX

A

B

C

D

E

F

G

Hipponicus: 402.
Hirophilus: 90.
Hitler: 76.
Homer: 14, 21, 22, 37, 46, 50,
   60, 79, 85, 86, 172, 176, 178,
   181, 182, 187, 188, 201, 208,
   216, 230, 250-257, 259, 262,
   280, 304, 312, 354, 355, 377.
Hymns: 194.
Iliad: 21, 22, 25, 28, 46, 63,
   64, 70, 79, 80, 83, 99, 130,
   144, 172, 179, 182, 188,
   200, 209, 215-217, 221,
   230, 253-256, 258, 312,
   316, 320, 333, 354-356,
   367, 377, 378, 380, 389,
   409, 417, 423.

Odyssey: 21, 22, 37, 50, 51,
   53, 72, 73, 92, 101, 165,
   172, 176-178, 182, 186,
   188, 200, 201, 209, 230,
   240-251, 253, 256, 259,
   260, 264, 270, 286, 304,
   309, 312, 327, 329, 333,
   367, 368, 378.
Horace: 255.
Hornblower, S.: 66.
Humphries, S.C: 362.
Hyacinthid: 399.
Hydra: 286, 335.
Hylax: 200.
Hyllus: 221, 334, 340, 341, 421.
Hyperbolus: 390.
Hyperides: 68, 106, 283.
Hypsipyle: 409; see Euripides.

I

Icarius: 240, 243, 251.
Ilium: see Troy.
Ilus: 67.
India: 221.
Infanticide: 146, 149-153.
Ino: 80, 151, 152, 348, 360; see
   Euripides.
Io: 83.
Iolaus: 396, 397.
Iole: 102, 187, 221, 313, 326,
   334, 336.
Ion: 38, 103, 132, 149, 151,
   236, 324, 345, 348, 395, 409,
   415.
Ionian: 28, 350, 352, 369.
Iophon: 117, 307, 308.
Iphicrates: 391.
Iphigenia: 17, 93, 61, 100, 101,
   192, 210, 215, 263, 313, 315,
   345, 363; see Euripides.
Iphis: 82, 216.

Ischomachus: 199, 371, 372.
Isaeus: 20, 56, 154, 167, 191,
   272, 277, 282, 294, 349.
   Apollodorus: 115, 271.
   Aristarchus: 167.
   Ciron: 66, 125, 191, 271, 349,
      361, 406, 412.
   Dicaeogenes: 115.
   Hagnias: 270.
   Menecles: 115, 154, 164, 236,
      269, 277, 362.
   Philoctemon: 164, 272.
   Pyrrhus: 125, 191, 269-271,
      283.
Ismene: 18, 129, 229-233, 283,
   382, 387.
Ismenus: 63.
Isocrates: 265.
Italy: 373, 401, 408.
Ithaca: 176, 188, 200, 201, 240,
   245, 250, 309.

J

Japan: 372.
Jason: 18, 78, 84, 139, 151,
   152, 185, 408.
Jew: 408.
Joan of Arc: 9.

Jocasta: 62, 151, 219, 229, 309,
   369, 384, 420, 421.
Johnston, S.I.: 122.
Jones, W.H.S.: 137.
J. Paul Getty Museum: see Getty,
   J.P.

K

L

M

N

O

P

T

Z

*

*

*